Refuting the allegation that the author of Luke–Acts showed no systematic thought about the significance of Jesus' death, this study affirms that Luke had a coherent *theologia crucis*. Peter Doble focuses sharply on the Gospel's death scene and explores those features which appear in Luke alone, then extends the exploration into the longer account of Jesus' final days in Jerusalem.

The three Lukan features are first, that the centurion calls Jesus 'dikaios' rather than the 'Son of God' of Mark and Matthew; Doble examines Luke's use of the word in his Gospel and in Acts, and shows that its presence and force come from the Wisdom of Solomon. Second, in Luke, Jesus' final word from the cross, different from that in Mark and Matthew, belongs to the same Wisdom model. Third, the centurion in Luke, seeing the manner of Jesus' death, is said to have 'glorified God', and this is shown to be a Lukan verbal signal which appears whenever the evangelist wants to show that an element in the salvation programme has been fulfilled.

In the final section Doble demonstrates how specific words and patterns from Wisdom shape and fill Luke's retelling of the story of Jesus' entrapment, trials and death. Luke wanted his readers to understand that what had happened to Jesus was not a humiliating rejection but in accord with scripture's presentation of God's plan, and issued in the paradox of his salvation.

SOCIETY FOR NEW TESTAMENT STUDIES

MONOGRAPH SERIES

General Editor: Margaret E. Thrall

87

THE PARADOX OF SALVATION

The paradox of salvation

Luke's theology of the cross

PETER DOBLE
Department of Theology and Religious Studies, University of Leeds

Published by the Press Syndicate of the University of Cambridge
The Pitt Building, Trumpington Street, Cambridge CB2 1RP
40 West 20th Street, New York, NY 10011-4211, USA
10 Stamford Road, Oakleigh, Melbourne 3166, Australia

First published 1996

Printed in Great Britain at the University Press, Cambridge

A catalogue record for this book is available from the British Library

Library of Congress cataloguing in publication data

Doble, Peter.
The paradox of salvation: Luke's theology of the cross / Doble, Peter.
p. cm. – (Society for New Testament Studies monograph series; 87)
Includes bibliographical references and index.
ISBN 0 521 55212 5 (hardback)
1. Bible, N.T. Luke XXIII, 13–49 – Criticism, interpretation, etc.
2. Salvation – Biblical teaching.
3. Jesus Christ – Crucifixion – Biblical teaching.
I. Title. II. Series: Monograph series (Society for New Testament Studies); 87.
BS2595.6.S25D63 1996
226.4′6–dc20 95-17438 CIP

ISBN 0 521 55212 5 hardback

CE

MPD
1956

EGD
1901–1991

HTD
1900–1994

ὅτι ὁ Θεὸς ἔκτισεν τὸν ἄνθρωπον ἐπ'ἀφθαρσίᾳ
καὶ εἰκόνα τῆς ἰδίας ἀϊδιότητος ἐποίησεν αὐτόν

CONTENTS

PREFACE

This monograph is a revision of a thesis sustained in the University of Leeds in 1992: parts I and III have been substantially rewritten to take up some implications of the earlier work; part II, the heart of the argument, has been much shortened, so that its accent now falls on Luke's composition rather than on his redaction of sources. In part III, chapter 7 develops an earlier detached note into a fuller treatment of echoes of Wisdom in Luke's narrative of Jesus' passion, while chapter 8 reflects on ways in which the preceding chapters point to Luke's theology of the cross.

Many people have supported the writing of this book: my thanks are most particularly due to Dr J. Keith Elliott, who proved an ideal supervisor; to Professor I. Howard Marshall, Dr Margaret Thrall, the Monograph Series editor, and to the anonymous reader, all of whom offered detailed comment on this work in ways which disclosed much about the generous yet rigorous spirit of our discipline. Two friends have been particularly helpful: Mary Hayward, a colleague for fourteen years, not only first prompted the writing of the thesis, but, during its emergence and during that of this book, generously encouraged and practically supported both, reading and commenting on successive drafts; Dr W.H. Burns marked forty years of friendship by reading, discussing and commenting on much of this work. Sandra Huxley was an admirable librarian, swiftly producing innumerable articles and books. Gwyneth, my wife, prospered this work by sharing our home with Luke, who has made increasing demands on time and space; I owe her large thanks for this – and for very much more that only she can know.

I also owe much to Cambridge – first, to my teachers. Among them, my largest debt is unquestionably to the Revd W.F. Flemington, who generously gave of himself and his learning to generations of his students while expecting much of them. Second, seminars and lectures for those reading part III of the Tripos stimulated particular interest in Luke–Acts which was the special study for part III; even then, discussion of Luke's passion narrative was lively, and teachers and taught certainly contributed more to this book than I can consciously recall and acknowledge. Third, when the University Press accepted this work for publication, I could not guess how much larger my debt to Cambridge would become: those charged with turning manuscript into book have been unfailingly helpful, meticulous and kind; perhaps, from all of them, I may particularly thank Peter Edwards, whose copy-editing kept my feet from many a pit. Acknowledging large debts to Cambridge does not overshadow more recent debts to colleagues in Leeds, among whom Dr Alan Lowe has been especially helpful, as the footnotes witness; I thank them for their interest in and contributions to my work, and for the Fellowship which makes them 'colleagues'.

Debts, however large, do not absolve an author from responsibility for what stands in his name. I hope that this little volume, with its defects, will contribute helpfully to continuing discussion of Luke's theology of the cross, and of the uses made by New Testament writers of Jewish scripture.

ABBREVIATIONS

ANQ	*Andover Newton Quarterly*
ATR	*Anglican Theological Review*
BC	Jackson, F.J.F. and Lake, K. *The Beginnings of Christianity*
BETL	Bibliotheca ephemeridum theologicarum lovaniensium
BJRL	*Bulletin of the John Rylands Library, Manchester*
BZNW	Beihefte zur ZNW
CBQ	*Catholic Biblical Quarterly*
CLS	Christian Literature Society
CUP	Cambridge University Press
DLT	Darton, Longman and Todd
Ephem Theol Lovan	*Ephemerides Theologicae Lovanienses*
EQ	*The Evangelical Quarterly*
Eus. *HE*	Eusebius, *Historia Ecclesiastica*
EWNT	*Exegetisches Wörterbuch zum Neuen Testament*
ExpT	*Expository Times*
HTR	*Harvard Theological Review*
IDB	*Interpreter's Dictionary of the Bible*
IVP	Inter-Varsity Press
JBL	*Journal of Biblical Literature*
JETS	*Journal of the Evangelical Theological Society*
JnlRel	*Journal of Religion*
JSNT	*Journal for the Study of the New Testament*
JSNTSS	JSNT Supplement Series
JSOT	*Journal for the Study of the Old Testament*
JTS	*Journal of Theological Studies*
MT	Masoretic Text

N-A 26	Nestle-Aland, Novum Testamentum Graece, 26.Ausgabe, 9.Druck 1987, Stuttgart: Deutsche Bibelgesellschaft
NewRSV	New Revised Standard Version
NIV	New International Version
NovT	*Novum Testamentum*
NTS	*New Testament Studies*
OUP	Oxford University Press
PerspRelStud	*Perspectives in Religious Studies*
REB	Revised English Bible
RevExp	*Review and Expositor*
RHPR	*Revue d'histoire et de philosophie religieuses*
RSV	Revised Standard Version
SB	Strack, H. and Billerbeck, P., *Kommentar zum Neuen Testament*
SBLMS	SBL Monograph Series
SBT	Studies in Biblical Theology
SCM	Student Christian Movement Press
SCM/TPI	SCM and Trinity Press International
SNTSMS	*Studiorum Novi Testamenti Societas* Monograph Series
SPCK	Society for Promoting Christian Knowledge
StANT	Studien zum Alten und Neuen Testament
TB	*Tyndale Bulletin*
TDNT	*Theological Dictionary of the New Testament*
Th. Wb.	*Theologisches Wörterbuch zum Neuen Testament*
THzNT	Theologisches Handkommentar zum Neuen Testament
Trin Sem Rev	*Trinity Seminary Review*
TS	*Theological Studies*
TWNT	*Theologisches Wörterbuch zum Neuen Testament*
TZ	*Theologische Zeitschrift*
UBSGNT	United Bible Societies Greek New Testament
UBS3	United Bible Societies Greek New Testament third edition, 1975
WCC	World Council of Churches
ZNW	*Zeitschrift für die Neutestamentliche Wissenschaft*

PART I

Luke's theology of the cross: preliminary matters

1

LUKE AND THE CROSS: SETTING THE SCENE

It is frequently alleged that Luke has no *theologia crucis*, or, at best, a weakened one.[1] Examination of three distinctive, interrelated elements at the heart of the Lukan passion narrative strongly suggests that this is a mistaken assessment and that Luke does have a clear, coherent understanding of Jesus' death within God's salvation plan, and not merely as a prelude to resurrection. This examination takes seriously the pervasive Lukan insistence on 'fulfilment' and finds a key interpretative element in Wisdom's δίκαιος-model; the case for this is developed throughout part II and extended in chapter 7. Although this examination originally worked with the two-document hypothesis and explored Luke's redaction of Mark,[2] because its argument stands without recourse to that hypothesis the work has been rewritten to examine Luke–Acts in its own right. One element in the original presentation has, however, been retained: the argument assumes throughout that Luke's purposes are directed to building up a mixed Christian community and not to developing a political apologetic.

A. Luke is alleged to have no *theologia crucis*

What, precisely, is the nature of this widespread complaint against

[1] Kümmel (1975, p. 134, n. 18), lists those who share this view. See George (1978, pp. 185–212): '. . . On est donc fort étonné de constater que l'oeuvre de Luc, qui parle si souvent de la mort de Jésus, fasse si peu de place à son efficacité salutaire, et ne dise rien de sa valeur expiatoire. Ce fait a été remarqué depuis longtemps et on l'a interpreté diversement.' George appends a list (1978, p. 185, n. 3) of 'recent' writers, including Lohse, *Martyrer und Gottesknecht*, Göttingen, 1955, [2]1963, pp. 187–91; Flender, *Heil und Geschichte*, Munich, 1965, pp. 140–2; Conzelmann, *Zur Bedeutung des Todes Jesu*, Gutersloh, 1967, pp. 51–3; Zehnle (1969), 'The Salvific Character of Jesus' Death in Lukan Soteriology', pp. 420–44; Marshall (1970), *Luke: Historian and Theologian*, pp. 170–5; *et al.*

[2] Doble, P., 'Dikaios at Luke 23:47 as a Lukan Christological Term', a thesis sustained in the University of Leeds, 1992.

Luke? It is alleged that in Luke–Acts Jesus' death is 'played down'. Kiddle (1935, p. 273) was sure that Luke systematically diminished the tragic, momentous colouring of the passion as it is recorded in Matthew and Mark. According to Kiddle, for Luke, Jesus' death is 'more political' and 'less religious' (1935, p. 272). This judgment is linked with his assessment of Luke's apologetic purpose in writing, but it epitomises a widespread sense that Luke's passion narrative is 'not theological'. The death is *there*, it *happened*, but this death *does* nothing. Cadbury, for example, maintained that the story of Jesus' death was 'told' rather than 'explained' (1958, p. 280), but this is also substantially true of the passion narratives in the other synoptics. Conzelmann (1960, p. 201) noted that Luke's Gospel had no 'passion mysticism'.

A strange necessity

On the other hand, many writers recognise that according to Luke this death was *necessary*. Creed's very brief comment on Luke's theology noted at least that much: ' there is indeed no *theologia crucis* beyond the affirmation that the Christ must suffer, since so the prophetic scriptures had foretold' (1930, p. lxxii). The frequent occurrence of δεῖ in Luke–Acts and its firm references to the necessity of the messiah's suffering according to the scriptures (Luke 24.25–7, 44–7) therefore requires comment.

One way of responding to a situation in which the evangelist appears both to emphasise the necessity of the messiah's suffering and to play down Jesus' death is to take very seriously one verse in the Emmaus story (Luke 24.26) and to claim that this death was a necessary prelude to the Lord's entering into his glory (so, e.g. Evans, 1990). The accent is thus shifted from the cross to one aspect or more of Jesus' vindication. Cadbury, for example, could write of this death as 'only a prelude' (1958, p. 280) and Kiddle was lyrical about his solution:[3]

> Much of the joy and confidence which mark [Luke's] gospel is actually due to his optimism concerning the future, an optimism which makes him gloss over the pangs and sorrows of the past. He wrote in the spirit of Easter and Whitsun, rather than that of Good Friday. He regarded the

[3] Although he ignored the weight of evidence gathered below in 'A Lukan emphasis'.

> latter as necessary, *but only as the short path to the unending glory which lay beyond* – a glory which illuminated even the way to the cross. (1935, p. 273, *italics added*)

According to many writers it is the ascension or the resurrection which focuses Luke's theology, so his is essentially a *theologia gloriae*. Cadbury saw the focus in resurrection (1958, p. 280); Keck (1967, p. 475) followed Talbert's arguments (1966) while Franklin (1975, p. 67, cf. p. 99 n. 36) found Luke's focus in the complex of resurrection and ascension: the cross served to make possible Jesus' resurrection and ascension.

Many complaints urged against Luke's treatment of Jesus' cross focus on his apparent policy of *exclusion:* he is said to have excluded Mark 10.45 (Cadbury, Conzelmann and Evans note this);[4] he excluded all covenantal reference in his account of the Last Supper (so, for example, Franklin; the textual question here is difficult, but if the shorter text is read, Franklin's point stands).[5] Franklin was also clear that Mark 10.45 was replaced in Luke's account of the Last Supper by the substituted 'I am among you as one who serves', thereby strengthening a case for a Servant soteriology in Luke.[6] It is

[4] Cadbury (1958, p. 280; cf. his treatment of παῖς, 1933, pp. 364ff.); Conzelmann (1960, pp. 201, 228); Evans (1990, p. 75). Jones (1984, p. 152) briefly discussed both Mark 10.45 and the shorter Lukan text of the word over the cup: he noted the absence from Luke of any hint that Jesus' death had atoning or redemptive significance.

[5] The longer text seems now to be preferred. Fitzmyer's careful treatment of the textual issues leads to the longer text (1985, pp. 1386–95); N-A 26 prints the longer text; UBS3 also prints the longer text but evaluates it only (and surprisingly) as a [C] reading. Marshall comments: 'The external evidence for the longer text is overwhelming. The weakness in this argument lies in accounting for the origin of the shorter text ... but this may be due simply to some scribal idiosyncrasy. On balance the longer text is to be preferred' (1978, p. 800). Evans (1990, pp. 786–8) notes that both Jeremias (*The Eucharistic Words of Jesus*) and RSV changed allegiance from the shorter text to the longer; he also describes Marshall's appeal to 'scribal idiosyncrasy' as 'somewhat desperate' (1990, p. 788), citing, but not supporting, a *disciplina arcani* as one reason for omission. It seems that on balance Evans prefers the shorter text.

If the longer text is now to be preferred, then Luke's τὸ ὑπὲρ ὑμῶν διδόμενον has a *vicarial* dimension (but appears not to be related to a Servant model). Fitzmyer's discussion (1985, pp. 1515–18) of Jesus' death as salvific is a corrective to much of what is said of Luke's want of a *theologia crucis*. Perhaps it is possible to see the Wisdom δίκαιος-model in a way which allows the death of the δίκαιος to initiate God's plan of salvation; for the implications of this discussion see chapter 8.

[6] See Doble (1992, Detached Note 1), for an argument *contra* Franklin – that Luke *transformed* Mark 10.45 into Luke 19.10. While Goulder (1989, pp. 675–9) is hesitant about Drury's account of the origins of this story, his own treatment of the

interesting to note how much store writers set by Luke's alleged policy of excluding references to ransom or redemption; it is particularly *this* that earns him so much disfavour among theologians. Kiddle noted that, for Luke, Jesus' death was not even vitally connected with redemption (1935, p. 277).

Luke's exclusion of these two key texts is closely linked with his firm divorce between a concern for and interest in forgiveness on the one hand and his narrative of Jesus' death on the other. Both Conzelmann (cited below) and Cadbury (1958, p. 282) particularly note this fact:

> The most important finding in this connection for our purposes is that there is no trace of any Passion mysticism, nor is any direct soteriological significance drawn from Jesus' suffering or death. There is no suggestion of a connection with the forgiveness of sins ... The fact that the death itself is not interpreted as a saving event of course determines the account given of it.
>
> (Conzelmann, 1960, p. 201)

Cadbury noted that Luke–Acts is imbued with a Lukan emphasis on forgiveness and that nowhere is this emphasis linked with Jesus' death. Keck (1967, p. 475) wrote of Luke's *avoiding* any explicit soteriological reading of Jesus' death and found the evidence in his two exclusions.

If, according to Luke, salvation is not to be found in the cross *per se* where may it be found? It is said to be found through Jesus' ministry or his present reign as Lord rather than through his death. This, for example, is Franklin's position: he insists that Jesus' cross is not the *means* of salvation – the activity of the risen Lord *is* (1975, p. 66). Tannehill argues in the same direction (1972, p. 74f.) making clear that salvation, forgiveness, was also to be found in the encounter between God and man in Jesus' ministry.

A Lukan emphasis

But a reading of the Gospel shows how odd these 'accusations' really are, for Luke emphasises Jesus' approaching passion more

passage depends on Luke's having extracted minute detail from Mark and Matthew before building it patiently into a piece of creative writing. Experience with the text suggests that Marshall rightly notes (Goulder, 1989 p. 675) that Luke does not create Jesus' sayings.

than either of the other synoptists; so why should an evangelist with no *theologia crucis* make so much of the passion? And why should his emphasis on the passion be so closely related to his great construct of Jesus' journey to meet his passion in Jerusalem?

If one reflects on the journey as it is announced in the transfiguration narrative (Luke 9.31), then the pressure of the evidence becomes clearer. It is of the essence of this Lukan scene that the transfigured Jesus is *standing together with* Moses and Elijah, the three of them talking about the ἔξοδος which he was about to complete in Jerusalem. At Luke 9.51, following this metamorphosis, Luke reports that Jesus 'set his face towards Jerusalem' and what awaited him there. What Luke might have intended here by ἔξοδος is explored in a later section,[7] but at present it is enough to note that it signals a theological map which the reader is invited to follow.

Within his journey narrative Luke takes up the three great passion predictions relating to the Son of man (9.21–2; 9.43b–5; 18.31–4), with distinctive Lukan elements which differentiate them from synoptic parallels. One of these, the second, omits any hint of a resurrection; both second and third draw attention to the hiddenness of these ῥήματα from the disciples, a theme more fully explored in the Emmaus narrative and beyond; the third spells out for a reader – thus drawing attention to – Ἰδοὺ ἀναβαίνομεν εἰς Ἰερουσαλήμ, with all its overtones from 9.31 and 51 before continuing: καὶ τελεσθήσεται πάντα τὰ γεγραμμένα διὰ τῶν προφητῶν τῷ υἱῷ τοῦ ἀνθρώπου. This use of τελέω in relation to Jesus' passion and death, a verb taken up at 12.50, 22.37 and Acts 13.29, will be examined below. Luke's composition thus includes not only what he probably found in sources still available, but an *emphasis* on the passion and its scriptural bases.

There are also unparalleled 'Lukan' sayings. At Luke 12.50 there is a curious and important little saying about a 'baptism' which most commentators understand as Jesus' suffering; again, there is a sense of its being brought to completion (... τελεσθῇ). Similarly, at Luke 13.33 there is reference to Jesus' prophetic martyrdom in Jerusalem; the verbs δεῖ and πορεύεσθαι root this saying in a distinct Lukan attitude to the coming passion. At Luke 17.25 stands a reference to the initial or supreme (πρῶτον δέ) necessity of the Son of man's sufferings (δεῖ αὐτὸν πολλὰ παθεῖν) before the 'Day of the Son of man', again, with no hint of resurrection or

[7] Chapter 7G below.

vindication. It is Jesus' suffering and death rather than vindication which are in view here.

Luke thus narrates the journey to Jerusalem as Jesus' journey to a destiny to which he adverts frequently on the way. Yet after the journeying has brought Jesus and his disciples to Jerusalem, the evangelist continues his interest in the purpose for their being in the city. It is surely no accident that in the parable of the Wicked Husbandmen (Luke 20.9–19) there is significant difference between what is found in Luke and what Matthew and Mark narrate: both the latter tell the reader that servants were also killed (Matt. 21.33–44; Mark 12.1–12); Luke has the son alone killed, leaving the servants traumatised and dishonoured yet with their lives intact (Matt. 21.35; cf. Mark 12.4ff.; *contra* Luke 20.10, 11, 12). While this is different from the picture he paints at Acts 7.51–53 it none the less focuses a reader's mind on the coming passion. Similarly, at Luke 22.37, in a citation of Isaiah 53.12, is another example of the strange necessity (δεῖ τελεσθῆναι) driving Jesus' life. It would, however, be a mistake to find in this verse reason to import the whole of the *'Ebed Yahweh* model;[8] what is stressed is that because Jesus' sufferings will be among the 'lawless', his will be a humiliating, shameful death (see chapter 7C).

How can such a composition as Luke–Acts be said to lack a *theologia crucis* while so emphasising the necessity of this death? Help is to hand in asking the question in another way.

A more focused question

As Kümmel rightly notes (1975, p. 141f.), the nub of these complaints against Luke is that he has not affirmed an unambiguously 'Pauline' doctrine of atonement. Even where he appears to have alluded to it, he either has Pauline teaching in a weakened form or it is probably not Pauline at all. Writing of Acts 20.22, Cadbury commented:[9]

> Superficially, this sounds Pauline enough, and no doubt Paul's work lies behind such a mode of expression, and yet one hesitates to assume that Paul's rather unique theology is shared understandingly by his biographer. Possibly the

[8] *Contra* Larkin (1977) *et al.*

[9] Houlden (1984, pp. 63f.), also reflected on Luke as theologian and came to no very encouraging conclusions.

> latter had no special penchant for such things; certainly he has no occasion in this work to elaborate such matters.
> (1958, p. 281)

Whether Luke was or was not a natural theologian is beside the point here. Kümmel argues that Luke's work should be assessed not by Paul's but by the central message of the New Testament, and this has to do with the canon, with taking history seriously, with the theological norm established by the agreement of Jesus,[10] Paul and John (1975, p. 141f.); by these criteria Luke's attempt to write for his own time coheres with the central proclamation of the New Testament. Kümmel urged that the question be posed in a new and different way: does Luke understand the history of Jesus as final event (1975, p. 142)? Fitzmyer came to the same general conclusion but framed his question rather differently. To find the right answer it is wise to ask the right question: in their own ways, both Fitzmyer and Kümmel affirm that there is diversity in the New Testament witness to Jesus, and each has chosen to provoke new ways of thinking about Luke's particular contribution.[11] This present study explores one small segment of Luke's passion narrative to clarify three distinctive elements through which this evangelist presented Jesus' death as in one sense 'final event', a fulfilment of the plan of God set out in scripture.[12]

B. Three distinctive elements in Luke's passion narrative

This evangelist's composition of Luke 23.44–7 relates to its parallels in Mark and Matthew. It has, however, three elements which deserve careful exploration: first, the Lukan Jesus' final word from the cross (23.46) is explored in chapter 6; second, the centurion ἐδόξαζεν τὸν θεόν (examined in chapter 2) before, third, he

[10] Kümmel's extraordinary mixing of categories here (*Jesus,* Paul and John) is probably indefensible, but his statement has the merit of reaffirming that Paul's is not the only NT witness to a theological position.

[11] Barrett's discussion (1979) of the term *theologia crucis* offers a helpful perspective on Luke's understanding of discipleship. The present argument follows a different path from his: Luke's is a *theologia crucis* in the sense that God's fulfilling his plan for salvation *entailed* the humiliation and martyrdom of the δίκαιος as an element in his 'career'. Only in so far as this death fulfilled scripture's paradigm was it an essential element in God's salvific work. This approach is explored in part III below where the relation of Luke's *theologia crucis* to discipleship is taken up.

[12] Squires (1993) explored Lukan usage in relation to the plan of God. It is, perhaps, a weakness in his case that he paid less attention than it deserves to the influence of LXX on Luke's thought.

affirmed Jesus as ὄντως ... δίκαιος (23.47); Luke's use of δίκαιος is explored in chapters 3 to 5. The thrust of this study is that these three elements belong together in one systematic and coherent Lukan narrating of the passion as an integral part of God's fulfilling his salvation plan in and through the agency of Jesus. Each of the chapters in part II constitutes an examination of one of these elements. Part III then extends the findings of part II into the larger Lukan passion narrative and into an approach to Luke's *theologia crucis*.

The distinctiveness and importance of these three elements has often been noted, but good reason for revisiting them may be found in C. J. Hemer's words (1977, p. 46): 'There is often ... a particular need to reopen and reformulate questions which have been prematurely closed. We need not so much novel answers as fresh leads to discrimination among those already canvassed or even discarded.' The particular need to reopen and reformulate questions about these three Lukan elements initially emerged from an examination of Luke's use of δίκαιος, results from which are incorporated in part II. Once that question had been reopened, its relation with the other elements became clearer, and, although each element has previously undergone careful separate scrutiny, their dynamic interrelation in Luke's thought appears not to have been explored.

C. Luke and the fulfilment of scripture

The force of these three interrelated elements and their place in Luke's understanding of God's plan of salvation should be given full weight in any assessment of Luke's *theologia crucis*. The reason for this is obvious from even a superficial reading of Luke–Acts: according to Luke, the risen Lord explained to his disciples how what had befallen him was essentially related to the scriptures – *Torah*, Prophets and Psalms (Luke 24.25–7, 44–6) – and that his shameful death was part of God's plan. While there is still dispute about the force of τῶν πεπληροφορημένων in Luke 1.1, a good case can be made for urging that because Luke saw the events he was narrating as in some sense God's fulfilling his saving purposes, this particular verb, whatever else it does, relates to such fulfilment. There is also a systematic appeal to scripture throughout the body of Luke–Acts, in the Nazareth sermon (Luke 4.16–30) and in Paul's address at Pisidian Antioch (Acts 13), in the Petrine speeches of

Acts 2–4 and in Stephen's long survey of Israel's relations with God (Acts 6.8–8.2), throughout the infancy hymns (Luke 1 and 2) and in the closing of the two volumes (Acts 28.23–31). Luke's apparent facility in interpreting the scriptures may perhaps be seen most clearly in his programmatic use of δοξάζειν τὸν Θεόν, a usage explored in chapter 2 below.

The thrust of this present work is that Luke found in scripture one particularly helpful model of God's saving activity. According to Wisdom, a scriptural book that Luke found illuminating,[13] it had been through a faithful Israel or through loyal and saintly individual people (δίκαιοι) that God had consistently saved his people. Historically, faithfulness to God had met opposition, enmity and persecution from other, less committed Israelites, and Wisdom offers in chapters 2–5 a paradigm of the δίκαιος in his conflict with cruel and cynical opponents, culminating in his open vindication by God. While this δίκαιος-model is initially presented in its singular form (e.g. Wis. 2.10–20; 4.16–5.8), there are passages where reference is clearly generalised as a plural (e.g. Wis. 3.1–9). So here one finds the kind of counterpoint between the one and the many which inhibits an interpreter from speaking of δίκαιος as a title, an oscillation also characteristic of Daniel's use of 'Son of man' and Deutero-Isaiah's use of 'Servant'. Consequently, throughout this study, δίκαιος in Luke–Acts is referred to more neutrally as a 'term' or 'descriptor'. A cumulative argument for Luke's use of Wisdom appears in chapter 7.

D. The question of Luke's sources

While an earlier form of this monograph worked with one possible solution to the synoptic problem, this present version makes its case on the basis of Luke–Acts itself. There are, however, one or two points at which remnants of the earlier form reappear. The reason for this change in approach is simply that the case for a Lukan *theologia crucis* based on Wisdom's model of the δίκαιος can be made independently of Luke's redactional activity. To tie a sound argument to a hotly debated hypothesis weakens the argument in

[13] This statement *assumes* that Luke's LXX included Wisdom. That the Muratorian canon appears to include Wisdom among the New Testament books points to its value to Christians as much as to the fact that it was not listed as 'scripture'. Chapter 7 below explores some 'echoes' of Wisdom in Luke–Acts.

the eyes of those who reject that hypothesis.[14] This revision clarifies issues by limiting the area of dispute.

The earlier version *assumed* that the two-document hypothesis was to be preferred to its rivals; it also reflected on experience of working with that assumption and concluded that, while the hypothesis remains precisely that, on the whole it worked well enough, although Talbert's claim, that each pericope's 'direction' had to be decided on its own merits, was to be taken seriously. Further, Dunn, Wenham and others have urged the continuing interaction of oral and literary relationships among gospels even after they were circulating in written form. Tuckett and Neirynck *et al.* have clarified issues raised, for example, by Farmer and Sanders, leaving the majority of students cautiously in possession of a suspect but still usable analytical tool.

Consequently, apart from clearly indicated passages, this version argues its case not from an assumption that Luke was editing and correcting Mark, but from the perceived character of Luke's own composition and the development of his narrative.[15] In this version, conclusions about Luke's *theologia crucis* no longer rest on the soundness of any particular hypothesis about synoptic relationships. But there remains one assumption which underlies the whole – something firm needs to be said about Luke's purposes.

E. The question of Luke's purposes

Why this question?

The basic answer to this question is that anyone attempting to demonstrate the coherence of Luke's *theologia crucis* needs to be aware of her or his assumptions about the Gospel's earliest readership. No one comes to the text without some notion of what it might be about and whom it might be for. So to what ends, for whom and for what reasons did Luke write his two-volume work?[16] Here, one of the thrusts of this study must be anticipated, because one of the three focal elements in the passion story is firmly tied to this

14 But, basically, the 1992 thesis tended to confirm that at points where it was tested, Markan priority seemed to make more sense than an alternative solution.

15 See, e.g., Johnson (1991 and 1992), Kurz (1993) and Tannehill (1986 and 1990).

16 Arguments for Luke–Acts being a two-volume work are probably stronger than those against; so Beck (1977), Maddox (1982) and Marshall (1983). Wenham (1991, p. 229f.) thinks the unity of Luke–Acts to be a baseless assumption; their unity is assumed throughout this study.

question. Translators and commentators alike have tended to see Luke's δίκαιος at Luke 23.47 as this evangelist's way of affirming Jesus' innocence (see chapter 3). For some, the reason for this Lukan affirmation was that political authorities might recognise there was nothing to fear from the nascent Church. Vigorous discussion of the question of Luke's purposes continues, but this study's interest in it is *primarily* to show that Kilpatrick's 'apologetic' argument has been considerably weakened.

For example, Kilpatrick (whose pivotal role in this discussion is noted in chapter 3A) argued for the possibility that at Luke 23.47 δίκαιος meant 'innocent'. 'To do this it must be shown both that the translation "righteous" is unsuitable and that δίκαιος does on occasion have the meaning "innocent". It must also be shown that the meaning accords more satisfactorily with the theme of the Lucan Passion story *and with the general purpose of the Gospel*' (1942, p. 34, italics added). Kilpatrick found this 'general purpose' in political apologetic. More recent discussion suggests that Luke's intention was to write for Christians rather than for 'outsiders', and that it is unlikely that the two volumes served some politically apologetic purpose.

While Kilpatrick rightly identified Jesus' innocence as one theme in Luke's passion story, he confused 'theme' with 'purpose'. Marshall (1983, pp. 290f.) carefully distinguished the evangelist's principal aims from his secondary, that is 'conscious purpose' from 'themes'. Cassidy (1983, p. 153) reflected on the tendency to confuse the two, concluding: 'The presence of an innocent Jesus in Luke's account does not thereby establish the presence of a political apologetic even though the two concepts have been linked in many previous analyses.' In chapters 3 and 4 below a case is urged that this Gospel's theme of Jesus' innocence is essentially part of a larger scriptural model of δίκαιος with which Luke was working.

Earlier discussion of Luke's purpose(s) was frequently closely tied to assessments of δίκαιος at Luke 23.47; Caird, Drury, Fitzmyer and Marshall are among those whose work will be examined below, where it becomes clearer that prior decisions about Luke's purposes in writing his work profoundly affect commentators' views of the centurion's 'confession'. Consequently, any reassessment of the 'centurion's' use of δίκαιος must include a reassessment of the evangelist's perceived purposes, and because this has been in process for some years, this study will work with *provisional assumptions*, based on what current research commends. From that body of opinion it is provisionally assumed that: Luke–Acts is addressed to a Christian readership; the two volumes address a Christian community's complex needs in a specific situation; the work's major themes would prove incomprehensible to someone outside the Christian community. The reasons for this provisional position are eclectic, drawing on recent discussion of the question from which the more influential factors are set out below.

Difficulties in discerning Luke's purposes

The absence of a current consensus concerning Luke's purposes shows the difficulties students have encountered in identifying them. They tend to work with three possible sources for learning of Luke's purposes: first, external testimony; second, the author's own statement of his purposes; third, a process of deduction from his work. Since there is no early external attestation of Luke's purposes – the so-called anti-Marcionite prologues shed no light on this (see Fitzmyer, 1981, pp. 35–41; see also Wenham, 1991, pp. 184ff.) – readers are left with only the second and third sources to help them, and the second source itself presents great difficulties.[17]

Apart from the Fourth Gospel's very different opening, a hymnic prologue possibly matched by that of Hebrews, Luke's two-volume work is unique in the New Testament in having prefaces, but Evans (1990, p. 115) probably speaks for most commentators:[18] 'Unfortunately, by reason of its extreme compression, its conventional character and its high-flown vocabulary [the preface to Luke] proves ambiguous at several points, and singularly uninformative as a whole.' The conventional character of Luke's opening sentence probably relates his work to contemporary Graeco-Roman literary models (Alexander, 1986 and 1993; Fitzmyer, 1981, pp. 287f.); this author's work is thus more obviously in the public domain than other New Testament writings. The editors of *BC* (II, pp. 133–7) note that 'preface' has to represent three distinct literary forms and that Luke's Gospel is preceded by a προοίμιον while Acts has a προέκθεσις, making Luke–Acts a reasonably neat parallel to Josephus' Contra Apion. So Brown (1978, pp. 99–111) explored the

[17] Discussion of the prefaces has been vigorous: see, e.g., Alexander (1986 and 1993); Aune (1981); Cadbury (1921); Minear (1973); Parker (1965); Robbins (1979); Talbert (1988, pp. 7f., 9f.).

[18] Alexander (1986, p. 53), in her checklist of characteristics of Luke's preface, notes a similar set to those offered by Evans.

interrelationships among Luke's two 'prefaces' and Talbert's list of five possible 'purposes' for Luke–Acts, noting that one's reading of the prefaces depended on whether he believed Luke–Acts to be a unitary work or Acts to be an afterthought. Only a unitary Luke–Acts will have προοίμιον and προέκθεσις; two separate works probably imply two distinct purposes and it is the existence of Acts which complicates the issues. 'The basic problem of Luke's theology is, quite simply, the fact that he wrote the Acts of the Apostles' (Franklin, 1975, p. 9). There is wide, though not unanimous, agreement that these two volumes comprise one work; what *kind* of work Luke produced remains the subject of continuing debate.[19]

Hypotheses of address to the Roman world

The notion of Luke's writing to secure for Christians the same legal status for their religion as that enjoyed by Jews has been effectively dismissed by both Esler and Maddox. Esler (1987, pp. 211–14) emphatically rejected the concept of *religio licita*, choosing instead to accept that Rome involved itself in only a pragmatic way in the religious affairs of its Jewish inhabitants. While Esler acknowledged that Judaism enjoyed a privileged position in the Roman world, he also noted evidence, primarily from Josephus, suggesting that such privilege derived principally from Rome's respect for ancestral custom, for what Jews actually did, rather than for what they believed. Rome was more interested in stability than in revelation. He further noted that after 70CE there was a positive financial disincentive to Christian search for legal parity with Judaism: Vespasian made the Jewish Temple tax, formerly paid for the upkeep of the Jerusalem Temple, now payable to Jupiter Capitolinus and due from all Jews over three years of age, both male and female.[20] Maddox (1982, pp. 91–3) also denied the existence of a legal category of *religio licita*, but further insisted that the institutional unity of Jew and Christian presupposed by Luke's alleged appeal to Rome is quite at variance with the position at the end of Acts where the writer's emphasis is on the separation of Church and synagogue.

Although commentators now tend not to appeal to the concept of *religio licita* they may wish to have Luke address more general

[19] Literature on the Lukan genre is extensive: see, e.g., Talbert (1974, pp. 125–43) or Sanders and Davies (1989) or Tuckett (1987) for surveys.

[20] Esler was drawing on Smallwood, E. M., *The Jews under Roman Rule*, Leiden, Brill, 1976.

political concerns and to argue a defence of Christianity in the face of public suspicion or attack. Barrett (1961, p. 63), writing of the purposes of Acts, dealt a devastating, frequently quoted, blow to all theories which present Luke–Acts as a political *apologia* to Rome:

> No Roman official would ever have filtered out so much of what to him would be theological and ecclesiastical rubbish in order to reach so tiny a grain of relevant apology. So far as Acts was an apology, it was an apology addressed to the Church, demonstrating Paul's anti-Gnostic orthodoxy, and his practical and doctrinal solidarity with the Church at Jerusalem.

One does not have to accept Barrett's hypothesis of an anti-Gnostic thrust in Luke–Acts to appreciate the strength of his brusque assessment of the political value of Luke's two volumes in a Roman setting.

These two considerations, taken in conjunction with Cassidy's and Marshall's distinction between theme and purpose, substantially weaken the case developed by advocates of a Lukan address to a Roman audience. It is this that makes one wonder why Evans (1990, p. 111) appears to decide marginally in favour of Luke–Acts' having been designed for a non-Christian audience before coming, by some route, to be part of Christian literature and, ultimately, canonical.

Hypotheses of address to a Christian audience

More recent writing takes seriously the probability that Luke's two volumes were designed for Christian reading.[21] Esler (1987), Franklin (1975), Karris (1978), Maddox (1982), Marshall (1970 and 1983) and Talbert (1974) agree in this assessment but differ substantially in the accounts they give of the composition of Luke's community and of its situation, needs and concerns.[22] Maddox is

[21] This raises the question why the volumes needed so grand an opening – if grand opening it be. Alexander (1986) identifies Luke 1.1–4 as a label with an address.

[22] Goulder (1978, pp. 1f.) offers indirect support to the Christian destination of Luke:

> How were ancient books advertised? It was often the practice of an author to become known by giving readings in public or at private dinner-parties. Did Luke perhaps give readings at dinner-parties? If so, to judge by the general tenor of the Gospel at least – the Septuagintal style, for example, the assumed background of Jewish ways, the stress upon perseverance and

sure (1982, p. 14) that a number of Lukan features demand a reader's prior acquaintance with and interest in the substance of Christian belief and practice: Luke's subtle use of the Greek Bible; his unexplained use of terms like 'Son of man' and 'Kingdom of God'; the fact that the 'Beatitudes and the eschatological discourses have an esoteric sound'; many parables are addressed specifically to Christians, others make more sense on the ground that the book is addressed to Christians. Maddox questioned whether Luke would have revealed the Lord's Prayer and the words of institution of the Lord's Supper to 'outsiders'. Because of such considerations, Maddox judged it right to read Luke–Acts as a work addressed to Christians. Esler (1987, p. 25) followed him approvingly, adding that a Lukan address to outsiders would have looked more like Paul's Areopagus speech or Justin Martyr's *Apology*. Cassidy (1983, p. 146f.) hinted at the great diversity of possible communities and originating circumstances. That diversity is exemplified below in the work of writers who were concerned principally with Luke's purposes as they might be disclosed by his themes or interests or redactional concerns.

Talbert (1966 and 1974 pp. 111–24) argued that Luke–Acts was written to combat Gnosticism; Barrett (1961, pp. 62f.) urged that Luke's rejection, root and branch, of Gnosticism constituted one of his two main theological concerns. But Talbert (1970, pp. 171–222) argued a far more complex case than at first might appear. Acknowledging that Conzelmann's lasting contribution to the study of Luke–Acts was his characterisation of Luke as a theologian (Conzelmann, 1960), Talbert demonstrated that Conzelmann's reading of Luke's theology was flawed by his profoundly mistaken understanding of Luke's eschatology.[23] Luke's redaction of his sources strongly suggested that he was rebutting an overrealised eschatology in his community: some people were spiritualising the parousia, saying that it had already happened. Talbert set great store by Luke's eschatological timetable (Luke 17.20–37; 21.8–36) and by the point on it where this evangelist and his community apparently stood – very near the End. This could be affirmed

the danger of apostasy – they will have been Christian dinner-parties; and Christian dinner-parties sound like Church services.

[23] See especially Marshall's critique of Conzelmann's work (1970, pp. 77–88; but judicious use of his index, p. 239, gives a much fuller picture.)

because much of the timetable had already been completed,[24] *but the End was not yet.* Luke's two volumes were written for a community facing a hermeneutical crisis (Talbert, 1970, p. 209); among them an overrealised eschatology was accompanied by a docetic transformation of christology. By identifying the *lived tradition* among the apostles (in the Acts),[25] and by prefixing to it an account of *the source of that lived tradition* (Jesus in the Gospel) Luke formally crystallised the apostolic tradition.

Franklin (1975, pp. 173–82) saw Luke as essentially a pastor and preacher seeking to reestablish 'faith in the Lordship of Jesus which his readers had once shared, but which was now in danger of being lost because of the problems such a belief faced' (1975, p. 174). Franklin's analysis of Luke–Acts had led him to identify three such problems: the failure of the parousia to happen; the failure of Jewish response to the gospel; the nature of Jesus' life and crucifixion.

Maddox (1982) also identified a real community with real needs: ecclesiological and eschatological. But these twin concerns prove to be different from what might have been expected, and much more like what has already been met in Talbert and Franklin. The major question underlying Luke's ecclesiology is 'Who are the Christians?' (1982, pp. 31–65, 183–6). For Maddox, this question was essentially about Israel as the community of salvation: Jews had mostly rejected the message about Jesus; but the promises of God were to Israel; were Christians in danger of thinking of themselves as divorced from the community of salvation? The same question underlies Maddox's understanding of eschatology – the Christians are people in a specific historical situation (1982, pp. 100–57, 186). Maddox was unconvinced by arguments seeking to show Luke's purpose as to teach his community that the parousia would be long delayed (1982, p. 115). For him, Luke's emphasis is both on the present fulfilment of eschatological hopes – for example, the presence of the Holy Spirit among them, the incoming of the Gentiles – and on the certainty of the consummation. Maddox (1982, p. 186) returned to Luke's preface to confirm his reading of it: the two

24 I have avoided discussion of dating Luke–Acts because that would involve too long an excursus. On balance, I incline to the view that an earlier date is to be preferred to a later: so, e.g., Robinson (1976) and especially Hemer (1989, ch. 9). It is possible to square Esler's overall position with an earlier date, probably a date *before* the Fall of Jerusalem, possibly pre-64–5.

25 See Talbert (1988, pp. 2–6) on legitimating the Gospel by demonstrating that the apostles were authorised by Jesus and lived consonantly with his teaching. This is taken up in chapter 8 below.

words which stood out for him were ἀσφάλεια and πεπληροφορημένα, words which spoke of the fulfilment of God's purposes expressed in scripture and of the confidence – assurance – which properly belonged to the evangelist's community (1982, p. 187).

Marshall (1983) wrote to clarify his earlier statement which had been characterised as 'vague' (1970, pp. 216–22). Noting that commentators tended to offer little in way of discussion of Luke's purposes, with some reservation Marshall welcomed Maddox's contribution. Marshall was able to identify a number of factors in recent writing which form a core around which he worked: van Unnik's view that Acts is the confirmation of the Gospel; Maddox's affirmation of a Lukan twofold view of fulfilment; Lohfink's view that Luke–Acts presents the story of how God gathered a new Israel, both Jew and Gentile. Binding together what happened before and after Easter, Luke concerned himself with Jesus and his followers in relation to the Kingdom of God and to salvation; there are clear continuities between the Gospel and Acts in its christology and eschatology, in its treatment of Jesus' teaching and its understanding of mission.

The ἀσφάλεια of the Gospel is located in a correspondence between prophecy and its fulfilment which legitimates the ministry of salvation. It looks as though Theophilus' catechism needed firming up and that he was offered the facts on ' how we got to where we are'. **Hemer**'s treatment of Luke's preface (1989, pp. 321–8), linking it with consideration of the 'we-passages', generally supports Marshall's reading of the situation. His references to τὸ ἀσφαλές within Acts are particularly supportive of what ἀσφάλεια may denote in the preface.[26]

Houlden (1984), in a critique of the second chapter of Maddox's book, appears to dissent from its thesis only in respect of the picture it presented of Luke's attitude to Judaism. After surveying Luke's enigmatic picture of Judaism, Houlden suggested (1984, p. 61) that Luke and his community lived at some distance from the time when relations between synagogue and Church were turbulent and that there were certain reasons for Luke's encouraging Christians to welcome and forgive Jews:

> The 'certain reasons' concern the chief source of threat as far as Luke was concerned. It came from within, as he shows Paul foreseeing in his one speech to a Christian

[26] – which was less than Mark but more than Acts 10.34–43!

> audience. Addressing responsible leaders, Paul puts his finger on the coming danger from Christians 'speaking perverse things' (Acts 20.30). And for Luke, I suspect, it was all too true, part of that general crisis in the Church of the late first and early second centuries about the location of authority, when there were diverse views on what Christianity really was.

Houlden's suggestion was that the evidence of Luke–Acts tended to support a view that the work was written in a context of uncertainty about Judaism's relation to Christianity in two temporal dimensions: the past – that is, how both traditions related to scripture and to Jesus; the present – that is, how they now related as two increasingly distinguishable institutions. Houlden's view was that part of the uncertainty had to do with where authority really lay in the Christian tradition and that the diversity of competing views included the option of cutting loose altogether from Jewish roots – that chosen, for example, by Marcion. While Houlden affirmed that it is hard to know what Luke is really about, at the end he focused on the Church's internal disputes:

> Internal conflict was, of course, not new – it went back to the time of Paul. What was new was that now it was in the context of a Church much clearer about its separateness from Judaism. In that new distinctiveness, there was less worry about Jews and more energy available for the fresh and never-ending problem of preserving Christian unity and identifying orthodoxy. (1984, p. 64)

Esler (1987, p. 58), dissenting from Houlden's account of the ambivalence in Luke's attitude to Judaism, offered a new sociological approach to the question of Luke's purposes. His work has the twin merits both of taking seriously the complex issues Luke appears to treat, and of offering a case study of a Christian community towards the end of the first century.[27] This community embodied both religious and socio-economic diversity: orthodox Jew and formerly idolatrous pagan gathered around one eucharistic table; a 'glittering elite', including Roman soldiers and officials, and the 'squalid urban poor' (1987, p. 221) were numbered among them. To set in motion the dynamics of this diverse group, Esler introduced the probability that they had recently become estranged from

[27] But see n. 24 above.

the local synagogue. Esler identified three basic problems faced by this community for which Luke wrote: there was a question of the community's relation to the God of Abraham; a question about social justice and Jesus' known teaching about wealth; a question of whether Roman members of the community might properly support a movement whose founder had been executed.[28] This was possibly a pressing problem for (former?) Roman soldiers and officials in Luke's community: how might they remain Christian when both Jesus and Paul had suffered at the hands of Roman courts? Esler argued that the politically sensitive Lukan material which has frequently been presented as evidence for Luke–Acts' apologetic purposes is, in fact, an element addressed to Roman Christians to legitimate their continuing allegiance both to the state and to Jesus (1987, pp. 201–19). (Esler might also have asked whether *Jewish* members of the community, disturbed by their recent rift with the synagogue, did not know what to make of the *manner* of Jesus' execution: his shameful death raised the question whether he was cursed by God (Deut. 21.22–3; see chapter 7) or *really* (ὄντως) a godly man (see chapter 8).)

Summary

Read in the light of these concerns and possible contexts, Luke's preface takes on a distinctly *Christian* tone. Its emphatic ἀσφάλεια now strongly suggests the work's normative nature. Its reference to the 'things fulfilled among us' probably anticipates Luke's theme of scriptural fulfilment.[29] Its avowed rooting in the testimony of those who were eyewitnesses and became ministers of the word indicates the work's interest in 'apostolicity'. Even Theophilus' having been

[28] It is to this group in the community that Luke addressed his apparently political apologetic, not to 'outsiders'. Given the likelihood of Jesus' shameful death as a cause of separation from the local synagogue, Luke's emphasis on Jesus' passion as an element in God's plan and on a δίκαιος-matrix as a way of understanding and resolving the problem is clearer. This is taken up in chapter 8 below.

[29] πεπληροφορημένων: 'The suggestion that the fulfilment of Scripture is what Luke means need hardly be taken seriously, though of course, πληρόω is so used' (Cadbury, 1922, p. 496). Fitzmyer (1981, p. 293) and Caird (1963, p. 48 by implication) offer good reason for dissenting from Cadbury's judgment. However tempting it is to see Luke's πεπληροφορημένων as somehow linked to the ἤρξατο of Acts 1:1 (so Cadbury, 1922, p. 496), read in the light of Luke's regular, even insistent appeal (overt or allusive) to scripture, this word should be taken to *include* fulfilment of scripture as well as the coming to fruition within the infant church of what began with Jesus' ministry.

catechised can safely stand; he and other readers may be assured that their practices, experiences and beliefs stand firmly within the mainstream of the Church's life *and within God's salvation plan*, which is now perceived also to embrace Jesus' apparently shameful death.

When one adds to this picture the widely acknowledged fact that Luke makes careful and profound use of the Bible (so, for example, Bock (1987), Cadbury, (1958, see index of 'Scripture' and 'Septuagint'), Clarke (1922), Drury (1976, esp. chapter 4), Fitzmyer (1981, esp. pp. 113–25), Franklin (1975, pp. 73f.)), not simply citing it but building into his work allusions, echoes, patterns and key concepts, it becomes clearer that Kilpatrick's initial assumptions were mistaken and that Luke's *Christian* interests go far beyond the needs or concerns of political apologetic.

Consequently, any argument which approaches Luke's account of Jesus' death as though it were simply part of a political apologetic must now be suspect. In part II it is assumed that the focus of this work – the tracing of a Lukan *theologia crucis* through exploring three distinctive Lukan elements – is unblurred by confusion over Luke's purposes. While scholars may not be certain of what those purposes were, they may *assume* enough of a consensus to detach this monograph's central concern from another disputed area of Lukan study.

PART II

Substantial matters: three distinctive elements at Luke 23.46, 47

2

LUKE'S USE OF ΔΟΞΆΖΕΙΝ ΤῸΝ ΘΕΌΝ

Luke's narrative of Jesus' death and its immediate sequel (Luke 23.47) places before his centurion's 'confession' of Jesus as δίκαιος, an enigmatic ἐδόξαζεν τὸν θεόν. Why, as Hanson demanded, glorify God for the shameful death of an innocent man? This is certainly more than a 'Lukan stock phrase',[1] but Franklin, while noting both that the phrase is significant[2] for Luke and that its appearance at Luke 23.47 underlines the validity of the centurion's response, underestimated its peculiar force in Luke–Acts (1975, p. 62; cf. Stanton, 1974, pp. 35–9 and Marshall, 1970, p. 203).

This 'peculiar force' derives from a number of factors at work in each of the pericopae where the phrase appears. First, it signifies a *worshipping response* by people who have recognised God's presence at work in Jesus; perhaps this hint of 'presence' is why δοξάζειν rather than its synonyms is the verb used here, echoing δόξα with all its Septuagintal overtones.[3] Second, the phrase is related to Luke's understanding of a *scriptural plan of salvation* so that wherever the phrase occurs it is accompanied by allusions to or reminiscences of scriptural passages. This feature echoes Luke's prologue where his work is described as a διήγησις περὶ τῶν πεπληροφορημένων ἐν ἡμῖν πραγμάτων. Third, taken together, the incidents which are linked to the phrase relate closely to the *programme*[4] set out in Luke 7.22, 23 as Jesus answers John's messengers, to an earlier statement of Jesus' programme in the Nazareth sermon (Luke 4.16–30), and to Simeon's canticle (Luke 2.29–32). Luke's notion of 'fulfilment' is thus twofold: directly or obliquely he recalls scriptural passages

1 Creed (1930, p. 288) speaks of the phrase as 'a characteristic Lucan addition'.

2 While this is the case, Franklin has not shown *in what sense or senses* the phrase is significant for Luke; see D below for an assessment of the phrase – its 'peculiar force' – in Lukan use.

3 See, e.g., *TDNT* II.242–5, 253f. Δοξάζειν τὸν Θεόν in LXX and NT is ultimately to affirm and to celebrate God's nature.

4 The evidence for this is set out in B below, 'A Lukan Programme'.

whose echoes allow people to perceive in Jesus an agent of God as, for example, Elijah was, but Luke also ties in such 'disclosure moments' with his outline of Jesus' salvation programme. Fourth, frequently, but not invariably, the phrase is used by Luke to distinguish sharply between those who *do* perceive God's activity in that of Jesus and those who are his opponents; there are appropriate responses to what is seen and heard and inappropriate responses.

The phrase thus acts as a Lukan signal for those moments when God's purposes, revealed in scripture, to save his people – purposes expressed also in Jesus' programme outlined in the Nazareth sermon – are being fulfilled in Jesus' activity. If that is the case, then its appearance at Luke 23.47 alerts a reader to the presence of much more than a stock phrase, rather to a 'disclosure moment' illuminated both by God's scriptural plan[5] and by Jesus' kerygmatic programme.

The remainder of this chapter sets out evidence for this 'peculiar force' in Luke's use of δοξάζειν τὸν θεόν.[6] The first section (A) examines Lukan usage in the Gospel. The second (B) explores the relation of this phrase to Luke's programme; the third (C) takes up Luke's practice in Acts.

A. Δοξάζειν τὸν Θεὸν in Luke's first volume

1. Luke 2.20

> καὶ ὑπέστρεψαν οἱ ποιμένες δοξάζοντες καὶ αἰνοῦντες τὸν θεὸν ἐπὶ πᾶσιν οἷς ἤκουσαν καὶ εἶδον καθὼς ἐλαλήθη πρὸς αὐτούς.

Pace Conzelmann's approach to Lukan theology,[7] the birth narratives belong to Luke's two-volume work, constituting an overture to a larger piece, and introducing many themes to be developed within his overall διήγησις. Their atmosphere is that of

[5] Throughout this monograph, phrases like 'God's scriptural plan' are shorthand for '*Luke's* understanding of God's plan, revealed in scripture, to save people'.

[6] See Doble (1992); Detached Note 3: 'Words of Praise in Luke–Acts'.

[7] Conzelmann's (1960) approach is one of studied neglect: his references to Luke's first two chapters are usually found in the notes and he makes no use of the infancy material in developing his work. Indeed, his note (1960, p. 16, n. 3) on using Acts 1.1 to fix the limits of Luke's Gospel appears to indicate his *formal exclusion* from consideration of the birth and childhood narratives. This neglect has earned him much criticism: e.g., Fitzmyer (1989, p. 63); Marshall (1970, pp. 96–105); see Oliver (1964) for a discussion of the unity of Lukan theology expressed in the birth stories.

first-century Jewish piety in a Septuagintal tone, and the people portrayed in them represent the Israel of God (this theme is explored in chapter 4A below). Among such people the shepherds play a minor role. R. E. Brown makes that point firmly: 'The shepherds are intermediaries who have no major importance in themselves ... They are forerunners, not of the apostles, but of future believers who will glorify God for what they have heard and will praise God for what they have seen' (1979, p. 429 n. 69). While the distinction apparently made in that statement between doxological responses to seeing and hearing is probably unsustainable, Brown has identified Lukan features which do attach themselves to the phrase δοξ- τὸν Θεόν wherever it occurs; at Luke 7.22, for example, Jesus' reply to John's messengers is built around an instruction to report what they *see and hear*, and in the other passages to be examined the verbs ἰδεῖν and ἀκούειν are never far from, and frequently are the efficient cause of, the response conveyed by δοξάζειν τὸν Θεόν. It can be argued that the stories cannot be told without using these verbs; perhaps so, but their regular presence, their relation to Luke's fulfilment theme and their echoing Luke 7.22 strongly suggest that, for Luke, glorifying God is a response to what eyes have seen and ears heard, one dimension of his theme of witnessing.

The shepherds return δοξάζοντες καὶ αἰνοῦντες τὸν Θεόν.[8] The verb αἰνέω and its related αἶνος are Lukan: six of the verb's eight occurrences in the NT are found in Luke–Acts and one of the noun's two uses is in the Gospel. Yet however Lukan, these words are not synonymous with the δοξάζειν group (in a more radical sense than a formal assertion that there are no synonyms, see chapter 3E below). The phrase as a whole is best taken as one of the pairings which mark Luke's style (Dawsey, 1989, pp. 48–66) and may also echo the LXX as, for example, Psalm 21.24 and Daniel 4.34. Such echoing fits Luke's evocation in these chapters of an atmosphere of Jewish piety.[9]

The reason for the shepherds' worshipping response is ἐπὶ πᾶσιν οἷς ἤκουσαν καὶ εἶδον καθὼς ἐλαλήθη πρὸς αὐτούς. What they had *heard* is to be found in the angel's message to them, itself

[8] In Luke's Gospel, apart from the disputed appearance of αἰνέω at 24.53 where the text of N-A 26 is surely to be preferred, these two words belong together in a kind of Septuagintal pairing. Αἰνέω, though not a synonym for the target phrase, lives in close harmony with it, figuring most frequently where the verbal or nominal form of δόξα is found: 2.13, 20; cf. 19.38. See note 5 above.

[9] See notes 6 and 8 above; the Detached Note comments on the relation of δοξ- τὸν Θεόν to other Lukan words of praise.

set in a 'seeing' context – καὶ δόξα Κυρίου περιέλαμψεν αὐτούς. That δόξα, recalling for a reader the rooting of the word in God's theophanies to his People during their wilderness experience, is the primary reason for the shepherds' response in ascribing to God the δόξα which is properly his. The angel announced good news: εὐαγγελίζομαι is Lukan while he seems studiously to eschew εὐαγγέλιον. Of the fifty three occurrences of the verb in the NT, Luke–Acts accounts for 47 per cent; of the fourteen occurrences of εὐαγγέλιον in the gospels and Acts, none is found in Luke's Gospel and only two in Acts (14 per cent). Announcement of good news is a Lukan theme expressed, for example, in Luke 7.22, πτωχοὶ εὐαγγελίζονται, a fact of which John's messengers were bidden take note – πορευθέντες ἀπαγγείλατε Ἰωάννῃ ἃ *εἴδετε* καὶ ἠκούσατε.

The angel's message is described as a source of joy for all people; τῷ λαῷ at this point strongly suggests that Israel is to be the recipient, although, because τῶν λαῶν at Luke 2.31 must refer to both Israel and the Gentiles, this conclusion cannot be final; Luke may have had his wider audience in mind from the beginning. Indeed, in view of Luke's overall purpose it is important to clarify this, particularly since Sanders (1987, p. 48) has claimed that a distinction is to be drawn between Luke's absolute use of λαός to signify the Church and 'People of Israel' to designate Jewish people – he cited Luke 2.32 to substantiate this. At this point, because of its setting, Luke probably intended the angelic message to be for Israel. Marshall notes that πᾶς ὁ λαός is typically Lukan (1978, p. 109) and argues for its referring to Israel rather than to Gentiles; in this he is supported by both Creed and Fitzmyer. In view of the Jewish colouring of Luke's narrative it is not easy to see how at this point τῷ λαῷ can mean anything other than Israel (*contra* Sanders). Deutero-Isaiah's opening verse addressed itself to the People of God; similarly, probably from the same theological provenance, this Lukan angelic messenger announced joyful news, namely, that a child had been born. Whether this echoes Isaiah 9.1–6 may be debated fiercely; so much of the Lukan passage's vocabulary and thinking is found in this Isaianic passage that a reader must ask whether Luke has produced a *midrash*[10] on it in line with his clearly

10 Both Brown (1979, pp. 557–62) and Fitzmyer (1981, p. 309) have reservations about the use of this word in relation to the infancy narratives. It is possibly safer to speak of Luke's having fused in his mind the language, thought patterns and hopes of Isaiah with the Christian sources which moved him.

announced fulfilment theme (Luke 1.1). Χώρα, σκότος, φῶς μέγα, λάμψει and a note of rejoicing are common to both passages. Central to both is the announcement of a birth; while the boy's titles differ, in each case his *stature* is spelt out. Further, the Lukan angelic chorus' announcement of 'peace' has its counterpart in Isaiah 9.6 and εἰρήνη is certainly a Lukan interest. The Isaianic child is destined for David's throne and his everlasting rule was to be marked by justice and righteousness; the Lukan announcement, echoing Isaiah's words, is of a child born in David's city. But this child has been born σήμερον, with all that that implies for Luke. His titles are also important: Σωτήρ is Lukan as is the absolute use of ὁ Κύριος for Jesus. Χριστός is probably to be read as 'messiah' rather than as an adjectival 'anointed,' so anticipating Acts 2.36. Yet each in its own way 'fulfils' not only the Isaianic passage, but also other scriptural anticipations.

There is to be a confirmatory sign for the shepherds that this fulfilment has in fact occurred. Again, commentators have found echoes of scriptural bases, most particularly in the reference to a φάτνη. Isaiah's oracles open with a complaint:

> Ἄκουε, οὐρανέ, καὶ ἐνωτίζου, γῆ, ὅτι Κύριος ἐλάλησεν. υἱοὺς ἐγέννησα καὶ ὕψωσα, αὐτοὶ δέ με ἠθέτησαν. ἔγνω βοῦς τὸν κτησάμενον καὶ ὄνος τὴν φάτνην τοῦ Κυρίου αὐτοῦ. Ἰσραὴλ δέ με οὐκ ἔγνω, καὶ ὁ λαός με οὐ συνῆκεν. (Isa. 1.2–3)

The confirmatory sign is thus that the φάτνη τοῦ Κυρίου is now known, where Κύριος is probably a designation of Jesus. Shepherds come and see and *understand* that God has acted and is made known in the act to all who can grasp its significance. Throughout the gospel there are to be those who hear, see and then glorify God for what they have perceived. Isaiah's oracle focuses sharply on Israel's rejection of her God: Luke's two-volume work witnesses to a renewed Israel's response to her Master. The σημεῖον itself contains echoes of scripture, linking with Luke's setting out of 'oracles fulfilled' or brought to completion.

Luke's shepherds also receive confirmatory witness to this message through the πλῆθος στρατιᾶς οὐρανίου αἰνούντων τὸν θεὸν καὶ λεγόντων,

> Δόξα ἐν ὑψίστοις θεῷ καὶ ἐπὶ γῆς
> εἰρήνη ἐν ἀνθρώποις εὐδοκίας. (2.13–14)

This passage has been extensively discussed and most of the issues are outside our present concern. Three matters are, however, important for this study. First, as at Luke 19.38, the phrase Δόξα ἐν ὑψίστοις functions as an acclamatory form of δοξάζειν τὸν Θεὸν and may need to be taken into account in this survey of Luke's uses of δοξάζειν. Presumably, the heavenly hosts are responding in worship because they too have seen and heard what God has done to complete his scriptural plan of salvation. The juncture of αἰνέω with an acclamatory δόξα acts as an antiphon to the shepherds' αἰνοῦντες καὶ δοξάζοντες. Second, on earth, εἰρήνη with all its connotations is to be the lot of humans towards whom God has shown his goodwill. Εἰρήνη picks up for Luke all that *shalom* implied, constituting a major component of 'salvation' in his Gospel and the Acts; it includes the results of healing and forgiveness. Of the twenty-nine occurrences of the word in the Gospels and the Acts Luke's work accounts for 70 per cent. Third, when δόξα ἐν ὑψίστοις occurs at Luke 19.38 it is curiously inverted: while disciples acclaim the king (*sic*) who comes in the name of the Lord (ὁ ἐρχόμενος) they locate εἰρήνη **ἐν οὐρανῷ**. Nearing Jerusalem, they had seen much already that led them αἰνεῖν τὸν Θεὸν, but in the Lukan scheme of things εἰρήνη lay the other side of Jesus' ἀνάλημψις.

The presence of the heavenly host is both confirmatory and explanatory. Their response to the event's significance is one of praise and the ascription to God of glory. The counterpoint of heaven and earth is complete.

The shepherds' response, however, is also to what they *saw* – τὸ ῥῆμα τοῦτο τὸ γεγονός. Here ῥῆμα must have the character of 'oracle'. God (ὁ Κύριος) had made it known to them and it had come to be. On seeing this sign (φάτνη), they had made this oracle known, presumably to a large number of people (πάντες οἱ ἀκούσαντες). Their glorifying God was prompted by all that they had heard and seen καθὼς ἐλαλήθη πρὸς αὐτούς. The note of fulfilment is unmistakable here, but there is one difference from Luke's usage in other pericopae culminating in the phrase δοξ- τὸν Θεὸν – in this case God's presence is discerned not in Jesus' deed but in his presence as sign.

2. Luke 5.25 and 26

καὶ παραχρῆμα ἀναστὰς ἐνώπιον αὐτῶν, ἄρας ἐφ' ὃ κατέκειτο, ἀπῆλθεν εἰς τὸν οἶκον αὐτοῦ δοξάζων τὸν

> θεόν. καὶ ἔκστασις ἔλαβεν ἅπαντας καὶ ἐδόξαζον τὸν θεόν, καὶ ἐπλήσθησαν φόβου λέγοντες ὅτι Εἴδομεν παράδοξα σήμερον.

Although it is substantially shared with Matthew and Mark, Luke's account of Jesus' healing of a paralysed man is distinctive. Only in Luke does the man whom Jesus healed respond by standing up and glorifying God as 'he went home' (5.25), a phrase which in Luke appears to suggest restoration to the way things ought to be. Here is a man who has identified God at work in Jesus' activity. There is, further, a sharp distinctiveness about the opening verses of Luke's version of this narrative. No longer set in Capernaum, this conflict story is generalised by Luke's formal gathering of scribes and Pharisees from every village of Galilee and Judaea and from Jerusalem (5.17); this somewhat surprising company was sitting nearby as Jesus happened to be teaching. Luke's formalised opening of public conflict between Jesus and other religious leaders created a context for the whole of Jesus' ministry as this and ensuing conflicts prepare a reader for the passion narrative and echo the testing of Wisdom's δίκαιος.[11]

The opening of Luke's narrative was significantly enlarged and formalised; its conclusion reflects this. Two words particularly demand attention: σήμερον and παράδοξα. 'Today we have seen paradoxa.' Putting 'today' at the very beginning of the onlookers' response gives it the emphasis found in Luke's own syntax. Σήμερον is a significant Lukan word whose appearance at this point draws a reader's attention to an event's place in the scheme of salvation (e.g. Luke 4.21).

Παράδοξα presents different problems: because it is *hap. leg.* in the New Testament there is no possibility of identifying a normative Lukan use. Its presence may be due entirely to chance. This evangelist's vocabulary is wide and rich so Fitzmyer may well be correct in saying that it is the nearest word to 'miracle' that can be found (1981, p. 586); such an understanding would echo Markan tradition. But why should Luke choose to formalise the opening of this conflict story only to rewrite the ending as a simple variant of the sort of thing found in Mark? He did, in fact, do something very much more precise as the presence of σήμερον shows.

Παράδοξος is not frequently used in the LXX, but its presence is

[11] See chapter 7C, 'The virtuous life of Wisdom's δίκαιος', for an account of 'testing' in the Just One's biography.

instructive. Judith 13.13; Wisdom 5.2, 16.17 and 19.5; Sirach 43.25; 3 Maccabees 6.33 and 4 Maccabees 2.14 appear to be its uses. The Judith and Maccabees occurrences take up the *unexpectedness* of an event, clearly one of its root meanings according to *TDNT*, and the Sirach passage lends weight to refuting Fitzmyer's suggestion that παράδοξος approaches 'miracle' because there it points to God's work in nature.

The Wisdom passages do offer help. This group not only echoes a pattern of thought with which the substance of this work is concerned, but actually suggests itself as a source for Luke's use of παράδοξος in his distinctive telling of this story (see chapter 7; see also Nickelsburg (1972) for a discussion of the humiliation / vindication patterning to be found in intertestamental literature). In full, Wisdom 5.2 reads:

> ἰδόντες ταραχθήσονται φόβῳ δεινῷ καὶ ἐκστήσονται ἐπὶ τῷ παραδόξῳ τῆς σωτηρίας.

The subject of this sentence is the τῶν θλιψάντων αὐτὸν of 5.1, earlier described as ἀσεβεῖς (1.16; 2.10; 4.16) or even οἱ λαοὶ (4.14). Something of the significance of Wisdom 5.1–14 needs to be noted here. Wisdom 1.16–5.23 sets out a *pattern* of God's dealings with those who are faithful to him (this has been exhaustively discussed by Nickelsburg, 1972). There is much here that echoes Daniel 7–12 without the immediacy of the Maccabaean struggle, but Wisdom's δίκαιος replaces υἱὸς ἀνθρώπου in Daniel and δίκαιοι the 'saints of the Most High'. Wisdom's δίκαιος is taunted by his oppressors and brought by them to a shameful death (2.20). The heart of this pattern is God's vindication of those who have trusted him even to death:

> Δικαίων δὲ ψυχαὶ ἐν χειρὶ Θεοῦ καὶ οὐ μὴ ἅψηται αὐτῶν βάσανος. ἔδοξαν ἐν ὀφθαλμοῖς ἀφρόνων τεθνάναι, καὶ ἐλογίσθη κάκωσις ἡ ἔξοδος αὐτῶν καὶ ἡ ἀφ'ἡμῶν πορεία σύντριμμα. οἱ δέ εἰσιν ἐν εἰρήνῃ. (Wis. 3.1–3)

As in Daniel, but without that book's vivid description of a court, a final judgment is taken for granted; here it is spoken of as God's vindication (3.7) or a reckoning of sin (4.20). Wisdom 3.8 echoes Daniel 7.27 in its affirmation that the righteous will judge nations, rule over peoples (cf. 1 Cor. 6.1f.); Wisdom 5.1 says that in that reckoning the δίκαιος will stand up boldly and face those who oppressed him.

A number of words in the Wisdom passages immediately call for attention. Of ἔξοδος (3.2) as a reference to Jesus' death or resurrection or 'salvation event' no more will be said until chapter 7, but ἰδόντες, φόβος and παράδοξος are of particular importance in relation to Luke 5.26. This leaves φόβος and ἰδόντες to be examined. A suggestion that Matthew and Luke were here using a common source should be discounted (Matt.: ἐφοβήθησαν; Luke: ἐπλήσθησαν φόβου – which might itself represent a Septuagintalising of φοβεῖσθαι – while Mark has no reference to φόβος); the evidence is hardly compelling (with Marshall (1978), p. 216) and it seems likely that Luke's version owes more to the Wisdom pattern than to chance. Confirmation of this hypothesis is more a matter of matching patterns than of counting words.

Wisdom's use of παράδοξος proves instructive. Its basic thought is of what is unexpected or unlooked for (*TDNT* 11.255). The word is also used at Wisdom 16.17:

> τὸ γὰρ παραδοξότατον ἐν τῷ πάντα σβεννύντι ὕδατι πλεῖον ἐνήργει τὸ πῦρ.

This, in context, is a way of thinking of the signs which accompanied Israel's exodus from Egypt and is probably a *midrash* on Exodus 14.24, but its detail does not concern us here. Wisdom 19.18–22 speaks of the transfiguration of the κόσμος at the Exodus, itself an unexpected and, consequently, astonishing journey – παράδοξον ὁδοιπορίαν (Wis. 19.5). Both passages pick up a note of transformation in that the writer is concerned with signs of God's saving presence; the word here indicates the unlooked for and astonishing nature of God's being at work in these situations. But all of these events were viewed as part of a vindication of the People of God (Wis. 19.22).

This reflection offers a probable meaning for παράδοξος at Wisdom 5.2 where the just one's opponents are overwhelmed by the reversal of his fortunes; this reflects the parallelism of individual and corporate senses of δίκαιος – what happened to Israel at the Exodus was παράδοξος just as the eschatological vindication of the 'abstract' δίκαιος was παράδοξος. Here indeed is a παράδοξον τῆς σωτηρίας, and Luke's concern for σωτηρία and its various forms has been widely noted (see, e.g., Marshall, 1970, pp. 77–115).

Luke's firm editing of the opening of this pericope (Luke 5.17–26), his distinctive use of παράδοξος and, in a lesser degree, his choice of a Semitic use for φόβος in the conclusion of the story, seem to owe their presence here to a pattern of thought which works its way through his two volumes. It is relatively easy to examine his work's use of quotations: Luke 24.44–8 offers a programme which has been thoroughly explored in so far as the evangelist has *quoted* scripture. If, however, Luke not only quotes scripture but *adverts to patterns* like that written of in Luke 24.46, the task of identifying possible patterns that he was working with becomes both pressing and problematic. (See chapter 7B for a discussion of issues relating to Luke's use of Wisdom.)

In Luke 5.26 the formally assembled scribes and Pharisees are reported to have glorified God. Luke placed their reason for doing so firmly in a context different from that he found in his sources; in what had happened before them the opponents of this man (these men?) had seen and recognised a sign of God at work. Luke's version of this event suggests that he saw it as a proleptic eschatological judgment based on Wisdom's δίκαιος pattern.

3. Luke 7.16

> ἔλαβεν δὲ φόβος πάντας καὶ ἐδόξαζον τὸν θεὸν λέγοντες ὅτι Προφήτης μέγας ἠγέρθη ἐν ἡμῖν, καὶ ὅτι Ἐπεσκέψατο ὁ θεὸς τὸν λαὸν αὐτοῦ.

Because the whole episode was so written as to evoke the LXX,[12] it is no surprise to find ἔλαβεν δὲ φόβος πάντας. Its formal parallel to Luke 5.26 should not be missed because this suggests that Luke's 'patterning' was still at work. In both cases people glorify God because fear or awe grips them as they recognise the hand of God at work among them; Luke's people spell out (λέγοντες) what it is that has moved them. Two reasons are offered in this pericope for such emotion and for glorifying God: a *great prophet* had been raised among them; God had indeed *visited his people*. Each of the reasons is deeply rooted in scripture and each contributes to understanding the special force of Luke's δοξ-τὸν Θεόν.

A great prophet

The literature on this phrase is extensive.[13] For this study's purposes

12 See Brodie (1986).

13 See, e.g., Cullmann (1963); Dubois (1973); Ellis (1974); Fitzmyer (1981); Lindars (1965); Marshall (1978); Miller (1988); Ravens (1990). See also Elliott, J. K. (1969) and *TDNT* VI.841–8.

it does not much matter which of the variant accounts of προφήτης is most acceptable. It may be that its very ambiguity allows the phrase to trail behind it a rich assortment of scriptural patterns.

First, *some sort of Elijah typology* is at work here. Apart from its direct echo of 1 Kings 17.23 (Luke 7.15), and more distant echo of 2 Kings 4.36, the passage cannot fail to recall Elijah's raising of a widow's son (1 Kings 17.8–24). Luke's apparent policy of offering two witnesses for each category of event – a *son* of Abraham (Luke 19.9) and a *daughter* (13.16); Jairus' *daughter* (8.42) and the *boy* at Nain (7.12); a crippled *man* (5.18) and an ankylosed *woman* (13.11) *et al.* – puts alongside the narrative of Jairus' daughter an unambiguous statement of Elijah-like prophetic activity which allows a reader little doubt about reasons for the crowd's belief that Jesus is none other than Elijah (e.g. Luke 9.19).[14] Questions of Elijah's place in Lukan writing are discussed at length by Dubois (1973), Fitzmyer, (1981, pp. 213–15), Miller (1988) and Jeremias (*TDNT* II.928–41).

Second, *the coming one* may be hinted at in this phrase. This term may itself be a reference back to Elijah because Malachi 3.1, which speaks of God's eschatological messenger, is amplified by Malachi 3.22 which plainly says that this messenger will be Elijah. A prime reason for suspecting that this reference in Luke 7.16 to a great prophet may be to the Malachian concept is Luke's use of it in 7.20, within a pericope examined later in this chapter in B, 'A Lukan Programme'.

A third possible approach takes up the concept of the *Moses-like prophet* promised in Deuteronomy 18.15, 18. Because Luke cited this promise in both Acts 3.22–3 and Acts 7.37 the concept was certainly in his mind and he probably counted it among those 'things that had been fulfilled' (Luke 1.1). Because the Moses-like figure also appears in the transfiguration narrative (Luke 9.28–36), where the triple tradition has ἀκούετε αὐτοῦ (Luke 9.35 αὐτοῦ ἀκούετε), one may safely conclude that this echo of Deuteronomy 18.15 (αὐτοῦ ἀκούσεσθε – so also Acts 3.22) is a hint of the way in which Luke took up and explored what was already in the tradition that had come to him; his Acts references strengthen the transfiguration scene's probable meaning for him. Both Moses and Elijah speak with Jesus concerning the ἔξοδος he was about to complete

[14] Miller (1988) affirms that Luke wants to present Jesus' *prophet-like* activity because peoples' response related him to the 'Moses' figure rather than to Elijah.

in Jerusalem (so Luke 9.31 *diff.* Mark 9.4; see chapter 7G). The language of this addition points to two underlying themes: one is Jesus' ministry as a kind of renewed exodus, leading God's people into a new liberty from whatever bound them and prevented their being the People of God; the second theme presents Jesus as the heir of *both* Moses and Elijah, the two great prophets of Israel's past, renewed in her present. The one had promised a prophet to succeed him; the other had been 'taken up' and was popularly expected to return to usher in God's rule (cf. Mal. 3.1).

The phrase ἠγέρθη ἐν ἡμῖν is most probably a theological passive, although the presence of ὁ Θεός in the following phrase may have prompted Luke to avoid repetition. At this point ἐγείρειν is best read as 'to raise up' rather than 'to resurrect' however tempting it may be to detect such subtlety in Luke's thought. Although the verb is most frequently used in Luke–Acts of resurrection (Gospel 47 per cent, Acts 58 per cent), it is also used of physically 'getting up' (Gospel 29.4 per cent, Acts 33.3 per cent), of 'rising up' (in anger?) at Luke 21.10 (5.8 per cent) and of 'raising up' in some other sense, usually in a Septuagintal style (Gospel 17.6 per cent, Acts 8.3 per cent) Among these uses are Luke's own construction at Luke 1.69 (which echoes Ps. 17.3 and Ps. 131.17); Luke's use of a passage from the Dual Tradition about God's being able to 'raise up' children for Abraham from 'these stones' (Luke 3.8 // Matt. 3.9); there is also at Acts 13.22 a reference to God's deposing Saul and 'raising up' David as king. Luke's Προφήτης μέγας ἠγέρθη ἐν ἡμῖν (Luke 7.16) does not match Deuteronomy's Προφήτην ... ὡς ἐμὲ ἀναστήσει σοι Κύριος ὁ Θεός σου (Deut. 18.15), but there is an echo of it; on the other hand, although the other references to ἐγείρειν in Luke 7 are to resurrections it seems unwise to postulate some kind of Lukan foreshadowing of the resurrection in this verse.

This presentation of Jesus as prophet coheres with Luke's broad christology.[15] For example, after narrating Jesus' reading from the Isaiah scroll in the synagogue at Nazareth (Luke 4.16–23), Luke reported Jesus' words, 'No prophet is accepted in his own town ...' (4.24).[16] The narration continued with two direct references to

[15] See, e.g., Fitzmyer (1981, p. 213–15); Marshall (1970, pp. 125–8) and Ravens (1990). Marshall's treatment of Jesus as prophet is notable for its argument that the word evokes a *Servant* and *messianic* dimension; for comment on this, see chapter 8 below.

[16] Marshall (1970, p. 125ff.): '... Luke took up a view of Jesus which saw him not merely as a prophet but as the final prophet, the Servant and Messiah' (p. 128).

prophets, one to Elijah (4.25), the other to Elisha (4.27; see 'A deed reminiscent of Elisha' section 5 below). During his recounting of the walk to Emmaus (Luke 24.13–35) Luke portrayed two disciples reporting of Jesus that ' . . . *he was a prophet*, powerful in word and deed before God and all the people' (Luke 24.19), a judgment echoed, but without the word 'prophet', at Acts 10.38. Luke's more *indirect* presentation of Jesus as a prophet continued this theme: the story of Jesus' rejection by Samaritan villagers (Luke 9.51–6) is plainly an allusion to 2 Kings 1.10, 12 (the Lukan text is probably irrecoverable, but the *varia lectio* in some MSS 'even as Elijah did' is not unLukan), while at Luke 9.61–2 there is an unmistakable echo of 1 Kings 19.19–21, although prophet Jesus responds differently from prophet Elijah. Luke's typology does not consist in imitation but is found in points of reference where frequently what is made plain is that a *greater* than Elijah is here (cf. Luke 7.26 where Luke presents Jesus' testimony to John the Baptist – ναὶ . . . καὶ περισσότερον προφήτου). This may even be the case in the Nain story where *this* prophet's raising of the dead proceeds without the trouble experienced by Elijah.

What remains clear through all this discussion of 'a great prophet' is twofold:

first, Elijah is, above all else, a prophet whose mission brought him conflict, pursuit and threats of death from ungodly opponents. It is a consistent theme of the Elijah story that he knew himself to be a lonely, faithful witness to God, a theme which emerges in the concept of a δίκαιος;

second, Luke's concept of prophethood embraces the notion of martyrdom: it cannot be that a prophet should die outside Jerusalem (Luke 13.33); 'which of the prophets did your fathers not persecute?' (Acts 7.52).

It is a measure of Luke's interest in this christological category that it is referred to twenty-nine times in his Gospel against, for example, five in Mark's.

God's visitation

They were awed because God had visited his people:

Ἐπεσκέψατο ὁ θεὸς τὸν λαὸν αὐτοῦ. (Luke 7.16b)

This is the language of Jewish expectation (*TDNT* II.599ff.). Already, in the infancy prologue to his Gospel, Luke had twice used the verb ἐπισκέπτομαι, once at 1.68b and again at 1.78, both within Zachariah's hymn of praise. Brown (1979, pp. 377–92) set out the problems and possibilities of the hymn. In this passage the LXX is never far away; the canticle is probably a florilegium of quotations or half-remembered quotations from and echoes of scriptural passages. Ἐπισκέπτομαι is an OT word put to NT uses carrying its essential meaning with it wherever the subject is God, a meaning derived from its scriptural contexts rather than from secular Greek. The word points to God's entering the life of his People to make his will known to them, either graciously or in judgment (so *TDNT* II.602). Such is the 'meaning' of the word both in the Benedictus and here at Luke 7.16. The word is Lukan in that 64 per cent of its uses are found in Luke–Acts, and that usage continues into Acts although at Acts 6.3 the verb's subject is ἀδελφοί, at Acts 7.23 it is Moses and at Acts 15.36 it is Barnabas and Paul. At Acts 15.14, however, the subject is God who has acted to take for himself a people from among the Gentiles.

This verse from Acts leads into a second layer of Luke's use of Ἐπεσκέψατο ... τὸν λαὸν αὐτοῦ. There can be little doubt that at Luke 7.16 λαός refers to Israel; by the time his ordered narrative had reached Acts 15.14 Luke had already begun to reshape the concept of the People of God. Of immediate concern is that Luke *both* portrays people who respond to God's visitation by glorifying him, who know a prophet when they meet one, *and* that some Jews opposed Jesus throughout his ministry and were ultimately responsible for his death. The evidence suggests that Luke carefully used a group of words to characterise Jesus' audiences:

he used ὄχλος when he had in mind a neutral mass of people who listened to Jesus' words and observed his deeds;

λαός where his thought was rather more formally of 'the People of God';

and he frequently used the plural ἄνθρωποι as a way of indicating humankind in opposition to God.

These uses appear to be distinct and to mark off such groups from Jewish leaders among whom there are some, like Joseph of Arimathaea, who are commended (Luke 23.50 – ἀνὴρ ἀγαθὸς καὶ δίκαιος – see chapter 4A4 below), and some who plot to bring about this prophet's downfall (see chapter 7E to G). It is difficult to see how Sanders concludes that Acts 7.52 constitutes evidence of anti-Semitism since it simply summarises what a reading of Jewish scripture makes abundantly clear, namely that it is the nature of prophethood to proclaim a message of God's judgment on a rebellious people. The problem with Sanders' criteria is that no Hebrew prophet escapes a charge of anti-Semitism.

The thrust of Luke's Nain narrative emerges clearly through its structure: two great crowds of people met, one of mourners, the other of disciples. An action ensued which could not fail to evoke an awed response. Luke's report of this action is redolent of Elijah's career and recounted in words borrowed from the scriptural account of the earlier prophet's raising a dead boy.[17] This action stimulated talk about Jesus throughout the whole of Judaea and the surrounding districts. The crowds' responses were reported in a thoroughly Septuagintal form which served to emphasise that God was at work in and through Jesus; recognising a great prophet, the crowds acknowledged that God had 'visited' his People, and by their responses they ascribed glory to God.

The Nain narrative prepares the way for much that follows in the Gospel: both John the Baptist's question (7.19) and the narrative of Peter's 'confession' (9.18–22) presuppose this sort of story which both accounts for Jesus' fame and the assessments which people were making of him. The Nain narrative also prepares the way for darker things, Luke's account of Jesus' arrival at Jerusalem ends in a prophetic lament over a city whose doom is sealed ἀνθ ὧν οὐκ ἔγνως τὸν καιρὸν τῆς ἐπισκοπῆς σου. (Luke 19.44). In this pericope the δοξάζειν phrase has rich scriptural associations.

4. Luke 13.13

καὶ ἐπέθηκεν αὐτῇ τὰς χεῖρας· καὶ παραχρῆμα ἀνωρθώθη, καὶ ἐδόξαζεν τὸν θεόν.

The setting

This scene is played out in triangular fashion: its players are Jesus, the ἀρχισυνάγωγος who represents the ἀντικείμενοι (Luke 13.17) and πᾶς ὁ ὄχλος (Luke 13.17b). The woman whose healing

[17] For his argument that Luke was writing a *mimesis* of the earlier story Brodie (1986) offers much more evidence than the καὶ ἔδωκεν αὐτὸν τῇ μητρὶ αὐτοῦ of

prompted her to glorify God remains a lay figure throughout except in so far as she recognises God's salvation when she sees it. Hers is the 'proper' response to what happened and by it she shows herself to be truly one of God's People – indeed, a daughter of Abraham – and her response judges the others.

The opponents

Luke's portrayal of the ἀρχισυνάγωγος is stylised in that the man is presented as an opponent of Jesus' action. The key verb is δεῖ. For this ruler, Ἓξ ἡμέραι εἰσὶν ἐν αἷς δεῖ ἐργάζεσθαι· ἐν αὐταῖς οὖν ἐρχόμενοι θεραπεύεσθε καὶ μὴ τῇ ἡμέρᾳ τοῦ σαββάτου (Luke 13.14), to which Jesus' response is οὐκ ἔδει λυθῆναι ἀπὸ τοῦ δεσμοῦ τούτου τῇ ἡμέρᾳ τοῦ σαββάτου; (Luke 13.16). The issue is *halachic*: what is the proper reading of *Torah?* The woman is in no doubt that God has graciously intervened for her and, for Luke, her response is entirely appropriate. The ἀρχισυνάγωγος, despite seeing what had happened, set a question against the action's appropriateness on *this day*, the sabbath. Luke, however, having widened the opposition to Jesus to include all present who agreed with the ruler, portrayed them as Ὑποκριταί ... καὶ ταῦτα λέγοντος αὐτοῦ κατῃσχύνοντο πάντες οἱ ἀντικείμενοι αὐτῷ (Luke 13.17). These words probably form a key part of the 'stylising' spoken of above for they echo Isaiah 45.16 (LXX): αἰσχυνθήσονται καὶ ἐντραπήσονται πάντες οἱ ἀντικείμενοι αὐτῷ ... Luke probably had this Isaianic passage in mind when writing the pericope under consideration; 'in mind' rather than 'before him'. It would be foolish to try to make the ruler's position parallel that of idol makers! Jesus' argument which put his opponents to shame is an extension of the argument at Luke 6.9; it is an extension in that it takes tradition concerning what is and what is not lawful and shows how much more what is *permitted* for animals is *necessary* for humans. In this case the human is a daughter of Abraham, bound by Satan. The argument is conclusive, but its effect is to show how scripture has been fulfilled in what was going on.

The crowd

There is a third element in Luke's triangular scene: πᾶς ὁ ὄχλος ἔχαιρεν ἐπὶ πᾶσιν τοῖς ἐνδόξοις τοῖς γινομένοις ὑπ' αὐτοῦ

Luke 7.15b//1 Kings 17.23, but even this single phrase suggests dependence. Why does not N-A 26 offer this phrase in italics?

(Luke 13.17). 'Ενδόξος here is an interesting foil to παράδοξος at Luke 5.26. The word almost certainly denotes God's wonderful acts towards Israel (so *TDNT* 11.254), echoing the notion of God's own δόξα. That *all the crowd* rejoiced over the wonderful deeds done by Jesus suggests again what Luke made clear at Luke 7.16b: τοῖς γινομένοις ὑπ' αὐτοῦ is a theological passive. So Luke has shown how Israel was divided between those who did and those who did not recognise the hand of God at work among them (see above on ὄχλος); most particularly, the freed woman ascribed glory to God because she recognised the source of her liberation.

This last comment introduces a further dimension to this triangular scene which bears on this study of Luke's use of δοξ-τὸν Θεόν, namely his *mode* of presenting what took place. He has so employed a group of words that the whole incident is now concerned with 'release' or 'liberation'. He seems to have taken his clue from a *halachic* argument indicated above: ἕκαστος ὑμῶν τῷ σαββάτῳ οὐ λύει τὸν βοῦν αὐτοῦ . . .; (Luke 13.15). This is similar to the argument set out in Luke 14.5, yet in this present narrative Luke pursued the λύειν root vigorously. To the woman herself he said ἀπολέλυσαι τῆς ἀσθενείας σου, which is somewhat odd in itself, although at both Luke 5.15 and 8.2 healing 'from' infirmity, or spirits of infirmity, or demons, is spoken of. But Luke pursued his chosen mode: the spirit which caused the woman's infirmity was evidence of Satan's having bound her, and her condition could be spoken of as 'this bondage' (δεσμός) (Luke 13.16). Luke did not hesitate to speak of Jesus' ministry as a conflict with Satan (cf. Luke 11.14–23, 10.18), so it should not be surprising to find this mode of narrating a healing in this Gospel; it is, however, unique. Luke continued Jesus' response to the ἀρχισυνάγωγος:

> ταύτην δὲ θυγατέρα 'Αβραὰμ οὖσαν, ἣν ἔδησεν ὁ Σατανᾶς ἰδοὺ δέκα καὶ ὀκτὼ ἔτη, οὐκ ἔδει λυθῆναι ἀπὸ τοῦ δεσμοῦ τούτου τῇ ἡμέρᾳ τοῦ σαββάτου; (Luke 13.16)

This mode of presenting her condition is a clue to Luke's understanding of the relation between his using the δοξ-phrase and the programme of Jesus' ministry.

5. Luke 17.15–16a

εἷς δὲ ἐξ αὐτῶν, ἰδὼν ὅτι ἰάθη, ὑπέστρεψεν μετὰ φωνῆς μεγάλης δοξάζων τὸν θεόν, καὶ ἔπεσεν ἐπὶ πρόσωπον παρὰ τοὺς πόδας αὐτοῦ εὐχαριστῶν αὐτῷ·

This is a puzzling pericope on almost every count. It is not easy to identify its literary form; its common 'title' frequently misses the point. There is no 'audience' – and that may well be the point. There is no agreement among commentators on the text about its composition: is it Lukan creation or redaction of an earlier source? Progress in grasping what Luke was about does not depend on resolving that question. Two principles can be offered:

first, Luke needs a second account of a leper's being cleansed so that he might have *two* witnesses;

second, his major theme in this pericope is indicated by a contrast between a Samaritan who recognised God at work and the other nine who apparently did not.

Two witnesses

The first principle need not be pursued in detail. What is important is that Luke already shared such an account with Mark (Luke 5.12–16 // Mark 1.40–45) and, apart from tidying its opening and closing, reported it much as Mark had done. By contrast, the second account (Luke 17.11–19) has Luke's fingerprints all over it, adding much to one's grasp of what Luke was about.

Contrasting responses

One of those cleansed ὑπέστρεψεν μετὰ φωνῆς μεγάλης δοξάζων τὸν θεόν. The others did not, and their absence, highlighted by three questions, culminated in Jesus' words: οὐχ εὑρέθησαν ὑποστρέψαντες δοῦναι δόξαν τῷ θεῷ εἰ μὴ ὁ ἀλλογενὴς οὗτος; (Luke 17.18). The contrast is crucial: δοξάζειν is probably synonymous with δόξαν δοῦναι which occurs elsewhere in Luke–Acts only at Acts 12.23 to characterise what was fundamentally missing in Herod. It is interesting, but hardly evidence of a normative Lukan use, that on its two appearances δόξαν δοῦναι signifies *what was wanting* as a proper response to God. Sanders may be correct in his assessment of the pericope's thrust: he sees it as a paradigm of varying responses to Jesus and notes the sole NT use of εὐχαριστεῖν with Jesus as its object. But that assessment misses what is evident in all the passages examined so far, namely that it is *God's action* which is central and *people's responses* to that which are then explored. At the same time, frequently by use of a theological passive, Luke portrays Jesus as God's agent. A response to Jesus is, at the same time, a response to God's act; at issue is whether or not God was active in and through him. (Chapter 5A takes up this question in its discussion of Stephen's speech.) The absent nine represent those who having seen παράδοξα (Luke 5.26) or ἐνδόξοι (Luke 13.17) fail to acknowledge that their agent is God's prophet and, consequently, fail to ascribe glory to God. It is not only synagogue rulers or scribes who do not see, indeed some of them see very well (see, e.g., Luke 23.50).

A deed reminiscent of Elisha?[18]

Some very Lukan fingerprints appear on this pericope. For example, the travel motif (ἐν τῷ) πορεύεσθαι εἰς Ἰερουσαλήμ also appears at Luke 9.51 and 13.22. The first example is the opening of Luke's travel narrative – where the phrase used is actually τοῦ πορεύεσθαι – and the second, πορείαν ποιούμενος εἰς Ἱεροσόλυμα, draws attention to the otherwise not very obvious fact that this *is* a travel account. Such passing notes remind readers of Luke's scheme, and one stands at the opening of this pericope. This motif also includes αὐτὸς διήρχετο διὰ μέσον Σαμαρείας καὶ Γαλιλαίας (17.11) echoing Luke 9.52 and its own memories of Elijah's treatment of a Samaritan village. Luke's apparent geographical innocence has generated its own literature[19] and needs no comment here. What does need to be remarked is its relation to the prophet theme discussed earlier. Another Lukan characteristic is in the call for pity or help, Ἰησοῦ ... ἐλέησον ἡμᾶς, which appears in the singular at Luke 18.38 where, like υἱὲ Δαυίδ, it is shared with Mark 10.47. Luke's ἐπιστάτα at Luke 17.13 is his own, the final occurrence of six on which this word, always in the vocative, always addressed to Jesus, appears in the NT – and only in Luke's Gospel. Of the six uses (Luke 5.5; 8.24, 45; 9.33, 49; 17.13) four seem to be Lukan variants on Mark while 5.5 and 17.13 are in L material. This cry for help looks like a Lukan construct. Further, ἡ πίστις σου σέσωκέν σε (17.19) occurs also at Luke 7.50; 8.48 and 18.42; this last occurrence is also from the Bartimaeus story and, again, the phrase is shared

[18] Brodie (1986) suggested that Hellenistic authors rarely confined themselves to imitating isolated passages; this seems to be another example of Lukan *mimesis*. Perhaps it is no accident that both this incident and that at Nain are 'fulfilments' of a plainly stated programme in Luke 4.16–30 and that the prophet Jesus evoked an awed doxological response from those who 'saw.'

[19] Especially in response to Conzelmann (1960, pp. 18–94).

with Mark 10.52, as is its presence in Luke 8.48 with Mark 5.34, a pericope dealing with the woman with an issue of blood. The number of phrases closely linked with the Bartimaeus narrative deserves note, as does the 'going' theme: πορεύου εἰς εἰρήνην (7.50; 8.48); ἀναστὰς πορεύου (17.19) and the reference to 'following' – καὶ ἠκολούθει αὐτῷ – in Luke 18.43.

The phrasing of the story is thus very Lukan. What of its content? While there is no direct parallel with the OT, a number of commentators have wondered whether the Elisha/Naaman material underlies Luke's story. This is a persuasive thought. Luke's interest in Jesus as 'more than' Elijah and Elisha has already been noted; he borrowed Markan material which brought out clearly for his readers the Elijah/Elisha-like qualities of this prophet. For example, Luke's narrative of the feeding of the five thousand (9.10–17) is written so as to leave its closing words a distinct echo of 2 Kings 4.44. Luke's ending now emphasised the narrative's scriptural precedent:[20] καὶ ἔφαγον καὶ κατέλιπον κατὰ τὸ ῥῆμα [τοῦ] Κυρίου, and, significantly, these words *immediately* precede the story of Naaman and Elisha (2 Kings 5.1–27).

Luke 17.11–19 does no more than *echo* Naaman's healing, but once one begins to read it with the knowledge that Luke tells his story of Jesus from a scriptural perspective the echoes are recognised as Luke's and not one's own.[21] The following clues suggest the

20 I.e., 2 Kings 4.44, which Luke's account now more clearly echoes. But that account of Elisha's feeding of a multitude itself follows a narrative of a raising of a dead son (2 Kings 4.25–37) while preceding that of a cleansing of a leper (2 Kings 5.1–19). Whether the 'according to the word of the Lord' (2 Kings 4.44) itself echoes Exodus 16 and Numbers 11 is not clear; what *is* reasonably clear is that Jesus' action *recalls* Elisha's (but is 'greater than' it) which itself echoes that of Moses.

21 Fitzmyer (1981, p. 97), discussing Talbert's (1974) argument for patterns or correspondences between Luke and Acts, wrote 'When one scrutinizes these correspondences, one sees that they are far from cut and dried. They raise an old question, who is seeing the correspondences, Luke or Talbert? ... When one looks at the details in Talbert's analysis of many of the alleged patterns, one constantly shakes one's head.' This problem, in relation to Wisdom, is addressed in chapter 7 below, 'Criteria for allusion', but the same question may be asked of all alleged correspondences between Luke–Acts and the Jewish scriptures. At present, one simply notes that Luke proposed to explore 'the things fulfilled among us' (Luke 1.1–4); that in his work there are *echoes* and *patterns* from the scriptures (see N-A 26, Appendix III; see also UBS3, p. ix); that this is not surprising since Luke's own text (e.g. Luke 24.25–7, 32, 44–6) strongly encouraged his readers to relate Jesus' life to the scriptures; that, on the whole, while respecting Fitzmyer's admonition, one suspects that if he finds echoes, patterns, correspondences *how much more did Luke's earliest readers*. It is not altogether clear how one *tests* the validity of such responses to the text; perhaps one should say to a critic – Look. Luke says that he

probability that Luke 17.11–19 is close-linked with 2 Kings 5.1–19 (Luke apparently has no interest in vv. 20–7).

First, the Aramaean soldier was *suffering from leprosy*. His wife's slave-girl suggested: Ὄφελον ὁ κύριός μου ἐνώπιον τοῦ προφήτου τοῦ Θεοῦ **τοῦ ἐν Σαμαρείᾳ** ... (2 Kings 5.3). In spite of his alleged geographical naïvety, Luke's narrative puts his prophet Jesus in the right place.

Second, Elisha's comforting words to the King of Israel are: ἐλθέτω δὴ πρός με Ναιμαν καὶ γνώτω ὅτι ἔστιν **προφήτης ἐν Ισραηλ** (2 Kings 5.8b). It has already been noted that this is a Lukan theme expressed in a variety of ways – in the person of Jesus there is a prophet in Israel. Just as Naaman's healing showed that this was the case, so these lepers might be expected to draw their own conclusions.

Third, while this narrative most probably 'borrowed' Jesus' command from Luke 5.14 this is, in itself, an echo from Elisha's instruction to Naaman: πορευθεὶς λοῦσαι ἑπτάκις ... (2 Kings 5.10). What is noteworthy at this point is that while both Mark and Luke agree in their shared narrative that the leper was cleansed **before** being instructed to do what *Torah* required, in this later construction Jesus brusquely sends all ten to the priests – it was as they went that they were cleansed, a distant echo of λοῦσαι καὶ καθαρίσθητι (2 Kings 5.13).

Fourth, both Naaman (2 Kings 5.15) and Luke's Samaritan (Luke 17.15, 16) return to their healer to thank him (Luke 17.16) and to acknowledge God's authorship of the cleansing: καὶ ἐπέστρεψεν ... ἔγνωκα ὅτι οὐκ ἔστιν Θεὸς ἐν πάσῃ τῇ γῇ ὅτι ἀλλ' ἢ ἐν τῷ Ισραηλ (2 Kings 5.15); ὑπέστρεψεν ... δοξάζων τὸν Θεόν (Luke 17.15). It has already been noted that εὐχαριστεῖν occurs only in this narrative with Jesus as its object (Luke 17.16); compare καὶ νῦν λαβὲ τὴν εὐλογίαν παρὰ τοῦ δούλου σου (2 Kings 5.15).

proposed to work in this way and invited readers to reflect on the scriptural dimensions of his account of Jesus; do you not also see how *this* telling echoes *that* passage? Wenham's appeal to the *plain man's* criterion (1991, p. 54) seems not to take account of a simple truth evident to anyone who has listened to an older generation of preachers recounting *any* story – the more their reading has been in the biblical texts, the more likely they are to tell their story in words, phrases, syntax etc. that reflect their 'treasured' scripture. (Bunyan's Pilgrim's Progress is a special English case of this phenomenon.) Since Luke tells his readers in general terms where to look for help in discovering the significance of Jesus' story in God's plan of salvation – the scriptures – readers would be perverse not to explore and to respond to them. The debate begun by Hays (1989) undergirds this monograph in a pragmatic way; see Chapter 7 below.

While these four parallels do not constitute proof of Luke's dependence on the Naaman story, least of all in any directly literal way,[22] they strongly suggest a memory of Elisha's action and, as in the earlier narrative, they draw a contrast between the foreigner and Israel. 'Lepers are cleansed'[23] and this leper, in particular, recognised the agent and source of his cleansing and *ascribed glory* to God who had done this thing.

6. Luke 18.43

καὶ παραχρῆμα ἀνέβλεψεν, καὶ ἠκολούθει αὐτῷ δοξάζων τὸν θεόν. καὶ πᾶς ὁ λαὸς ἰδὼν ἔδωκεν αἶνον τῷ θεῷ.

Throughout his telling the Bartimaeus story Luke tends to preserve Jesus' words as they appear in the Triple Tradition while tidying the others' narratives; this is typically Lukan. But, most significantly, in Luke's narrative *both* Bartimaeus *and* πᾶς ὁ λαός recognise God's hand in this event and both respond appropriately. It is what people *see* – that the blind have sight – that elicits their praise; it is what Bartimaeus *experienced* that brought him to ascribe to God the glory that is properly his.

Evidence so far examined in the Gospel shows that the δοξ- τὸν Θεόν phrase is one element in Luke's composition and that its 'peculiar force' is derived from scriptural allusions and patterns clustered in its immediate contexts, as well as from a persistent Lukan appeal to what was seen and heard. The scriptural allusions suggest that this phrase may be closely linked with Luke's concern for the fulfilment of scripture; this notion of fulfilment as it relates to Luke's use of δοξ- τὸν Θεόν must now be examined more closely.

B. A Lukan programme

The previous section explored how Luke used the phrase δοξ- τὸν Θεόν in his Gospel. This use appears to be intentional and has to do with people recognising God at work in Jesus' activity and responding worshipfully. In Luke 5.26 in particular there is strong suggestion that Luke was interested in the notion that scripture was being fulfilled. In Luke's special material his focus was on recognition, or non-recognition of God's being at work in τὰ περὶ Ἰησοῦ. These

[22] But see Brodie (1986) for a case which makes transformation and adaptation of the LXX a *literary* rather than an *aural* act.

[23] Luke 7.22; see B., 'A Lukan Programme', below.

pericopae emphasised contrasts among people's responses to Jesus' activity and disclosed allusions to and citations from scripture.[24]

Initially, these pericopae suggest that in his deployment of δοξ- τὸν Θεόν Luke may have had motives other than a fondness for Septuagintalising. The greater part of the pericopae concerned healings, but not exclusively so; Luke 2.20 and 23.47 dealt with other concerns. These pericopae can be listed in *text* order:

2.20 the shepherds' response to the angelic announcement
5.25 a paralytic responds to his healing
5.26 a crowd's perception of God's hand in that healing
7.16 a crowd's perception of God's activity in Jesus' raising of a widow's son
13.13 the ankylosed woman's response to liberation
17.15 a Samaritan leper's response to his cleansing
18.43 a blind man's response to restored sight – and a crowd's recognition of God at work in him
23.47 a centurion's response to the manner of Jesus' death.

This list immediately suggests another grouping of most of the same material:

a *lame* man *walks*	5.25, 26
a *dead* son *raised*	7.16
a *'captive'* woman *freed*	13.13
a *leper cleansed*	17.15
a *blind* man *sees*	18.43

As soon as the material is listed in this way it recalls Luke's use of Isaiah: if the occurrences of δοξ- τὸν Θεόν do mark moments of recognition of God's activity in the actions of Jesus, then it seems that they are *also* related to the programme sketched in Luke 4.16–30, Jesus' rejection at Nazareth, and taken up in 7.18–23, his response to John's messengers.

Rejection at Nazareth[25]

There is wide agreement that Luke 4.16–30 is programmatic,[26] in some senses Luke's own creation and a key to the whole of his

[24] See Stanton (1974), pp. 37–9.

[25] See also Chilton (1981); Houston (1987); Keck (1967); Tannehill (1972); Young (1949). Talbert (1988, pp. 51–7) suggests that Luke has made this unit the frontispiece of his account of Jesus' *public* career and that Luke 1.5–4.15 is thus an account of his *pre-public* life. Talbert also treats Acts 13.13–52 as a literary and conceptual parallel to the Nazareth incident; Paul's rejection is modelled on that of his Lord (1988, p. 54f.).

[26] So, e.g., Marshall (1978), Fitzmyer (1981).

two-volume work, reflecting his mind in similar ways to the speeches in Acts.

This Lukan synagogue scene – it can hardly be called a sermon – stands at the opening of Jesus' public ministry. In the matter of the scene's *placing*, Luke differs from both Matthew and Mark;[27] the evangelist probably wanted to make a clear statement of the perspective from which Jesus' life was properly to be viewed (so Keck, 1967; Marshall, 1970, 1978). It stands, consequently, at the end of a sequence in which Luke presents Jesus as Son of God (Luke 1.32; 3.22–38; 4.3, 9) and in which the Spirit's presence and activity characterise the development of Luke's plot.[28] The *essence* of this scene appears to be Jesus' rejection by the Nazareth synagogue, although its construction does not always help a reader decide why this should have happened. The scene also focuses on the relation of Jesus' ministry to scripture: it was in Jesus, the home-town boy they knew, that God's salvation was even then (σήμερον) being fulfilled. By its careful placing in Luke's composition; by its systematic setting out of core Lukan themes such as the Spirit, the fulfilment of scripture through Jesus, his rejection, his mission to 'others' (a theme extended in Acts in line with Simeon's oracle, Luke 2.29–32), Luke's opening scene encapsulated his story.

There is substantial, though not unanimous, agreement that this scene is a Lukan construction,[29] probably a redaction of Mark 6.1–6. Caird (1963, pp. 23ff.), for example, noted that this passage is a crux for the arguments for and against the Proto-Luke hypothesis which he preferred to the Markan hypothesis; this latter strongly implied Lukan creativity rather than fidelity to tradition. Others like Grässer, Keck, Tannehill, Franklin, Dunn and Fitzmyer see this scene as a reworking of Mark's account (see also Talbert, 1988, pp. 54–7). Dunn's brief analysis (1975, p. 54) leads to a recognition of Luke's hand redacting Mark's somewhat different story; this

[27] Grässer (1969) has shown that the pericope probably came to Mark without a fixed position in the tradition and that each of the synoptists has placed it according to his own redactional interests.

[28] E.g. Luke 1.35, 67; 2.25, 26, 27; 3.16, 22[NB]. Tannehill (1972) finds the ἔχρισεν used of the Spirit in 4.18 a clear link among the Spirit's empowering of Jesus at his baptism, the Nazareth programme and primitive Christian use of Χριστός to denote Jesus' role in God's economy of salvation. Marshall strongly related the *content* of the Nazareth incident to Jesus' being a prophet and, consequently, to his Servant role.

[29] . . . whatever this phrase means: he probably had a version of Mark, information from other sources (see Luke 1.1–4) and his Greek Bible, presumably meditated on by the churches.

scene is reminiscent of the Acts speeches (e.g. 10.34–43) which are generally held to be Luke's work and to represent a Lukan theology.[30] So Luke crafted this scene out of his Markan source and by reflection on Jesus' fulfilment of scripture. However, it does not much matter for the analysis below if Caird, Taylor and Streeter are right: the facts of a new placing for the pericope and a vivid statement of themes which cohere with those characteristic of the two volumes combine to give the scene its very special place in Luke's work (so Marshall, 1970).

Of particular interest to us is the scene's concern with scripture and its fulfilment in Jesus. For the present, one must ignore questions about the text of the Isaiah scroll handed to Jesus: it is probably that of the LXX (Isaiah 61.1–2a) with a single Lukan insert from Isaiah 58.6 placed there to emphasise Luke's concern with ἄφεσις in Jesus' words and deeds.[31] Dunn's exploration of Luke's use of Isaiah 61.1ff. (1975, pp. 54–62) highlights Luke 6.20; 7.18–23 (see below) and Acts 10.38.

This Isaianic prophet's anointed task may be set out as follows:

πτωχοῖς εὐαγγελίσασθαι
κηρύξαι ... ἄφεσιν
τυφλοῖς ... ἀνάβλεψιν
ἀποστεῖλαι τεθραυσμένους ἐν ἀφέσει
κηρύξαι ἐνιαυτὸν Κυρίου δεκτόν

His task may be summarised in three verbs (εὐαγγελίσασθαι, ἀποστεῖλαι, κηρύξαι), two 'blessings' (ἄφεσις, ἀνάβλεψις) and four classes of recipient (πτωχοῖς, αἰχμαλωτοῖς, τυφλοῖς and τεθραυσμένους).

The remaining paragraphs of this section link the elements of this Lukan and scriptural programme for Jesus' ministry with Luke's use of δοξ- τὸν Θεόν, showing that this is not simply a Lukan catch-phrase drawn from the Septuagint but a significant indicator of important steps in God's fulfilling through Jesus his plan of salvation revealed to Israel in her scriptures. Franklin (1975, p. 62) had glimpsed something of the meaning of this δοξ- phrase, but neither worked it through nor discussed its possible link with Luke's 'programme'.

30 But as Hemer (1977 and 1989) has argued, reworking is not mere invention.

31 See also Bailey (1980, p. 103f.) on the *structural* significance of Luke's adding Isa. 58.6. Part of 61.1b is also missing, ἰάσασθαι τοὺς συντετριμμένους τῇ καρδίᾳ, and Luke altered the beginning of v. 2, replacing καλέσαι by κηρύξαι and omitting all that follows Κυρίου δεκτὸν. Luke's role in this structuring remains the subject of debate.

Table 2.1. *Comparison of Nazareth 'sermon' and response to John*

Nazareth	Response to John
τυφλοῖς ἀνάβλεψιν	τυφλοὶ ἀναβλέπουσιν
....	χωλοὶ περιπατοῦσιν
(ref. Elisha)	λεπροὶ καθαρίζονται
....	κωφοὶ ἀκούουσιν
(ref. Elijah)	νεκροὶ ἐγείρονται
πτωχοῖς εὐαγγελίσασθαι	πτωχοὶ εὐαγγελίζονται
κηρύξαι ἄφεσιν	....
ἀποστεῖλαι ἐν ἀφέσει	....
κηρύξαι ἐνιαυτὸν Κυρίου δεκτόν	....

John Baptist's enquiry

Jesus' reply to John Baptist's enquiry (Luke 7.18–23) also appeals to a florilegium of Isaianic passages about the blessings of the end time:[32] the messengers were bidden report to John what they had seen and heard. This list may be set out:

τυφλοὶ ἀναβλεπούσιν
χωλοὶ περιπατοῦσιν
λεπροὶ καθαρίζονται
κωφοὶ ἀκούουσιν
νεκροὶ ἐγείρονται
πτωχοὶ εὐαγγελίζονται

Jesus' activity is here summarised in six verbs for six classes of recipient. It is possible, but not more, that there is a link between this narrative and the Nazareth 'sermon' in a beatitude – καὶ μακάριός ἐστιν ὃς ἐὰν μὴ σκανδαλισθῇ ἐν ἐμοί (Luke 7.23) – which possibly takes up the concluding verses (Luke 4.28–30) of Luke's Nazareth pericope in a single verb, σκανδαλίζειν, the very verb employed at Mark 6.3 which Luke may have expanded into two verses.

A table of comparisons

While there are differences between the two lists, there are also clear relations as table 2.1 shows. If the Nazareth incident is taken *as a whole*, then this prophet's self-comparison with Elijah and Elisha must be taken seriously: they raised the dead and cleansed the leper.

32 Marshall (1970, p. 118f.) also relates the two incidents.

Luke clearly had in mind his list of Isaianic blessings when developing his account of the incident. Again, both κηρύξαι ἄφεσιν and ἀποστεῖλαι ἐν ἀφέσει look odd until one recalls the manner of Luke's telling the story of an ankylosed woman: he made much of her being bound by Satan and of her being set free (see above, A4, *contra* Conzelmann). Similarly, Luke's account of the 'paralytic' emphasises both his forgiven-ness (ἀφέωνταί σοι αἱ ἁμαρτίαι σου is assumed in the 'greater' release) and his being 'sent' home (ἔγειρε ... πορεύου εἰς τὸν οἶκον σου clearly fulfils both χωλοὶ περιπατοῦσιν and ἀποστεῖλαι ἐν ἀφέσει).

The only elements left unaccounted for are κωφοὶ ἀκούουσιν in the responses to John and κηρύξαι ἐνιαυτὸν Κυρίου δεκτόν in the Nazareth list. The former is probably a lost cause: the only treatment of 'deafness' in Luke's Gospel is at Luke 11.14–23 where, as in 13.10–17, the issue is primarily Jesus' conflict with Satan. To be consistent with himself Luke should have added δοξάζων τὸν Θεόν immediately after ὁ κωφός at 11.14; that he did not do so weakens a little but does not collapse the case, largely because Luke's narrative is about the man's *speaking* rather than *hearing*. It is worth asking whether it is significant for synoptic studies that Mark's account of the deaf mute, whose *hearing* is reported, falls in the 'great omission', so one of Luke's (alleged) sources offered no story of Jesus making the deaf hear. If this were the case, then this is a little piece of evidence that Luke resisted creating a story which would nicely complete his full house of Isaianic blessings worked by Jesus. The second phrase – κηρύξαι ἐνιαυτόν κτλ[33] – seems to be a comprehensive one, embracing the sum of Jesus' preaching and activity, which probably has a bearing on the centurion's response at Luke 23.47 in that, for Luke, Jesus' life, death and vindication are a visible fulfilment of God's salvation plan revealed through scripture.

Luke was working here with two distinct but related notions of fulfilment: one is that in which Jesus' *ministry* is seen by the evangelist as in some sense fulfilling Isaianic prophecies; the other is that in which Luke uses δοξ- τὸν Θεόν to 'tick off' for his readers those narratives in which someone has genuinely perceived the earlier fulfilment taking place.

[33] We bracket off Yoder's interesting suggestion that Jesus' synagogue address was an appeal to his hearers to observe the Year of Jubilee (1972, esp. pp. 34–40, 64–77). See also Trocmé (1973).

Table 2.2. *Healing narratives in Luke*

Locus in text	Healing	Geographical *locus*
Nazareth incident		
4.38–9	Peter's mother in law	Capernaum
4.40–1	Sick at evening	Capernaum
5.12–16	Healing of leper	Galilee
5.17–26	Paralysed man *walks**	Galilee
6.6–11	Withered hand	Galilee
6.17–19	Healing of crowds	Galilee
7.1–10	Centurion's servant	Capernaum
7.11–17	Widow's son *raised**	Nain
John Baptist's question		
8.40–56	Jairus' daughter	Galilee
9.37–43	Epileptic child	Galilee
Travel Narrative begins		
11.14–23	Beelzebul/dumb spirit	Journey
13.10–17	Ankylosed woman *freed**	Journey
14.1–6	Dropsical man	Journey
17.11–19	Thankful leper *cleansed**	Journey
18.35–43	A blind man *sees**	Jericho

Luke's healing narratives

But not every Lukan narrative of a healing has the δοξ- phrase attached to it; those starred in table 2.2 have. To exclude the possibility that the target phrase may be related to a source or a place, this table also indicates the *locus* of an event, both textual and geographical.

Clearly, the starred incidents do not relate to source, geographical feature or to order of events; they are, however, rooted in the Isaianic programme in that δοξ- τὸν Θεόν signals **one** instance of an event *conceptually very close* to the Nazareth programme. For example, the raising of the widow of Nain's son echoes Elijah's action specifically noted in Luke 4.25, 26, so it is starred rather than the raising of Jairus' daughter. The cleansing of the Samaritan leper is starred because it echoes Elisha's healing of Naaman reported in Luke 4.27, while the cleansing noted in Luke 5.12–16 is not. This argument suggests only that *one instance* of each type of healing is starred and that this is then *related to Luke's understanding of Jesus'* *programme*. It was noted above why κωφοὶ ἀκούουσιν is not handled in this way.[34]

Two examples of the target phrase remain outstanding. Luke 2.20 is almost certainly Luke's way of indicating in his infancy prologue that the poor were having good news proclaimed to them: the verb is present; there is a cluster of Lukan christological 'triggers' – σήμερον, David, Christ, Lord, Saviour; the angelic host's chorus focuses on δόξα and εἰρήνη (*shalom*). This birth is of one who **is** God's proclaiming good news to the *anawim*. Readers are intended to understand that from this beginning the deeds and words of Jesus are such proclamation. Luke 23.47 remains to be spoken of, but given that each of the δοξ- phrases appears to have a programmatic significance in the Gospel, it would be odd were this instance (Luke 23.47) not to be equally significant. So this phrase does act as a clear Lukan signal for those moments when God's purposes to save people, purposes already revealed in scripture, are now being fulfilled in Jesus' activity. Those same purposes are expressed also in Jesus' programme outlined in the Nazareth sermon and confirmed in his encounter with John Baptist's disciples. If this is so, then ἐδόξαζεν τὸν θεόν at Luke 23.47 draws a reader's attention to the presence here of much more than a 'stock phrase' – rather to a 'disclosure moment' illuminated *both* by God's scriptural plan and by Jesus' kerygmatic programme.[35] That is, Luke made[36] *his* centurion a witness who perceived in Jesus' death an act of God, and the Lukan form of that witness prompts his reader to ask what scriptural dimensions are implied by its context. Before that context is examined, Luke's use in Acts of the δοξ- phrase must be tested.

C. Δοξάζειν τὸν Θεὸν in the Acts

A fundamental difference discernible in Luke's use of the phrase δοξ- τὸν Θεόν in Acts from that in his Gospel derives from his perspective that the Lord, now exalted in heaven, is normally encountered through his disciples rather than immediately. God's

[34] There is another perspective. Mark 7.31–7 records a healing of a deaf mute. This is part of the so-called 'great omission' which may imply that the Jesus-tradition known to Luke contained no such healing. Consequently, it seems that Luke's practice was to 'signal' those significant events rooted in the Isaianic programme; this case is stronger than the text suggests.

[35] See p. 26 above.

[36] . . . or found this version in a source which appealed to him.

action remains the focus of each incident, but in a changed perspective.

Five passages are to be studied: Acts 3.13; 4.21; 11.18; 13.48 and 21.20. Each opens huge areas of discussion, but in this chapter analysis is limited, as far as possible, to confirming what was learnt from the Gospel's pericopae. An exception to this follows from an earlier assessment of the purposes of Luke's second volume (see chapter 1E above). Following Maddox, Esler *et al.*, it is provisionally assumed that Luke 1.1–4 is a prologue to Luke's two volumes; that the two key words in this prologue are πεπληροφορημένα and ἀσφάλεια; that the two volumes are about the Christian Church in its relation on the one hand with the Lord Jesus, on the other with Judaism; that Luke's community needed to be assured that God's saving purposes revealed in scripture were not limited to the House of Israel but had unambiguously flowed into and found fulfilment in their own community; that social, political and religious pressures upon Luke's mixed community were being answered in Luke's portrayal of the lives and teaching of Jesus and his apostles. These provisional assumptions strongly relate to the programme outlined in Acts 1.1–6. Franklin's view of Acts makes plainer why this is the case: 'in Jesus the prophetic expectations were fulfilled and . . . God's final promises to the Jewish people, *and through them to the nations,* were being realised' (1975, p. 34; italics added). It is this purpose, an extension of the fulfilment of the scriptural plan of salvation, which is the standpoint for a changed perspective in Acts.

In the name of Jesus (Acts 3.13; 4.21)

> ὁ θεὸς Ἀβραὰμ καὶ ὁ θεὸς Ἰσαὰκ καὶ ὁ θεὸς Ἰακώβ, ὁ θεὸς τῶν πατέρων ἡμῶν, ἐδόξασεν τὸν παῖδα αὐτοῦ Ἰησοῦν, ὃν ὑμεῖς μὲν παρεδώκατε καὶ ἠρνήσασθε κατὰ πρόσωπον Πιλάτου, κρίναντος ἐκείνου ἀπολύειν.
> (Acts 3.13)

> οἱ δὲ προσαπειλησάμενοι ἀπέλυσαν αὐτούς, μηδὲν εὑρίσκοντες τὸ πῶς κολάσωνται αὐτούς, διὰ τὸν λαόν, ὅτι πάντες ἐδόξαζον τὸν θεὸν ἐπὶ τῷ γεγονότι. (Acts 4.21)

Luke can be surprisingly expansive when setting out a narrative of more than ordinary significance for his purposes. Acts 3.1–4.21 is a long account of the events surrounding a lame man's healing at a

Temple gate. The account falls into three parts: first, a *narrative* of Peter and John's healing in Jesus' name; second, a *speech* by Peter to 'Israel' interpreting both how such deeds might happen and their significance; third, a *conflict* about what had been done and said, in which ultimately, although the Sanhedrin dissented, πάντες ἐδόξαζον τὸν Θεὸν ἐπὶ τῷ γεγονότι.

The narrative

The narrative reminds a reader of deeds done by the Jesus of Luke's Gospel; for example, Luke 5.17–26 reports a similar incident, though recorded more briefly. Here is also an echo of the Isaianic programme succinctly presented in Luke 7.22, but at Acts 3.7–10 allowing its roots to be seen:

> παραχρῆμα δὲ ἐστερεώθησαν αἱ βάσεις αὐτοῦ καὶ τὰ σφυδρά, καὶ ἐξαλλόμενος ἔστη καὶ περιεπάτει, καὶ εἰσῆλθεν σὺν αὐτοῖς εἰς τὸ ἱερὸν περιπατῶν καὶ ἁλλόμενος καὶ αἰνῶν τὸν θεόν.

The presence of αἰνῶν τὸν θεόν is merely noted here,[37] but why should Luke repeat ἅλλομαι? The NT has three occurrences of ἅλλομαι and only one of ἐξάλλομαι (the others are at John 4.14 and Acts 14.10 where Paul is allotted a parallel 'sign'). Bruce (1952, p. 105) refers a reader to Isaiah 35.6; Conzelmann (1987, p. 26) says that the 'demonstration' is *reminiscent* of that verse: τότε ἁλεῖται ὡς ἔλαφος χωλός. Isaiah's τότε contrasts with the σήμερον of Luke 4.21; what once was future has been completed in Nazareth's present. According to Luke, that present continued in the activity of Peter and John.

Peter's speech

Peter's speech πρὸς τὸν λαόν began, *pace* Sanders, Ἄνδρες Ἰσραηλῖται (Acts 3.12). They must be the same group as those referred to in Acts 3.9–10 (cf. Luke 5.26) – καὶ εἶδεν πᾶς ὁ λαὸς . . . καὶ ἐπλήσθησαν θάμβους καὶ ἐκστάσεως ἐπὶ τῷ συμβεβηκότι αὐτῷ. They were bidden look beyond the apostles for the source of the healing (Acts 3.12) and were, rather, to recognise that what had happened was ἐν τῷ ὀνόματι Ἰησοῦ Χριστοῦ τοῦ Ναζωραίου (Acts

[37] See note 6 above.

4.10); that it was the God of the patriarchs who had *glorified his child*, or his servant Jesus (Acts 3.13; see chapter 5, pp. 128–31 and 151–8) whose role was to be understood as that of the Deuteronomic prophet (Acts 3.22–3 cf. Deut. 18.15–19). Indeed, all the prophets had spoken of 'these days'; in that last phrase Luke again took up his emphasis on the present as the time of salvation's fulfilment. The speech is a complex passage and a source of vigorous debate; here, one simply notes that it was the occasion for a conflict.

The conflict

The conflict is outlined in Acts 4.1–22. As in Luke's treatment of the narrative of the paralysed man at Luke 5.17–26, there is a stylised statement of the apostles' opponents (Acts 4.1–5) from which Pharisees are noticeably absent; this is different from the Gospel parallel where Pharisees play a key role.

It would be myopic to ignore two levels of conflict continuing in this passage. The first is a sharp reminder to the Sanhedrin that it had crucified Jesus whose conflict with the authorities resulted in his humiliation. Luke contrasts the Sanhedrin's response to Jesus with God's response.[38] This contrast is epitomised at Acts 4.11 in a reference to Psalm 118.22 (117LXX): ὁ λίθος ὁ ἐξουθενηθεὶς ὑφ' ὑμῶν τῶν οἰκοδόμων ὁ γενόμενος εἰς κεφαλὴν γωνίας. The second level of conflict in this passage is between the Sanhedrin and the apostles as Jesus' *sheluchim* and is summed up in Peter's response to his being forbidden to teach ἐπὶ τῷ ὀνόματι τοῦ Ἰησοῦ –

> Εἰ δίκαιόν ἐστιν ἐνώπιον τοῦ θεοῦ ὑμῶν ἀκούειν μᾶλλον ἢ τοῦ θεοῦ, κρίνατε· οὐ δυνάμεθα γὰρ ἡμεῖς ἃ εἴδαμεν καὶ ἠκούσαμεν μὴ λαλεῖν. (Acts 4.19b–20)

This particular conflict is not pursued because the Sanhedrin has to reckon with the people (Acts 4.21b). Luke's reason for the Sanhedrin's retreat from further conflict is that πάντες ἐδόξαζον τὸν Θεὸν ἐπὶ τῷ γεγονότι. The use of τῷ γεγονότι is interesting: at one level it refers to the healing of the lame man; at yet another level it must refer to the claim that this happened in Jesus' name – both Peter's speech and his defence before the Sanhedrin make this

[38] This separation between the rulers who are *directly* addressed in Acts 4.8 and the People Israel to whom the facts should be known allows substantial guilt for Jesus' death to remain with the rulers. See also chapter 7H, 'Ignorance and guilt: a Lukan theme'.

certain. At a still deeper level Luke must have included the people's response to the κήρυγμα about Jesus. The phrase ἐπὶ τῷ γεγονότι replaces the explanatory clauses found in the Gospel pericopae, but the consonance between this use of δοξ- τὸν Θεόν and that identified in earlier sections should be noted. It confirms that God makes the lame walk (Luke 5.25, 26; 7.22), thus continuing through the apostles Jesus' fulfilment of God's salvation plan.

Through them to the nations (Acts 11.18; 13.48; 21.20)

The remaining instances of Luke's using δοξ- τὸν Θεόν relate to the admission of the Gentiles. This is so large an issue and its details press so hard on each of the incidents now to be discussed that a brief caveat must precede them. There are those, like Sanders (1987) and Beck (1994, pp. 199–284), who (mistakenly) see in Luke's work fertile seeds of Christian anti-Semitism or anti-Judaism. On the other hand, the notion that Luke's primary concern is with reconstituting the People of God is supported strongly by Maddox in his exhaustive treatment of Luke's purposes:

> He writes to reassure the Christians of his day that their faith in Jesus is no aberration, but the authentic goal towards which God's ancient dealings with Israel were driving. The full stream of God's saving action in history has not passed them by but has flowed straight into their community life, in Jesus and the Holy Spirit. (1982, p. 187)

Some of the evidence in the studies in this section tends to support Maddox, Fitzmyer, Jervell and others who take 'reconstitution' rather than 'rejection' of Israel to be the keynote of Luke's work. Consequently, the reasons for glorifying God in these passages lie in God's having offered salvation to the Gentiles also, thus fulfilling what scripture, for example, Isaiah, had promised.

This dual response to God by Jew and Gentile is possibly related to δοξάζειν from its very inception in Luke's work, particularly in Simeon's oracles (Luke 2.29–32, 34–5). Brown (1979) has argued that Luke adapted the canticles in his infancy narrative from an *anawim* source, fitting them into his existing framework. Thus, Simeon's oracle concerning Jesus, Ἰδοὺ οὗτος κεῖται εἰς πτῶσιν καὶ ἀνάστασιν πολλῶν ἐν τῷ Ἰσραὴλ καὶ εἰς σημεῖον ἀντιλεγόμενον (Luke 2.34b), represents for Brown an early stage of Lukan thought. This 'rising up' as well as the 'falling' of many in Israel reflects a conflict evidenced throughout the Gospel and the Acts. It also reflects what Sanders tends to ignore, the strong sense within Israel's prophetic tradition flowing into Qumran and the *anawim* of a need for Israel to be purified. As a symbol (σημεῖον) of God's salvation Jesus is to be contradicted (Luke 2.34); a remnant motif is rarely far from an oracle and some who hear it embrace its truth while others reject it. This simple fact with all its consequences is what underlies the ῥομφαία of Luke 2.35 and the διαμερισμόν of Luke 12.51. Consequently, at the beginning of his two volumes Luke spelled out that Jesus' presence would be a crisis for Israel, dividing the House, and sifting the 'rising' from the 'falling'. A similar pattern occurs at Daniel 12.1–4, a pattern examined by Nickelsburg (1972).

Simeon's oracles

Simeon's canticle, however, goes beyond identifying Jesus as the occasion for Israel's crisis. The canticle blesses God for fulfilling his promises and identifies three specific elements within that fulfilment. First, Luke makes plain that what Simeon (and all those like him) had been waiting for had arrived, namely God's salvation (Luke 2.30); second, that fulfilment of God's salvation plan involved the child's being a light for the Gentiles' revelation (2.32a); third, and here δόξαν, like φῶς, is taken to be the object of ἡτοίμασας in 2.31, that fulfilment entailed God's δόξαν being restored to Israel.

R. E. Brown (1979, p. 485) argued that Simeon's canticle is a pastiche of a group of Isaianic passages: Isaiah 52.9–10; 49.6; 46.13; 42.6 and 40.5. The themes in these passages – seeing salvation, the sight of all the peoples, a light to the Gentiles, glory to Israel – are also those of the Nunc Dimittis, but Luke's arrangement of the canticle made plain that the word 'peoples' comprises both Jew and Gentile. The σωτήριον which had been prepared for all people, neither solely for Israel nor excluding her, is accompanied by two key words: ἀποκάλυψις and δόξα. In the Acts Luke unfolds the ἀποκάλυψις to the Gentiles; in the Gospel he sets out in an orderly fashion how Israel both rejected and accepted God's δόξα in the person of Jesus.

Simeon's canticle is echoed at Acts 13.47, Τέθεικά σε εἰς φῶς ἐθνῶν τοῦ εἶναί σε εἰς σωτηρίαν ἕως ἐσχάτου τῆς γῆς, a passage yet to be examined in detail because the hearers' response was, ἀκούοντα δὲ τὰ ἔθνη ἔχαιρον καὶ ἐδόξαζον τὸν λόγον τοῦ κυρίου, καὶ ἐπίστευσαν ὅσοι ἦσαν τεταγμένοι εἰς ζωὴν αἰώνιον (Acts 13.48). This theme of light to the Gentiles – and to Israel – is taken up in Paul's testimony before Festus and Agrippa at Acts 26.19–23 confirming the programmatic nature of Simeon's canticle:

> ἄχρι τῆς ἡμέρας ταύτης ἕστηκα μαρτυρόμενος μικρῷ τε καὶ μεγάλῳ οὐδὲν ἐκτὸς λέγων ὧν τε οἱ προφῆται ἐλάλησαν μελλόντων γίνεσθαι καὶ Μωϋσῆς, εἰ παθητὸς ὁ Χριστός, εἰ πρῶτος ἐξ ἀναστάσεως νεκρῶν φῶς μέλλει καταγγέλλειν τῷ τε λαῷ καὶ τοῖς ἔθνεσιν.

Similarly, Luke's second volume effectively ends with a summary of the canticle's thrust:

> γνωστὸν οὖν ἔστω ὑμῖν ὅτι τοῖς ἔθνεσιν ἀπεστάλη τοῦτο τὸ σωτήριον τοῦ θεοῦ· αὐτοὶ καὶ ἀκούσονται.
>
> (Acts 28.28)

Examination of the remaining instances in Acts of δοξ- τὸν Θεὸν takes place in the context of a provisional assumption that Luke's purposes include his affirmation that God's saving plan embraces both Jew and Gentile, fulfilling Simeon's oracle.[39]

Acts 11.18

> ἀκούσαντες δὲ ταῦτα ἡσύχασαν καὶ ἐδόξασαν τὸν θεὸν λέγοντες· Ἄρα καὶ τοῖς ἔθνεσιν ὁ θεὸς τὴν μετάνοιαν εἰς ζωὴν ἔδωκεν.

Luke gave the Cornelius incident a large space. Peter's vision, recounted in Acts 10.9–16, was repeated in 11.4–10, while vv. 11–15 repeated the narrative of Peter's encounter with Cornelius and the gift of the Spirit to the Gentiles. Acts 11.16 is a crucial reference to what the Lord had said before his ἀνάλημψις (Acts 1.5 cf. Luke 3.16); the Cornelius event and its reception by some of the Judaean believers was clearly important in Luke's scheme.

According to Bruce (1952) the δ text adds 11.1b, καὶ ἐδόξαζον τὸν Θεόν,[40] the effect of which is sharply to divide the apostles and

[39] This position, however, is a tentative one, grounding itself basically on Fitzmyer (1981, pp. 188–91) and Jervell (1972, pp. 41–74).

[40] Because this is clearly a secondary reading the phrase will not be explored here. It is worth noting, however, that its presence approaches the conditions identified for its 'special force' in Luke: God at work, fulfilment of scripture and of Simeon's oracle. What is lacking is their seeing and hearing these things *for themselves*.

brethren of Acts 11.1 – because the presence of the δοξ- phrase numbers these among those recognising that God was fulfilling his salvation plan in what had happened – from οἱ ἐκ περιτομῆς of 11.2. Without this addition it is possible to think of a circumcision party within the Jerusalem church.[41] The δ text also recast 11.2, reducing the shock of the transition from God's gift of the Spirit to the Gentiles to a spirit of acrimony. N-A 26 notes only the δ addition to 11.2 at this point; the existence of these additions indicates how difficult even earlier readers found the stark contrast between Jerusalem and Caesarea: among the apostles and brethren in Judaea was a circumcision party swift to challenge Peter's behaviour.

Luke also set up a contrast between Acts 11.1 and 11.3 in his account of what had been heard in Judaea of the events in Caesarea. According to Luke, the apostles and brethren heard that the Gentiles had received the word of God. The circumcision party had a more robust version of what they had heard: 'You went into men who had foreskins and you ate with them.' This is the only occurrence of ἀκροβυστία in Luke; all the other NT instances are Pauline. The overtones of the biblical Greek word seem to be lost; its more usual form, ἀκροποσθία, has undergone a transformation whose process and rationale seem now inaccessible. Whatever the overtones, its occurrence at Acts 11.3 vigorously indicates the disputed ground: Peter not only associated with such men, he *ate* with them. Peter's opponents were divided from him, διεκρίνοντο; the dispute was sharp.

The nub of Peter's response to his opponents appears to be in Acts 11.17 and needs only brief exploration:

> εἰ οὖν τὴν ἴσην δωρεὰν ἔδωκεν αὐτοῖς ὁ θεὸς ὡς καὶ ἡμῖν πιστεύσασιν ἐπὶ τὸν κύριον Ἰησοῦν Χριστόν, ἐγὼ τίς ἤμην δυνατὸς κωλῦσαι τὸν θεόν;

The force of this sentence depends on the preceding statement: 'I remembered the Lord's word, how he said, John baptised with water but you shall be baptised in Holy Spirit' (Acts 11.16). Taken together, the statements provide an understanding of the events in Cornelius' house: their 'Pentecost' is a parallel to that of the earliest believers and fulfils Jesus' oracle in the same way. The event itself continues Peter's vision with its new insight into God's dealing with

[41] Marshall (1980, p. 194), dissenting from RSV, reads οἱ ἐκ περιτομῆς as 'those of Jewish birth', not as a reference to a circumcision party.

people: κἀμοὶ ὁ θεὸς ἔδειξεν μηδένα κοινὸν ἢ ἀκάθαρτον λέγειν ἄνθρωπον (Acts 10.28b), which was, of course, precisely what οἱ ἐκ περιτομῆς (Acts 11.2f.) had done.

Together, the vision, events and disputes of Acts 10.1–11.18 argue that the extension of the mission to the Gentiles was God's act which fulfilled Jesus' ῥῆμα. It is these which comprise the ταῦτα of Acts 11.18.

Luke presented Peter's interrogators' response as simple: ἡσύχασαν καὶ ἐδόξαζον τὸν Θεόν ... A reader may deduce that this was a unanimous judgment; Luke appears to leave one with the impression that the 'thatness' of this extension of the community of believers was now accepted in Jerusalem, leaving until later his account of the disputes over the conditions on which it might take place. 'They kept their peace' should not be read as a truculent response because Luke clearly signified that the erstwhile opponents had perceived God at work in what had happened, and that they saw its significance (see λέγοντες ... Acts 11.18a).

This explanatory clause (Acts 11.18b) contains a καὶ which must mean either 'also' or 'even', strongly implying the fulfilment of what Luke had set out in the infancy narratives (and, incidentally, throwing light on the καὶ at Acts 28.28). Luke set out these events at length: he highlighted his conviction that they were 'disclosure' events in which God acted; in his scheme they hark back to Simeon's oracle and its sense of fulfilment of God's σωτήριον **both** for Gentile (ἀποκάλυψις) and for Jew (δόξα).

In this passage, ἐδόξαζον τὸν Θεόν thus signals another 'moment' in Luke's setting out of 'what has been fulfilled among us', *confirming* the 'special force' of this Lukan phrase.

Acts 13.48

ἀκούοντα δὲ τὰ ἔθνη ἔχαιρον καὶ ἐδόξαζον τὸν λόγον τοῦ κυρίου, καὶ ἐπίστευσαν ὅσοι ἦσαν τεταγμένοι εἰς ζωὴν αἰώνιον.

It may be that this passage has no place in a final assessment of Luke's use of the phrase δοξ- τὸν Θεόν simply because it is different; whether it is fundamentally different remains to be explored.

There is certainly so close a connection between the function and setting of this formula and those of δοξ- τὸν Θεόν that it must be examined. The setting of this verse is at the end of Luke's narrative of Paul's first 'turning to the Gentiles' and is, consequently, a parallel to the author's treatment of Peter and Cornelius. Some features of this narrative are soon obvious: there is a stress on scripture's being fulfilled (Acts 13.47); on its relation to a word of Jesus (cf. Acts 1.8–9 – ἕως ἐσχάτου τῆς γῆς, itself an Isaianic echo); there is a link with Luke's overall programme (cf. Luke 2.32, treated earlier in this section); there is a division, a conflict which from this point forward shapes the development of Luke's second volume; finally, God's action – this time in Paul's decision to address the Gentiles – is recognised as part of his saving plan, so glory is ascribed to him.

Further, within the framework of Luke–Acts, Paul's Antioch sermon is structurally a counterpart to Jesus' Nazareth sermon. First, Paul, with Barnabas, is invited to preach in a synagogue; this is where Luke, unlike the other canonical evangelists, had set Jesus to outline his programme (Luke 4.16–30) and, as in the case of Jesus, apparently based his words on the *Haftorah*. However, while Jesus had pointed to prophecy's being fulfilled in his hearers' presence (Luke 4.21), Paul summarised Israel's experience of salvation history including what had happened concerning Jesus. As Jesus had drawn attention to the normal fate of prophets, highlighting the attention paid by Elijah and Elisha to non-Israelites, so Paul indicates that he is to turn to the Gentiles. Like Jesus (Luke 4.28–30), Paul was hurried out of town (Acts 13.50–1), although Acts 13.49 implies the passage of some time before that event.

Second, Paul's citation of scripture points in a number of directions. He has compressed the LXX of Isaiah 49.6, omitting εἰς διαθήκην γένους; the concluding clause is identical – τοῦ εἶναί σε εἰς σωτηρίαν ἕως ἐσχάτου τῆς γῆς. It is probable that at Acts 1.8 ἕως ἐσχάτου τῆς γῆς is an echo of this Isaianic passage; Luke summarised in one verse the programme for this volume. It is also plain that at Luke 2.32 he foreshadowed the wider mission in his allusion (it is no more – but no less) to this passage – φῶς εἰς ἀποκάλυψιν ἐθνῶν.

Third, at Acts 13.46, Luke presented a principle: that the order of salvation required Israel to hear the word of God first and, when they refused to believe it, the Gentiles might be addressed. Again, this formally corresponds to Luke's account of Jesus' response to the Nazareth congregation. But this principle should not be over-pressed in the way that Sanders (1987, p. 276) has done.[42] If one reads the evidence in the light of those conclusions properly drawn from Simeon's canticle rather than from a conviction that Luke is the begetter of Christian anti-Semitism, a very different picture emerges: both Jew and Gentile are 'today' called to respond to God's σωτήριον. From this perspective, Luke's work does *not* write off the Jews; he thinks rather of the People of God as Jews and Gentiles who have responded appropriately to what they have seen and heard of God.

It may be that this framework is what justifies including this section in this study. If it be the case that ὁ Κύριος is understood both as Jesus and as God; if ἐντέταλται (Acts 13.47) refers both to the Isaianic oracle adapted by Luke and to Jesus' commissioning of the apostles (Acts 1.8), then Luke's Gentiles in this narrative perceived God's promise of salvation being fulfilled in Jesus and did what was appropriate. But their ascribing glory to the word of God requires comment.

Fitzmyer's lengthy treatment of Luke's use of λόγος is helpful though not altogether satisfactory (1981, p. 157f.). He notes Cadbury's judgment that it may be intended by Luke as a general term applicable to the story of Christian origins; that would certainly be the case here, cohering with the prologue, especially Luke 1.2 and 4. But this is rather bland. Fitzmyer takes matters further by noting that used absolutely (cf. Acts 8.4; 10.36; 11.19; 14.25, cf. Luke 8.12–15) it tends to have the significant overtone of 'the word of God'. What that means is not clear, unless Fitzmyer is thinking of this being a move which allowed increasingly, but almost imperceptibly, the attribution to Jesus of characteristics of 'the Word of God' (e.g. Wis. 7.22–9.18) as this concept developed in Alexandrian thought, a way of talking about God's action become a hypostasis.

There is, however, one instance in the Acts which may throw light on what Luke had in mind. At Acts 20.32 Luke wrote: καὶ τὰ νῦν παρατίθεμαι ὑμᾶς τῷ θεῷ καὶ τῷ λόγῳ τῆς χάριτος αὐτοῦ . . . It is not easy to see how people might be entrusted to a message. In the context of Paul's taking leave of the elders from Ephesus before setting off to Jerusalem and to all that was to befall him there (strongly reminiscent of the Gospel's travel narrative), the verb παρατίθεμαι has especial poignancy. It is a form of the verb in

42 Sanders seems to *generalise*. For example, in the extract noted in the text he speaks of 'the Jews everywhere'; it would be sounder to write of 'some Jews'.

which Luke couches the word of Jesus from the cross, citing Psalm 30.6.[43] It is, consequently, just possible that Luke knew that Christians were already speaking of 'the proclaimer' as 'the proclaimed'; that the message was focused in the person of Jesus; that the 'word of the Lord' was a way of speaking about the 'Jesus event'. If this be the case, then Acts 13.48 becomes comprehensible and relevant to this study because the 'word of the Lord' stands for the exalted, regnant Jesus, the Son of man come in his glory – cf. Luke's use of δόξα in Stephen's speech, explored in chapter 4 below – and who was the consummation of the divine salvation set out in prophetic oracles and in God's gracious dealings with Israel recorded in scripture. Ascribing glory to Jesus thus conceived may have been a theological jump peculiar to Hellenist and Gentile circles; at this point one can only note possibilities.

Acts 21.20

> [19] καὶ ἀσπασάμενος αὐτοὺς ἐξηγεῖτο καθ' ἓν ἕκαστον, ὧν ἐποίησεν ὁ θεὸς ἐν τοῖς ἔθνεσιν διὰ τῆς διακονίας αὐτοῦ. [20] οἱ δὲ ἀκούσαντες ἐδόξαζον τὸν θεόν, εἶπόν τε αὐτῷ, Θεωρεῖς, ἀδελφέ, πόσαι μυριάδες εἰσὶν ἐν τοῖς Ἰουδαίοις τῶν πεπιστευκότων, καὶ πάντες ζηλωταὶ τοῦ νόμου ὑπάρχουσιν.

The setting of this narrative is crucial to Luke's scheme: it falls within one of the 'we sections'; it records Paul's final encounter with the Jerusalem church; the meeting provides the efficient cause of the meetings and journeys of the book's concluding chapters.

It is not easy to weigh the significance of this narrative's falling within a 'we section'; there is a sense in which the setting is of no significance for this present study, simply because it is concerned with Lukan composition rather than an assessment of the historicity of its narrative.[44] Discussion of Luke's use of 'we passages' appears to be indecisive at present. Robbins' argument from classical parallels (1978, pp. 215–42), that the literary form is of no evidential value at all, needs to be weighed carefully in the light of earlier work by people like Bruce and Ramsey and, later, by Hemer (1977, 1989),

[43] See chapter 6C, 'Psalm 30.6 in Luke's Composition'.

[44] This comment neither ignores the importance of assessing Luke's 'historical' dimensions nor minimises his achievements; rather, it acknowledges a path along which this study does not *at present* go.

whose appreciation of Luke as historian is more generous than that of, for example, Haenchen. On the whole, those arguments which point in the direction of the 'we sections' constituting a source with some claim to historicity appear at present to have the edge; this study *provisionally* assumes that although the material has been edited to fit Luke's purposes, it none the less bears relation to the way things were.

The place of Jerusalem in Luke's scheme of things has been frequently and thoroughly explored; it is the focus of Jesus' journeying and the centre of the Church's missionary activity following Jesus' ἀνάλημψις. Acts 1.8 not only takes up the implied programme of Simeon's oracle but becomes a plan of Luke's second volume:

> ἀλλὰ λήμψεσθε δύναμιν ἐπελθόντος τοῦ ἁγίου πνεύματος ἐφ' ὑμᾶς, καὶ ἔσεσθέ μου μάρτυρες ἔν τε Ἰερουσαλὴμ καὶ ἐν πάσῃ τῇ Ἰουδαίᾳ καὶ Σαμαρείᾳ καὶ ἕως ἐσχάτου τῆς γῆς.

However the Paul of the letters might have responded to the notion of the Jerusalem church's primacy, Luke's plan involved both Peter's (Acts 11.1–18) and Paul's reporting to the Jerusalem church. In this narrative Paul spelled out clearly, step by step what God had been doing among Gentiles through his (Paul's) ministry (21.19). His readers were expected to supply from Luke's earlier chapters what this ministry was. What is interesting is that at this point Luke's habit of repeating what had happened, as he did, for example, in the case of Peter and Cornelius, is absent. Was there just too much? The whole of Paul's διακονία is summed up in a single phrase which has been strongly implied in all the earlier occurrences of δοξ- τὸν Θεὸν, namely ὧν ἐποίησεν ὁ Θεὸς. Here the author spelled out succinctly what is implied throughout: there are some actions and events in which some people see God at work while others do not. ... ὧν ἐποίησεν ὁ Θεὸς contrasts, in this case, with what the generality of Jewish Christians believed to be true with respect to Paul:

> Θεωρεῖς, ἀδελφέ, πόσαι μυριάδες εἰσὶν ἐν τοῖς Ἰουδαίοις τῶν πεπιστευκότων, καὶ πάντες ζηλωταὶ τοῦ νόμου ὑπάρχουσιν· κατηχήθησαν δὲ περὶ σοῦ ὅτι ἀποστασίαν διδάσκεις ἀπὸ Μωϋσέως τοὺς κατὰ τὰ ἔθνη πάντας Ἰουδαίους λέγων μὴ περιτέμνειν αὐτοὺς τὰ τέκνα μηδὲ τοῖς ἔθεσιν περιπατεῖν. (Acts 21.20b–21)

Whether this is an eyewitness account of what James said; whether it accurately reports the composition and numbers of the Jerusalem church does not matter. The thrust of Luke's narrative is a stark contrast between what James and the presbyters recognised and what was commonly believed among a section of believers.

Opposition within the church to Paul's activity is alleged to be based on a misreading of the case: he appeared to be teaching rebellion against *halachic* living, including the circumcision of Jewish children, an activity summarised as rebellion against Moses. How successfully, if at all, the leaders had told the church of their approval of Paul cannot be known. The immediate cause of his arrest is said to be οἱ ἀπὸ Ἀσίας Ἰουδαῖοι who, mistakenly, alleged that Paul had introduced Gentiles on to the Temple Mount; their report of his ἀποστασία was that Paul was teaching against 'this holy place' and against the *Torah*, a parallel charge to that against Stephen (Acts 6.13). Luke's pointed contrast between what God was doing through Paul, recognised now by the leaders of the Jerusalem church, and what was popularly believed about his activity coheres with this evangelist's use of the δοξ- phrase throughout his two volumes: some who see and hear recognise God's work and give him the glory.

D. Summary

Exploring Luke's use of δοξ- τὸν Θεόν throughout his two volumes revealed a number of tendencies. Because he alone has the phrase at Luke 23.47 these tendencies need to be carried forward to fuller discussion of Luke's composition of the story of Jesus' death. Perhaps the soundest reason for carrying forward these tendencies lies in the phrase's apparent relation to a Lukan programme (see B above) which set Jesus in the role of God's agent who acted to fulfil God's salvation plan revealed in scripture. Luke's volumes were addressed to Theophilus that he might know the certainty of the things that he had been taught; their content was spelt out in a distinctive phrase at Luke 1.1 – τῶν πεπληροφορημένων ἐν ἡμῖν πραγμάτων – which sets out at the beginning of his work Luke's interest in 'fulfilment'.[45] Simeon's canticle added a second element to

[45] *Contra* Cadbury (1922, p. 496), who dismissed this notion out of hand. In the light of Luke's *whole* work, it seems clear that Luke's verb must at least *include* the fulfilment of scripture (see Dillon, 1981, p. 211ff.). It is a pity that in his engagement with Cadbury, Bock (1987, p. 27f., 286, nn. 57–62) did not actually

Luke's salvation programme: Isaiah had not only seen the blessings of salvation for Israel, but had also spoken of God's intentions for 'the nations'. Adverting to Isaiah 49.6 and 42.6, Luke gave to Simeon a song which affirmed that he had seen God's salvation, a child who was to be a light to lighten Gentiles and to be glory for Israel. The fact that this notion is echoed in the important 'Pauline' sermon at Pisidian Antioch (Acts 13.47; see Doble, 1992, 6C2) and in Paul's testimony before Agrippa and Festus at Acts 26.19–23 tends to confirm the programmatic nature of Simeon's canticle:

> ἐπικουρίας οὖν τυχὼν τῆς ἀπὸ τοῦ θεοῦ ἄχρι τῆς ἡμέρας ταύτης ἕστηκα μαρτυρόμενος μικρῷ τε καὶ μεγάλῳ, οὐδὲν ἐκτὸς λέγων ὧν τε οἱ προφῆται ἐλάλησαν μελλόντων γίνεσθαι καὶ Μωϋσῆς, εἰ παθητὸς ὁ Χριστός, εἰ πρῶτος ἐξ ἀναστάσεως νεκρῶν φῶς μέλλει καταγγέλλειν τῷ τε λαῷ καὶ τοῖς ἔθνεσιν.

Luke attended to both elements in his programme, thereby assuring Theophilus of the ways in which Jesus' life 'fulfilled' scriptural promises; both the Nazareth synagogue incident and the answer to John's disciples help one see how firmly rooted was Luke's portrait of Jesus in the prophetic idiom of his own community; they presumably treasured these oracles. It is probable that the evangelist 'ticked off' his reports by the δοξ- phrase which alerted a reader to the fact that this event evoked a worshipping response from someone who had seen what was *really* happening. Additionally, Acts 1.8 not only set out formally the plan of Luke's second volume, but echoed the Isaianic ἐσχάτου τῆς γῆς (Isa. 49.6; cf. Acts 13.47, itself another echo of the φῶς ἐθνῶν noted above). At this point it is enough to notice that the evangelist was aware of the significant role of properly understanding the scriptures:

> τότε διήνοιξεν αὐτῶν τὸν νοῦν τοῦ συνιέναι τὰς γραφάς· καὶ εἶπεν αὐτοῖς ὅτι Οὕτως γέγραπται παθεῖν τὸν Χριστὸν καὶ ἀναστῆναι ἐκ νεκρῶν τῇ τρίτῃ ἡμέρᾳ, καὶ

discuss this enigmatic πληροφορέω, although it is clear that he understood Cadbury's position to be near to viewing Luke 'as a theologian who presents salvation history' and who used the OT as proof from prophecy. It is interesting that Cadbury (1958, pp. 303–5) later used the notion of *fulfilment* in a more positive sense than is implied in his *Expositor* (1921) article. Bock's statement that the Jesus-event and the OT are in active interaction with each other (1987, p. 279) summarises well the experience of at least this reader, and his characterisation of Luke's hermeneutic as *proclamation from prophecy and pattern* fits well this study's experience with δίκαιος. *Fulfilment* is used in this sense in the text.

κηρυχθῆναι ἐπὶ τῷ ὀνόματι αὐτοῦ μετάνοιαν εἰς ἄφεσιν ἁμαρτιῶν εἰς πάντα τὰ ἔθνη – ἀρξάμενοι ἀπὸ Ἰερουσαλήμ. (Luke 24.45–7)

Consequently, one finds the δοξ- phrase not only marking off the apostles' role as Jesus' *sheluchim* in making the lame man leap like a hart, but also indicating key moments at which the Gentiles were being enlightened and people were acknowledging God's hand in it. It thus becomes possible to ask whether this unfolding of God's salvation σήμερον may not be the missing κηρύξαι ἐνιαυτὸν Κυρίου δεκτόν of Luke 4.19 (see section B above).[46] If it is, then by his participation in the δοξ- phrase the centurion at the cross may conceivably be thought to be Luke's way of representing a Gentile[47] recognising and responding worshipfully to God's salvation being unfolded before him.

In sum, ἐδόξαζεν τὸν Θεόν at Luke 23.47 draws attention to two elements in Luke's programme. First, because the phrase acts as a programme signal, it invites the reader to focus carefully on what is happening on and around the cross and to relate those events to the Isaianic signs set out at Nazareth (Luke 4) and in dialogue with John's disciples (Luke 7). Such a conclusion is contrary to the thrust of Kilpatrick's argument that this Lukan δίκαιος is 'mere bathos' if it stands for 'righteous'.[48] Second, because this key phrase is extended in Acts to signal 'moments' in the process of fulfilling God's salvation plan for the Gentiles, the centurion's whole response (Luke 23.47) may in some sense look forward as well as back, both anticipating the later chapters of Acts and reflecting on the significance for salvation of Jesus' deeds, including his dying.

This first exploration of a Lukan compositional element at Luke 23.47 confirms the special force attaching to the phrase δοξ- τὸν Θεόν. This centurion glorified God 'by saying' (λέγων); Luke's use of ἐδόξαζεν τὸν Θεόν at this point strongly suggests that his readers should, consequently, take seriously what his centurion said. Because the term δίκαιος is central to this centurion's appreciation

[46] See note 32 above.

[47] There is no *evidence* for his being a Roman (*pace* Klostermann, 1929, p. 226 '... bezeugt der Römer die Unschuld Jesu ...'), nor for his being Gentile; the position simply reflects popular opinion. If, however unlikely, Luke's centurion was a Jew, then Kilpatrick's argument would fall anyway.

[48] It is contrary to the thrust of Kilpatrick's argument because it roots δίκαιος firmly in *scripture fulfilled*. The text anticipates to some degree the conclusions of the remainder of part II.

of Jesus and his dying, and because the Lukan δοξ- phrase has been shown to signal God's fulfilling his plan of salvation announced in scripture, Luke's own use of δίκαιος needs to be examined now to establish how it might have worked for him at this point and whether it might be associated with some 'scriptural dimension'.

3

ΔΊΚΑΙΟΣ AND 'INNOCENT': LUKE 23.47

Because Luke's use of δοξ- τὸν Θεόν suggests that at Luke 23.47 the centurion's 'δίκαιος' has programmatic significance, there is a need to identify what Luke might have intended by his use of that word. Unfortunately, that task has been made more difficult by a lengthening tradition in which translators have fixed on 'innocent' as their preferred rendering of δίκαιος at this point. The extent of this practice is illustrated in table 3.1. This rendering of δίκαιος is now to be found in many languages,[1] but is, perhaps, most interestingly focused in the recent Greek translation where the δίκαιος of N-A 26 is transmuted to ἀθῷος.[2] This confirms a strengthening orthodoxy which, if justified, plainly makes Luke's passion narrative a reductionist version: despite his suffering, this man is innocent. There is, as yet, little sign of challenge to this commitment to 'innocent'.[3]

A. Kilpatrick and 'innocent': an orthodoxy emerges

For English readers the focal point of this strengthening orthodoxy is an article written by G. D. Kilpatrick (1942). He did not invent the tradition; indeed, both German- and English-speaking translators or commentators had earlier made 'innocent' their lexical choice; some had even argued their case. But what is impressive is the extent to which commentators readily acknowledge their indebtedness to Kilpatrick's article. There is an apparent tendency to assume that his case for 'innocent' had won the field and that they need only

[1] E.g., the modern, ecumenical Catalan translation (1979) which moved away from the translation produced by liberal catholics in 1972.

[2] 'ὅταν ὁ ἑκατόνταρχος εἶδε τὶ ἔγινε, ἐδόξασε τὸν Θεὸν καὶ εἶπε "Πραγματικὰ ὁ ἄνθρωπος αὐτὸς ἦτο ἀθῷος"' (Η Καινη Διαθηκη, Athens, 1990). I am grateful to Dr Paul Ellingworth who drew my attention to this translation and discussed its implications with me.

[3] But see below for discussion of the work of Beck, Houlden, Ruppert and Matera.

Table 3.1. *Δίκαιος in English Translations of Luke 23.47 and Commentaries*

	Innocent	Righteous/just	Other
1611		Authorised Version	
1881		Revised Version (NT)	
1900		Young	
1902	Weymouth		
1904		C20th Bible	
1913	Moffatt (NT)		
1919	*S. C. Carpenter*		
1922			*Plummer*
1930	*Manson*		*Creed*
1932	*Cadbury*		
1937	C. B. Williams		
1942	*Kilpatrick*	*Hanson*	
1946	RSV	Knox	
1952		E. V. Rieu	C. K. Williams
1952			J. B. Phillips
1960	New Amer St		
1961	NEB		
1963	*Caird*		
1966			Jerusalem Bible
1966			Good News Bible
1968	W.Barclay		
1973	*J. Drury*		
1973	Translator's NT		
1974	*L. Morris*		
1975	*E. Franklin*		
1978	*Marshall(?)*	NIV	
1985	*Fitzmyer*		New Jerusalem
1989	REB		
1989	New RSV		
1990	*C. F. Evans*		Cassirer
1990	*K. Grayston*		
1990	[Η Καινη Διαθηκη, Athens]		
1990	*G. Schneider* [*EWNT*]		

Note: translations in roman type, other writers in italics.

refer readers to *JTS* for 1942 to confirm this. If readers are to discover what Luke was about in using δίκαιος, they must first question the accepted wisdom concerning this word at this point. and Kilpatrick's argument does not stand.

This chapter examines Kilpatrick's fourfold case, noting its weaknesses. The following two chapters are an exercise in semantic analysis to establish not a general sense of δίκαιος in the New Testament nor even in the gospels, but what may confidently be said of *Luke's* usage, first, in his Gospel, then in the Acts. A succeeding chapter explores the Lukan Jesus' word from the cross and confirms that at this point in the passion narrative Luke was probably working with a model of *the just man*, his sufferings and his vindication. This model, lived out in the ministry, death and vindication of Jesus, is the framework for Luke's *theologia crucis*. To establish this, there is need first to see why the argument found in Kilpatrick (1942) will not stand.

Kilpatrick and Hanson (1942)

A brief interchange between these two scholars clearly marked out issues in discussion of Luke 23.47. Consequently, it will be helpful to summarise what each contributed to the debate.

Kilpatrick, G. D. (1942)

Kilpatrick's first sentence seizes one's attention:

> At Luke xxiii.47, as the usual translation of δίκαιος by 'righteous' makes the evangelist's alteration of Mark's phrase υἱὸς Θεοῦ seem mere bathos, it seemed, in view of a suggestion by Klostermann, worth while to investigate the possibility that δίκαιος in this passage of Luke means 'innocent'.

To sustain his argument Kilpatrick followed four lines of enquiry:

Theological: understood as 'righteous' δίκαιος 'would be obscure to any but a religious Jew' and the word itself allegedly plays no part in the thought of the Gospel comparable to υἱὸς Θεοῦ in Mark;

Linguistic: Kilpatrick thought δίκαιος might 'on occasion' carry the sense of 'innocent'. His occasional evidence was drawn from the LXX of Proverbs 6.7 (*sic*), Joel 4.19, Jonah 1.14 and Genesis 20.5 (*sic*) supported by Matthew 23.35, 27.19;[4] James 5.6 and 1 Peter 3.18;

[4] There is a large difference between the use of δίκαιος at Matt. 23.35 and 27.19. The former is clearly Hanson's 'conventional phrase' while the latter is not. Matt. 27.19 has been rendered 'innocent' by NIV, REB and Cassirer; NewRSV has changed its

Thematic: Luke's passion narrative was concerned to show Jesus' innocence. Pilate, Herod and the thief had all testified to Jesus' innocence and now the centurion's voice joined those of the other 'disinterested parties';

Luke's purpose: Kilpatrick urged that Luke's Gospel was to some extent apologetic. This might be seen in the evangelist's substitution of clearly political charges for those in Mark, a ploy which enabled him to deal with the scandal of Jesus' execution by demonstrating that what happened was a travesty of justice and that Jesus was not politically dangerous.

Kilpatrick's article ended with a claim that his argument also effectively laid to rest the Proto-Luke hypothesis.

Hanson, R. P. C. (1942)

His article's title announced Hanson's principal concern: 'Does δίκαιος in Luke XXIII.47 Explode the Proto-Luke Hypothesis?' It did not, and on the way to that conclusion Hanson dealt with two of Kilpatrick's lines of argument.

Linguistic: Hanson argued that Kilpatrick's case was flawed because in three instances the LXX evidence was drawn from a conventional phrase which did not justify the assumption that in the NT *without an accompanying αἷμα* δίκαιος might be rendered 'innocent'.[5] Consequently, Kilpatrick's citing Matt. 23.35 in support of his case is acceptable because it is in the conventional phrase αἷμα δίκαιον. Hanson pointed out that in the light of James 5.17 (*sic*) it is not possible to read 'innocent' at James 5.6; and while 'innocent' is *possible* at 1 Peter 3.18 it is neither certain nor obvious.[6] Hanson asked whether there were other examples in Luke's writing of δίκαιος used for 'innocent', and concluded (1942, p. 76) that there were two indications that Luke did not use it so: first, in Luke's treatment of the parallel to Matthew 23.35 there is no reference to δίκαιος; if Luke borrowed from Matthew, then he dropped this use of δίκαιος; if from 'Q', then it did not have the phrase and Luke did

mind in favour of 'innocent' and against 'righteous' in RSV. C.B. Williams has 'righteous' although he has 'innocent' at Luke 23.47. See Schrenk's comment on Matt. 27.19 (*TDNT* II, p. 187); cf. discussion of Schrenk's comment, Doble (1992, p. 25f.).

5 Hanson corrected Kilpatrick's *Prov. 6.7* to *Prov. 6.17.*

6 See also chapter 6D, 'Discipleship, trust and Jesus' passion: 1 Peter and Acts'.

not add it. Second, because the evangelist used the adverb δικαίως in the sense 'justly' at Luke 23.41, it was almost impossible to believe that he should use the adjective δίκαιος in the opposite sense six verses later. So the linguistic evidence for 'innocent' outside the conventional phrase was very weak indeed.

Theological: Hanson offered two approaches to an answer to Kilpatrick's assertion that Luke's change of Mark's use led to mere bathos: first, he rightly raised a question about the significance of the centurion's glorifying God – '. . . if we wish to see in this change the influence of one of Luke's themes we have first to explain the point of ἐδόξαζε τὸν Θεόν'.[7] Second, he briefly suggested that Luke changed Mark's υἱὸς Θεοῦ to δίκαιος because the former might not have meant much to his readers or they might have misinterpreted it. The bulk of Hanson's reply was then given over to his defence of the Proto-Luke hypothesis.[8]

Clearing ground

This exchange mapped out some of the ground on which the argument of this monograph depends: there are *linguistic, literary, theological and redactional matters* to be considered. The heart of the argument in the following chapters takes up one of Hanson's questions which he did not pursue in detail: how does *Luke* use δίκαιος? Surprisingly, Hanson's rebuttal of Kilpatrick's claim has received much less notice than its target. Perhaps fewer people then read *Hermathena* than read the *JTS*; perhaps his article's title as well as the thrust of his argument directed attention towards concern with the Proto-Luke hypothesis rather than to the issue of the centurion's 'confession'. English translations and commentators now tend to follow the path indicated by Kilpatrick when they address themselves to Luke 23.47, but three possibilities lie before them. Δίκαιος is rendered in one of the following senses:

- *forensic*, that is, in a legal sense, e.g. 'innocent' in the passage under discussion;
- *moral*, that is, in a sense which echoes in some measure the thrust of δίκαιος in both general Hellenistic use or in a more technical, ethical sense, e.g. 'good';

[7] This is why it was essential to examine the phrase in the preceding chapter. *Real* bathos, as Hanson noted, would be glorifying God for the execution of an innocent man.

[8] See the discussion in Doble (1992, 2B2 and 3).

– *religious*, that is, in a context where a person's uprightness before God and his willingness to endure persecution for his faith makes the sense clear, e.g. 'just' or 'righteous' in the Psalms, in Wisdom, in Habakkuk and in other places. This sense *includes* both moral and forensic dimensions: this δίκαιος *is* innocent of charges against him and he does live a good life. These virtues, however, flow from his commitment to God and to living by *Torah*.

Before these possibilities are examined in detail, to tease out more carefully issues of some concern, in the three sections below examples are considered of how translators and commentators have dealt with Luke 23.47. A fuller list of modern English translations is given in Ellingworth (1990); those which appear in the sections below and are referred to in table 3.1 above were selected because they are popularly used in Britain[9] or are representative of a trend or offer some interesting feature.

B. Forensic uses: post-1942 English examples where δίκαιος at Luke 23.47 is rendered 'innocent'

Translations

The *Revised Standard Version* appeared in 1946, a product of American scholarship. At Luke 23.47 it reads: 'Certainly, this man was innocent.' The *New American Standard Bible* (1960), implicitly laying claims to recover for evangelical interests the right to inherit the mantle of the *American Standard Version* (1901), used exactly the same sentence as the RSV. In Britain the *New English Bible* (1961) followed the same line: 'beyond all doubt, this man was innocent.' *The Living Bible* (1971) hedged its bets by offering 'Certainly this man was innocent', while adding the footnote 'Literally "righteous"'; but the text shows where the translators' decision lay. The *Revised English Bible* (1989) differs only marginally from NEB: 'Beyond all doubt, he said, this man was innocent.' The *New Revised Standard Version* (1989), under Metzger's chair-

[9] This study concerns itself only with *English* writing: this is not 'wilful parochialism'. Recent translations in French, German, Greek and Spanish have also broken a link between δίκαιος at Luke 23.47 and the Acts passages, but exploration of a wider field would have made this study unwieldy. The *principles* underlying the argument concern the Greek text of Luke and are readily translatable.

manship, is a translation – 'as literal as possible, as free as necessary' (1989, p. 14) – based on the best text available at the time. The translators made no change at Luke 23.47 from the 1946 version: 'Certainly, this man was innocent.'

One puzzling fact needs to be noted. Kilpatrick's article reports that his exploration of δίκαιος as 'innocent' followed a suggestion by Klostermann. Because he offered no clue to the nature or location of this suggestion, one cannot be sure whether it was verbal prompting or whether, with Marshall (1978, p. 876), it is to be found in Klostermann (1929).[10] There were, however, *already* in existence popular English translations of the New Testament offering precisely what Kilpatrick suggested.[11] For example, in 1903, when Weymouth published The New Testament in Modern Speech he was clear that he wanted nothing to do with *literal* translations:

> Dr Welldon, recently Bishop of Calcutta, in the Preface (p. vii) to his masterly translation of the *Nicomachean Ethics* of Aristotle, writes, 'I have deliberately rejected the principle of trying to translate the same Greek word by the same word in English, and where circumstances seemed to call for it I have sometimes used two English words to represent one word of the Greek' – and he is perfectly right.
> (Weymouth, 1903, p. vi)

There seems to be no evidence of what 'circumstances' led Weymouth to render δίκαιος at Luke 23.47 as 'innocent' while at Acts 3.14, 7.52 and 22.14 he chose 'Righteous One' consistently. That his was a deliberate step cannot be doubted. Further, Moffatt (1913) offered: 'This man was really innocent.' Whatever one thinks of Moffatt's treatment of ὄντως his decision to render δίκαιος as 'innocent' presumably reflected his thinking about Luke's passion narrative. While it is not clear what led Moffatt to his decision, his popular translation became the basis for a series of commentaries. C. B. Williams, *The New Testament in the Language of the People* (1937), a popular American translation, famed for its attention to

[10] Klostermann (1929, p. 226): 'δίκαιος ... mit diesem ethisch gewandten Bekenntnis bezeugt der Römer die Unschuld Jesu.' Klostermann's Lukan text read: 'Dieser Mensch ist wirklich ein Gerechter gewesen.'

[11] Why these offered the translations of Luke 23.47 which they did deserves exploration; there is almost certainly an American connection. This study of Luke's *theologia crucis* has worked via Kilpatrick's article because it is so often cited by writers as sufficient ground for their use of 'innocent'.

the tenses and moods of verbs, offered in the text 'He certainly was an innocent man', while adding the footnote 'righteous'. Like Weymouth, at Acts 3.14, 7.52 and 22.14 Williams rendered δίκαιος as 'Righteous One'. There was thus ample precedent for Kilpatrick's move.

Commentaries (pre-1942)

Manson (1930, p. 262), working with the Moffatt translation, offers no clue to Moffatt's reason for choosing 'innocent' and little to his own for supporting it:

> The army captain who is looking on is shaken with religious emotion, and his words, 'This man was really innocent' doubtless prefigured for Luke the coming conversion of the heathen world. In Mark the exclamation takes the form, 'This man was certainly a son of God', a confession that in Jesus a divine or superhuman personality had been manifested to the world.

Manson's reference to 'the coming conversion of the heathen world' just may have a hint in it of an apologetic motif in which the heathen needed assurance of Jesus' political or criminal innocence, but his is too shadowy a comment to build on. Nor, in his later christological study (Manson, 1943), does he make use of the Lukan passion narrative when developing his Servant model. Consequently, there is no firm evidence which throws light on either the commentator's or translator's reasons for choosing 'innocent'.

It is nearly inconceivable that Kilpatrick was unaware of **Cadbury**'s contribution **(1933, p. 364 n. 3; cf. 1958, p. 310)** to the study of δίκαιος:

> So of Jesus in Luke xxiii.47 δίκαιος (not ὁ δίκαιος) replaces Mark xv.39 υἱὸς Θεοῦ (not ὁ υἱὸς τοῦ Θεοῦ). Here, unless we see a far-fetched echo of Wisdom of Solomon ii.18 . . . Luke is simply putting in the centurion's mouth the more colourless 'innocent' for the more technical or 'superstitious' Son of God.

It is not clear why Cadbury should have thought the allusion to Wisdom 2.18 'far-fetched', nor why he should have chosen Wisdom rather than the Psalms as his reference, but he sets a question mark against the case for Luke's knowledge and use of the Wisdom of Solomon,[12] particularly that work's δίκαιος model.

Dodd (1935), writing in 1934, contributed to an understanding of δίκαιος by his study of the religious vocabulary of Hellenistic Judaism (1935, pp. 42–59, 64f.). While his work is not a commentary, it was widely available and greatly respected. Dodd summarised his position thus:

> We may take it that the Greek-speaking public, on the whole, meant by δικαιοσύνη doing the right thing by your neighbour, however the right thing might be conceived; while if it used the term in a narrower and more precise sense it meant by it the virtue of acting towards your neighbour with a strict and impartial regard to his merit. It would probably be fair to say that the narrower sense tended to colour the wider sense – i.e. that the Greek tended to think of 'righteousness' in terms of 'justice'.
>
> (1935, p. 43)

Dodd's 'on the whole' and 'tended' must be noted before turning to his exploring of δίκαιος in the LXX – the use noted in the extract above would probably be that of a Greek-speaking, non-Jewish centurion. In the LXX, however, δίκαιος might be rendered rather differently, because the translators had stretched the concept δικαιοσύνη in a Jewish setting. Dodd offered some forty instances in which δίκαιος or δικαιοσύνη appeared to represent Hebrew roots outside the *zdk* group and where the 'normal' LXX sense was enlarged; among these 'enlarging' uses were 'trustworthiness', 'uprightness' and 'innocence'. So the word **can** represent 'innocent'? Three facts need to be noted:

- *first*, in the LXX one finds a *general appropriation* of the concept δίκαιος to serve *Jewish* religious experience, practice and belief; that is a fact on which to build in the following chapter;
- *second*, one needs to be aware of the *proportions* employed in Dodd's 'enlarging' terms in the LXX vocabulary. Hatch and Redpath (1975) offer roughly six columns of δίκαιος

[12] Evidence for Luke's use of the Wisdom of Solomon, particularly in his treatment of Jesus' passion, is gathered in chapter 7 below. It cannot be too strongly emphasised that this evidence is derived only from those pericopae with which the body of this study of Luke's *theologia crucis* is concerned; there may well be more. Cadbury was mistaken; this echo is not far-fetched.

and five for δικαιοσύνη. At approximately 70 entries per column this amounts to around 770 instances of the two words in the LXX. Consequently, Dodd's 'enlarging' set constitutes about 5 per cent of the total. More precisely, for present purposes, it is noteworthy that Dodd wrote of *four* cases where δίκαιος should be rendered 'innocent' – which represents about 0.52 per cent of the whole. It is *possible* that even so small a percentage indicates the availability to Luke of a concept of δίκαιος synonymous with 'innocent', but its *probability* is rapidly approaching vanishing-point.[13] This is especially the case if one takes account of Hanson's note on the technical phrase within which δίκαιος stands;

- *third*, one has to deduce Dodd's evidence because he offered no detailed references to the LXX. There can be little doubt, however, that his four supporting uses are those appealed to by Kilpatrick and briefly examined by Hanson. Rarely can so large an exegetical industry have flourished on so small and doubtful a base![14]

As was noted above, Dodd's discussion began with a summary of general usage, illuminated by Plato and Aristotle. He then examined those instances where δίκαιος or δικαιοσύνη represented Hebrew terms other than those derived from the root *zdk*; the bulk of his note, however, explored the terms' general thrust (95 per cent of their use) in the thought of the translators. Our present purpose has been simply to identify and tentatively evaluate evidence in English work before 1942 for rendering δίκαιος as 'innocent'.

Commentaries (post-1942)

Because commentators in English usually work on a given translation, they tend to comment on this passage in detail only when they dissent from, or in some way wish to vary, the published translation. There are exceptions. **Caird**, commenting on the RSV translation of Luke 23.47, positively confirmed his approval of 'innocent':

> Pilate and the penitent criminal have declared Jesus innocent; now the centurion adds his testimony. According

[13] See the discussion of Fitzmyer's comment on pp. 82–6 below.

[14] Cf. Hemer (1977, p. 45f.): see especially the final paragraph of his section II.

> to Mark he said, 'Truly this man was a son of God'; but the version given here better fitted Luke's apologetic purpose. (1963, p. 253)

Caird's reference to 'apologetic purpose' clearly indicates the hinterland of his approval of 'innocent'. Kilpatrick (1942) had begun to expose the coherence of such translation with judgments about the evangelist's overall purposes; in 1963 Caird offered his support to this aspect of Kilpatrick's case.

Caird saw Luke's two-volume work[15] addressed to Theophilus, who held high office in the Roman government, as a publication to the world outside the Christian community. Almost all of this can be – and has been – challenged; the weight of present scholarship suggests Christian roots for Luke's purposes (see chapter 1E above). For the present, one simply notes Caird's supporting arguments (1963, pp. 14–15). Christians lived in a dangerous post-Neronic world where their safety depended on their neighbours' goodwill, and where ill-informed rumour represented them as dangerous: their religion was an eccentric, foreign superstition; they were revolutionaries, turning the world upside down; they indulged in antisocial behaviour; they were felonious followers of an executed criminal. Caird saw Luke's purpose as supplying 'Theophilus and all like him with the solid truth about this calumniated movement'. This solid truth might be summed up in four general, answering propositions: first, '[Luke] will prove that [Christianity] is the true fulfilment of the religious aspirations of the Old Testament, deserving all the tolerance that Rome has shown to the Jews'; second, 'His story will tell how Christ turned his back on political revolution in order to accomplish a profounder revolution in the realm of ideas and values'; third, 'He will portray the author of their faith as a figure of nobility, grace and charm, able to reproduce these same qualities in the lives of his followers and to raise to decency and dignity even the outcasts from the society of men'; fourth, 'He will show that Christ and his disciples have been pronounced innocent by the representatives of Roman law.'

Whether Caird thought that Theophilus would be impressed by the legal acumen of a centurion is not clear, and the judgment of an executed thief, however penitent, is unlikely to have carried much

15 Most commentators (*pace* Wenham, 1991) now hold Luke's work to comprise two volumes. See, e.g., Beck (1977), Dawsey (1989), Mánek (1958), Marshall (1969b, 1989), O'Toole (1977), Talbert (1976, 1983 and 1985), Tatum (1967).

weight in the Praetorium, but Luke's focus on Pilate's judgment (Luke 23.22) makes it plain that Caird's fourth proposition probably is the case. To sustain that case, however, neither entails rendering δίκαιος as 'innocent' nor requires that one subscribe to the theory that Luke's purpose was apologetic in Caird's sense. Readers need to continue to distinguish carefully between a *theme* of Luke's passion narrative and his overall *purposes*.

Drury (1973, p. 211), commenting on Phillips' translation, changed 'good' to 'innocent' ('good' understood technically), 'a lesser and more comprehensible assessment'. His reasons for the change are rooted in his understanding of Luke's aim, 'to present Christianity to the wider world by means of telling its story as clearly and attractively as possible in the hope of winning (possibly) converts and (certainly) respect for this new religion.' (1973, p. 12). This is achieved by Luke's 'editing of Mark's dark and ambiguous narrative into something lighter and more intelligible: the good death of an innocent man' (1973, p. 204). Drury's talk of Luke's more intelligible telling of the story of Jesus' death is distantly, but essentially, related to Kilpatrick's article in that it echoes his reference to 'righteous' as 'obscure to any but a religious Jew': Drury seems to assume a non-Jewish audience – and a non-Jewish centurion. (These matters are revisited in later reflections on the place in Luke's narrative of scripture's fulfilment, which might also be thought obscure to any but a religious Jew.) Further, his reference to 'the good death of an innocent man' suggests that Drury views Jesus' death as a martyrdom, a strand of discussion resumed in chapter 7 below. In this he is supported by Nineham (1963, p. 430) who, while commenting on the centurion's response according to Mark's passion narrative, noted: 'so what we have here is not simply a case of an executioner being won over to the side of a martyr (something which often occurs in the martyrologies and is all that Luke sees here – Luke 23^{47}), but a much greater miracle, the conversion of one unbeliever by the dying Saviour'.

Marshall (1978, p. 876) also takes up the martyrdom theme but notes that some writers dissent:

> In the death of Jesus the centurion sees the sacrifice of a martyr who has perished innocently, (*sic*) For this use of δίκαιος cf. Klostermann, 226; AG s.v.; and especially G.D. Kilpatrick ... Thus a Lucan theme in the passion story reaches its final statement. Luke's description alters

> Mark's form of the statement in which the centurion confesses that Jesus is the Son of God. It may well be that Luke's stress on innocence is sufficient to motivate the alteration, but some scholars argue that Luke is unlikely to have weakened Mark's statement (Lagrange, 593).

Marshall's 'especially G.D. Kilpatrick' strongly suggests that he approved the thrust of that writer's 1942 article and wedded it to the 'martyrdom' theme discussed by Beck (1981) and others.

Goulder (1989, p. 770) holds that Luke was fearful of misleading his readers if he took over Mark's υἱὸς Θεοῦ, 'so Luke contents himself with the now standard testimony to Jesus' innocence: "Really this man was righteous"'. One does not discover what Goulder understands by 'now standard', but he plainly joins those who choose to translate δίκαιος as 'innocent'.

Fitzmyer (1985) presents a complex range of issues for consideration. These issues are so basic to any discussion of Luke 23.47, so intricately interlocked, so difficult to present clearly yet briefly, that it is simplest to explore them through an annotated excerpt from Fitzmyer's commentary.

> The comment of the centurion in the Lucan story stands in striking contrast to that in Mk 15:39 'Truly this man was the Son of God.' Luke has chosen not to follow Mark, but rather a tradition from 'L'.[(A)] On the lips of the historical centurion,[(B)] *dikaios* would have meant 'innocent.' This meaning is found in the LXX[(C)] where it translates Hebrew *naqi*, 'clean, guiltless' (Prov. 6:17; Joel 4:19; Jonah 1:14) cf. Matt. 23:35; 27:19. See further E.J. Goodspeed, *Problems of New Testament Translation* (Chicago: University of Chicago, 1945) 90–1; G.D. Kilpatrick, 'A Theme of the Lucan Passion Story'; but cf. R.P.C. Hanson, 'Does *dikaios* in Luke xxiii.47 Explode the Proto-Luke Hypothesis?' *Hermathena* 60 (1942) 74–78. That suits the problem of Stage I of the gospel tradition,[(D)] but at Stage III[(E)] one can ask whether Luke may not have meant more, since Jesus is at times called the 'Righteous One' in Lucan writings (Acts 3:14; 7:52; 22:14; cf. M.-J. Lagrange, *Luc*, 593). The centurion's reaction to Jesus joins those of Pilate (23:4, 14–15, 22), Herod (23:11) and the criminal (23:41).[(F)] (Fitzmyer, 1985, p. 1520)

(A) The question of Luke's sources remains unanswered although in principle it is probably not unanswerable. (See Goulder (1989), Evans (1955 and 1990)) Fitzmyer, working with a two-document hypothesis, appears to use 'L' to signify what in Luke is not-Mark, not-Q and not-Lukan composition. He understands 'source' in a broad sense, either oral or written 'but which is not to be put on a par with "Mk" or "Q"' (Fitzmyer, 1981, p. 83). What, then, might Fitzmyer have intended by 'Luke has chosen not to follow Mark, but rather a tradition from "L"'? In any answer to this question two elements need to be distinguished:

- *first*, many Lukan scholars agree with Fitzmyer's judgment that Luke is not a scissors and paste editor, but a creative writer. 'Indeed, it is above all necessary to stress today what Streeter once wrote years ago, that Luke "though not, as has been rashly alleged, 'a great historian' in the modern sense, is a consummate literary artist" (*The Four Gospels,* 548). For he composed his narrative (diegesis) not merely as an ancient historian of the Hellenistic mode, nor merely as a theologian of the early church writing in a biblical mold, but also as a conscious littérateur of the Greco-Roman period' (Fitzmyer, 1981, p. 92).
- *second*, the evangelist has a high regard for his sources; Luke *tends* to preserve intact Jesus' words as he found them in sources where he can be checked; he readily transformed their contexts, but showed great respect for the traditions of the Lord's words as they came to him through others. There is some evidence that Luke might *transform* a saying of Jesus in accord with some principle of conformity with scripture (Doble, 1992, pp. 349–56), but might he attribute to Jesus a saying *derived from scripture* without its already appearing in a tradition of the Church? and has he *created* this word of the centurion, or has he *drawn it from one of his sources?* Given Luke's record of fidelity where it is checkable, one must be cautious; given his known concern with fulfilment of scripture, one must be prepared not to be inflexible, *particularly if the saying relates to, arises from or clearly echoes a passage from scripture.*

Consequently, to answer the question posed above about Fitzmyer's claim, until readers can more certainly distinguish between 'L' and Luke's own theological and literary activity, they cannot confidently judge how far this evangelist *created* material.

Neither Drury (1976) nor Goulder (1989), who frequently offer sparkling insights into Luke's 'creative' activity, offers much help in relation to Luke's choice of δίκαιος in Luke 23.47.

(B) The Gospels agree that there was a centurion at the cross; legend has given him a name – Longinus or Petronius (see Taylor, 1952, p. 354). But in writing of the *historical centurion* Fitzmyer presents his reader with a new set of problems:

- *first*, he has assumed (reasonably) that the soldier spoke Greek and one may also assume that it was *Koine*;
- *second*, Fitzmyer also appears to have assumed that the centurion was thoroughly acquainted with the LXX (see (C) below). The *thrust* of Fitzmyer's comment is to support, with some reservation, 'innocent' as a proper translation of δίκαιος at Luke 23.47 and he has located his *linguistic* support in that part of his comment which deals with the historical centurion. This is unwise.

(C) Fitzmyer has made Luke's historical centurion:

- *first*, intimately acquainted with the LXX which here forms the language bank from which his use of δίκαιος is drawn; to the present, no one appears to have identified any classical or *Koine* example where δίκαιος requires 'innocent' as its translation. The absence of such evidence is problematic. While one may not argue from silence, the brooding weight of this silence certainly adds to the importance of a search for a more secure understanding of Luke's use. Were such usage to be discovered, its presence would add to the language bank available to Luke, but would not necessarily diminish the force of the present argument about Lukan *use*;
- *second*, acutely sensitive to one *very* specialised and abnormal use which, as emerged above in the note on Dodd (1938), comprises about 0.5 per cent of the occurrences of δίκαιος and δικαιοσύνη in the LXX;
- *third*, indifferent to the *normative* uses of δίκαιος in the LXX which had a religious rather than forensic reference (see chapter 4 below).

But this discussion of a *historical* centurion will not do at all. If this so-called historical centurion was a *Koine*-speaking non-Jew he would almost certainly not have thought of using δίκαιος to express his conviction of Jesus' innocence. It cannot be over-emphasised that no one has yet produced an example from the *Koine* of δίκαιος being used in this forensic sense; there was an adequate range of suitable words commonly available: ἄκακος, ἀναίτιος, ἀθῷος, ἄμεμπτος or ἀπρόσκοπος. On the other hand, had he been a *Koine*-speaking proselyte to Judaism or a God-fearer who knew his Greek Bible thoroughly, he would have been much more likely to know and *use* δίκαιος in the *religious* sense found in 95 per cent of its occurrences in the LXX rather than in the very specialist sense adduced by Fitzmyer, Kilpatrick *et al.* If a historical centurion's use of δίκαιος is in focus, then 'just' or 'righteous' must be overwhelmingly the more likely translation. Much more to the point, however, at Luke 23.47 one is probably dealing with Luke's own use and not that of an otherwise unknown warrior, and he can offer surer comments on the evangelist's use of this word.

(D) But, as emerged in (C), this does *not* suit Stage I of the gospel tradition. It is also, according to Fitzmyer's own principles, a secondary issue because his commentary seeks to elucidate *Luke*'s work: 'The primary concern of this commentary is to interpret the Lucan form of Stage III: how has Luke presented his Jesus in his two-volume work, especially in its first part, the Gospel. At times questions about Stage I will arise – inevitably – and an attempt will be made to handle them; but it should be noted at the outset that such questions are secondary to the aim of this commentary' (Fitzmyer, 1981, p. viii). What is uncharacteristically odd about Fitzmyer's procedure here is that he has allowed his unsafe conclusions about Stage I (the historical centurion) to decide his final translation of δίκαιος at Stage III.

(E) 'What immediately confronts the reader of the Lucan Gospel is a form of Stage III of that tradition. It is the result of literary composition, based on material inherited by the author from Stages I and II and fashioned by him into a synthesis, an interpretation of the Christ-event. Stage III should not be confused with Stage I' (1981, p. viii). Fitzmyer recognises that there are connections to be made between the Gospel and Luke's second volume. Having raised the question of what *more* Luke might have meant, Fitzmyer neither explored it nor allowed it to colour his judgment in (F).

(F) Fitzmyer's sentence is reminiscent of Caird's (see above) where the argument depends not on language but on a judgment about Lukan apologetics: Pilate and the criminal have testified to Jesus' innocence, now the centurion adds his voice. Because Fitzmyer stood by his printed translation, because this is his final viewpoint (so 1981, p. 218), it must be concluded that he has himself confused Stages I and III and that he stands by his confused judgment of Stage I.

C. Moral uses: δίκαιος as 'good' etc. at Luke 23.47

Some translators have drawn back from rendering δίκαιος as 'innocent' while apparently recognising the force of arguments against 'righteous'. The problem here is that it is difficult to learn why they decided on the translation they chose. That they found the verse problematic is clear: what their problem was is not.

Translations

C. K. Williams' *The New Testament: A New Translation in Plain English* (1952) reads: 'When the sergeant saw what was done he praised God and said, Truly this was a good man.' J. B. Phillips (1952) has, 'That was indeed a good man.' *The Jerusalem Bible* (1966) offers, 'This was a great and good man.' *The Good News Bible* (1966), now probably the most widely used translation in English churches,[16] reads, 'Certainly, he was a good man.' *The New Jerusalem Bible* (1985) dropped its predecessor's 'great' and moved from 'good' to 'This was an upright man,' which may be a move, but not far enough, in the right direction.

Commentaries

At present it is not easy to find work which supports the translations noted above. Two earlier commentaries appear, however, to encourage translators to fudge the issues. Plummer (1922, p. 539) wrote: 'Harmonists suggest that the centurion said δίκαιος before the earthquake and Θεοῦ υἱός after it. More probably the two expressions represent one and the same thought: "He was a good man and quite right in calling God his Father."' Whether Plummer

[16] The evidence for this is largely impressionistic, supported by the *Guinness Book of Records*, 1989.

had made a firm conceptual link between δίκαιος and υἱὸς Θεοῦ (see Wis. 2.18) is not clear, nor is it possible to establish whether 'good' is a reduced form of the *religious* commitment normatively implied by δίκαιος in the LXX. So influential a commentary cannot have failed to play its part in translators' decisions at Luke 23.47. That is also true of Creed (1930), whose comment on this verse raises a new crop of problems: 'Lk. prob. felt his own version of the centurion's words to be more fitting in the mouth of a stranger than the full confession of Jesus as Son of God.' Creed suggests no English rendering of δίκαιος; he does affirm that it is less than υἱὸς Θεοῦ as a description of Jesus.[17]

D. Religious uses: English translations of δίκαιος as 'righteous' or 'just'

Translations

Both the *Authorised Version* (1611) and the *Revised Version* (1881) read, 'Certainly this was a righteous man.' Young (1900), confident that a literal translation into English was safer than any other, produced, 'and the centurion having seen what was done, did glorify God saying, "Really this man was righteous"; and all the multitudes . . .' The *Twentieth Century New Testament* (London, 1904) rendered δίκαιος as 'good', but is placed in this section because it invites a reader to refer to Wisdom 2.18, a passage we shall later examine in detail. By doing this, the translators firmly linked the centurion's words with a basic model of δίκαιος, helping a reader grasp what the word might mean in this context. Ronald Knox (1946) not surprisingly rendered the Vulgate's *iustus* as 'This . . . was indeed a just man.' His footnote, however, takes a reader much further: 'St Augustine suggests that the centurion did not recognise in our Lord the unique Son of God, but only a "son of God" in the general sense in which "a just man" would be the equivalent of that term; cf. Wis. 2.16. But it is possible that "the Just One" was used in very early times as a cipher-word for "Son of God"; cf. Acts 3.14; 7.52; 22.14' (1946, p. 233). The significance of this linkage is explored

[17] Whether δίκαιος is 'less than' υἱὸς Θεοῦ depends on one's understanding of the function of each of these terms, so judgment about their relative status is frequently a result of circular argument. Δίκαιος at Luke 23.47 most probably *includes* υἱὸς Θεοῦ; Wisdom's δίκαιος was persecuted because of his 'claim' to be God's son (see chapter 7E, 'The Sanhedrin's Decision (Luke 22.66–71)').

throughout the remainder of this monograph. Knox had correctly identified a relation of Mark's υἱὸς Θεοῦ to Luke's δίκαιος, while ignoring the questions posed by Augustine's distinctions among senses of 'sonship'.

'Commentary'

The only substantial post-war work on Luke that appears to affirm 'righteous' at this point is Franklin's (1975), who firmly links 'righteous' with the Isaianic suffering servant. But not every example of 'righteous'[18] is what it first appears to be. S. C. Carpenter (1919), in his 'Luke the Psychologist', opined: 'But on the other hand, he will not overstate. For example S. Matthew and S. Mark relate that the centurion at the Cross said, when all was over, "Truly, this was the Son of God." There is, of course, no possibility that he meant what we mean by such words. He was a pagan, and he meant "a son of the gods", "a demi-god", "no ordinary man", "there's more in this than meets the eye". S. Luke, himself a Greek, would appreciate this and, *lest he should seem to encourage an illegitimately theological idea,* he interprets, "Truly, this was a righteous man" (xxiii.47)' (Carpenter, 1919, p. 183; italics added). So, for Carpenter, δίκαιος is a Lukan creation; it brackets off a possible misunderstanding; it has a definite theological purpose; it makes links with Hellenistic rather than Hebrew thought. This centurion's ethnic or religious identity presents no problem to Carpenter.

[18] There are problems with current English use of 'righteous' which now has distinctly negative connotations for most people. An informal survey of two disparate groups showed that a translator would now be unwise to employ 'righteous' to communicate what Luke intended by δίκαιος (as understood in this monograph). Members of Christian congregations agreed that they did not use 'righteous' in everyday speech except when conjoined with 'self'; the word had simply ceased to function for them, *even in a religious context.* Members of an academic community gave the word largely negative values: priggishness, pride, hypocrisy, an overweening sense of one's own moral worth were among its associations for them. The one exception to this negative response was in the pairing *righteous indignation.* The basic problem for translators now is to identify a usable English word which takes up the Lukan associations of δίκαιος including its representing a group of people profoundly committed to God whose own character is δίκαιος. 'Just' barely works, particularly as a title, but is to be preferred to 'righteous'. Whichever word is chosen, it should be used at Luke 23.47, Acts 3.14; 7.52 and 22.14 to ensure that a reader is aware of Luke's using *a single term to communicate a single christological model.* The body of this work amply demonstrates that it is not arguing a case for a simple word-for-word equation but for increased sensitivity to this author's apparent intention.

It is time to examine systematically issues that have emerged from this survey.

E. On rejecting conventional wisdom

This brief survey, focused in table 3.1, indicates both the weight of conventional wisdom and the representative nature of Kilpatrick's argument for 'innocent' at Luke 23.47. To establish Luke's *theologia crucis* it was necessary to question this conventional wisdom as crystallised in Kilpatrick's work. The tiny, insecure *linguistic* basis of his case became apparent;[19] his appeal to Luke's *purpose* is, at the least, profoundly suspect;[20] his *thematic* case for Jesus' innocence does not require Luke 23.47 for its support nor does it entail the translation 'innocent' at that point. Kilpatrick's sole remaining argument has to do with the coherence or comprehensibility of δίκαιος understood *theologically*; he could not bring himself to believe that Luke's use might have a theological reference. Con-

[19] In a lengthy study of dik-words, Hill (1967) preferred 'innocent' at Luke 23.47 (1967, p. 123). He claimed that Luke was either altering Mark or using a special source. If altering Mark, we are obliged to say that *he did so solely for the sake of variety of expression* or possibly to avoid conveying a notion of θεῖος ἀνήρ – but δίκαιος does little to clarify υἱὸς Θεοῦ. Hill noted Wis. 2.18 but made nothing of it; he also briefly noted Kilpatrick's 1942 article. In a substantial critique of *TWNT* Hill set out his method (1967, pp. 18–22): he attended to context, to Hebrew roots and other influences; he also explored synoptic uses and those in epistles–*but not the Acts*. For example, he explored Matt. 27.24 (1967, p. 122), Pilate's examination of Jesus, concluding that it is the task of judicial proceedings to declare culpability or innocence rather than to measure goodness. So Hill stressed an apologetic motif in relation to the scene and opined 'We are obviously in touch with the Hebrew-based meaning of δίκαιος, "in the right", which, with special reference to Jesus may be *extended* to *connote* innocence' (1967, p. 122, italics added). If Hill really intended *connote* rather than *denote* then we cannot fault him; if, however, he wanted to say something of Luke's intentions, we must protest. Hill's own background work is careful and helpful. Comparing LXX and MT he confirmed that the *zdk*-root was represented by δίκαιος in 462 out of 476 occurrences showing that the semantic overlap between the two was very great; 'innocent' (*naqi*) was represented by δίκαιος at Job 9.23 and 17.8 and the phrase 'innocent blood', usually rendered αἷμα ἀθῷον, is δίκαιος at Prov 6.17; Joel 4.19 and Jonah 1.14. He notes the Greek word as 'in the right' or 'just' (1967, pp. 98–103).

This is helpful, but his judgment with respect to Luke 23.47 is methodologically unsound. First, he failed to deal with the most pressing problem, 'Was wollte Lukas?' To discover this he needed to attend to *Lukan* usage in both volumes. Second, he only lightly dealt with the difference between *language* and *speech*. In relation to the present study's examination of δίκαιος at Luke 23.47, Hill is thus an insecure guide. For a more detailed critique of Hill's work, especially in relation to his assessment of Barr (1961), see Cotterell and Turner (1989, p. 124).

[20] See 1E, 'The question of Luke's purposes'.

sequently, if it can be shown that in Luke 23.46 and 47 the evangelist was *probably* working with a christological descriptor that made sense of Jesus' death in scriptural terms, then Kilpatrick's case falls and those who wish to argue for 'innocent' at this point will have to do so on much firmer grounds.

Semantic analysis

The following two chapters comprise an extended word study of δίκαιος. This *lexical method*, semantic analysis, needs only a brief word of comment.

During the second half of this century students of the New Testament have increasingly drawn insights from linguistics. G. B. Caird described his own *The Language and Imagery of the Bible* as a book written by an amateur for amateurs (1980, p. i), thus signalling to his readers that the writer was not himself a professional linguistician but one whose proper concerns were prospered by what linguisticians had to offer.[21] Among their wares was the sub-discipline of *semantics*, concerned to grasp the meaning of lexical units. Because this monograph seeks to identify the 'meaning' of δίκαιος at Luke 23.47 – and because one of the issues identified in Kilpatrick's case was *linguistic* – a semanticist's insights are indispensable. Caird spelled out carefully what he understood those insights to imply (1980, pp. 37–61): 'When we turn from language and what words are capable of meaning to what they actually do mean in any given item of speech, then, as we have already seen, *the user is in control*' (1980, p. 49; italics added). Kilpatrick attended to *language* in this sense while *this* enquiry's concern is with Luke's *speech*. 'The user is in control' is Caird's way of saying much the same as Haenchen's 'Was wollte Lukas?' In all that follows the argument stays closely with that question: this study's interest is not in lexicography in general but in *Luke's* use of δίκαιος.

Grayston's study (1990, pp. 374–81) of the δικ-group of words is a style of word study which will not much help the present quest because he is more concerned with *language* than with *speech*. His brief attribution of 'innocent' to δίκαιος at Luke 23.47 (1990,

[21] He was being overly modest. Henry Chadwick in his Memorial Address for Caird at St Mary the Virgin, Oxford (13 October 1984), told of a cable sent by Micklem in response to the question 'Can Caird teach Hebrew?': 'Yes – and if you give him an hour or two's notice, he can also teach Aramaic, Syriac, Coptic, Akkadian, Soghdian and Sumerian.' His firsts in both parts of the Classical tripos also testify to his linguistic skills; Caird was well placed to reflect on the Bible's speech and language.

p. 375) is undefended. His kind of survey acts as a paper with which to argue, but it studiously ignores the problem of what Grayston means by 'means'. Cottrell and Turner (1989), for example, will not countenance this 'older' form of word study which, in the end, shows what range of connotations *might* have been open to the user (*language*) but not what he or she actually intended (*speech*) – which is the focus of this study.

Perhaps the single most important indicator of the seriousness with which students of the New Testament now treat semantic issues and styles was the publication of Louw and Nida's *Greek English Lexicon of the New Testament based on Semantic Domains* (1988). This work is a product of the age of the computer and of language sciences: 'The data base for this Greek New Testament lexicon consists of the entire vocabulary of the third edition (both text and apparatus) of the Greek New Testament published by the United Bible Societies. The vocabulary, including both individual words and idioms, consists of some 5000 lexical items, with more than 25000 meanings in all.' (1988, p. vi). This ratio of *meanings* to *lexical items* indicates something of the dimensions of a translator's task. In such a setting, where may Luke's δίκαιος be found? To answer this question, Louw and Nida's five basic principles of semantic analysis (1988, pp. xv–xix) are used, and are related to Caird's fuller, but slightly different, description of this tool: they are set out briefly below.

There are no synonyms. In practice, this principle entails formally distinguishing δίκαιος, for example, from παῖς and χριστός to discover what Luke was about when using this word. Procedurally, this involves a refusal to go along with some analyses of passages, however interesting or helpful they may seem to be, simply because they import, without proper consideration, the sense associated with one word into the connotation of another. (One of the most elusive of New Testament words in this respect is 'Messiah' or 'Christ'.)

Differences in meaning are marked by context, either textual or extra-textual. Textual contexts can vary from the phrase within which a word stands to the whole work of which it is a part, taking in sentences, units and chapters on the way, but it also has wider contexts:

> The first and weightiest rule of speech is that context determines meaning. But what do we mean by context? The words we use have at least four types of setting, verbal,

> situational, traditional and cultural, all of which have an influence on their sense. (Caird, 1980, pp. 49f.)[22]

We shall use this 'weightiest' principle extensively to try to identify the circumstances, concepts and images Luke associated with δίκαιος. Such associations clustering around a word indicate what a writer wished to convey by using it. Here is a guide to Luke's speech which cannot, of course, be unrelated to the *language* available to him and to his readers.

Meaning is defined by a set of distinctive features: a verbal item is marked out by a set of boundary indicators, the sum of which constitutes the body of what the writer is trying to say, so the present search is for 'markers' around Luke's δίκαιος.

Figurative meanings differ from their bases with respect to three fundamental factors: diversity in domains, differences in the degree of awareness of the relationships between literal and figurative meanings, and the extent of conventional usage. In Luke's δίκαιος one encounters a form of *Koine* with a Hebrew accent; the δικ-base is not far distant, but in the Greek Bible the word acquired a range of conventional discourse specific to Hebrew religious life and thought.[23]

Both different meanings of the same word and the related meanings of different words tend to be multi-dimensional and are only rarely orthogonal in structure, by which Louw and Nida appear to say that relations among words are messy and cannot be neatly organised diagrammatically. A later chapter explores the semantic overlap among, e.g. δίκαιος, Son of man and Servant, and also the differences found between *Luke's* use of δίκαιος and that found in, e.g. 1 John.

The following two chapters are essentially an exploratory exercise in semantic analysis through these five principles, an attempt to resist the seductive power of conventional wisdom concerning δίκαιος at Luke 23.47.

22 This study has not systematically followed through Caird's fourfold division because, as becomes more evident in the course of part II, while his formal structure is useful, a more flexible approach to the notion of context allows 'what is there' to appear.

23 'Conventional' in this sentence is roughly equivalent to Caird's 'traditional'; see the preceding extract.

4

ΔΊΚΑΙΟΣ IN LUKE'S GOSPEL

If Luke is unlikely to have intended 'innocent' when he used δίκαιος at Luke 23.47, what may confidently be said about his use of the word? A word study *via* the principles outlined in the previous chapter is an obvious way of approaching Luke's meaning, but two factors need first to be taken into account.

First, δίκαιος has its roots in classical Greek, Hellenistic Greek and the LXX. The *TDNT* article on δίκαιος explores what happened to the word during its history, offering a clear picture of the change that came over it when the word was used to convey religious concepts in Jewish traditions.[1] No interpreter can be unconcerned for the word's history and range of meaning available to a writer who used it. Consequently, all of that 'pool of meanings' which belongs to Israel's religious concerns must be *assumed* by this study, at least provisionally, to be available to Luke. What remains to be explored in this chapter and the next is the extent to which (if at all) Luke made this pool his own, and the extent to which he was indebted to a more forensic or ethical usage.

Second, δίκαιος and its cognates are also used elsewhere in the New Testament. This simple fact is complicated by a stress placed

[1] Hill (1967, pp. 18–22) reflects interestingly on his method of word study. He chose a group of words which, in his judgment, show in their NT usage a large indebtedness to Jewish biblical Greek of the Septuagint. 'Greek *words* changed their meaning, or added a new meaning in Jewish and Christian usage, and the change was due to the influence of the Greek version of the Old Testament scriptures' (1967, p. 18). Hill's insistence on the importance of understanding how the LXX translators viewed the relation of Greek words and Hebrew meanings proved helpful; in his treatment of δίκαιος, however, he did not focus on *Lukan* usage nor did he seek to identify *associated* factors in the immediate context.

He noted a wider humiliation/vindication pattern in the LXX than a narrow 'Servant' model (1967, p. 79) and made specific reference to Wis. 2–5; he did not, however, choose to develop a method for exploring Luke's use of this group of chapters, concluding, rather, that at Luke 23.47 δίκαιος is best rendered 'innocent' *because that translation best coheres with Luke's special interest in the legal guiltlessness of Jesus*; he calls Kilpatrick (1942) in support (1967 p. 122).

on the word group during the Reformation and by Protestant Churches since that time. Christian history might lead some readers to anticipate a Pauline-style underpinning wherever the δικ- words appear; such eisegesis is comparatively rare and can be ignored here. But the *diversity* of New Testament Christianity is such that it would be equally unsound simply to import a 'general' New Testament usage into any particular setting in Luke's work.[2] While one cannot remain indifferent to the fact that, for example, Paul used the word, and particularly its verbal cognates, this study systematically addresses only evidence associated with Luke–Acts. This is not to deny that there may be some link between Paul's use and Luke's, but that link would itself need to be established only after one had identified as far as possible what *each* of these writers probably intended to convey by his uses of δίκαιος.

Because exploration of δοξ- τὸν Θεόν has shown that Luke attached special significance to his narrative around Luke 23.47, one may properly assume for the present that Luke's δίκαιος also carried a weighty meaning for his readers' understanding of his passion account. Consequently, this word study attends solely to the ways in which Luke uses the noun and adjectival forms of δίκαιος, and attends to them by analysing whole discourses. Within a paragraph, or group of paragraphs, containing the root word Luke has events, ideas, memories and allusions which illuminate the way in which δίκαιος is operating at that particular moment. It is from such whole discourses that Luke's characteristic use of the word can be deduced, in accord with the semantic analytical principles of chapter 3E above. But exploring a larger context to determine Luke's use of δίκαιος offers its own difficulties. As Cadbury noted long ago, this writer's facility with Greek is such that it is frequently almost impossible to pin down what is Lukan composition, Lukan redaction or one of his sources.

Occurrences of δίκαιος in Luke–Acts can be clustered in four large classes:[3] as a positive description of specific people; to contrast

[2] Like many writers on Luke, Grayston (1990) offers a summary of his views on δίκαιος but does not argue his case (1990, pp. 374–5). Because he does not attend to an analysis of the word's use within each writer's work and within each context, his appendix on δίκ-words does not help this present study.

[3] To save space, studies of δίκαιον as 'fitting' or 'proper' (e.g. Luke 12.57; Acts 4.19) and δικαιῶς, 'justly' (Luke 23.41), have not been included here. Words do, of course, operate in more than one semantic domain and τὸ δίκαιον and εἰ δίκαιον ἔστιν are seen to function differently from the substantive or adjectival form δίκαιος.

with ἁμαρτωλός κτλ; when used ironically of adversaries; when used, apparently, as a christological title or descriptor. This fourth class will be examined in chapter 5, so the remainder of this chapter is divided into three main sections.

A. Δίκαιος used of specific people

On five occasions Luke refers to *specific* people as δίκαιος; since one of these is Luke 23.47, the target verse of this study, only four will be explored in this section. (A short paragraph on Luke 1.17 is also included although formally it contributes little to the study.) Presumably, Luke and his readers drew on a pool of shared meaning. One way of rediscovering that pool is to ask what characteristics of the persons so described are noted in each pericope; it should then be possible to ask what qualities, ideas or allusions are commonly *associated* with Luke's uses of δίκαιος, thus placing markers around the concept. The number of Lukan uses is too small for certainty, but a trend certainly appears.

1. Luke 1.6. Zechariah and Elizabeth

Commentators quickly note the abrupt change of style from v. 5 to v. 6; the reader is thrown into a Septuagintal milieu.

> ἦσαν δὲ δίκαιοι ἀμφότεροι ἐναντίον τοῦ θεοῦ, πορευόμενοι ἐν πάσαις ταῖς ἐντολαῖς καὶ δικαιώμασιν τοῦ κυρίου ἄμεμπτοι.

Bock's assessment of Luke's use of the Greek *Tenakh* may be trusted (1987, pp. 88f.): Luke's allusions, appeals to patterns, echoes of language, hints – all these are much more difficult to handle in an analytical way than a more pedestrian writer's careful citation. Marshall (1978, p. 52f.) makes much the same point in drawing attention to the fact that while there is no direct quotation from the LXX, this passage is very *evocative* of it. Luke's mind is saturated with the language of the LXX and he draws on it as he also employs *typical patterns* based on the lives of particular characters.

R. E. Brown's examination of the infancy narratives (1979) suggests a two-stage process of composition; he also offers rich insight into the unity of the narratives with the remainder of Luke's work. His drawing attention, for example, to similarities between the narratives and the Acts in matters of 'spirit' (1.15, 41, 67, 80;

2.25–7 cf. Acts 2.17 *et al.*), 'angelic appearances' (1979, pp. 243f.) and in attention to the 'titles' of Jesus (1979, pp. 243f.) is a way of correcting Conzelmann's refusal to allow the narratives to contribute to an assessment of Luke's theology. Provisionally, we shall work on the principle that Luke's *prooimion* (Brown, 1979 p. 242) ensures that a reader grasps the author's purposes.[4] Just as Acts 1–2 is a transition from the story of Jesus to the story of the Church, so Luke 1–2 is a transition from the story of Israel to that of Jesus. The characters of these two chapters are drawn almost straight from the pages of scripture and embody the flowering of Israel's piety among first century groups.

There seems to be general agreement that Abram and Sara were called to sit for Luke's portrait of John's parents: arguing that case need not detain one here. What does require examination is the portrait's delineation of the pair who were δίκαιοι ἀμφότεροι ἐναντίον τοῦ θεοῦ. Luke provides two *associated characteristics*: Zechariah and Elizabeth were both πορευόμενοι ἐν πάσαις ταῖς ἐντολαῖς καὶ δικαιώμασιν τοῦ κυρίου and ἄμεμπτοι. These characteristics contribute to an understanding of their being δικαίοι.

Although commentators have urged the absence of any clear allusions to the LXX in these verses, *it is almost certain that Luke had in mind a specific passage from scripture* when fleshing out his sketch of John's parents. Marshall notes that πορεύομαι used in an ethical sense is uncommon; that ἐντολή and δικαίωμα appear together in Genesis 26.5 and Deuteronomy 4.40. This is so, and a pursuit of these words and combinations of words through a concordance emphasises just how Septuagintal is Luke's writing at this point; pursuit of his ἄμεμπτοι uncovered a possible source for Luke's characterisation of John's parents. Hatch and Redpath, vol. I p. 65, offer in brackets at the end of their entries for ἄμεμπτος

Al Pss. 1.1; 18(19).8; 100(101).2; 118(119).1

It was the last entry which proved most illuminating when Psalm 118.1–8 was set out according to the reading offered in 'Al'.[5]

1 Μακάριοι οἱ **ἄμεμπτοι** ἐν ὁδῷ
οἱ **πορευόμενοι** ἐν νόμῳ Κυρίου
2 μακάριοι οἱ ἐξερευνῶντες τὰ μαρτύρια αὐτοῦ·
ἐν ὅλῃ καρδίᾳ ἐκζητήσουσιν αὐτόν.

[4] See chapter 1E above and notes.
[5] It remains unclear which MSS are referred to within Hatch and Redpath's *Al.*

3 οὐ γὰρ οἱ ἐργαζόμενοι τὴν ἀνομίαν
ἐν ταῖς ὁδοῖς αὐτοῦ ἐπορεύθησαν.
4 συ ἐνετείλω **τὰς ἐντολάς σου**
φυλάξασθαι σφόδρα.
5 ὄφελον κατευθυνθείησαν αἱ ὁδοί μου
τοῦ φυλάξασθαι **τὰ δικαίωματά σου**.
6 τότε οὐ μὴ ἐπαισχυνθῶ,
ἐν τῷ με ἐπιβλέπειν **ἐπὶ πάσας τὰς ἐντολάς σου**.
7 ἐξομολογήσομαί σοι, **Κύριε**, ἐν εὐθύτητι καρδίας
ἐν τῷ μεμαθηκέναι με τὰ κρίματα τῆς δικαιοσύνης σου.
8 **τὰ δικαιώματά σου** φυλάξω
μή με ἐγκαταλίπῃς[6] ἕως σφόδρα.

Both the *language* and *content* of these verses suggest that they are a probable source for Luke's description of Zechariah and Elizabeth.

a. Language. Luke's *words* appear in the psalm: in v. 1 πορεύεσθαι works ethically as Fitzmyer noted (1981 p. 323). In vv. 4 and 6 τὰς ἐντολάς and πάσας τὰς ἐντολάς are followed by τὰ δικαιώματα in vv. 5 and 8. The psalm opened with μακάριοι [ἄμεμπτοι]; Luke used ἄμεμπτος as a brief signal of his intention at the very end of his description of the pair. Not only the vocabulary but *the sense of both passages coheres.* Luke could hardly have bettered his descriptive clause as a summary of the virtues of the psalm's opening verses: πορεύεσθαι is linked to νόμος Κυρίου which itself comprises αἱ ἐντολαί and τὰ δικαιώματα; those who walk in that way are ἄμεμπτοι. Careful searching has so far failed to trace another scriptural passage in which Luke's sequence of words and summary of sense are found; in the absence of any such passage it can be said that an argument from vocabulary, sequence and sense strongly suggests that Luke had this part of this psalm in mind when filling out what might be said of John's parents.[7]

6 For the significance of this verb for an understanding of Luke's passion narrative, see chapter 6B below, 'Why might Luke abandon Psalm 21(22).1?' Within that section see especially ''Εγκαταλείπω in the Psalms'.

7 It is true that Job is both ἄμεμπτος and δίκαιος; see, e.g., Job 1.1, 8; 2.3; the figure of Job as a δίκαιος needs to be explored, but initial examination suggests that the root of *Luke's use* is more surely in Wisdom than in Job. See chapter 7 and n. 28 to chapter 6. My colleague, Mary Hayward, drew my attention both to the δίκαιος passages in Job and to Plato's discussion in *The Republic* of the truly just man. The former are clearly a significant element in the development of the concept of the δίκαιος in Jewish piety, and the sole reason for their exclusion from this study was that Job's testing was by God (cf. chapter 7C, 'The testing of Jesus'); Job's *motives* are being tested – by Satan rather than by the ungodly. There remains an interest-

Ἄμεμπτος as a *varia lectio* needs no attention here – the argument outlined above derives from the fact that such a *varia lectio* exists and that translators could choose either ἄμωμος or ἄμεμπτος to render the opening of the psalm. The latter's presence *may* indicate that Luke had available, or knew, a version of the psalm like that in 'Al'; it *may* reflect Luke's tendency to paraphrase. Ἄμεμπτος is *hap. leg.* in the Gospels, so one cannot attempt an evaluation of the word in Luke–Acts, but, as Louw and Nida indicate, ἄμεμπτος and ἄμωμος occupy the same semantic domain; Luke, paraphrasing, might easily have supplied a closely related word. If, however, his *written* version of the psalm supplied ἄμεμπτοι, then this constitutes another piece of evidence for establishing the nature of the Greek Bible with which Luke worked.

b. Content. If, as seems probable, Luke's clause echoes the opening verses of Psalm 118(119), then a perceptive reader's mind resonates with the 'orchestration' of the rest of the psalm, creating a mood. This is **the** great psalm of exultation, delight, confidence in God's *Torah*. In it the ultimacy of God's word or law or instruction or decrees is *joyously affirmed*. If Luke was trying to evoke a general sense of the kind of people John's parents were, this psalm offered him a rich source on which to draw. A reader knows them to be ἄμεμπτοι, the μακάριοι of Psalm 118(119).1 and of all that follows; they represent the best of Jewish piety.

What has this to do with δίκαιος? The Lukan clause discussed above is a participial clause qualifying the main clause ἦσαν δὲ δικαίοι ἀμφότεροι ἐναντίον τοῦ Θεοῦ. Consequently, it seems safe to infer from its associations that for Luke, at this point in his Gospel, δίκαιος was a way of talking about people who are ἄμεμπτοι, who live by God's *Torah*, and who delight in that word while obeying its *mitzvot* carefully.

2. Luke 2.25. Simeon

Καὶ ἰδοὺ ἄνθρωπος ἦν ἐν Ἰερουσαλὴμ ᾧ ὄνομα Συμεὼν καὶ ὁ ἄνθρωπος οὗτος δίκαιος καὶ εὐλαβής, προσ-

ing question of the relation of Plato's portrait of the truly just man to the development of Jewish thought on these matters. However one renders ὄντως into English at Luke 23.47, it distantly echoes both Plato's and Job's concern with *genuine* uprightness. Cf. Danker, (1988, p. 382).

δεχόμενος παράκλησιν τοῦ Ἰσραήλ, καὶ πνεῦμα ἦν ἅγιον ἐπ' αὐτόν.

Luke's *description* of Simeon is long, similar in structure to that of Joseph of Arimathaea: καὶ ἰδοὺ, ἀνὴρ, a linked pair of adjectives (ἀγαθὸς καὶ δίκαιος, δίκαιος καὶ εὐλαβής), ᾧ ὄνομα, ὀνόματι, προσδέχομαι ... Because many of these features are similar to those in Luke's parallel to Mark's account of Joseph (see section 4 below) it is likely that one is dealing with a stylised form of introduction.

Luke's *context* for the story is the Temple where Simeon and Anna make a representative pair; Brown sees them as representing *Torah* and prophets. Set in Jerusalem, the discourse is shot through with emphasis on conformity with *Torah* – '... a Samuel-like story involving the parents, the child and an aged figure at the sanctuary' (Brown, 1979, p. 451). Each of them is presented as having recognised in the child the fulfilment of God's promises (see below). But this section concentrates on Simeon, for he alone of the pair is called δίκαιος. Three statements about him call for comment:

- καὶ εὐλαβής
- προσδεχόμενος παράκλησιν
- πνεῦμα ἦν ἅγιον ἐπ' αὐτόν.

a. καὶ εὐλαβής. In the New Testament the word εὐλαβής is Lukan; apart from this occurrence it appears only in Acts 2.5; 8.2 and 22.12. Bruce comments on its use only of Jews (1952, p. 83). Related words occur only in Hebrews: εὐλάβεια – 5.7; 12.28; εὐλαβέομαι– 11.7. Bultmann (*TDNT* II.751ff.) speaks of 'nervous fear' as an essential part of a concept that seems primarily to be about 'cautious care in respect of religious duties'. Strangely, at Acts 8.2 Luke describes as εὐλαβεῖς those who defied Jewish provision that there should be no lamentation for an executed man (Bruce, 1952, p. 182); they seem neither nervous nor cautious, paralleling for Stephen the humanity shown by Joseph to Jesus' body. But that the word points to care about religious duties is clear from Acts 22.12 where Ananias is described as εὐλαβὴς κατὰ τὸν νόμον.

For present purposes, whatever εὐλαβής signified for Luke is *probably additional to rather than constitutive of* the concept δίκαιος. They may, to some extent, be overlapping concepts as, presumably, a δίκαιος is also ἀγαθός as in Joseph's case. It is more likely that the participial clause προσδεχόμενος παράκλησιν κτλ qualifies δίκαιος as well as ἄνθρωπος.

b. προσδεχόμενος παράκλησιν κτλ. A participial clause spells out more fully the character of this ἄνθρωπος δίκαιος καὶ εὐλαβής. He was *waiting:* he was in a state of expectancy (Louw and Nida, II.730) with respect to παράκλησιν. On balance it seems preferable to render προσδεχόμενος as 'waiting' rather than 'welcoming' at this point despite Simeon's canticle, or, possibly, because of it. Luke's intention seems to have been to portray people who were living in expectation that God would do what scripture promised them that he would do; the canticle's thrust then portrays a Simeon whose hopes had been realised – Simeon had seen the Lord's *Christ*, he had seen God's *salvation*, both terms apparently elements within whatever παράκλησις might mean. There are scriptural roots for the notion – e.g. Isaiah 66.12–13; Marshall relates the notion to Isaiah 40.1. Fitzmyer also points to Isaiah 40.1 and then to Isaiah 61.2 as possible sources for the concept παράκλησις. Given Luke's general depiction of Simeon, Fitzmyer seems nearer the mark in thinking of παράκλησις as indicating Israel's post-Exilic hope for God's restoration of theocracy. Creed (1930, p. 40) notes that παράκλησις was in frequent use among the rabbis for the fulfilment of messianic expectations; he cites SB II p. 124f. as evidence.

By this clause Luke conveyed a *mood* of expectancy. The plural at Luke 2.38 makes clear Luke's view that just before Jesus' birth there was a body of people eagerly anticipating God's promised act, an act described in many different ways – at Luke 2.38, e.g. it is λύτρωσιν Ἰερουσαλήμ.

c. καὶ πνεῦμα ἦν ἅγιον ἐπ' αὐτόν (2.25)

> καὶ ἦν αὐτῷ κεχρηματισμένον ὑπὸ τοῦ πνεύματος τοῦ ἁγίου μὴ ἰδεῖν θάνατον πρὶν ἢ ἂν ἴδῃ τὸν Χριστὸν κυρίου. (2.26)

Two features are significant here: one is the probable relation of this description to Luke's wanting to portray the mood of the 'last days'. In Acts 2.17–21 he offered his scriptural base for the now-democratised holy spirit: through Joel, God had promised to pour out holy spirit on everyone. Simeon was an earnest of that promise: three references to (holy) spirit in as many verses suggest Luke's emphasis on this 'last day' mood (Luke 2.25–7) in which Simeon's encounter with and recognition of Jesus is not accidental, but part of God's salvation plan.

A second feature is the relation of this mood to Simeon's canticle and what follows: *the spirit's revelation is authenticated.* Simeon's portrait more nearly resembles the atmosphere of Acts, where holy spirit's guidance of the nascent community pervades Luke's writing, than that of the body of the gospel in which Jesus alone is spirit-led.

In Simeon's case δίκαιος is associated with those earnestly longing for God's salvation, a man to whom God reveals himself.

3. Luke 1.17. Gabriel's canticle: John Baptist

καὶ αὐτὸς προελεύσεται ἐνώπιον αὐτοῦ
ἐν πνεύματι καὶ δυνάμει Ἠλίου,
ἐπιστρέψαι καρδίας πατέρων ἐπὶ τέκνα
καὶ ἀπειθεῖς ἐν φρονήσει δικαίων,
ἑτοιμάσαι κυρίῳ λαὸν κατεσκευασμένον.

This passage links only indirectly with the present theme in that δικαίων does not refer to John Baptist but to his task, so the 'specific' persons are neither named nor described. All that can be reasonably inferred from this passage for present purposes is that φρόνησις is a quality associated with a δίκαιος and that in some, as yet indistinct, sense ἀπειθεῖς is at the other end of a religious spectrum from δικαίων.

Φρόνησις is a Wisdom word, the *practical wisdom* of those loyal to God, an attitude of the whole person; such an attitude is clearly portrayed in Psalm 118(119), while δικαίων takes up what has been said of Zechariah and Elizabeth. If John's task is to prepare for the Lord a people 'at the ready' presumably the previous two lines indicate something of the content of that notion.

It is clear from Luke's reference to Elijah and brief allusive citation from Malachi 4.5 (cf. LXX 3.23) that a reader is invited to reflect on John as a fulfilling of what God had promised in scripture. In the absence of any other clear allusion, it is probably safe to suggest that the two lines following the citation are a summary of what Elijah had been about – the restoration of God's people from its disobedience to faithfulness. Φρονήσει δικαίων thus has 'remnant' overtones, suggesting *a group of people who have held fast to God* amid a rebellious nation.[8] This picture fitted what Luke believed to be the case just before Jesus' birth. It is reasonable, then, to infer that δίκαιος at this point also refers to those who are a faithful remnant.

4. Luke 23.50. Joseph of Arimathaea

> Καὶ ἰδοὺ ἀνὴρ ὀνόματι Ἰωσὴφ βουλευτὴς ὑπάρχων καὶ ἀνὴρ ἀγαθὸς καὶ δίκαιος ... ἀπὸ Ἁριμαθαίας πόλεως τῶν Ἰουδαίων, ὃς προσεδέχετο τὴν βασιλείαν τοῦ θεοῦ, οὗτος προσελθὼν τῷ Πιλάτῳ ᾐτήσατο τὸ σῶμα τοῦ Ἰησοῦ ...

While Luke shares this account with both Matthew and Mark, he narrates the event in his distinctive manner. Essentially, Luke has omitted εὐσχήμων and added ἀνὴρ ἀγαθὸς καὶ δίκαιος, preferring to number Joseph among the *anawim* rather than among the aristocracy.

Discussing εὐσχήμων at Mark 15.43, Greeven (*TDNT* II.771ff.) correctly notes that Joseph is called εὐσχήμων βουλευτής. He seems then to assume that Matthew and Luke search for ways of explaining what is *meant* by Mark's εὐσχήμων because he comments that Matthew 25.57 'rather narrows the sense by using πλούσιος' and that in Luke 23.50 the word 'seems to be given the sense of moral quality: ἀνὴρ ἀγαθὸς καὶ δίκαιος. οὗτος οὐκ ἦν συγκατατεθειμένος τῇ βουλῇ καὶ τῇ πράξει αὐτῶν'. His *assumption* that Luke is simply spelling out what εὐσχήμων means to him cannot stand because when this evangelist himself used the word at Acts 13.50 and 17.12 he clearly conveys a notion of 'aristocracy'. It is, consequently, safest to assume that if Luke shared Mark's understanding of εὐσχήμων then he probably intended by his redaction to say something quite different. Just as Matthew simply wanted to say that Joseph was rich and had become a disciple of Jesus, Luke, on the other hand, chose to number him among the δίκαιοι such as Simeon, Elizabeth and Zechariah.

Luke's portrait of Joseph shares its essential features with Mark: βουλευτής ... προσδεχόμενος τὴν βασιλείαν τοῦ Θεοῦ ... Luke knew of those who were προσδεχόμενοι – faithful Jews whose

[8] This is the picture of life painted in Wis. 1–5. Ἀπειθής is not a Wisdom word, nor is it to be found in the Psalms. Marshall (1978, p. 59) notes that Schürmann suggested that this was a paraphrase of Mal. 4.5b.

Table 4.1. *Luke's portrayal of the δίκαιοι*

Δίκαιος	qualifier	participle
1 Zechariah and Elizabeth	ἄμεμπτοι	προσδεχόμενοι κτλ to evoke atmosphere of Ps. 118.1–8.
2 Simeon	εὐλαβής	προσδεχόμενος παράκλησιν to evoke sense of pious expectation.
3 Joseph	ἀγαθός	προσδεχόμενος τὴν βασιλείαν τοῦ Θεοῦ to evoke a sense of pious expectation.
4 Cornelius (Acts 10.22)	φοβούμενος τὸν Θεὸν	μαρτυρούμενος κτλ to indicate the Jewish community's approval of his life.
Cornelius – εὐσεβής (Acts 10.2)	φοβοῦμενος τὸν Θεὸν	ποιῶν, /δεόμενος to indicate the quality of this centurion's life

disposition to welcome the Kingdom of God, or whose expectation that God would really act to fulfil his promises, was the necessary context of Jesus' ministry. Examination of Luke's substructure shows that he tends to portray such people by a rough formula: δίκαιος plus another *qualifier* plus a *participial* qualifying clause. This becomes plainer when tabulated (see table 4.1).

While this sample is far too small to draw any assured conclusions it seems to indicate a small straw blowing in a compositional wind.[9] Luke shares the 'Markan' tradition's προσδεχόμενος κτλ., and did not go down Matthew's path of making the councillor a disciple. By a clumsy parenthesis Luke distanced Joseph from the rest of the Sanhedrin's treatment of Jesus (Luke 23.51a). His want of a 'Markan' τολμήσας does not imply that Luke thought Joseph other than a brave and generous man – that is strongly implied in the narrative and, anyway, Luke wanted to place his emphasis elsewhere. Refusing to number Jesus among the criminals, Joseph gave him a reverent burial. Fitzmyer rightly notes (1985, p. 1527) the consonance between this scene and the infancy narrative; this is a clue to what Luke was doing – redrawing Joseph's portrait so that at

[9] *Contra* Conzelmann (1961, p. 89 n. 2)

the end as at the beginning of Jesus' ministry the Lord was recognised by Israel's faithful and pious: whatever Rome had said, this honourable representative of Israel did not number Jesus among the criminals. Consequently, it seems safe to affirm that rather than interpret tradition's εὐσχήμων, Luke was developing its clues in line with his own interest in faithful Israel to say plainly that he numbered Joseph among the δίκαιοι. We may now add to the collection of words, phrases and ideas associated with δίκαιος Joseph's looking forward to God's Rule.

5. Acts 10.22. Cornelius

An apparent exception to a general rule now begins: to this point δίκαιος has proved to be a term for the faithful pious of Israel but Cornelius is evidently a Gentile,[10] as the dispute over his baptism makes clear. The general **context** of this whole event is discussed above in chapter 2 (C, 'Through them to the Nations'). The sharp controversy between Peter and the circumcision party over his baptising the Gentiles centred on Peter's not only associating but eating with men who had foreskins; Luke had earlier been at great pains – twice in this lengthy episode – to describe the character of the man of whom the circumcision party complained. That description, containing the word δίκαιος, begins at the point at which Cornelius' carefully chosen messengers, arrived at Joppa, give Peter their message:

> οἱ δὲ εἶπαν, Κορνήλιος ἑκατοντάρχης, ἀνὴρ δίκαιος καὶ φοβούμενος τὸν θεόν, μαρτυρούμενός τε ὑπὸ ὅλου τοῦ ἔθνους τῶν Ἰουδαίων, ἐχρηματίσθη ὑπὸ ἀγγέλου ἁγίου μεταπέμψασθαί σε εἰς τὸν οἶκον αὐτοῦ καὶ ἀκοῦσαι ῥήματα παρὰ σοῦ. (Acts 10.22)

As indicated above in table 4.1, Luke worked with a formula, δίκαιος plus qualifier plus participle. Here, two things are said of Cornelius which are significant for an exploration of δίκαιος: he reverenced God (φοβούμενος τὸν Θεόν, the added qualifier) and was borne testimony to by the whole Jewish community (μαρτυρούμενος κτλ, the participial clause). There can be little doubt that Luke intended to stretch his church's conception of a world waiting for the fulfilment of God's promises. He had begun this process in

[10] That is, in Sanders' terms, Cornelius was one of *them*, not one of *us*.

Table 4.2. *Luke's portrayal of Cornelius*

10.2 εὐσεβὴς	καὶ φοβούμενος τὸν Θεόν	ποιῶν ἐλεημοσύνας δεόμενος τοῦ Θεοῦ
10.22 δίκαιος	καὶ φοβούμενος τὸν Θεόν	μαρτυρούμενος κτλ
	cf.	
10.35 δεκτὸς	ὁ φοβούμενος αὐτόν	ἐργαζόμενος δικαιοσύνην

Simeon's canticle. Its full stretching is probably seen in Acts 10.34–5:

> Ἐπ' ἀληθείας καταλαμβάνομαι ὅτι οὐκ ἔστιν προσωπολήμπτης ὁ θεός, ἀλλ ἐν παντὶ ἔθνει ὁ φοβούμενος αὐτὸν καὶ ἐργαζόμενος δικαιοσύνην δεκτὸς αὐτῷ ἐστιν.

What Luke wanted to say about Cornelius actually matches this formula neatly, but his process of description had begun much earlier:

> Ἀνὴρ δέ τις ἐν Καισαρείᾳ ὀνόματι Κορνήλιος, ἑκατοντάρχης ἐκ σπείρης τῆς καλουμένης Ἰταλικῆς, εὐσεβὴς καὶ φοβούμενος τὸν θεὸν σὺν παντὶ τῷ οἴκῳ αὐτοῦ, ποιῶν ἐλεημοσύνας πολλὰς τῷ λαῷ καὶ δεόμενος τοῦ θεοῦ διὰ παντός ... (Acts 10.1–2)

This fuller description of Cornelius can be set out in tabular form (table 4.2 above).

Setting out the description in this way reveals a possible inner logic in Luke's treatment of Cornelius. First, he is consistently referred to as φοβούμενος τὸν Θεόν. The concept of 'God-fearer' has been thoroughly explored and requires no attention here (see, for example, *TDNT* IX.213; Bruce (1952, p. 215); Conzelmann (1987, p. 81); Esler (1987); Haenchen (1971, p. 346); Wilcox (1981)). Marginal members of the Jewish community, distinct from proselytes, God-fearing Gentiles were a feature of the first century world.[11] Peter's position toward this group, as Luke understands it,

[11] But see also Sanders' discussion of the existence or non-existence of God-fearers (1991, pp. 434–55), particularly his references to the Aphrodisias inscription (1991 p. 440f.). While this discussion remains open, the phrase is an undoubted part of Luke–Acts and one may properly work with it; whether it is a Lukan invention is another matter. See Jervell (1972, pp. 49–69).

is clearly set out in Acts 10.34, and its exposition later causes those who had objected to Cornelius' baptism to keep their peace while ἐδόξασαν τὸν Θεόν (11.18).

Second, table 4.2 suggests that he is δίκαιος who is ἐργαζόμενος τὴν δικαιοσύνην, which, *pace* Bruce (1952, p. 215) and Haenchen (1971, p. 346), is not simply to be rendered as 'charity' even though the first-century synagogue tended to use the term in this way. Δικαιοσύνη should be understood in the sense in which *Luke* appears to use it at Luke 1.75, Acts 13.10; 17.31 and 24.25, where it probably signifies both God's self-consistent justice in his dealings with his creation and a human quality, that of pursuing a life which 'answers' God's righteousness by doing his will. 'A man is righteous when he meets certain claims which another has on him in virtue of a relationship. Even the righteousness of God is primarily his covenantal rule in fellowship with his people' (*TDNT* II.195).

Cornelius is first described as εὐσεβής, a word used by Luke only once more, five verses later at Acts 10.7.[12] Foerster (*TDNT* VII.181ff.), noting the New Testament's reserve with respect to this word group, suggested that this is 'associated with the fact that in Hebrew and in the mother tongue of most of the New Testament authors there was no direct equivalent for these Greek terms' (p. 182). Luke thus introduced Cornelius *to the reader* as one whose conduct was shaped by virtues outside a Jewish context; he was among those awed by 'the divine' and who respected the relations implied by it. But Luke immediately added a dimension which his readers would understand: while εὐσέβεια knew nothing of one's being under the unconditional claim of a personal power,[13] φοβεῖσθαι τὸν Θεὸν meant precisely that to Jewish and Christian readers. Luke further qualified the term in ways which were well known to the synagogue: first, Cornelius was distinguished for his compassion and generous almsgiving (ποιῶν ἐλεημοσύνας πολλάς) to the People of God (τῷ λαῷ); second, he was diligently prayerful (δεόμενος τοῦ Θεοῦ), a virtue encouraged by Luke as basic to discipleship.

Luke introduced Cornelius *to Peter* by summarising the earlier introduction in words suitable for Jewish ears: Cornelius remains φοβούμενος τὸν Θεόν but now he is δίκαιος rather than the 'strange' εὐσεβής, and it is hard not to see δίκαιος here as a

12 Outside Acts only at 2 Pet. 2.9, although its cognates appear fifteen times, mostly in the Pastorals.

13 Foerster, *TDNT* VII, p. 182.

distillation of 'generous almsgiving and diligent prayer by one who reverences God'. The wider Jewish community would also give Cornelius a good reference – μαρτυρούμενός τε ὑπὸ ὅλου τοῦ ἔθνους τῶν Ἰουδαίων (Acts 10.22).[14] The unambiguous statement that 'Cornelius is δίκαιος' must not be undervalued; it has been carefully explored by Luke and encapsulates the principle adumbrated by Peter at Acts 10.34–5, namely that God is not to be thought of as interested only in ethnic Jews, but accepts Gentiles who reverence him and behave consonantly with that reverence. Luke has taken such pains over the Cornelius story that a reader must ask what might have been happening in Luke's church to evoke such careful writing about the place of Gentile converts in God's economy of salvation. One must assume a *corpus mixtum* living with tensions deriving from divergent ways of understanding God's will (see, for example, Maddox (1982), Esler (1987)); Luke helps these groups grasp the ἀσφάλειαν τῶν πεπληροφορημένων ἐν ἡμῖν πραγμάτων (Luke 1.1–4) by detailing the things concerning Cornelius.

Just as Zechariah and Elizabeth, then Simeon and, later, Joseph were representatives of Israel's patient, faithful piety, so Cornelius epitomised those 'among the nations'[15] whose hope would also be realised by God's saving acts in Jesus and who might properly be called δίκαιος. Further, God had spoken to Cornelius as to Simeon and to Zechariah. For Simeon the word had come by holy spirit:

> καὶ ἦν αὐτῷ κεχρηματισμένον ὑπὸ τοῦ πνεύματος τοῦ ἁγίου μὴ ἰδεῖν θάνατον πρὶν ἢ ἂν ἴδῃ τὸν Χριστὸν κυρίου. (Luke 2.26)

For Cornelius as for Zechariah, the word of God came by angelic vision:

> . . . ἐχρηματίσθη ὑπὸ ἀγγέλου ἁγίου . . .
> (Acts 10.22b cf. Luke 1.8–20)

Thus, by his reverencing God, by his virtues and by an angelophany Cornelius was installed among Luke's δίκαιοι.

[14] Sanders' suggestion (1991, p. 449) that *God-fearer* may be an honorific title among Jews for Gentiles who contributed towards the building of synagogues is probably eroded by the *Jewish* associations of the Lukan use of δίκαιος.

[15] See Sanders' careful discussion of the ambiguities inherent in τὰ ἔθνη (1991, pp. 443–51): *nations* or *Gentiles*? and by what criteria may one choose an appropriate rendering?

This is Luke's 'saints' gallery' of δίκαιοι: they are the faithful to God, Jew and Gentile alike, who delight in his will, revealed through scripture, and whose lives evidence their commitment.

B. Δίκαιος contrasting with ἁμαρτωλός, κτλ

This section focuses on contrasts: first between δικαίοι and ἁμαρτωλοί; second, between those who are raised from the dead and those who are not. These contrasts indicate something of Luke's thought about the concept δίκαιος, and his 'indicators' are gathered at the end of the section. Provisionally, one notes that these contrasts tend to confirm the findings of section A – that Luke uses the word in contexts which emphasise the Jewishness of its underlying thought by relating it to terms and ideas which belong to the piety and theology of first-century Israel.[16]

Δίκαιος /ἁμαρτωλός

Luke offers two instances of such clear-cut contrasts: Luke 5.32; 15.7. There is, however, an extended Lukan treatment of the contrast at Luke 18.9–14, the 'parable' of publican and Pharisee, respectively ἁμαρτωλός (Luke 18.13) and, ironically(?), δίκαιος (18.9). Because of its importance *in its own right* for exploring Luke's concept of δίκαιος, detailed examination of Luke 18.9–14 is deferred to section C below. The two instances examined in this section are both summarising *logia* attributed to Jesus, relating to the purposes of his activity. Luke's interest in statements about Jesus' purpose runs throughout his Gospel and is explored in section C.

The first contrast is found at Luke 5.32, οὐκ ἐλήλυθα καλέσαι δικαίους ἀλλὰ ἁμαρτωλοὺς εἰς μετάνοιαν. Apart from a perfect, where Mark has an aorist, and a characteristic εἰς μετάνοιαν, Luke shares this *logion* with Mark's Gospel. The question of how fittingly the *logion* coheres with the little parable about the physician is of no importance to this present enquiry. What is clear is that Luke intended ἁμαρτωλός to stand over against whatever he understood by δίκαιος. The same is true of the second instance (Luke 15.7):

[16] The more certain interpreters can be that Luke's pool of meaning for δίκαιος is in Jewish religious thought, the firmer will be their assessment of δίκαιος at Luke 23.47. It has become increasingly clear that Luke's interest is in *commitment* rather than in *innocence*, and this positive element of the word persists.

λέγω ὑμῖν ὅτι οὕτως χαρὰ ἐν τῷ οὐρανῷ ἔσται ἐπὶ ἑνὶ ἁμαρτωλῷ μετανοοῦντι ἢ ἐπὶ ἐνενήκοντα ἐννέα δικαίοις οἵτινες οὐ χρείαν ἔχουσιν μετανοίας. Standing at the end of Luke's version of the parable of a lost sheep, this *logion* holds all the elements of Luke's theme: sinners and repentance, righteous and sinners, God's joy – all reflect what Luke understood a significant part of Jesus' ministry to be about.

Consequently, when one identifies how ἁμαρτωλός operated for Luke, the nature both of this contrast with and, by implication, of his understanding of δίκαιος becomes clear. This contrast almost certainly reached Luke both from the tradition and from his pondering on the Psalms where the contrast between δίκαιος and ἁμαρτωλός is frequent and instructive.[17]

Ἁμαρτωλός in Luke–Acts

In the Gospel ἁμαρτωλός appears, as adjective or noun, in seventeen places, but is absent from Acts. It may focus a contrast with godly behaviour (Luke 6.32, 33, 34.), suggest a notoriety of life (Luke 7.37, 39), or link 'sinners' with penitence (Luke 15.7, 10; both of these are in Lukan parables). The word may describe a person (Luke 5.8; 9.7; 24.7 – where it is not clear whether it refers to Gentiles or to the sinfulness of Jewish authorities in bringing about Jesus' death); it may also link sinners with publicans (Luke 5.30; 7.34; 15.1; 18.13 – where the publican's offence probably lay in his

[17] We ought now to examine *all* occurrences of this contrasting pair in the Psalms and summarise our conclusions. There is neither space nor time in this study for so substantial a piece, but enough of the evidence has been worked through in a preliminary way to know that this frequent pairing consistently portrays δίκαιοι as people who delight in God's *Torah*. Ps. 1, e.g., encapsulates the atmosphere of Zechariah and Elizabeth's blamelessness (see 1.1–3; cf. A1 above) then –

> οὐχ οὕτως οἱ ἀσεβεῖς, οὐχ οὕτως,
> ἀλλ' ἢ ὡς ὁ χνοῦς, ὃν ἐκριπτεῖ ὁ ἄνεμος ἀπὸ
> προσώπου τῆς γῆς.
> διὰ τοῦτο οὐκ ἀναστήσονται ἀσεβεῖς ἐν κρίσει
> οὐδὲ **ἁμαρτωλοὶ** ἐν βουλῇ **δικαίων**·
> ὅτι γινώσκει Κύριος ὁδὸν **δικαίων**
> καὶ ὁδὸς ἀσεβῶν ἀπολεῖται. (Ps 1.4–6)

Consequently, in what follows, this study will assume that Luke had pondered on and worked with the Psalms. The *Index loci citati vel allegati* in N-A 26, pp. 752–7 offers evidence of Luke's use in Luke–Acts of sixty-seven psalms, including the studied use of Ps. 118.1–8 (examined in A1 above); given this evangelist's unambiguous inclusion of the Psalms in his appeal to scripture (e.g. Luke 24.44), it is reasonable to assume that wherever this pairing is found, there is an indicator of Luke's psalm-like understanding of δίκαιος.

office rather than his person). In one instance it raises the question of a link between sin and suffering (Luke 13.2).

In most cases the word has strong negative connotations, particularly in the form of complaints: Luke 5.30; 7.34, 39; 15.2; 19.7. An affirmation of Jesus' concern for ἁμαρτωλοί is found in 5.32; 15.7, 10 (see 18.9–14; 19.10). But in general, Luke's use of the word appears to be that outlined by Rengstorf (*TDNT* I.327ff.). Rengstorf traced through Judaism's use of the word the process by which δίκαιος / ἁμαρτωλός emerged as a contrasting word pair to polarise two perspectives on *Torah*, and ultimately to separate Pharisaic from non-Pharisaic approaches to it. Apart from the Lukan story of a notorious woman (Luke 7.37, 39), the evangelist's use of ἁμαρτωλός seems to cohere with that indicated by Rengstorf: generally, he indicates not those who were rebellious against God's *moral* law or who denied God's claim on them but rather those who did not give themselves to *Torah* study and to scrupulous observance of its detail. It is at this point that one becomes aware of a possible irony in Luke's use of the word; in section A above δίκαιος works far more positively than simply as an indicator of meticulous *Torah* observance. If, as indicated in the two quotations above, Luke truly contrasted δίκαιος and ἁμαρτωλός, then there is a possibility that the word δίκαιος in this context might be taken to refer to those who were meticulously concerned with the minutiae of *Torah* study. At present, however, one is left with a clear impression that, whatever might be implied in the contrast between δίκαιος and ἁμαρτωλός, this word pair operates in a thoroughly Jewish way, relating primarily to God's will as revealed in *Torah* and to ways of responding to it.

Ἀνάστασις δικαίων καὶ ἀδίκων

At two points Luke relates 'resurrection' to δίκαιος; each hints at a contribution to the Lukan pool of meaning for which this study is searching. The first instance is to be found in Luke's account of a meal at which Jesus offered his host advice about the guests he really should invite (and the guests advice on how they really should behave); to the host, having invited not friends and relations but the poor and disadvantaged, it is said:

> καὶ μακάριος ἔσῃ, ὅτι οὐκ ἔχουσιν ἀνταποδοῦναί σοι, ἀνταποδοθήσεται γάρ σοι ἐν τῇ ἀναστάσει τῶν δικαίων.
>
> (Luke 14.14)

The second instance is of interest because it is a rare example of talk about resurrection of the *unjust* as well as of the just. Its context is Paul's defence speech before Felix; the historicity or formal structure or relation of this speech to the rest of Luke–Acts cannot be explored here, only the probable relevance of one verse to a pursuit of the Lukan concept δίκαιος:

> ἐλπίδα ἔχων εἰς τὸν θεόν, ἣν καὶ αὐτοὶ οὗτοι προσδέχονται, ἀνάστασιν μέλλειν ἔσεσθαι δικαίων τε καὶ ἀδίκων. (Acts 24.15)

The question of Jesus' resurrection is broached only later; what is of concern here is the general concept. Luke is well aware of its contentious place in Jewish thought (Acts 23.6–9) and tells the story so as to focus on Christian emphasis on what Pharisees hold to be true – that there is to be a *resurrection*. Before Felix, Paul's assertion is that resurrection is of both δικαίων and ἀδίκων. It is not easy to decide what sort of hinterland of meaning is to be discovered within this reference; nor is it possible to be certain whether one is dealing with Paul or Luke.

Although the developing notion of resurrection is found in prophetic writing, its relation with a concept of the δίκαιος appears to be explicit at only two places in Jewish writing before the Christian movement – in Daniel 12.2–4 and in Wisdom 2–5 (see Nickelsburg (1972 and 1980)). In each case a firm link is made between the word δίκαιος on the one hand and, on the other, notions of a commitment to God which is held in spite of great suffering, even to the point of death. In the Wisdom passages this suffering appears to be at the hands of the ungodly (ἀσεβεῖς) who are also, at Wisdom 4.10, spoken of as ἁμαρτωλοί. In Daniel, the oppressors and persecutors are alien, earthly, political authorities – the Seleucids and their supporters.

A formal link between δίκαιοι and the saints of the Most High, the suffering yet faithful people of God, is made in Daniel 12.1b–3 (Θ):

> ... ἐν τῷ καιρῷ ἐκείνῳ σωθήσεται ὁ λαός σου, πᾶς ὁ εὑρεθεὶς γεγραμμένος ἐν τῇ βίβλῳ. καὶ πολλοὶ τῶν καθευδόντων ἐν γῆς χώματι ἐξεγερθήσονται, οὗτοι εἰς ζωὴν αἰώνιον, καὶ οὗτοι εἰς ὀνειδισμὸν καὶ εἰς αἰσχύνην αἰώνιον. καὶ οἱ συνιέντες ἐκλάμψουσιν ὡς

> ἡ λαμπρότης τοῦ στερεώματος καὶ ἀπὸ τῶν δικαίων τῶν πολλῶν ὡς οἱ ἀστέρες εἰς τοὺς αἰῶνας καὶ ἔτι.

Daniel's vision of an end in which God's persecuted faithful are vindicated in glory is matched by Wisdom's reflection on the sufferings of the δίκαιος. This connection will be explored in some detail in part III; here it need only be noted that there is a close conceptual relation between the δίκαιος of Wisdom and of the Psalms, and that the 'resurrection' of the just man's persecutors (τῶν θλιψάντων, Wis. 5.1) is essential for his vindication to be *seen*, and to be the source of their shame and confusion.

Consequently, Luke's references to resurrection of the just and unjust suggest a pool of meaning which cannot be very different from that implied in the Daniel and Wisdom passages and which may, in fact, be dependent on one or both of them. The long, bitter conflict between the δίκαιοι on one hand and, on the other, their persecutors, whether from inside or from outside the House of Israel, is all part of what Luke is about. The δίκαιος in Psalms and Wisdom looks to God for rescue from, or vindication before, his oppressors; talk of ἀνάστασις τῶν δικαίων καὶ ἀδίκων is talk of a hope that in the end God would certainly deal justly with those who had staked their all on him. This is a part of Luke's pool of meaning and must be considered in any search for his concept of δίκαιος.

C. Δίκαιος used ironically or of opponents

There are two cases of Luke's employing the word δίκαιος in relation to people very different from those discussed in section A; the examples are close together but they differ in character – Luke 18.9 and 20.20.

1. Luke 18.9–14. Publican and Pharisee

The parable of these two men is a focal passage for understanding Luke's use of δίκαιος (see also Beck, 1989, p. 36). Its *characters* raise the question of who is genuinely δίκαιος; its *context* is within a larger scheme whose major concern is 'discipleship'; its *concluding verse* links the pericope firmly with a basic Lukan concern; above all the 'parable' was addressed to those who were self-confident because or that they were δίκαιοι and accounted others of no worth. It is this last clause which focuses the defining characteristics of δίκαιος in Luke's thought.

The characters

Luke assembles three key groups in the gospel's drama: the audience, Pharisees, publicans or toll-collectors.

The audience. Although Luke does not say that Jesus told the parable specifically to Pharisees many commentators take this to be the case; that would match other contexts for parables, e.g. that of the two brothers in Luke 15.11–32 which stands in a sequence headed by

> καὶ διεγόγγυζον οἵ τε Φαρισαῖοι καὶ οἱ γραμματεῖς λέγοντες ὅτι Οὗτος ἁμαρτωλοὺς προσδέχεται καὶ συνεσθίει αὐτοῖς. εἶπεν δὲ πρὸς αὐτοὺς τὴν παραβολὴν ταύτην λέγων ... (Luke 15.2–3)

But Luke's address in 18.9 may be much wider; one probably errs in making the assumption that *only* Pharisees and their scribes had an arrogant concept of δίκαιος. The possibility that Luke focused his discussion on a problem within his own church should not be too quickly dismissed. As becomes increasingly obvious, he took care to spell out a coherent description of δίκαιος – and of its more corrupt versions. His own church, like every other institutional church, faced the possibility of reading the gospel in a way which encouraged pride in personal piety and its concomitant tendency to see people who were not obviously *inside* to be *outside* God's chosen people. That his church probably faced such divisiveness within its own life can be seen to be the case as one traces Luke's rewriting of Jesus' story in a direction which emphasises the deadliness of such pride, culminating in the affirmation that it was the publican rather than the Pharisee who went back to his home δεδικαιωμένος.

The Pharisee. Pharisees[18] have had a bad press through most of Christian history and this is no place to confirm stereotyping which led to anti-semitism. There is, however, real difference between recognising that Jesus died as the result of a deep and bitter conflict within the Judaism of his time, a conflict reported in all the

[18] See also Carroll (1988); Ziesler (1978) and *TDNT* IX. 11–48.

Gospels, and allowing that recognition to pass into a condemnation of all Jews. Luke reports a conflict between Jesus and a specific group, or, more properly, with members of that group.

Jeremias' account of the Pharisees (1969, pp. 246–67) makes plain their honoured place in the Israel of Jesus' time; he highlights the risks involved in Jesus' call to such people to repent. The profoundly shocking nature of Jesus' teaching and, in particular, of his address to and comments on both scribes and Pharisees can hardly be overemphasised. Modern readers can probably never recover the shock of the earliest presentations of the Christian gospel. Pharisees were honoured, trusted, committed men whose personal and social ideals led them to form communities which took God's *Torah* so seriously that, to echo Jeremias, they fought on two fronts: on one side they were profoundly opposed to the Sadducaean hegemony, on the other they were separated from the *am ha'aretz* by their meticulous, scrupulous attention to living by *Torah*.

Luke's treatment of the conflict which led to Jesus' death is complex. Pharisees do not figure in his passion narrative; other forces operate there (see Ziesler (1978) pp. 146–57). Throughout the remainder of the Gospel, however, Luke has systematically arranged his material so that a distinctive account is given of Jesus' conflict with them.

First, in his composition Luke tends to pair Pharisees and scribes,[19] sometimes adding 'Pharisees' where Mark has none (e.g. Luke 5.21). **Second,** for Luke the *distinctive* encounter among Jesus and the scribes and Pharisees is around a meal.[20] As a setting for material he possibly shares with a sayings source, Luke may have constructed his picture of Jesus invited to eat with a Pharisee – ἐν δὲ τῷ λαλῆσαι ἐρωτᾷ αὐτὸν Φαρισαῖος ὅπως ἀριστήσῃ παρ' αὐτῷ (Luke 11.37) – followed by material parallel to that in Matthew 23 (see Huck (1951) 154). There are two similar situations in purely Lukan material:

> Ἠρώτα δέ τις αὐτὸν τῶν Φαρισαίων ἵνα φάγῃ μετ' αὐτοῦ (Luke 7.36)

and

> Καὶ ἐγένετο ἐν τῷ ἐλθεῖν αὐτὸν εἰς οἶκόν τινος τῶν

19 Note the diversity of Lukan words for 'scribe'– e.g. νομοδιδάσκαλος (5.17); γραμματεύς (5.21, 30); νομικός (7.30; 10.25; 11.45–53; 14.3).

20 On the place of meals and hospitality in Luke–Acts see, e.g. Cadbury (1958, pp. 251–3), Esler (1987, ch. 4), Just (1993), Robinson, B.P. (1984, pp. 485–7).

ἀρχόντων τῶν Φαρισαίων σαββάτῳ φαγεῖν ἄρτον καὶ αὐτοὶ ἦσαν παρατηρούμενοι αὐτόν. (Luke 14.1)

Such context-giving suggests a distinctive Lukan view of relations between Jesus and the Pharisees: they felt able to welcome him as they would not have felt able to welcome one indifferent to *Torah*'s commands. Luke's portrayal of the conflict is thus *within* a circle where Pharisees operated. **Third,** Jesus' systematic attack on Pharisees is set by Luke within the context of such a table fellowship (Luke 11.37–44, 49. Luke 11.45–8 is directed formally to scribes; see chapter 7). Luke's giving it a table-context points up the fierceness of this attack. **Fourth,** meals are elsewhere occasions for conflict between Jesus and Pharisees: in Luke 7.36–50 the issue is one of an unacceptable person; in 14:1–6 it concerns sabbath healing. In both cases the table context sharpens the conflict. **Fifth,** the issues on which Jesus and Pharisees were in conflict include cleanliness (washing, 11.38; people, 7.37–9) and the sabbath (5.17–26; 14.1–6) but, according to Luke, above all, a self-confident, arrogant trust in one's having completed *Torah*'s requirements. It may be the case that Luke has over-egged the pudding, and that alongside this unattractive presentation of Pharisees in his Gospel there existed in the real world a Pharisaism meticulous in its piety yet without an exclusivism which accounted those outside its circle as of no worth. Ziesler (1978) reached broadly similar conclusions (cf. Carroll (1988)).

However, because much of the evidence for this period derives from the New Testament, particularly the Gospels and Paul's letters; because **some** conflict led to Jesus' death, a conflict deep and strong enough to stir religious authorities to action; because each layer of gospel tradition points strongly to an unattractive exclusivism among Pharisees, it seems safe to focus the conflict within the circle of Jews who took their commitment very seriously indeed. According to Luke, Jesus identified three elements in the Pharisees' piety which constituted a basic ungodliness: first, while they were meticulous in observing *Torah* they missed the innerness of true faith (Luke 11.37–41, 42); second, their religious observance tended to enhance their standing in their contemporaries' eyes, but they failed to 'please God' (Luke 11.43; 16.15 cf. 5.17–26; 5.27–32); third, their exclusiveness led to their despising others and remaining aloof from them; this accounting others to be worthless underlies much of

Luke's portrayal of Jesus' animus against Pharisees (Luke 7.36–50; 15.11–32) and is openly expressed in this parable (18.9).

By the time his readers reached the parable of the Pharisee and the publican Luke had set out all the constituent elements in one of his characters. He had done the same with the other.

The publican, or toll-collector, symbolised those despised by this Pharisee. Jeremias' account of the τελῶναι (1969, pp. 304f. cf. pp. 32, 56) indicates that theirs was a despised trade because they were robbers (cf. *TDNT* VIII.101–5). Luke's picture of τελῶναι is complex, concentrated in a few passages.

Luke related publicans to John Baptist's activity. In Luke 3.12 they form one of the groups seeking ethical guidance from John. Their τί ποιήσωμεν; is answered by an instructive Μηδὲν πλέον παρὰ τὸ διατεταγμένον ὑμῖν πράσσετε (Luke 3.13), advice which would make sense only if Luke believed the popular view to be that the contrary was the case. (In relation to this belief Luke 19.8b may be an ironic conditional.) The curious conjunction of ὁ λαὸς and οἱ τελῶναι appears again at Luke 7.29, there contrasted with Pharisees and scribes; they fall on opposite sides in relation to Jesus' estimate of John:

> λέγω ὑμῖν, μείζων ἐν γεννητοῖς γυναικῶν Ἰωάννου οὐδείς ἐστιν. ὁ δὲ μικρότερος ἐν τῇ βασιλείᾳ τοῦ θεοῦ μείζων αὐτοῦ ἐστιν. (Luke 7.28)

Luke's presentation of John's role in the economy of salvation seems to place the Baptist at the turn of the ages,[21] but his call to repentance had already evoked a positive response from 'the People' among whom publicans are specifically noted.[22]

[21] Conzelmann's periodisation of salvation history (1960, p. 26) remains problematic. On the whole, he appears to have been justified in his appeal to Luke 16.16 (note the frequency of Conzelmann's appeal to this verse, e.g., 1960, p. 250) but his understanding of μέχρι was probably mistaken, which then implies that John the Baptist should be *included with Jesus at the beginning of the new order*. This is substantially Fitzmyer's position (see 1989, p. 62f.; cf. 1981, pp. 181–7) and also takes account of Marshall's reservations concerning (among other things) Conzelmann's non-use of the birth narratives (1970, pp. 124, 130f. and esp. 145f.). See also Barrett (1961, pp. 40–6) for an early summary of and reflection on Conzelmann's work.

[22] Talbert (1988, pp. 84f.) suggests that at Luke 7.35 σοφία is a periphrasis for God and that δικαιόω is used in respect of God; he calls in support Pss. Sol. 2.16; 3.3; 4.9; 8.7, 27. He appeals also to Ps. 51.4 (50.6LXX) as a further example of this use – namely, the verb is used of God's people 'justifying' him, vindicating *his* sentence, judgments, name, accepting them and acknowledging them to be righteous. So, at

Luke presented publicans as a group who also responded to Jesus' message: two cameos particularly encapsulate this response. First, the story of Levi's abandonment of his trade to become Jesus' disciple is parallel to that in Mark (Huck p. 42, sect. 53) but different enough to ensure that no reader could miss the point that not only Jesus but his disciples also ate and drank with publicans and sinners – anticipating Luke 7.33–4. Second, Luke's story of Zacchaeus' repentance (Luke 19.1–10) crystallises his understanding of the relation of Jesus with this class of despised, rich penitents. Drury's account of the genesis of this Lukan encounter, showing how the LXX might be a rich source for such Lukan stories, is compelling (1976, pp. 72–5, although many cannot share his conviction that Luke was dependent on both Mark and Matthew).[23] Yet even were the story to owe more to Luke's creative and imaginative use of scripture than to events which may or may not have occurred at an ancient oasis during Jesus' ministry, it none the less presents a reader with a vivid portrayal of an important relationship in the gospel – that of Jesus and this despised group of toll-collectors.

Luke made clear to his reader that the publicans' generous response was to deliberate activity by Jesus which, in its own way, fulfilled scripture. **First,** in Levi's case two distinct *logia* sum up this activity: Οὐ χρείαν ἔχουσιν οἱ ὑγιαίνοντες ἰατροῦ ἀλλὰ οἱ κακῶς ἔχοντες (Luke 5.31) parallels Mark except for ὑγιαίνοντες which differs from Mark's ἰσχύοντες. This proverb offers a perspective on Jesus' purpose which is sharply focused by Luke's differences from Mark. Luke's ἐλήλυθα presumably indicates the continuity of past action into his present; Mark's aorist lacks this linear sense. Εἰς μετάνοιαν coheres with a Lukan emphasis: like John Baptist (Luke 3.3, 8), Jesus summoned people to repentance (Luke 5.32) and in his parables (cf. Luke 15.7) reinforced his purpose; indeed the calling in Jesus' name of all nations to penitence is part of scripture's presentation of God's plan of salvation as Luke understands it (Luke 24.47).

Second, in Zacchaeus' case there are two more *logia* which bind this cameo to Jesus' purposeful activity. The first, Σήμερον σωτηρία τῷ οἴκῳ τούτῳ ἐγένετο, καθότι καὶ αὐτὸς υἱὸς 'Αβραάμ ἐστιν (Luke 19.9b), hammers home the integrity of Zacchaeus' place in the People of God, Israel, thus matching the case of the ankylosed

Luke 7.35 people and tax collectors acknowledged the rightness of God's call in John and Jesus; lawyers and Pharisees did not.

[23] See Doble (1992, chapter 2B).

woman at Luke 13.10–17. The second *logion*, ἦλθεν γὰρ ὁ υἱὸς τοῦ ἀνθρώπου ζητῆσαι καὶ σῶσαι τὸ ἀπολωλός (Luke 19.10), is probably intended to provide a summarising saying not only for this story but also for Jesus' ministry to this point in the Gospel (See Doble, 1992, Detached Note 1). As in the Levi story, it functions here as a brief summary of the purpose of Jesus' activity; this time it is based on Ezekiel 34.16, once more demonstrating Luke's interest in the fulfilment of scripture.

The result of Luke's composition is that a reader (hearer?) can actually grasp what God's 'seeking the lost' meant to Luke; in the parable with which this study is basically concerned (Luke 18.14) one **sees** God's judgment on ὁ ὑψῶν and ὁ ταπεινῶν; it is important to note that the publican's self assessment echoes Luke's earlier teaching on discipleship (17.10) – when you have done all you ought, you remain unprofitable servants.

Thus, in the phrase 'publicans and sinners' Luke has a catch-phrase which pairs two quite distinct groups and makes possible his stylised introduction at Luke 15.1. It is interesting that the publican of Luke 18.9–14 and Zacchaeus (19.7) are characterised as ἁμαρτωλός. Throughout his presentation of οἱ τελῶναι Luke affirms that these people are of worth and the objects of God's care. This little parable at Luke 18.9–14 makes sense only in this overall context. He now has a contrasting pair,[24] a Pharisee and a publican, each representing a group of people related in one way or another to *Torah* and the People of God while together symbolising the tension and conflict that marked Jesus' ministry.

The parable's context in the Gospel

This parable stands within an enigmatic, loosely ordered collocation of material which has so far defied attempts by critical scholarship to discover within it an overarching, logical, editorial principle; even

[24] – in more than one sense. If Talbert (1988, p. 85) is right, then there is a formal parallel between this parable and the story of a penitent woman in Luke 7.36–50 so that this woman makes a pair with the publican in the Temple. Each 'incident' places a Pharisee on the wrong side of judgment and vindicates a man and a woman whose manner of life might be questioned. Luke's narrative at 7.36–50 may be seen as an explanatory expansion of the saying in Luke 7.35 – καὶ ἐδικαιώθη ἡ σοφία ἀπὸ πάντων τῶν τέκνων αὐτῆς. In this case δικαιόω, while functioning here in relation to God rather than a human, is, none the less, an immediately present concept: reversal and δικ-words are related in Luke's two accounts of a Pharisee in relation to a sinner.

its names are the subject of debate – Travel Narrative, Central Section, Perean Section.[25] Within that longer, looser sequence Luke has a more particular linkage among the three pericopae of which the parable of the publican and Pharisee is central. Each draws attention to a strange reversal of how people at large – and Pharisees in particular? – thought matters might stand in relation to the Kingdom. According to Luke's form of Jesus' teaching it is those with childlike qualities [26] who enter the Kingdom; it is the powerless and disadvantaged, as was a widow, but with *persistent piety* who are numbered among God's vindicated people; it is those whose unassuming, honest self-appraisal leads to genuine penitence who go home δεδικαιωμένος.[27] Luke's own church was learning of the qualities attaching to true discipleship, surprisingly different from those frequently prized by people. In fact, the final *logion* of the parable takes up an issue which runs throughout Luke's Gospel.

The parable's final logion

πᾶς ὁ ὑψῶν ἑαυτὸν ταπεινωθήσεται, ὁ δὲ ταπεινῶν ἑαυτὸν ὑψωθήσεται. (Luke 18.14)

25 See also Bailey (1976, pp. 79–85); his structural analysis offers a 'double ten inversion' pattern which does not attempt to include all the material in Luke 9.51–19.48. Bailey (1980, pp. 142–56) offers an exegesis of the parable under consideration; his insights are fascinating, but not always compelling. For example, his move to reading 'atonement' into the publican's prayer needs rather more support than he offers. As a hypothesis it might suffice, and, in itself, it offers richness to the scene. Yet his *use* of this hypothesis arrives at a christological conclusion very different from that reached in this study. Bailey writes: 'Jesus proclaims that righteousness is a gift of God made possible by the atonement sacrifice which is received by those who, in humility, approach as sinners trusting in God's grace and not in their own righteousness ...' (1980, p. 156) and he approvingly cites Jeremias' judgment: 'Our passage shows ... that the Pauline doctrine of justification has its roots in the teaching of Jesus' (Jeremias, 1972, p. 114).

26 but presumably only their *good* qualities.

27 It is better formally to separate this use of δικαιόω by Luke from its place in 'Pauline' thought. Bailey's conclusion to his consideration of this parable is not altogether convincing, but there is not space at this point to enter into dialogue with him. He claimed: 'This understanding (we would suggest) then becomes the foundation of the early Church's theology. In short, the starting point for the New Testament understanding of righteousness through atonement is traceable to no less than Jesus of Nazareth' (1980, p. 156). There are two problems here: first, this conclusion is not borne out by *Lukan* use; second, and an important principle, is it wise now to talk of '*the* New Testament understanding'? Whether the sinful publican went home δεδικαιωμένος because of the efficacy of the atonement sacrifice or whether it was his attitude to God and his fellows that numbered him among the δικαίοι needs further careful exploration.

Here is Luke's answer to those who trusted in themselves because (that?) they were δίκαιος. His reversal of judgment – it was the publican, not the Pharisee, who went home δεδικαιωμένος – is based on the clear principle cited above. It presents a word of Jesus basic to discipleship and is a Lukan theme.

Manson writes of this as a 'floating saying' which 'only serves to weaken the conclusion in v. 14a' (1949, p. 312). Moreover, Manson identified v. 14a as Jesus' comment on the story, assigning 14b to a Lukan role which obscured the story's meaning. But Luke's form of the story is all there is. Jeremias offers the same kind of comment as that made by Manson: 'V. 14b contains a generalising conclusion which affirms a favourite gospel theme, the eschatological reversal of existing conditions' (1972, p. 142). But this quite overlooks Luke's treatment of the matter:[28] it is a theme in his work because he sees it as a *disposition* to which disciples are summoned in the present, a *principle* which underlies the evangelist's depiction of Jesus' conflict with Pharisees and, almost certainly, a *defining characteristic* of who is, and who is not, δίκαιος. Moreover, this notion of reversal was deeply embedded in a scriptural passage on which it is likely that Luke had pondered long (see York, 1991, pp. 71–5 and 78–80).

This 'generalising statement' clearly belongs to the Dual Tradition, whatever that might imply. It appears at Matthew 23.12 in a context which has to do with true greatness: ὅστις δὲ ὑψώσει ἑαυτὸν ταπεινωθήσεται, καὶ ὅστις ταπεινώσει ἑαυτὸν ὑψωθήσεται. The *structure* of Matthew's sentence is that of Luke's at 18.14, Luke's πᾶς and participial forms only thinly cover a common saying. Further, Matthew has a related form of the saying which links closely with **both** a dispute about true greatness **and** with childlike qualities: ὅστις οὖν ταπεινώσει ἑαυτὸν ὡς τὸ παιδίον τοῦτο, οὗτός ἐστιν ὁ μείζων ἐν τῇ βασιλείᾳ τῶν οὐρανῶν (Matt. 18.4). The *logion* also appears elsewhere in Luke's Gospel, Luke 14.11, at the end of what initially appears to be appallingly devious advice about a strategy for one-upmanship when invited to dinner. The phrase reads:

> πᾶς ὁ ὑψῶν ἑαυτὸν ταπεινωθήσεται
> καὶ ὁ ταπεινῶν ἑαυτὸν ὑψωθήσεται.

[28] See also Bailey (1980, p. 155f.); Marshall (1978, pp. 680f.) *contra* Ellis (1974, p. 215); Talbert (1988, p. 170) *implies* that the concluding *logion* belongs to Luke's parable by affirming that 'the story fits into the general theme of status reversal in the Third Gospel . . . we meet this theme in the birth narratives (1:51–53) and in the Sermon on the Plain (6:20–26)'.

Apart from καὶ rather than δὲ in line 2 the two Lukan *logia* are identical. This instance sits in a conflict context, with Pharisees and scribes prominent, just as Matthew 23.12 sits in Matthew's terrible indictment of Pharisees; the Lukan saying emerges during a meal on a sabbath in a senior Pharisee's company.

To treat Luke 14.7–14 simply as advice on how to behave at meals suggests a policy of hypocritical rather than flagrant ambitiousness. Perhaps the advice offered to the host on his choice of guests throws light on what is really happening in vv. 7–12. What Jesus called for was a radical overthrow of conventional wisdom and practice; *this* Lukan table prefigures another and greater because God will honour (ἔσται σοι δόξα – a theological passive) the one who does not push for seats among the mighty. Jesus' hearers are invited to nurture a *disposition* deriving from their numbering themselves among the lowly.

Echoes of the Magnificat reverberate around the passage and an attentive reader, already conscious that Luke 1.47–55 is probably a Lukan *midrash* on 1 Samuel 2.1–10, recognises yet another firm link with scripture:[29]

καθεῖλεν δυνάστας ἀπὸ θρόνων
καὶ **ὕψωσεν ταπεινούς**, (Luke 1.52)

which itself echoes

Κύριος πτωχίζει καὶ πλουτίζει
ταπεινοῖ καὶ ἀνυψοῖ. (1 Sam 2.7)

Luke already had this saying in the Dual Tradition from which he drew; another form of it stood in a scriptural passage on which he had pondered for the creation of his infancy prologue. On those occasions when he deployed this deeply significant saying – significant *because scripture had told him that this was what God would do* – he placed it where there was conflict with Pharisees. It is possible that tradition told Luke that such was the case in Jesus' ministry. It is also just possible that the isolated saying at Luke 16.15b echoes the same principle in the same sort of context and is quickly followed by the story of Dives and Lazarus: τὸ ἐν ἀνθρώ-

[29] Fitzmyer (1985, p. 1047) suggests that the scriptural allusion is to Ezek. 21.31 – ἐταπείνωσας τὸ ὑψηλὸν καὶ τὸ ταπεινὸν ὕψωσας. In view of Luke's creative use elsewhere of Ezek. 34 (see Doble 1992, Detached Note 2) and of the antithetic structure of the saying in Ezekiel, Fitzmyer's attribution is interesting, although the *logion*'s relation with Luke's birth narrative must be taken seriously.

ποις ὑψηλὸν βδέλυγμα ἐνώπιον τοῦ θεοῦ. The saying is addressed to Pharisees: ὑμεῖς ἐστε οἱ δικαιοῦντες ἑαυτοὺς ἐνώπιον τῶν ἀνθρώπων. (Luke 16.15) This use of δικαιόω brings the discussion full circle.

Some conclusions

At Luke 18.14 the evangelist has spelt out the scriptural and dominical principle of judgment which allows the publican to return home δεδικαιωμένος.[30] *His* disposition, physically in the parable as well as spiritually, was of unassertive recognition of his real stance before God. The Pharisee's confidence in personal achievement was accompanied by his despising the other. Luke's Jesus is quite clear: it is the publican who in this judgment is pronounced δίκαιος, not the Pharisee.

Consequently it seems highly likely that for Luke one of the defining characteristics of δίκαιος is that disposition marked out by ταπεινῶν ἑαυτὸν.[31] It seems equally likely that Luke systematically

[30] *Contra* Bailey, see note 27 above. This is the sole appearance of this word in the Synoptists; Luke *knows* Paul's language, cf. Acts 13; see also Pelikan (1988, p. 144).

[31] It was not only Luke who did this: it is no accident that this writer represented Paul as one who valued ταπεινοφροσύνη as a prime Christian virtue (Acts 20.19). Although some commentators have dismissed this farewell speech as a Lukan composition, others carefully draw attention to its distinctive character and its evocation of a Paul-like letter (e.g. Stanton (1974, p. 111) and Marshall (1980, pp. 329f.); see also their references to other writers such as Cadbury, Bruce *et al.*).

It is instructive to note that the Paul of this Lukan speech characterised his Ephesian ministry as one marked by ταπεινοφροσύνη, an active disposition to be ταπεινός. It is significant that the Paul who wrote to the Philippians *also* set great store by this prime Christian virtue. He strongly appealed to his readers (as a church) to have a common disposition – φρονῆτε. ... φρονοῦντες (Phil. 2.2); φρονεῖτε (2.5) – a disposition of ταπεινοφροσύνη (2.3), a word characterised by its immediate associations (see also Eph. 4.2; Col. 2.18, 23 contrast with 3.12; 1 Pet. 5.5).

It seems equally clear that this 'mindedness' was exemplified by Christ Jesus and that the Philippian Christians were exhorted to look to him as their model. There is widespread, though not unanimous, agreement that Phil. 2.5–11 may be a pre-Pauline hymn; there is not widespread agreement about its exegesis (see, e.g., Dunn, 1989, pp. 114–21 and xviii–xix). In understanding the hymn's thrust a great deal depends on the reader's perspective: if this is a hymn of Christ's pre-existence, specific words will have one meaning, if Adamic, another. This is the case with ἐταπείνωσεν ἑαυτὸν (2.8), but what *is* clear is that Christ Jesus ἐταπείνωσεν ἑαυτὸν while God αὐτὸν ὑπερύψωσεν (2.9).

The point to note here is that while this contrasting pair (ταπεινόω / ὑψόω) may belong to a pre-Pauline hymnic tradition relating to Jesus, it certainly forms the ground for an ethical appeal for ταπεινοφροσύνη. Luke seems to have known of

excluded πᾶς ὁ ὑψῶν ἑαυτὸν from the category δίκαιος. It is, consequently, probable that Luke's use of both δίκαιος and δικαιόω in this parable confirms his understanding of these as religious rather than forensic words.[32] Neither word appears in the preceding parable of the unjust judge: that parable is set in a courtroom, this in the Temple. Luke knows which words belong to which form of discourse. It does not help matters to suggest that both toll-collector and Pharisee were appearing before the supreme judge. While it is true that thought about someone's standing before God has its judgmental dimension, it is no longer *overtly* forensic; in Luke, δίκαιος seems to be reserved for use in that domain where loyalty, genuine faithfulness to God, is at issue. At the opening of this parable, the word δίκαιος had plainly passed beyond signifying simply 'innocent'; it contained all the qualities noted in section A. According to Luke, the self-confident person, Pharisee or Christian, *enrolled himself or herself* with Simeon, Cornelius, Zechariah and Elizabeth – and with Jesus? At the end of his Gospel Luke was to imply – by his use of ὄντως at Luke 23.47 (see chapter 6) – that the role model for δίκαιος was Jesus.[33]

2. Luke 20.20. Honest spies?

Καὶ παρατηρήσαντες ἀπέστειλαν ἐγκαθέτους ὑποκρινομένους ἑαυτοὺς δικαίους εἶναι . . .

The immediate context is far too complex to take into account in its entirety. Both F.F. Bruce (1984) and H. St John Hart (1984), writing in *Jesus and the Politics of His Day*, edited by Bammel and Moule, have drawn attention to the wider and disputed issues in this pericope. For present purposes the issue is more limited: how should one understand δίκαιος in this verse?

Translators have vacillated between a religious sense and a moral.

this Pauline grasp of discipleship (Acts 20.19; see 2 Cor. 11.7; 12.21; Phil. 4.12). So one should not be surprised that for Luke this disposition towards being ταπεινός is characteristic of being δίκαιος. What he found in the Dual Tradition and in Paul (probably in Peter also) became for Luke a crucial virtue for those who followed Jesus (see also chapter 6 note 20). Cf. Vermes (1993, p. 80).

32 Presumably Luke 10.29 is an exception in being used in a secular sense: the *Torah* expert wanted to vindicate himself professionally. The issue is altogether different from that at Luke 18.9–14.

33 'It must be pointed out that a Jesus who makes an Adamic choice is more of a model for Christian behaviour (Phil. 2:1–13) than a pre-existent Christ . . .' (Dunn, 1989, p. xxxiv n. 23). But that is another story.

Caird (1963 p. 221) chose 'sincere', while REB, substantially following NEB, prefers 'honest'. (They all prefer 'innocent' at Luke 23.47.) Cassirer rendered δικαίους as 'seekers after uprightness' while C.B. Williams elected 'upright men'. Evans (1990) chose 'sincere' on the ground that δίκαιος might mean 'pious' or 'righteous' in the sense of being concerned with *Torah*; it might signify 'honest' in the sense of having a genuine question of conscience (1990, p. 704). Fitzmyer (1985) leaned towards 'upright' as an appropriate sense.

Luke's carefully worked introduction to this pericope suggests that he had in mind a picture of the entrapment of a good man, and that the hired agents (ἐγκαθέτους) *pretended* to be numbered among those concerned with the minutiae of *mitzvot*. In the battle between good and evil δίκαιοι stood for good and, as emerged in the parable of the Pharisee and the publican, it was possible to lay claim to the descriptor δίκαιος without, in fact, being the genuine thing (Luke's ὄντως at Luke 23.47 may be an affirmation of genuineness in Jesus' case). These spies (a paraphrase interpreting their having been paid to do this job) were to play the role of those genuinely interested in the propriety of images and coins on the Temple Mount. Ὑποκρίνομαι is *hap. leg.* in the New Testament; it figures in Job, in Sirach and in Maccabaean writing; the word refers to playing a role. The hired agents in this story played a role different from that of the Pharisee in Luke 18.9–14: he had convinced himself that he was numbered among the δίκαιοι, but had got it wrong; these agents were paid to *act*.

Παρατηρήσαντες (cf. Luke 6.7 and 14.1; Acts 9.24) is strongly Lukan in that of its six appearances in the New Testament, four instances of παρατηρέω occur in Luke–Acts. Its sense of keeping a close watch on someone certainly echoes the narrow observation of a δίκαιος implied in Wisdom 2.10, 12, 17, 19, 20. The word also appears at Psalm 36(37).12 –

> παρατηρήσεται ὁ ἁμαρτωλὸς τὸν δίκαιον
> καὶ βρύξει ἐπ' ἀυτὸν τοὺς ὀδόντας αὐτοῦ.

Luke stepped up a sense of entrapment by his use of παραδοῦναι at this point;[34] this might be implied by Mark 12.13 and emerges as a metaphor in Matthew 22.15. But Luke's narrative made quite clear that the action in Luke 20.20 was to hand over Jesus to the rule and authority of the governor. The way Luke wrote the introduction to

34 See chapter 7F, 'Entrapment', for fuller treatment of this Lukan theme.

this pericope both strongly *recalls* the plotting described in Wisdom 2.10–20 and quite *changes* the character of the interchange; it also shapes a reader's approach to Luke's narrative of Jesus' death. The perpetrators of this betrayal were apparently the scribes and principal priests referred to in Luke 20.19. Cassirer is mistaken in his importing of 'Pharisees' into 20.19; Luke, for his own reasons, systematically excluded Pharisees from the immediate encompassing of Jesus' death and they make no appearance in his narrative after Luke 18.39.

Because of Luke's treatment of this narrative, it seems wisest to think of δίκαιος at this point as a word which enshrines the virtues encountered so far in his 'saints' gallery' and to acknowledge that some of Luke's contemporaries interpreted the word in a restricted sense, as did the Pharisee, for example, in Luke 18.11–12. The paid agents of Luke 20.20 are presented as pretending to be among those whose loyalty to God issued in a meticulous observing of the *mitzvot*. What is important here is to listen to Luke's echoes of the entrapment plotted by the ἀσεβεῖς of Wisdom 2.10–20. This *may* be confirmation of his shaping Jesus' story around a matrix drawn from Wisdom (see chapter 7).

D. Summary of preliminary conclusions

Before surveying Luke's use of δίκαιος as a christological descriptor, it will be useful to summarise his usage in relation to people other than Jesus. Associated with Luke's concept of δίκαιος is a pool of meaning made up of:

- leading a life of blameless devotion to God and delighting in *Torah*;
- ταπεινῶν ἑαυτὸν;
- longing for God's Kingdom – his saving acts promised in the scriptures – to be realised;
- committing oneself to God, even to death, in the face of alien oppression or of intra-communal contempt or persecution;
- trusting that in the end God will vindicate his faithful people even beyond death and in the face of their persecutors;
- recognising that the word might be misappropriated by religious zealots who despise those not willing to share their particular enthusiasm for and reading of *Torah*.

Consequently, to this point, Luke's use of δίκαιος seems consistently to reflect a Septuagintal notion of one whose life responds fully to God as Δίκαιος himself; for Luke it is a religious rather than a forensic concept, drawing heavily on scriptures, particularly the Psalms, 1 Samuel, Daniel and Wisdom. There remain, however, four instances of Luke's using δίκαιος of Jesus.

5

ΔΊΚΑΙΟΣ AS A CHRISTOLOGICAL DESCRIPTOR:[1] ACTS

In the previous chapter, most of Luke's uses of δίκαιος were examined, but there remain four occasions when he used this word to refer *specifically* to Jesus. Of these one, Luke 23.47, is that verse whose 'meaning' is the focus of this whole enquiry, consequently it will not be analysed in this section. The others are found in Acts 3.14; 7.52 and 22.14. Their distribution is of interest in that they belong to what Conzelmann wrote of as the period of the Church. Luke assigns these uses of δίκαιος to Peter, Stephen and Paul, and always in a Jewish context.

These occurrences of δίκαιος have been thoroughly explored by commentators, but the present approach – seeking a pool of meaning on which the evangelist drew – allows further comment, largely because it differs from what has frequently been the case: there seems to be wide agreement that δίκαιος is explained best as a title or quality of the messiah, a term drawn from Deutero-Isaiah's *'ebed Yahweh* and (or) from 1 Enoch. This study's approach differs from the apparent consensus in that it proceeds on the principle that there are no synonyms:

> The first principle of semantic analysis of lexical items is that there are 'no synonyms,' in the sense that no lexical items ever have completely the same meanings in all of the contexts in which they might occur. Even if two lexical items seem not to be distinguishable in their designative or denotative meanings, they do differ in terms of their connotative or associative meanings. This principle of 'no synonyms' may also be stated in terms of the fact that no

[1] A neutral word, recognising that δίκαιος is hardly a *title* at Luke 23.47, where it may be anarthrous or may be used as a complement. This study uses 'term' to cover Lukan usage, but *at this stage* one knows only that Luke used δίκαιος to *describe* Jesus and his significance for the reader.

> two closely related meanings ever occur with exactly the same range of referents, much less the same set of connotative or associative features. (Louw and Nida, p. xv)

This seems to imply that instead of simply asserting that δίκαιος is a way of talking about the 'messiah' a commentator needs to attend to the context where it is used and to seek the word's associations.

Δίκαιος, messiah and Παῖς Θεοῦ

The principle of 'no synonyms' invites one to fish with a finer mesh and in the case of δίκαιος to examine the catch to determine with a reasonable degree of probability what Luke may have had in mind. Preliminary analysis of the relevant material suggests that Luke had in mind a precise christological model not normally identified by commentators who assign δίκαιος to a qualifier of messiah or Παῖς Θεοῦ. Cullmann, for example, has conjoined δίκαιος with παῖς, offering as Luke's 'pool of meaning' ideas, words and patterns drawn from Deutero-Isaiah's Servant Songs. Others have written of δίκαιος as a messianic 'title' (Bruce, 1952, on Acts 3.14) or 'epithet' (Haenchen, 1971), thus drawing on yet another range of scriptural patterns and thoughts. Both Conzelmann and Haenchen have found δίκαιος to be coloured by notions of 'guiltlessness' or 'innocence'. These positions fail to do justice to Luke's rather more subtle use of δίκαιος, but a further brief comment on each will make this claim clearer.

In *The Christology of the New Testament* (1963), Cullmann placed great emphasis on two titles of Jesus. From the moment of his baptism, Jesus himself was conscious of carrying out God's plan. 'He knew first that he must accomplish the forgiveness of sins through his death in fulfilment of the prophecy about the "Suffering Servant of God"; and he anticipated this goal already during his life by preaching and healing the sick' (1963, p. 318). Second, he knew himself to be the 'Son of man' whose task was to introduce the Kingdom of God. Discussing the first of these titles, Cullmann drew attention to the early Church's use of a 'Paidology' to explain Jesus' person and work. 'We may even assert that this is probably the oldest known solution to the Christological problem' (1963, p. 73). Cullmann's argument from here depends on the LXX use of Παῖς Θεοῦ to render *'ebed Yahweh*. He affirmed that 'Jesus is called *Pais* exactly as he later is commonly called "Christ".' In his first footnote to p. 73 Cullmann added: 'Those passages in Acts which, following Isa. 53.11, designate Jesus δίκαιος also come into consideration here: Acts 3.14; 22.14 and especially 7.52.'[2]

There are, however, considerations which question the wisdom of Cullmann's relegation of δίκαιος to a footnote, particularly one which subordinates it to another category, thereby importing a pool of meaning into δίκαιος without examining it. **First,** while παῖς is certainly the word used in the Greek OT to render *'ebed Yahweh*, it also appears in other contexts used in ways which might have given rise to its christological use in the early church. See, for example, Psalms 69.17 (LXX 68.18) and 86.16 (LXX 85). **Second**, in precisely the same way that Cullmann takes δίκαιος as a *qualifier* of παῖς so Wisdom employs δίκαιος as its *substantive* category, using παῖς as a qualifier or related term. Wisdom's author presents his opponents as saying of the δίκαιος: ἐπαγγέλλεται γνῶσιν ἔχειν Θεοῦ καὶ παῖδα Κυρίου ἑαυτὸν ὀνομάζει. (Wis. 2.13) Cullmann, like Franklin (1975), appears to have overemphasised the *Servant* category in Luke's thought; one might reasonably invite him to reread the passage with δίκαιος as its central category,[3] but, like many commentators, and for unclear reasons, he ignores material which should be taken into account. **Third,** and related to the previous point, in Deutero-Isaiah δίκαιος is used only once adjectivally of παῖς Θεοῦ (Isa. 53.11), while there is a far more frequent comparable use of the term in scriptural reservoirs from which Luke probably drew. Rarely has so large a result stood on so singular a base. **Fourth,** παῖς in Wisdom operates much like *'ebed Yahweh* in Deutero-Isaiah in that each can carry a corporate sense; **but** Wisdom 18.7–9 also closely relates παῖς Θεοῦ, ὅσιος, δίκαιος and δοξάζειν. Here is, consequently, a model in which most of what Cullmann calls a paidology is already subsumed, but which also contributes to an understanding of τὸν ἅγιον at Acts 3.13–14:

> προσεδέχθη ὑπὸ λαοῦ σου
> σωτηρία μὲν **δικαίων**, ἐχθρῶν δὲ ἀπώλεια·
> ᾧ γὰρ ἐτιμωρήσω τοὺς ὑπεναντίους,
> τούτῳ ἡμᾶς προσκαλεσάμενος **ἐδόξασας**.
> Κρυφῇ γὰρ ἐθυσίαζον **ὅσιοι παῖδες** ἀγαθῶν
> καὶ τὸν τῆς θειότητος νόμον ἐν ὁμονοίᾳ διέθεντο,

[2] It is *because* these are the passages to be discussed in the body of this chapter that a preliminary discussion of Cullmann's Paidology is appropriate here.

[3] See part III.

τῶν αὐτῶν ὁμοίως καὶ ἀγαθῶν
καὶ κινδύνων μεταλήμψεσθαι **τοὺς ἁγίους**,
πατέρων ἤδη προαναμέλποντες αἴνους. (Wis. 18.7–9)

Consequently, on these four grounds, a firm question mark needs to be set against Cullmann's attempt to incorporate Luke's δίκαιος into a paidology derived solely from the '*ebed Yahweh* category.

But another question forms itself: if Luke had intended Stephen's speech to culminate in such a paidology *why did he write* δίκαιος *rather than* παῖς? Had this happened once, it might be easier to understand, but both Peter and Paul are also reported to have said δίκαιος when they apparently meant to say παῖς. Assuming that Luke used δίκαιος at Acts 3.14; 7.52 and 22.14 *because he wanted to convey to his readers something other than what was associated with* Παῖς then one may examine each occurrence afresh to determine whether the 'no synonym' principle has illuminated the passages under scrutiny.

Three other influential writers, Bruce, Haenchen and Taylor, muddied Luke's pool of meaning by urging that δίκαιος is a function of 'messiah', a word which is frequently expanded to a point of near meaninglessness. It becomes a basket into which so much of the vocabulary of God's action is loaded that 'messiah' both covers too many separable significations and obscures the vitality and flexibility in much early discussion of Jesus' place in God's economy of salvation.

Bruce (1952), referring to Acts 3.14 (his principal note on the term), says simply that both δίκαιος and ἅγιος are messianic titles. He indicates those places in Luke–Acts where the two words are applied to Jesus. He finds the roots of messiah's righteousness in 2 Samuel 23.3; Isaiah 32.1 and 53.11; Zechariah 9.1 and notes that the Son of man is linked with righteousness in 1 Enoch 38.2 and 46.3. (By this move 'Son of man' has gone into the 'messiah' basket.) Mowinckel (1959, pp. 366 and 377ff.) also rooted the concept δίκαιος in the Son of man in 1 Enoch. Turning to Acts 7.52, Bruce notes that ἔλευσις is 'a messianic term', calling to his aid an article by Kilpatrick (1945). This may well be the case, but certainly not the *whole* case. First, it is not the whole case because Bruce did not explore thoroughly Luke's *specific* use of δίκαιος and consequently worked with a restricted range of evidence. Second, it is not yet certain that 1 Enoch may legitimately be summoned to give support to this equation of messiah, Son of man and δίκαιος: when did that work appear?[4] Third, even were 1 Enoch sufficiently early, there is no evidence that Luke used the work or, having used it, embraced its denotation of δίκαιος.

Haenchen (1971), commenting on Acts 3.14, speaks of ἅγιος and δίκαιος as 'messianic epithets', citing 1 Enoch and emphasising Luke 4.34. In relation to Acts 22.14 he calls Schrenk in support of his contention that δίκαιος is 'an attestation of the executed guiltless' (Th.Wb.II.188 cf. *TDNT* II.187f., 'the attestation of this innocent Victim in the resurrection.'). To describe δίκαιος simply as a messianic epithet does not help a reader grasp what Luke might have been about in his passion narrative. Because there are real differences among these terms, it is proper to make distinctions among them.

Taylor (1952, chapter 14) placed 'The Righteous One' in the 'second division' of messianic titles: he denied its titular use in the gospels but affirmed its messianic use in Acts (p. 82), citing Cadbury, (1933, p. 364) in support. He continued: 'These passages recall 1 Enoch xxxviii.2, "And when the Righteous One shall appear before the eyes of the righteous, ... where then will be the dwelling of sinners?"' (1952, p. 82) Taylor briefly noted that the term might have derived from Isaiah 53.11, but he also noted that Cadbury (1933), dissented from this view.

There are, then, good reasons for reassessing attitudes towards δίκαιος as they are focused in comments by Cullmann, Bruce, Haenchen and Taylor on these three passages in Acts.[5]

The order of the following sections is not Luke's. The Stephen-unit (Acts 6.8–8.2) is taken first because, while it proved the most complex passage, it was also the richest source of hints of possible pools of meaning. Paul's *apologia* (22.14) follows because it soon became clear that results from the Stephen-unit would have to serve as a hypothesis for the meaning of δίκαιος here; it fits as no alternative hypothesis does. Acts 3.14 sits in a context densely packed with christological terms and with few clues to Luke's source of reference. Some of the problems facing an interpreter of Peter's speech have already been noted, but, again, the model, inferred

[4] This question receives many answers: early second century AD (Hindley J.C., *NTS* 14 (1968), pp. 551–65); about 40AD (Mearns C.L., *NTS* 25 (1979), pp. 360–9); end of first century AD (Knibb M.A., *NTS* 25 (1979), pp. 345–59); more likely to fall outside 'our period' than in it (Bock, 1987, p. 326, n. 113).

[5] These 'good reasons' include those offered above in preliminary comments on Cullmann's Paidology.

from Acts 7.52 and confirmed by 22.14, fits more comfortably than any other.

A. Acts 7.52. The Stephen-unit (Acts 6.8–8.2)

τίνα τῶν προφητῶν οὐκ ἐδίωξαν οἱ πατέρες ὑμῶν;
καὶ ἀπέκτειναν τοὺς προκαταγγείλαντας
περὶ τῆς ἐλεύσεως τοῦ δικαίου
οὗ νῦν ὑμεῖς προδόται καὶ φονεῖς ἐγένεσθε . . .

This is an extended, tightly written unit, comprising introduction, speech, peroration and martyrdom. The speech and peroration are substantially concerned with fulfilment, a fact most obviously the case in Stephen's bearing public witness to the Son of man's vindication. The unit is christological in character and purpose (see Doble, 1985). The literature on this unit is vast, but comparatively little has been written on the issue which is this study's central concern.

Within the Stephen-unit one finds possibilities for a Lukan pool of meaning for δίκαιος. **First**, the target verse, Acts 7.52, falls within Stephen's countercharge: it was the Sanhedrin and its witnesses who were guilty, not he. The **nature** of this countercharge and its **link** with the long, preceding speech offer two fruitful areas for exploration (see below 'Scriptural roots of the Stephen-unit'; cf. Esler, 1987, pp. 122–5, 135–45). **Second**, because Luke made Stephen's peroration (Acts 7.51–3) the immediate cause of his martyrdom, and because this smaller context contains δίκαιος as a christological descriptor, exploration will initially focus on this smaller unit. But, clearly, this peroration crystallises the preceding speech in which there is a remarkably high density of scriptural quotations and an even higher density of scriptural allusions or echoes – a far more typical Lukan technique.[6] Although this exploration is characterised more by questions and balancing probabilities than by clear proof, there are reasonably strong hints of thought patterns underlying the Stephen-unit. One of these thought patterns focuses on the humiliation and vindication of a δίκαιος whose sufferings through conflict with the ungodly and whose ultimate

[6] In chapter 7B, 'Criteria for allusion', there is further exploration of what is understood here by 'echoes' or 'allusions'. The work of Hays, R.B. (1989) and of Marcus, J. (1993) has proved immensely important for the development of this argument.

Table 5.1. *Scriptural roots of the Stephen-unit*

Acts 7	Nehemiah 9
51 stiffnecked (σχληροτράχηλοι)	16, 17, 29 stiffnecked and arrogant (ἐσχλήρυναν τὸν τραχηλὸν αὐτῶν)
uncircumcised ears	17, 29 they refused to listen
just like your fathers	16 they, our forefathers
resist the Holy Spirit	20a you gave your good spirit to instruct them
	30 by your spirit you admonished them through your prophets
52 was there a prophet your fathers did not persecute?	26 they killed your prophets
53 you who have received the *Torah* but have no obeyed it	13 you gave them commands, decrees and laws through your servant Moses
	16, 26, 29, 34 they did not obey

vindication by God are explored in both the Psalms and Wisdom. Luke probably derived the matrix for his underlying model from Wisdom rather than from any other source;[7] that intertestamental book's concept of δίκαιος sheds light on Luke's use of the term in this passage.

Scriptural roots of the Stephen-unit

In Stephen's counter-charge, Luke's view of Israel's history echoes one strand in Israel's own scripture. A number of brief summaries evaluating Israel's religious performance occur in a variety of settings. Analysis of these passages reveals a similarity between the thrust and content of Nehemiah 9 and that of Stephen's counter-charge (table 5.1).[8] Nehemiah's relentless insistence on Israel's chronic disobedience of God is set in a context of a renewed and re-discovered *Sukkoth* among newly returned former exiles, committed

[7] The scattered arguments for this conclusion are gathered in chapter 7 below, although the remainder of chapter 5A contributes to this result.

[8] This chapter was completed before I encountered Karris (1985). His exploration of the notion of 'rejected prophet' (1985, pp. 18–20) includes an italicised extract from Neh. 9.26–31 which, while different from this comparative analysis of it and of Stephen's countercharge, offers significant, independent corroboration of the argument.

to reestablishing Jerusalem's theocracy in obedience to *Torah*. If one abstracts the 'negative' elements from Nehemiah's prophetic survey, placing them beside Stephen's counter-charge, the similarity is clear. Luke's few verses are a thoroughly prophetic, *authentically Jewish* appreciation of God's dealings with Israel. They are not, as will be seen in the next section, the *only* perspective from which the national history might be viewed, but they are certainly not evidence for Luke's alleged anti-Semitic disposition.[9] Luke's Stephen is here presented as a Christian prophet who owed much to something very like Nehemiah's recital; structure, words and thrust cohere throughout but are now written in the light of the cross and resurrection.

Further, Luke's question τίνα τῶν προφητῶν οὐκ ἐδίωξαν οἱ πατέρες ὑμῶν; (Acts 7.52) summarises a persistent Lukan theme:[10] κατὰ τὰ αὐτὰ γὰρ ἐποίουν τοῖς προφήταις οἱ πατέρες αὐτῶν (Luke 6.23b); διὰ τοῦτο καὶ ἡ σοφία τοῦ θεοῦ εἶπεν, 'Αποστελῶ εἰς αὐτοὺς προφήτας καὶ ἀποστόλους, καὶ ἐξ αὐτῶν ἀποκτενοῦσιν καὶ διώξουσιν (Luke 11.49); ὅτι οὐκ ἐνδέχεται προφήτην ἀπολέσθαι ἔξω 'Ιερουσαλήμ. 'Ιερουσαλὴμ 'Ιερουσαλήμ, ἡ ἀποκτείνουσα τοὺς προφήτας καὶ λιθοβολοῦσα τοὺς ἀπεσταλμένους πρὸς αὐτήν ... (Luke 13.33b–34).

This theme, pursued into Jesus' death and Stephen's martyrdom, should not be attributed to Luke's alleged anti-Semitism,[11] rather it takes up an established theme in Jewish scripture, namely, continuing conflict between God's prophets on one hand and, on the other, political or religious authority or a complacent nation. The following is a representative rather than exhaustive list illustrating that theme: Amos 7.10–17; Jeremiah 26.20–4; 38.4–6; 1 Kings 18.4, 13; 19.10, 14; 2 Kings 21.10–16 (cf. 24.4); 2 Chronicles 24.17–22; Nehemiah 9.26. Conzelmann noted that this kind of thinking was also alive in Judaism, citing Josephus *Ant.* 9.265–6 and 10.3–4 (1987, p. 57). *Pace* Haenchen (1971, p. 290) Stephen's summary is more prophetic than anti-Semitic; he knows that those who speak for God have always been vigorously opposed in Israel, a position shared by some surveys of Israel's history.

9 *Contra* Sanders (1987); cf. Dunn (1991, pp. 149–51).

10 This is a Lukan theme in two senses: first, by including Luke 13.33b, the evangelist made this theme his own; second, although all the other references are drawn substantially from the Dual Tradition they constitute an important element in his work.

11 E.g. Sanders (1987, pp. 190, 309f. cf. p. 25).

Scriptural surveys of Israel's history

Not all historical surveys in scripture are prophetic in character. For example, Sirach 44–50, Psalms 105, 135 and 136 are examples of a more positive appreciation of Israel's spiritual biography. None of them ignores the perils and folly of idolatry and Sirach adopts a thoroughly Deuteronomic evaluation of Israel's 'royal' history (Sir. 49.4–7) – all, save three, of Israel's rulers were defective because they abandoned or sat light to God's *Torah*. Although there is nothing in these surveys of the bitter reflection on Israel's history found in some books, it is clear that prophets were not altogether safe in the land:

> . . . ἐκάκωσαν γὰρ αὐτόν,*
> καὶ αὐτὸς ἐν μήτρᾳ ἡγιάσθη προφήτης,
> ἐκριζοῦν καὶ κακοῦν καὶ ἀπολλύειν,
> ὡσαύτως οἰκοδομεῖν καὶ καταφυτεύειν.
> (Sir. 49.7; * referring to Jeremiah)

In two psalms, however, one finds a thoroughly 'prophetic' view of Israel's biography.

Psalm 77(78) focusing primarily on the Exodus experience, especially the Wilderness period, also reflects on the Settlement; David is celebrated as God's servant. This 'history' is one in which 'the fathers' or 'forefathers' are systematically presented as people disloyal to God:

> ἵνα μὴ γένωνται ὡς οἱ πατέρες αὐτῶν,
> γενεὰ σκολιὰ καὶ παραπικραίνουσα,
> γενεά, ἥτις οὐ κατηύθυνεν τὴν καρδίαν αὐτῆς
> καὶ οὐκ ἐπιστώθη μετὰ τοῦ Θεοῦ τὸ πνεῦμα αὐτῆς.
> (v. 8, cf. 17–20, 32, 36–37, 41, 56–58)

> καὶ ἀπέστρεψαν καὶ ἠσυνθέτησαν καθὼς καὶ οἱ πατέρες αὐτῶν καὶ μετεστράφησαν εἰς τόξον στρεβλόν . . . (v. 57)

The principle of 'as the fathers, so the children' runs through this survey of Israel's *Heilsgeschichte*.

Psalm 105(106) also recognises Israel's solidarity with the fathers' sins:

> ἡμάρτομεν μετὰ τῶν πατέρων ἡμῶν
> ἠνομήσαμεν, ἠδικήσαμεν·
> οἱ πατέρες ἡμῶν ἐν Αἰγύπτῳ οὐ συνῆκαν τὰ θαυμάσιά σου . . . (vv. 6–7)

A specific instance of their lawlessness is highlighted in the incident of the Horeb calf:

> καὶ ἠλλάξαντο τὴν δόξαν αὐτῶν
> ἐν ὁμοιώματι μόσχου ἔσθοντος χόρτον (v. 20)

a further example is drawn from 'Meribah'

> ὅτι παρεπίκραναν τὸ πνεῦμα αὐτοῦ
> καὶ διέστειλεν ἐν τοῖς χείλεσιν αὐτοῦ (v. 33)

where τὸ πνεῦμα probably refers to God's spirit; but central here is the psalm's concern with Israel's tendency to idolatry (vss 28–9, 35–39), a continuation of their apostasy at Horeb (cf. Acts 7.39–43).

Wisdom of Solomon 10–19

The 'historical' section of this book stands within a pseudonymous work dating probably from the first century BC (but see Winston, 1979). Attributed to Solomon (see Horbury, 1994), its main thrust is the establishing and demonstrating that God acts in history by the agency of Σοφία. Wisdom 2–5, examined more fully below, considers the 'unwise' and their relation to the δίκαιος. Chapters 6–9 are an imaginative and occasionally poetic reflection on the notion and getting of Σοφία. Chapters 12–15 are a studied, mocking repudiation of idolatry, while in chapters 10, 11 and 18 the writer surveys Israel's history, especially the Exodus, to demonstrate *Wisdom*'s administration of God's care for Israel through a succession of δίκαιοι.

The 'historical' section of this work is a roll call of Israel's major characters of whom all, save three, are simply called δίκαιος, their identity being established by qualities or events associated with them: Noah (Wis. 10.4b), Abraham (10.5b – τὸν δίκαιον, ἄμεμπτον), Lot (10.6), Jacob (10.10), Joseph (10.13) and even the Israel that came out of Egypt is δίκαιος (10.20; cf. 15, 17 – λαὸν ὅσιον καὶ σπέρμα ἄμεμπτον). In this section at least, δίκαιος refers both to individual people and the corporate People.

There is a trio not called δίκαιος: Adam, for obvious reasons, although the writer is certain that *Wisdom* helped him survive his fall (Wis. 10.1); Cain is not called δίκαιος, again for obvious reasons, and his fate is obscurely noted for a modern reader (10.3 cf. Gen. 4.8–13). While Moses is not called δίκαιος, the writer notes that *Wisdom* entered his soul (10.16) and that his hands did her work (11.1) thereby obliquely affirming his status as δίκαιος, even though he is spoken of as the Lord's servant (θεράποντος Κυρίου, 10:16) and holy prophet (προφήτης ἅγιος, 11.1).

While the work's historical survey lacks the 'prophetic bite' of the Psalms or Nehemiah, it does have an implied critical view. It opens with a survey of the unwise and of their calculating, cynical oppression of the δίκαιος; the unwise are also idolaters, and the space Wisdom's author devotes to the folly of idolatry strongly suggests its threat to Israel (see Wis. 14.27) – even Israel's therapeutic serpent needed to be sanitised for his readers (16.6–7).

In some psalms, in Nehemiah and in Wisdom there is precedent for 'Stephen's' survey. Whether there is evidence for one source rather than another's being at the heart of the Stephen-unit must await exploration of the presence of δίκαιος as a descriptor.

Δίκαιος in the Psalms and in Wisdom[12]

Earlier, we provisionally set aside Deutero-Isaiah's Παῖς Θεοῦ as a source for Stephen's use of δίκαιος, preferring to ask first whether other sources offered pools of meaning on which Luke drew. There appear to be two *major* sources in which δίκαιος figures in its own right as a descriptor of a humiliated, suffering, longing-to-be-vindicated man of God – the Psalms and the Wisdom of Solomon.[13]

Δίκαιος in the Psalms

In the Psalms δίκαιος normally appears in a conflict setting, usually with 'sinners', 'the ungodly' *et al.* The δίκαιος and his enemies are contrasted (e.g. Pss. 1.4–6; 33.15–16, 20–1; 74.11), enemies by whom he is oppressed (e.g. Pss. 30.19; 36.12, 32–3; 63.3 – where there is a *conspiracy* of the wicked; 93.21). Israel of the Psalms is a *corpus mixtum* in which the δίκαιοι understand themselves to be an isolated, oppressed, identifiable group. The psalmists are sure that God watches over, cares for, loves, blesses the δίκαιος (e.g. Pss. 7.10; 31.10; 32.20–2; 33.16–20; 36.28) and that he will ensure the just one's ultimate vindication (e.g. Pss. 1.4–6; 33.20; 36.17; 54.23; 57.12; 117.15–16, 20–21; 124.3 cf. 36.25, 29, 39; 67.4; 68.29). God is himself δίκαιος (e.g. Pss. 114.5; 118.137–8; 128.4; 144.17–20) and his

12 See also Donahue (1976); Ruppert (1972) and Nickelsburg (1972 and 1980).

13 Job is also a potential candidate, but because his testing is not by human agents examination of the book has been excluded from this work. (See chapter 4, note 7.)

δίκαιοι trust him (e.g. Ps. 111.6–9). Consequently, the δίκαιοι are generous (e.g. Pss. 36.21; 111.5–6) and find themselves 'illuminated' (e.g. Pss. 96.11; 111.4).

Δίκαιος frequently appears towards the end of a psalm, summarising much of what preceded it, particularly in psalms which speak in the first person singular (e.g. Pss. 5.13; 31.11; 141.8 cf. 63.11; 74.11; 91.12–15; 96.11–12; 139.14). Δίκαιος is *associated with* many other words such as 'saints' (e.g. Ps. 30.24), 'the upright' (Pss. 31.11; 96.11; 111.2–3), 'the godly' (e.g. Ps. 31.6), 'those who fear God' (e.g. Pss. 33.8; 111.1) and those who take refuge in him (e.g. Ps. 30.20). While this group of words probably represents one varied referent group, it is preferable to sustain the principle that *there are no synonyms*. A clear image emerges of the δίκαιος whose rule of life is *Torah (*e.g. Pss. 118.137–8; 36.30–1) and utter commitment to God, facing enemies who are quite other than he.

Δίκαιος is also defined by *what it negates*. His opponents are arrogant and boastful (Pss. 5.5; 30.19; 51.3–4; 72.3–9); their tongues are a special source of evil (Pss. 5.7; 30.19; 57.3–4; cf. 139.10–12); they are deceitful (Ps. 5.10), wicked (Ps. 1.5–6) and plot their mischief together (Pss. 5.10; 36.14; 63.6–7); they are rebellious (Ps. 5.11), violent (Pss. 7.17; 139.12), pregnant with evil (Ps. 7.14–17) and unjust (Pss. 57.2–6). They are proud (Ps. 30.19), sure that there is no God (e.g. Ps. 13.1–6) and careless of the poor. Because Luke's work frequently quotes from or alludes to psalms (see N-A 26 Appendix III), it is reasonable to suppose that he knew the psalmists' vividly drawn picture of a persecuted δίκαιος, and chapter 6 below suggests reasons for Luke's substitution of Psalm 30 for Mark's Psalm 21 at Luke 23.46. Of the sixty-seven psalms of which Luke shows some knowledge, thirteen contribute to the psalmists' model(s) of the δίκαιος.[14] A reader may be reasonably

[14] This measure is a comparatively crude one, noting in the *Index loci citati vel allegati* of N-A 26 each psalm which has at least one entry against Luke or Acts, then identifying those of that cohort which clearly make reference to a δίκαιος: Pss. (LXX) 1(.5, 6); 7(.10); 10(.5); 30(.19); 32(.1); 33(.16, 18, 20, 22); 36(.12, 16, 17, 21, 25, 29, 30, 32, 39); 67(.4); 68(.29); 96(.11, 12); 111(.6); 117(.15, 20); 145(.8, 9). Luke has shown knowledge of *these* psalms and they belong to that class which uses δίκαιος to speak of God's People.

Certain features of this group need further investigation. For example, are the ungodly of Ps. 1.5 not to 'rise' at the judgment or not to 'stand'? But they are strongly contrasted with δίκαιοι, so one properly infers that at the judgment δικαίοι 'rise' or 'stand' – see the following discussion of ἑστῶτα. Similarly, the close connection of Pss. 36.12 and 111.10 with Acts 7.54 gives one pause; in each case 'teeth gnashing' is an ungodly gesture against a δίκαιος, and the *formal*

confident that Luke was aware of a pool of meaning for δίκαιος, far more extensive than that for the Παῖς Θεοῦ and certainly within an element of scripture which Luke specifically named – the Psalms – as contributing to his theology (Luke 24.44–8).

Δίκαιος in Wisdom

In Wisdom chapters 2–5 the model of a δίκαιος which appears in the psalms in a scattered, informal fashion has been systematised. The sources for Wisdom's model are not important here: there are literary allusions to Isaiah (so, e.g., Jeremias, *TDNT* V.684; cf. Marcus, 1993, pp. 190ff.) and to the Psalms; the book has possibly been affected by Daniel and its perception of the 'saints of the Most High' and of the related, symbolic figure of the Son of man. As an early reader listened to these four chapters (s)he was probably conscious of a very wide range of 'scriptural harmonics' (see Young, 1990).

The emphasis of these four chapters is on the ungodly: their rejection of Σοφία resulted in a mind-set not unlike that of the cynical,[15] pessimistic materialism of Ecclesiastes, a view utterly repudiated by Wisdom's writer: Σοφίαν γὰρ καὶ παιδείαν ὁ ἐξουθενῶν ταλαίπωρος, καὶ κενὴ ἡ ἐλπὶς αὐτῶν καὶ οἱ κόποι ἀνόνητοι, καὶ ἄχρηστα τὰ ἔργα αὐτῶν (Wis. 3.11). Because of their indifference to and rejection of Σοφία the life of the ungodly is ultimately fruitless:

> ἐάν τε γὰρ μακρόβιοι γένωνται, εἰς οὐθεν
> λογισθήσονται,
> καὶ ἄτιμον ἐπ'ἐσχάτων τὸ γῆρας αὐτῶν·
> ἐάν τε ὀξέως τελευτήσωσιν,
> οὐχ ἕξουσιν ἐλπίδα οὐδὲ ἐν ἡμέρᾳ διαγνώσεως
> παραμύθιον·
> γενεᾶς γὰρ ἀδίκου χαλεπὰ τὰ τέλη. (Wis. 3.17–19)

relation of this passage with Acts 7.52 is not to be overlooked. Again, Ps. 68 appears in the passion narrative (v. 22 cf. Luke 23.36) but also in relation to Judas' fate (Acts 1.20 cf. Ps. 68.26); this psalm contrasts the ungodly (who will *not* be written into the book of the living with the δίκαιοι, v. 29) and the righteous. Ps. 36 (whose vs 12 *may* be echoed at Acts 7.54) offers a very wide range of convictions about the nature of a δίκαιος, some of which appear to relate strongly to the Lukan portrayal of Jesus (see, e.g., v. 25 in relation to Jesus' word from the cross; cf. 6B, esp. ''Εγκαταλείπω in the Psalms').

15 See, e.g., Eccles. 9.1–16. Ps. 36.25 also affirms the contrary.

Throughout these chapters their calculating oppression of the δίκαιος is described so that a paradigm of righteous suffering emerges.

First, in these four chapters there is an oscillation between the singular and plural forms of δίκαιος which strongly suggests that as in other cases, for example, υἱὸς ἀνθρώπου and παῖς Θεοῦ, the one represents the many.[16] Again, the virtuous man (sing.) stands up boldly before his accusers (Wis. 5.1–14) whose futile lives are then contrasted with the lot of the δίκαιοι (plur. Wis. 5.15–23). There is also a similar change from the singular of Wisdom 2.10–24 to the plural of Wisdom 3.1–9. A paradigm of the singular δίκαιος is established in comparatively few verses: he 'stands for' a corporate experience.[17]

Second, his oppression by the ungodly is described:

> ἐνεδρεύσωμεν τὸν δίκαιον (Wis. 2.12)

and

> ὕβρει καὶ βασάνῳ ἐτάσωμεν αὐτόν (2.19)

and

> θανάτῳ ἀσχήμονι καταδικάσωμεν αὐτόν. (2.20)

Their plotting issues in his suffering and death, but even in that moment:

[16] This is taken up in chapter 8 below as an important strand in Luke's *theologia crucis*. Perhaps one should emphasise at this point that use of 'the one and the many' in no way implies the presence of 'corporate personality'. A descriptor may oscillate between singular and plural uses so that its singular, symbolic form stands for and represents the plural reality.

[17] This poses an interesting problem for modern translators. The LXX of Wis. 5.1–5 clearly presents a singular form and supports it thereafter: στήσεται ... αὐτὸν ... αὐτοῦ ... οὗτος ... αὐτοῦ ... αὐτοῦ ... ἔστιν. The *figure* is singular although we know him to be *representative*. The NewRSV, however, systematically turns each singular in Wis. 5.1–5 into a plural. Their reason is almost certainly that offered on p. xiv – their avoiding linguistic sexism: they were mandated to eschew that orientation to the masculine gender which 'has often restricted or obscured the meaning of the original text' (p. xiv). While their general case is admirable, in *this* instance they have themselves obscured a model which worked for Luke. Δίκαιος should be rendered as a masculine singular because the evangelist seems to have read it as a word about Jesus. By changing its *number* the translators have obliterated the *model*. (This was inevitable because at Luke 23.47 RSV had rendered δίκαιος as 'innocent' and was followed in this by NewRSV.) At Wis. 5.1–2 the singular δίκαιος stands for a plural and the masculine for the feminine. The translators left Isa. 52.13–53:12 untouched; why did their mandate regarding linguistic sexism not apply here also?

ὄψονται γὰρ τελευτὴν σοφοῦ,
καὶ οὐ νοήσουσιν τί ἐβουλεύσατο περὶ αὐτοῦ
καὶ εἰς τί ἠσφαλίσατο αὐτὸν ὁ Κύριος.
ὄψονται καὶ ἐξουθενήσουσιν ... (4.17–18a)

Wisdom 2.12 reveals that this conflict centres on *Torah* and tradition, and that the ungodly allege a powerful motive for their behaviour – resentment: εἰς κίβδηλον ἐλογίσθημεν αὐτῷ καὶ ἀπέχεται τῶν ὁδῶν ἡμῶν ὡς ἀπὸ ἀκαθαρσιῶν (2.16a).

Third, the writer reports that the δίκαιος

ἐπαγγέλλεται γνῶσιν ἔχειν Θεοῦ (2.13)

παῖδα Κυρίου ἑαυτὸν ὀνομάζει (2.13, cf. 2.18)

ἀλαζονεύεται πατέρα Θεόν. (2.16c)

This collection of words – father, son or servant,[18] and knowledge of God – is notable for its relation to Jesus' story, as is

μακαρίζει ἔσχατα δικαίων (2.16b)

A post-resurrection Christian writer might understandably find in these allusions a prefiguring of what Christian tradition reported as Jesus' words and deeds.

Fourth, the writer describes God's eschatological vindication of his δίκαιος before his tormentors, those who had sought his death to see what God would do (2.6–20):

τότε στήσεται ἐν παρρησίᾳ πολλῇ ὁ δίκαιος
κατὰ πρόσωπον τῶν θλιψάντων αὐτὸν
καὶ τῶν ἀθετούντων τοὺς πόνους αὐτοῦ ... (5.1)

The δίκαιοι also experience such a *post mortem* vindication:

Δίκαιοι δὲ εἰς τὸν αἰῶνα ζῶσιν,
καὶ ἐν Κυρίῳ ὁ μισθὸς αὐτῶν,
καὶ ἡ φροντὶς αὐτῶν παρὰ Ὑψίστῳ. (5.15)

This hope takes form in a word that was apparently not available to the psalmists:

καὶ γὰρ ἐν ὄψει ἀνθρώπων ἐὰν κολασθῶσιν,
ἡ ἐλπὶς αὐτῶν **ἀθανασίας** πλήρης ... (3.4)

Is Wisdom 3.7–10 a *midrash* on Daniel 12.1–9 and its earlier stories of suffering? This *post mortem* vindication is characterised as παράδοξος τῆς σωτηρίας (5.2; see 2A2 above), but is παράδοξος only

[18] See the discussion of παῖς in Doble (1992) at 6D3c.

to the good man's persecutors, among whom his salvation is now understood to be God's doing.

Fifth, like Daniel's 'saints of the Most High' the δίκαιοι inherit God's Kingdom, or exercise its rule with him:

> κρινοῦσιν ἔθνη καὶ κρατήσουσιν λαῶν
> καὶ βασιλεύσει αὐτῶν Κύριος εἰς τοὺς αἰῶνας
> (3.8, cf. Dan. 7.22, 26; cf. 1 Cor. 6.2)

> διὰ τοῦτο λήμψονται τὸ βασίλειον τῆς εὐπρεπείας
> καὶ τὸ διάδημα τοῦ κάλλους ἐκ χειρὸς Κυρίου.
> (Wis. 5.16)

That Wisdom's author has drawn heavily from the Psalms, probably from Daniel and certainly from Isaiah (Jeremias, *TDNT* V.684) does not negate the probability that he worked out in his own language what others had also struggled with, namely what meaning attaches to the suffering of God's People at the hands of those who oppress them? Wisdom's paradigm of the δίκαιος with its clear grasp of *immortality* as God's way of vindicating his People offered to the young church a model which made sense *in scriptural terms* of Jesus' suffering and shameful death.

Wisdom and Luke's use of Δίκαιος (Acts 7.52)

There are persuasive grounds in Acts 7.52–6 for holding that Luke's use of δίκαιος at this point was *focused* by Wisdom's model. Although interpreters cannot avoid bringing their existing baggage into the hermeneutical circle, they must ensure that, as far as possible, each piece of evidence they call is assessed in its own right. In chapter 7 below, cumulative, mutually supporting evidence is adduced for Luke's writing his passion narrative around Wisdom's δίκαιος-matrix, and in the light of that evidence the Lukan Stephen's use of δίκαιος at Acts 7.52 becomes much more understandable. But to ensure that the later cumulative argument is spiral, not circular, one must first survey the 'persuasive grounds' in this particular case.

First, in Acts 7.52–6 there are two mutually supportive elements from Wisdom's model of the δίκαιος: they are the linked words δίκαιος and ἑστῶτα (see chapter 7B, 'Criteria for allusion').

Luke chose to focus Stephen's talk of the betrayal and 'murder' of Jesus in the descriptor δίκαιος (Acts 7.52). Although, a few verses later (Acts 7.56), he would uniquely bring to its conclusion Christian tradition's ὁ υἱὸς τοῦ ἀνθρώπου theme,

- at *this* critical point in his narrative;
- placing this event at the climax of his long survey of Israel's tendency to resist God's plan;
- in Jerusalem;
- directly confronting Jesus' oppressors with their guilt both in respect of his death and of their sharing their fathers' resistance to God's spirit;

Luke chose to have his Stephen epitomise Jesus as δίκαιος, *thus pulling into one semantic basket all of these associated ideas*. There is much here that echoes Wisdom.

There is, moreover, a confirmatory clue close at hand in the same scene. In his account of Stephen's witnessing to the vindicated Jesus, by his twofold repetition of ἑστῶτα (Acts 7.55, 56) Luke *also* chose to emphasise the Lord's unexpected posture. This emphasised feature points to Wisdom rather than to the Psalms. Stephen's vision sets out the christological certainties on which the Gentile mission might proceed, but it *also* functions as a vindication scene in which Stephen faces opponents who had brought Jesus to his death. Luke has carefully distinguished two stages: in the first stage the evangelist reports what Stephen **saw**:

> ὑπάρχων δὲ πλήρης πνεύματος ἁγίου
> ἀτενίσας εἰς τὸν οὐρανὸν εἶδεν δόξαν θεοῦ
> καὶ **Ἰησοῦν ἑστῶτα** ἐκ δεξιῶν τοῦ θεοῦ. (Acts 7.55)

Then, Luke reports what Stephen **said**:

> Ἰδοὺ θεωρῶ τοὺς οὐρανοὺς διηνοιγμένους καὶ **τὸν υἱὸν τοῦ ἀνθρώπου** ἐκ δεξιῶν **ἑστῶτα** τοῦ θεοῦ.
> (Acts 7.56)

thereby clearly identifying the Son of man's vindication (cf. Dan. 7.13) as that of the same Jesus who had just been spoken of as the δίκαιος betrayed and murdered by Stephen's hearers (Acts 7.52); Luke's readers are intended to understand his move here. But the form of each of these reports prompts an urgent question: why 'standing'?[19] At his trial Luke's Jesus had affirmed:

[19] See note 14 above; cf. Ps. 1.5, 6. Derrett (1988) explores this question. While I remain committed to the view that Luke drew ἑστῶτα from Wisdom's δίκαιος-model, Ms Alison Jack of Edinburgh has drawn my attention to the 4Q385 Second-Ezekiel *targum* on Ezek. 37, where at line 8 'a great crowd of people shall

> ἀπὸ τοῦ νῦν δὲ ἔσται **ὁ υἱὸς τοῦ ἀνθρώπου καθήμενος** ἐκ δεξιῶν τῆς δυνάμεως τοῦ Θεοῦ. (Luke 22.69)

That verse alone, a clear prophecy both from the Lord and from scripture, should have guaranteed that in any later vision of the vindicated one he would be **seated** at God's right hand. Behind this picture probably lie passages like Psalm 79.16; Psalm 109.1 and Daniel 7.13; certainly καθήμενος is the posture appropriate to Jesus' post-vindication Lordship in the remainder of Luke–Acts, so prompting the question, what pressures led Luke twice over to write ἑστῶτα at this point?

Wisdom's δίκαιος was also vindicated *post mortem* by God:

> τότε **στήσεται** ἐν παρρησίᾳ πολλῇ ὁ δίκαιος
> κατὰ πρόσωπον τῶν θλιψάντων αὐτὸν καὶ τῶν
> ἀθετούντων τοὺς πόνους αὐτοῦ. (Wis. 5.1)

His vindication is in his facing his tormentors after they had done their worst;[20] it is not simply the regnant Lord whom Luke portrays, but the *vindicated.* Luke, having in mind Wisdom's δίκαιος-matrix, having identified Stephen's accusers as Jesus' προδόται καὶ φονεῖς (7.52, cf. 22.8 cf. Luke 10.16), continued his basic thought pattern and emphasised Jesus' vindication in Wisdom terms, that is, Jesus *stood.* If this be the case, then the Wisdom model must have exercised a powerful influence in Luke's thought, overriding both a word of the Lord and other scriptural words. Suggestions that the Lord stood to greet his first martyr are charming tokens of a courteous disposition from an age of chivalry; Wisdom's picture of a δίκαιος, once humiliated but now standing in God's presence, vindicated, to face his accusers, reflects Luke's coherent, systematic *theological* model of Jesus' ministry.[21] Luke's betrayed and

stand up'. Given the presence of both Son of man and δίκαιος in the primary text's near context, and Fitzmyer's suggestion (n. 29, chapter 4 above), Luke's relation with Ezekiel should be further explored.

20 'Wis. 2:12–20 is a dramatic, hellenistic portrayal of a conspiracy against the despised godly man; and 5:1–7 shows his escape and triumph, though not, of course, his resurrection' (Grayston, 1990, p. 175). But what *is* clear is that the vindication of the δίκαιος is *post mortem,* so Grayston's 'escape' is a misleading word. Wis. 5.1–14 is a vindication scene of the *martyred* δίκαιος in the presence of his astonished opponents.

21 Moule (1967, pp. 82–99) has drawn attention to Zech. 3 as a vindication/trial scene in which Joshua is *standing*: Καὶ ἔδειξέν μοι Ἰησοῦν τὸν ἱερέα τὸν μέγαν ἑστῶτα πρὸ προσώπου ἀγγέλου Κυρίου, καὶ ὁ διάβολος εἱστήκει ἐκ δεξιῶν αὐτοῦ τοῦ ἀντικεῖσθαι αὐτῷ (3.1). Here is an insight into lawcourt imagery similar to that found in Wis. 5.1. Moule commented on how attractive Christians

murdered Jesus was described as δίκαιος; his vindicated Jesus is standing. Here are two verbal clues which *together* point to Wisdom's δίκαιος; this particular piece of evidence is carried forward for further examination in chapter 7.

Second, Stephen's speech has affinities with Wisdom's survey of Israel's history.

Stephen's speech and Wisdom's survey of Israel's history have in common a twofold *perspective* on the ways things were: both writers set out their vision of God's having chosen a succession of men – for Wisdom they are δίκαιοι; for Luke they culminate in the δίκαιος – through whom he acted to bring about his saving purposes; both writers trace Israel's tendency to resist, oppose, even ill-treat these men; in this opposition Israel is resisting God's spirit. This shared perspective passes into the *content* of the two pieces: in their surveys of Israel's history both Wisdom and Stephen's speech concentrate on the Exodus and on Moses' role in that event. Although Wisdom does not call Moses δίκαιος, both writers agree in identifying him as a prophet (Wis. 11.1; cf. Acts 7.37 which *obliquely* refers to his being a prophet by citing Deut. 18.15).[22] Stephen's speech has many sources; its model was probably Wisdom.

B. Paul's *apologia* in Jerusalem: Acts 22.14

ὁ δὲ εἶπεν, Ὁ θεὸς τῶν πατέρων ἡμῶν
προεχειρίσατό σε γνῶναι τὸ θέλημα αὐτοῦ
καὶ ἰδεῖν τὸν δίκαιον
καὶ ἀκοῦσαι φωνὴν ἐκ τοῦ στόματος αὐτοῦ.

Contexts and problems

The immediate context of this verse is Paul's speech in his own defence before both a lynch mob and a Roman centurion; its boundaries are thus fixed at Acts 22.1 and 22.21. There is, however,

found these chapters in Zechariah – did this picture influence Luke? The strength of an underlying Wisdom model in shaping Luke's narrative is more fully explored in chapter 7 below.

22 For a discussion of the suffering prophet/Just One see Donahue (1976) and Ruppert (1972): 'Die besondere theologische Leistung des historischen Jesus hätte somit darin bestanden, dass er sich als leidenden Gerechten *und* leidenden Propheten begriff, wobei er seine in oder nach dem Tode erwartete *Verherrlichung* als *Erhöhung* und zwar in der Weise der Einsetzung *zum* eschatologischen *Menschensohn* verstanden haben kann' (Ruppert, 1972, p. 75).

a larger context which begins at 19.21 and continues to the end of the volume. Its 'text' might be its first verse: ὡς δὲ ἐπληρώθη ταῦτα, ἔθετο ὁ Παῦλος ἐν τῷ πνεύματι διελθὼν τὴν Μακεδονίαν καὶ Ἀχαΐαν πορεύεσθαι εἰς Ἱεροσόλυμα, εἰπὼν ὅτι Μετὰ τὸ γενέσθαι με ἐκεῖ δεῖ με καὶ Ῥώμην ἰδεῖν (Acts 19.21). The δεῖ με is possibly a theological irony; the Jerusalem theme and Paul's consequent journey to Rome now occupy the forefront of Luke's mind (cf. Acts 1.8). Within this larger context Paul's *apologia* is pivotal, surveying what has happened to the present while pointing to what is yet to come. Although commentators profess to finding it hard to account for this speech at this moment in Luke's scheme, its pivotal function helps a reader move forward more surely.

In its larger context stand four elements: Paul's journey through Macedonia and Achaia; his visit to Jerusalem; a series of legal processes; his journey to and sojourn in Rome. Throughout that journey to Jerusalem runs a threat of suffering in the city.[23] For example, in his speech at Miletus to the Ephesian elders Luke has Paul say: καὶ νῦν ἰδοὺ δεδεμένος ἐγὼ τῷ πνεύματι πορεύομαι εἰς Ἰερουσαλήμ, τὰ ἐν αὐτῇ συναντήσοντά μοι μὴ εἰδώς, πλὴν ὅτι τὸ πνεῦμα τὸ ἅγιον κατὰ πόλιν διαμαρτύρεταί μοι λέγον ὅτι δεσμὰ καὶ θλίψεις με μένουσιν (Acts 20.22–3) Again, at Caesarea the prophet Agabus enacted a prophetic parable to show the fate awaiting Paul in Jerusalem: Τάδε λέγει τὸ πνεῦμα τὸ ἅγιον, Τὸν ἄνδρα οὗ ἐστιν ἡ ζώνη αὕτη οὕτως δήσουσιν ἐν Ἰερουσαλὴμ οἱ Ἰουδαῖοι καὶ παραδώσουσιν εἰς χεῖρας ἐθνῶν (Acts 21.11b). Consequently, the Pauline *apologia* at 22.1–21 is more securely read within the larger scheme that Luke proposed. Many problems are posed by this *apologia*, one of which is that Luke reports Paul's Damascus Road experience three times over and each version differs from the others. For present purposes one notes that two elements unique to this version offer help in the search for Luke's concept of δίκαιος. **First**, Ananias' words to Paul are succinctly offered in Acts 22.12–16; these do not figure in Luke's account in chapter 9 of Paul's conversion and Ananias does not appear in the version in chapter 26. (Ananias has himself undergone considerable

[23] This journey's parallel with the Gospel is part of the Lukan patterning identified by Talbert (1974, pp. 15–23, see esp. p. 17) as an 'architectural feature' of the two volumes. While his detailed work is impressive, Talbert is surely mistaken in placing item 23 where it is on his 'Pauline' list (1974, p. 17) – this particular sacramental meal relates to the journey to Rome, not in or near Jerusalem; and even if one extends Talbert's sense of 'after', there is a *very* different context, quite disciple-free.

change between Acts 9 and 22. In the first he was plain μαθητὴς in the second he is – ἀνὴρ εὐλαβὴς κατὰ τὸν νόμον, μαρτυρούμενος ὑπὸ πάντων τῶν κατοικούντων Ἰουδαίων. Probably, only Luke's reservation of the term to Jesus at 22.14 prevented his calling Ananias δίκαιος, another in the succession from Zechariah and Elizabeth to Cornelius.) Because these explanatory words are an *addition*, their function here is clearly important and they are considered in detail below. **Second,** in 22.17–21 Luke offers an account of a further Pauline vision, this time in the Temple, in Jerusalem – a vision otherwise unreported. This account leaves the reader in no doubt that Paul's quitting Jerusalem for the Gentile mission was Jesus' will – constituting Paul also a *shaliach.*

Together, these additional features indicate that Luke, through this *apologia*, was continuing his exposition of the christological basis for the Gentile mission. This *apologia* stands at the very end of Paul's mission journeys; affirms Paul's former role as a persecutor of Jesus' followers; emphasises the encounter between Paul the former persecutor and Jesus the ascended Lord; focuses on Ananias' explanatory role. These features must be explored more fully.

Emphases in Paul's *apologia*

Because of his addition to this account of details not found in the Acts 9 version *one may be reasonably confident that Luke wished here to emphasise Paul's role as a persecutor*. These additions are basically amplifications of what is known from the earlier version, but their form none the less marks them out as emphases. This particular sketch of Paul begins with Jesus' question

Σαοὺλ Σαούλ, τί με διώκεις; (Acts 22.7 // 9.4b)

answered by Paul's question

Τίς εἶ, κύριε; (22.8 cf. 9.5a)

and, in both accounts, the answer ἐγώ εἰμι Ἰησοῦς [add ὁ Ναζωραῖος–22.8b] ὃν σὺ διώκεις (9.5b). The term ὁ Ναζωραῖος is possibly used by Luke to identify *which* Jesus is referred to, but in a christologically neutral way (Doble, 1985, p. 73); it is an *outsider's* way of speaking of Jesus and is here a way of letting Paul know that the one addressing him is the Galilaean prophet, condemned and executed, whose followers Paul is presently hounding (Doble, 1985, p. 73; see also *TDNT* IV.874–879).

Luke tends to emphasise the solidarity of Jesus with the suffering of his disciples: Luke 10.16 affirms a *shaliach*-relation of disciple and Lord; this is focused by the follower-relation set out in Luke 9.23 with its addition of καθ' ἡμέραν to Mark's version: Εἴ τις θέλει ὀπίσω μου ἔρχεσθαι, ἀρνησάσθω ἑαυτὸν καὶ ἀράτω τὸν σταυρὸν αὐτοῦ καθ' ἡμέραν, καὶ ἀκολουθείτω μοι. In practice, according to Luke, this taking up of a cross – or persecution or suffering – came early to the infant church and was understood by the evangelist to be an element in discipleship: Οἱ μὲν οὖν ἐπορεύοντο χαίροντες ἀπὸ προσώπου τοῦ συνεδρίου ὅτι κατηξιώθησαν ὑπὲρ τοῦ ὀνόματος ἀτιμασθῆναι (Acts 5.41). Luke reported a more general attack on the disciples immediately after Stephen's martyrdom, associating it with a dispersion of the Jerusalem church (8.1b). Acts reports that Paul, whose connivance (but not active participation) in Stephen's death was noted (8.1a), sought commission from the High Priest to return this Christian *diaspora* to Jerusalem (9.2); his disposition was not friendly: Ὁ δὲ Σαῦλος, ἔτι ἐμπνέων ἀπειλῆς καὶ φόνου εἰς τοὺς μαθητὰς τοῦ κυρίου ... (9.1).

This general picture has been filled out by Luke in one of the elements added to his second version of Paul's conversion with its connecting Jerusalem vision: Κύριε, αὐτοὶ ἐπίστανται ὅτι ἐγὼ ἤμην φυλακίζων καὶ δέρων κατὰ τὰς συναγωγὰς τοὺς πιστεύοντας ἐπὶ σέ ... (Acts 22.19). Luke has made plain to his readers that Paul was once diligent in persecuting Christians; he has made equally clear that *at the same time, by virtue of this behaviour the apostle was persecuting Jesus.* Consequently, a reader rightly infers that Paul had enrolled himself among those who were Jesus' enemies.[24]

[24] This is indeed confirmed by the voice in Paul's Damascus Road experience (Acts 9.4–6; 22.7–9; 26.14–15). In each case the verb 'to persecute' is repeated and Paul's action against followers specifically related to Jesus. There is another dimension to Paul's experience which deserves much fuller exploration than it can be given here: essentially it has to do with the parallels between Luke's describing Paul's career as a persecutor and the conflict passages in Wisdom. These parallels can be briefly indicated:

a. *Light shining around:* Wis. 5.6/Acts 9.1–3; 22.6, 9; 26.12–18
b. *Way:* Wis. 5.7/Acts 9.2; 22.4, 6 (see Haenchen (1971, p. 320 n.1) who notes the uncertain origin of ὁδός used absolutely for 'Christianity'; cf. *TDNT* V.84–91; note especially the link between 'go astray' and 'wander' – Isa. 35.8/Wis. 5.6; 'unclean', Isa. 35.8/Wis. 5.16).

This version of Paul's *apologia* also emphasises his encounter with the ascended, vindicated Lord. Two such encounters are noted: the first in Acts 22.6–11; the second at 22.17–21. In Acts, visions play an important part in the narrative by disclosing to men what the true state of affairs is in the heavens; like Stephen's, Paul's vision is of Jesus. Luke may have intended the reference to light (22.6) to parallel Stephen's seeing the δόξαν Θεοῦ (7.55). Luke probably intended this light to represent Jesus also. Whatever the best reading at 22.11 might be – and B's οὐδὲν ἔβλεπον surely conveys the sense of this passage – Luke seems to have wanted to affirm that Paul was unable to see because of the light. No account of this encounter suggests that Paul 'saw Jesus' in the direct way attributed to Stephen at Acts 7.55, although the added story of a Jerusalem vision unequivocally does this (καὶ ἰδεῖν αὐτὸν λέγοντά μοι – Acts 22.18, cf. v. 14). A distinction is made between Paul's Jerusalem vision and that on the road to Damascus: the former is said to be ἐν ἐκστάσει while the latter is 'objectivised' by Luke's reference to Paul's companions also having seen the light (22.9).[25] Unlike Paul, his companions heard no voice (22.9 *contra* 9.7), yet, according to Luke, Paul was left in no doubt that he was in the presence of the One he had persecuted by his persecuting those who put their faith in him (22.19); these included Stephen (τοῦ μάρτυρός σου – 22.20) whose death Paul had approved. No careful reader can avoid the impression that Luke is describing an encounter between the vindicated Lord and his persecutor. Paul is plainly depicted as ἀσεβής in this context; his persecution of 'the saints' reflects that of the δίκαιος by the ἀσεβεῖς of Wisdom 2–5, and, given the case (see chapter 7 below) that can be urged for Luke's use of Wisdom, there may be an

c. *Jesus as 'Son of God':* Wis. 5.5/Acts 9.20, cf. 22.15.
d. *Lawlessness:* Wis. 5.7, 23; cf. 4:20/Acts 9.1, 13–14, 21–2; 22.3–5; 26.9–12a.
e. *Shaken with fear, amazed:* Wis. 5.2/Acts 9.4; 22.7; 26.14 ('when we had all . . .')

At present, this relation between Paul's career and Wisdom remains uncertain. If these parallels do stand up, then this note should be carried forward into chapter 7, offering further evidence of Luke's 'gravitational attraction' by Wisdom's δίκαιος-model.

[25] This is not the place to discuss problems posed by the portraits of Paul offered on one hand by Luke and on the other by the 'Pauline' letters. There is, however, an interesting sidelight shed on Acts 22.6, 11 by 2 Cor. 3.18–4.6. It is also possible – but no more – that the description of this light is intended to recall the *light of righteousness* which did **not** shine upon the ἀσεβεῖς (Wis. 5.6), among whom, assuming that the previous note is correct, the pre-conversion Paul should be numbered.

echo of Wisdom 5.7 in Luke's speaking of Christian commitment as 'the Way'.

There is also a Lukan emphasis on Ananias' role in Paul's enlightenment; this becomes clearer when one contrasts the information offered by Acts 22.14–16 with that offered in 9.17b. In Paul's *apologia* Ananias' function is undoubtedly to clarify for Paul *the significance of what had happened.* His explanation is – as one would expect from a Jerusalem context in which there is emphasis on the Jewishness of events – thoroughly Jewish and one which overtly identifies the ascended Jesus with τὸν δίκαιον, a move which in Stephen's speech had to be inferred. Its Jewishness is heralded by the *apologia*'s opening:

- **its address** – Ἄνδρες ἀδελφοὶ καὶ πατέρες (22.1)
- **its language** – τῇ Ἑβραΐδι διαλέκτῳ (21.40b; 22.2)
- **its author's biography** – ἀνὴρ Ἰουδαῖος (22.3)
  γεγεννημένος ἐν Ταρσῷ (22.3)
  ἀνατεθραμμένος δὲ ἐν τῇ πόλει ταύτῃ (22.3)
  πεπαιδευμένος –
    παρὰ τοὺς πόδας Γαμαλιὴλ
    κατὰ ἀκρίβειαν τοῦ πατρῴου νόμου (22.3).

This Jewishness reaches into Ananias' explanation:

- **the vision's source** – Ὁ Θεὸς τῶν πατέρων ἡμῶν (22.14)
- **its message** – προεχειρίσατό σε (22.14)
- **its content** (22.14) – γνῶναι τὸ θέλημα αὐτοῦ (22.10 cf. vv. 15, 21)
  – ἰδεῖν τὸν δίκαιον (cf. Wis. 5.2, ἰδόντες . . .)
  – ἀκοῦσαι φωνὴν ἐκ τοῦ στόματος αὐτοῦ (cf. 22.8, 10, 18, 21)

Consequently, because the first and third elements in Ananias' explanation unquestionably relate to elements in the remainder of the *apologia*, the phrase ἰδεῖν τὸν δίκαιον **must** refer to the brilliant light associated with the voice which announced to Paul 'I am Jesus whom you are persecuting.'

Summary

Examination of 'Stephen's' and 'Paul's' uses of δίκαιος suggests some preliminary conclusions. **First**, as a christological descriptor in Acts δίκαιος appears only in Jewish contexts. **Second**, the term seems to be shorthand for a christological model which highlights the unexpected vindication in the presence of his persecutors of

God's humiliated man. In both cases so far examined there has been emphasis on a confrontation between the Lord and his persecutors; in both cases a vision confirmed that the once-humiliated Jesus is not only with God but exercising authority; in both cases the writer clearly intends his readers to associate the word δίκαιος with what had befallen Jesus. **Third,** the aptness of this reading of Paul's vision to his own circumstances at this point in Luke's volume is clear. The erstwhile persecutor is himself facing trials such as Stephen and Jesus faced, standing where they once stood. Luke did not accidentally refer to Stephen in this narrative (Acts 22.20); the two visions and the two defences are closely linked in Luke's scheme, two witnesses to one christological truth, namely that Jesus the Nazarene, the humiliated one, is, however unexpectedly, with God. **Fourth,** this Pauline *apologia* not only sets out the Church's christological confidence but retrospectively validates the Gentile mission. Stephen's vision and speech in Jerusalem stand at its beginning; Paul's exposition before a hostile crowd in Jerusalem of his Damascus road vision stands at its end. Luke has neatly brought *the testimony of two witnesses* to the possibility that δίκαιος, with its powerful scriptural overtones, is one way of encapsulating an understanding of Jesus' career within which the Lord is now both the source of and authority for the Gentile mission. A third, and disputed, witness must now be heard.

C. Peter's speech: Acts 3.14

ὑμεῖς δὲ τὸν ἅγιον καὶ δίκαιον ἠρνήσασθε,
καὶ ᾐτήσασθε ἄνδρα φονέα χαρισθῆναι ὑμῖν . . .

This passage is examined last because of the difficulties it presents to an interpreter. One of its greatest is the consensus that seems to have emerged among commentators that δίκαιος is related to παῖς, and that because of ἐδόξασεν at Acts 3.13, echoing, as it is thought, Isaiah 52.13, it is reasonable to conclude that Luke was working with a model derived from Deutero-Isaiah's Servant Songs. The introduction to this chapter noted that procedurally it was preferable not to *assume* this to be the case.[26] In the two studies already outlined a case has been argued for Luke's using a model derived primarily from Wisdom's δίκαιος. Consequently, *the thrust* of this section is, first, further to question the consensus on this verse and,

[26] See pp. 128–31 above.

second, to explore its context to determine whether or not the hypothesis can be defended that Luke worked with a δίκαιος-model different from that derived from its association with παῖς. These preliminary conclusions are carried forward into a fuller discussion of the issues in chapter 7, where δίκαιος in this speech is shown to be most probably rooted in the Wisdom model.

Context

The immediate context of this verse is Peter's speech to a crowd gathered at the 'Beautiful Gate' of the Temple in Jerusalem. The speech appears to be a kerygmatic explanation of how a lame man came to walk and, because he walked ἁλλόμενος καὶ αἰνῶν τὸν Θεὸν while the crowd ἐδόξαζον τὸν Θεὸν ἐπὶ τῷ γεγονότι, this study has already explored many of the implications of the unit in chapter 2C above. One of the unit's features is that its fuller context also includes Peter's defence of his action before the Sanhedrin, during which Luke appears to substitute Psalm 117.22 for the christological 'titles' of Acts 3.

Δίκαιος and paidologies

A key issue in the speech is the christological difference between Jesus' followers and others. For both the lame man (3.6)[27] and for the Sanhedrin (4.10) Peter fixes clearly which *Jesus* he is speaking of – the Nazarene. In each speech there is then an amplification of Jesus' significance for the speaker, usually an amplification derived from scriptural models – and the plural is important for, as has already been noted, to reduce them to one basket is to abandon any hold on the vitality and flexibility of the infant Church's christology. In an unpublished public lecture delivered at Cambridge on 10 February 1954, R. Newton Flew began, 'Christologies are made of countless stones of adoration and innumerable titles of love.' While his accent was rightly on the rooting of christology in worship, his noting its 'countless' or 'innumerable' elements should warn against attempts to reduce δίκαιος to a mere adjective. The truth of Flew's assertion is exemplified in this scene in Acts where Luke has the apostles speak of Jesus as: παῖς (Acts 3.13, 26; 4.27, 30); τὸν ἅγιον

[27] Isa. 5.6 stands close behind this account of the lame man and the reference to the 'Holy Way' (Is. 35:8) is nearby.

καὶ δίκαιον (3.14); τὸν ἀρχηγὸν τῆς ζωῆς (3.15); τὸν Χριστὸν (3.18, 20; 4.10, 26 cf. 27); προφήτην (implied by 3.22); λίθος (4.11 cf. Ps. 117.22).

While it is clear that παῖς is one of the two most frequent categories in this unit it should not be simply equated with Deutero-Isaiah's *'ebed*. In addition to the considerations noted in the introduction to this section, one factor immediately erodes so simple an equation – David is unambiguously called παῖς at Acts 4.25 and two of the references to Jesus as παῖς follow it immediately in the same context–that of worship. There is a strong likelihood that what is meant by παῖς in one Lukan use is what should be read in the other. So either David is to be thought of as a servant figure, which seems unlikely, or the word refers more generally to a man who in some way is God's man. It may have the overtone of 'son' here, in which case, again, it is not the *'ebed Yahweh* model which is at work.

The strongest argument for παῖς at Acts 3.13 to be read as *'ebed Yahweh* is probably its association with ἐδόξασεν. 'Ιδου, συνήσει ὁ παῖς μου, καὶ ὑψωθήσεται, καὶ δοξασθήσεται σφόδρα (Isa. 52.13). Interestingly, N-A 26 does not italicise the ἐδόξασεν at Acts 3:13 although it does refer to Isaiah 52.13 in the outer margin. (Readers of *The Jerusalem Bible*, DLT (1966), p. 206 (NT) may well (wrongly) infer from its italicising that they are dealing with an undisputed quotation.) The presence of ἐδόξασεν may, or may not, be confirmation that Luke had the *'ebed Yahweh* in mind here; certainty is not possible. But the references to δόξα may be much wider than this one Isaianic reference and relate more to what was known of Jesus' life – including the transfiguration narrative – than to the *'ebed Yahweh*.[28] At present, a connection with Isaiah is simply not proven; but another factor needs to be noted. In the little doxological passage (4.23–31) which speaks of David as παῖς, Jesus is called:

– τὸν ἅγιον παῖδά σου 'Ιησοῦν (4.27)

– τοῦ ἁγίου παιδός σου 'Ιησοῦ (4.30)

Nobody, it seems, argues, as they do for δίκαιος, that ἅγιος is a function of παῖς in Deutero-Isaiah; but this christological formula, set in the context of worship, cannot be divorced from the clear reference to David at Acts 4.25.

[28] For example, Wisdom's judgment was that God had always 'glorified' his People: 'For in everything, O Lord, you have exalted and glorified your people, and you

A final factor needs to be taken into account: even if παῖς at Acts 3.13 should, on balance, be taken to be an allusion to *'ebed Yahweh*, there is no *necessary* connection with δίκαιος in the following verse where it is linked with ἅγιος. Indeed, as was noted in the introduction, the *'ebed Yahweh* is only once called δίκαιος – that is, δίκαιος is not a major qualifier in the model. There is, however, strong evidence from both Paul's and Stephen's speeches examined above that Luke worked with a christological model in which δίκαιος was both primary and relatively frequent.

Scripture fulfilled

Typically of Luke, this unit has a strong emphasis on scripture's having been fulfilled in Jesus' ministry. This appears in two ways. First, there are frequent citations from or close allusions to scripture: e.g. Acts 3.13 = Exodus 3.6; 3.22 = Deuteronomy 18.18–19; 3.25 = Genesis 22.18; 4.11 = Psalm 117.22; 4.25 = Psalm 2.1–2. The density of other possible allusions can be deduced from the outer margins of the N-A 26 text. Second, Luke presents Peter's drawing attention to the fact of fulfilment. Acts 3.17–26 distils Luke's perspective: neither the people nor their leaders understood what they were really doing in their treatment of Jesus (3.17);[29] Jesus is properly understood both as the prophet foretold by Moses (3.22 cf. Deut. 18.15, 18–19) and as the eschatological Christ (3.20); through all his prophets God had foretold that the Christ would suffer (3.18 but see below);[30] the prophets anticipated a time of God's ἀνάψυξις (3.20) or ἀποκατάστασις (3.21). It is quite clear to impartial readers of Jewish scripture that the prophets had **not** foretold the sufferings of Christ, indeed this appears to have been the very christological issue that divided the apostles so clearly from their compatriots and fellow Jews.[31] Here is a reviewing and reworking of the concept 'messiah'. Bruce is sure that this is the case: 'The

have not neglected to help them at all times and in all places' (Wis. 19.22) cf. 'For by the same means by which you punished our enemies you called us to yourself and glorified us' (Wis. 18.8).

[29] See Wis. 2.22; cf. Houlden (1984, p. 64f.) who deals briefly with the oppressors' ignorance as an 'excuse' both in Luke–Acts and in Wisdom. This issue is considered in chapter 7H, 'Ignorance and guilt: a Lukan theme'.

[30] 'That the *Christ* would suffer?' Young (1977, pp. 13–47), in a much-praised essay, opens up the question of a christology for today, and particularly the significance of *soteriology* (pp. 30 and 38) for its formulation.

[31] Doble (1992, pp. 205–6).

Messiah as such is not represented as suffering in OT. The Isaianic Servant is so represented, and the apostles followed Jesus Himself in interpreting His Messiahship in terms of the Servant prophecies.' (1952, p. 111).

But all that has gone before indicates just how wide was the scriptural reservoir on which Luke had to draw (as had possibly Jesus and his disciples); Luke's intention is, apparently, to elucidate what Israel's leaders had not grasped, namely that in Jesus, God had acted.

Conflict and vindication

As in the previous two cases, this accusation occurs in a confrontation with those who oppose Jesus and his followers. In his own way Luke portrayed Peter and John as Jesus' *sheluchim*: this is probably intended by the frequent use of 'in the name of' (Acts 3.6, 16; 4.7, 10, 12, 30), and is possibly supported by μάρτυρες at 3.15. In this sense, then, Peter and John, like Stephen and Paul, are one with and represent their risen Lord. Speaking in his name, and arguing from scripture to help both people and leaders grasp what had been going on, they contrast 'your' treatment of Jesus with God's: 'you' (at 3.13, referring to the crowd, the ὑμεῖς is emphatic)[32]

– παρεδώκατε καὶ ἠρνήσασθε [αὐτὸν] (3.13)

– ἠρνήσασθε [τὸν ἅγιον καὶ δίκαιον] (3.14)

– ᾐτήσασθε ἄνδρα φονέα. (3.14)

Reference back to the crowd's part in Jesus' humiliation and unjust death is clear; 7.52 reflects the same countercharge against both crowd and leaders. In Peter's defence before the Sanhedrin (parallel to those of Stephen and Paul) there is another emphatic ὑμεῖς

– ὃν ὑμεῖς ἐσταυρώσατε. (4.10)

Jesus' *shaliach*, Peter, confronting both crowd and Sanhedrin, affirmed that the humiliated Jesus had been vindicated by God:

[32] So also Tannehill (1991, esp. p. 405). This is an important article which examines Peter's speeches in Acts from a *narrative-critical* perspective. Its thrust generally supports the view taken in this study, namely that there is development from speech to speech, and that together they take forward Luke's case. Tannehill's treatment of the Cornelius episode (1991, p. 413f.) and of the Pisidian Antioch sermon (1991, p. 403) also offers support to this study's work in those areas (cf. Doble, 1992, 3D2a and 6C2).

– ὁ Θεὸς . . . ἐδόξασεν τὸν παῖδα αὐτοῦ Ἰησοῦν (3.13)

– ὃν ὁ Θεὸς ἤγειρεν ἐκ νεκρῶν. (3.15; 4.10)

The apostles were witnesses to the resurrection (3.15), but, more to the point, so now was the once-lame man whose cure was called in confirmation of their testimony (cf. 4.30).

There is further evidence that this unit is a vindication scene – the presence at Acts 4.11 of Psalm 117.22 as a summary of what Luke had spelt out in 3.13–16 . . . οὗτός ἔστιν ὁ λίθος, ὁ ἐξουθενηθεὶς ὑφ' ὑμῶν τῶν οἰκοδόμων, the note of rejection (cf. Luke 18.9 and 23.11) by those who ought to have known better. This contrasts sharply with . . . ὁ γενόμενος εἰς κεφαλὴν γωνίας a dramatic reversal of fortune so like that attributed by Wisdom to the Just One's vindication (Wis. 5.1).

One further small hint of a connection with that vindication scene should be noted: the word παρρησία occurs twice in this unit (Acts 4.13, 29), more often than might be expected from its frequency throughout Luke–Acts. In itself this might be of little consequence, but its *use* adds to the word's importance: 'when the Sanhedrin saw the apostles' παρρησία they recognised that they were with Jesus' (4.13); 'after their release by the Sanhedrin they continued to speak God's message with παρρησίᾳ' (4.31). Jesus' *sheluchim* thus exhibit *in this context* that quality which distinguished Wisdom's δίκαιος as he confronted his tormentors:

τότε στήσεται ἐν παρρησίᾳ πολλῇ ὁ δίκαιος
κατὰ πρόσωπον τῶν θλιψάντων αὐτὸν
καὶ τῶν ἀθετούντων τοὺς πόνους αὐτοῦ.

This may amount to little; on the other hand, because there are many echoes in Luke–Acts of this evangelist's appeal to Wisdom (see chapter 7 below), the presence of παρρησία *may* be another, quieter echo of the model with which Luke was working.

Some tentative conclusions may be drawn from analysis of this unit. First, it is far from certain that one should look to the '*ebed Yahweh* model for Luke's pool of meaning for δίκαιος. Second, the richness of Luke's christological models in this unit encourages one to look for *diversity* of imagery rather than for *convergence*. Third, given the word's context – a long vindication scene in which confrontation is to the fore – Luke probably had in mind that δίκαιος pattern with which he worked in two other settings (see chapter 7 below).

Δίκαιος as a christological descriptor – preliminary conclusions

First, in the event, the choice of 'descriptor' rather than 'title' or 'name' was justified. 'Title' suggests something more formal and consensual than is intended here; 'name' signifies a word proper to its referent, as Χριστός soon became in the Christian tradition. 'Descriptor' was intended to identify a word or phrase which, by its metaphorical or associative roots in Jewish scripture, elucidated Jesus' ministry and person for his followers.

Second, the principle that a word's signification is illuminated by its context has also been justified by results from each passage studied: the word occurs only in *Jewish* passages, not in those where the focus is on Gentiles.[33] While the passages are too few to affirm a Lukan *Tendenz,* their uniquely Jewish setting is almost certainly necessarily associated with their also being *vindication* scenes in which Jesus, through his disciples (*sheluchim*), confronts his persecutors. Consequently, each unit has its defence speech, obviously so in the case of Paul and Stephen, but also important in Acts 3.14 and its contexts.[34]

Third, the root of each confrontation is *christological*: what may properly be said of the Jesus who had suffered a shameful death by hanging on a tree? The speeches in Acts show Jesus' disciples identifying and exploring scriptural passages which helped them understand that God had been at work in their Lord; they could confidently relate him *and his death* to God's salvation plan revealed in the scriptures. Luke emphasised that this tradition of scriptural interpretation was handed down to his disciples by the Lord himself (see, e.g., Luke 24.27, 45–8); the Acts speeches reveal them as heirs of his tradition. Within the scriptures they found, and worked with, a variety of 'models' of God's men – son of man,

[33] This assessment is one of the strengths of Longenecker's discussion of δίκαιος as a christological term (1970, pp. 46f.). Longenecker, however, saw Luke's use of δίκαιος as evidence of the evangelist's tendency to 'downplay' distinctive Jewish motifs in the Gentile mission (1970, p. 98 n. 158). His inconsistency at this point is instructive. Had he taken seriously his own note 109 on p. 47, he might have registered that Luke's use was far from a downplaying. There is no evidence in his work that he knew or used Kilpatrick's 1942 article, but he *may* have been influenced by the general climate of opinion *re* Luke 23.47 as expressed in American translations and commentaries.

[34] Strictly speaking, the 'defence speech' is Acts 4.8b–12, cf. 19–20. The prayer of thanksgiving for their deliverance (Acts 4.24b–30) appears to allot responsibility to *Gentiles* (4.27) as well as to Jews.

servant, son of God, messiah, saint, prophet *et al.* among which was δίκαιος.

Fourth, a survey of these three passages has adduced evidence which strongly suggests that in them Luke worked with a model of δίκαιος drawn largely from Wisdom.[35] This evidence emerged cumulatively and positively from a study of Acts 7.52; analysis of Acts 22.14 and its contexts showed δίκαιος to function as it did at 7.52; after bracketing-off Deutero-Isaiah's παῖς model as Luke's resource for δίκαιος at Acts 3.14, it emerged that the passages' contexts and content cohered with Luke's Wisdom model.

D. Luke's use of Δίκαιος in Luke–Acts: a summary of conclusions

What may be said of Luke's use of δίκαιος lies in the field of *probability* rather than of proof. Chapters 4 and 5 sought Luke's pool of meaning[36] for this word in its contexts and found Luke consistent in his using it.

The major, if not exclusive, pool from which Luke drew was his Greek Bible. Analysis of the word's contexts strongly suggests that δίκαιος belongs to a specific realm of discourse – the piety and theology of first-century Judaism. Luke's consistency in use also suggests that he shared this pool of meaning with his readers, and that he expected them to be able to hear the 'harmonics' of δίκαιος as he used it.

Luke's usage falls naturally into two quite distinct but closely related phases: first, that phase which continues from the word's past, still shared with Israel, into the Church's present, in which the *general term* δίκαιος identifies God's loyal men and women; second, that phase which followed Jesus' cross and resurrection, marking him out as a *special case* of the general term δίκαιος.

The first, general use of δίκαιος reflects the LXX notion of one whose life responded freely to God who is himself δίκαιος. Here it is unquestionably a religious rather than formal, legal concept and within the Greek Bible it draws heavily on Psalms, 1 Samuel, Daniel

[35] See chapter 7: 'Wisdom in Luke's passion story'.

[36] That is, *discourse meaning*; cf. Cotterell and Turner (1989, pp. 68–72; 77–102) who write of a 'presupposition pool' to include a rather wider range of evidence than is appealed to here, where interest has been substantially in *lexical semantics*: what 'components' of δίκαιος have been identified, what *associated features* in its immediate contexts? This study's search is primarily for the concept of δίκαιος at Luke 23.47. Caird's discussion of meaning is also helpful (1980, esp. pp. 54–61).

and Wisdom. For Luke it comprised a number of elements: leading a life of blameless devotion to God and delighting in *Torah;* being disposed to count others better than oneself (ὁ ταπεινῶν); longing for God's Kingdom or his salvation to be realised; committing oneself to loyalty to God, even to death, in the face of alien oppression or intra-communal contempt or persecution; trusting that in the end God would vindicate his faithful people even beyond death, and in the face of their persecutors; recognising that the word might be misappropriated by religious zealots who despised those not willing to share their particular forms of enthusiasm for *Torah.*

The second, unique use in relation to Jesus takes up all those elements of trust and loyalty into an affirmation by apostolic witnesses that God had actually vindicated one δίκαιος. God's act of vindication enabled Christians to think and speak of Jesus not as **a** δίκαιος but rather as **the** δίκαιος, evoking scriptural images and allusions which clarified for them what God had been doing in Jesus and, most particularly, in his shameful death. Luke used δίκαιος only in contexts which emphasised **both** Jesus' vindication by God **and** the presence of those who engineered his humiliation and death.

If this be the case, what may be said of Luke's use of δίκαιος at Luke 23.47? Because the ways in which Luke normally used δίκαιος have now been more surely identified, a reader is better able to evaluate Kilpatrick's advocacy of 'innocent': while he *assumed* that 'righteous' was a bathetic translation, Luke most probably worked with an underlying, explanatory δίκαιος-model drawn from scripture. Evidence examined in this chapter suggests that Wisdom's model offered a scriptural matrix around which Luke was able to rework the passion story as a defence of Jesus' death: it was one element in God's plan of salvation. Consequently, an interpreter needs to produce very good reasons for *not* rendering δίκαιος at Luke 23.47 in a way which reflects Luke's normative twofold use, that is, a general case of God's loyal saints, within which Jesus was a special case.[37]

[37] Throughout this chapter the appearance of Ἰοῦστος has been systematically ignored (Acts 1.23; 18.7; cf. Col. 4.11), treated as a 'neutral' *cognomen* rather than a Latinised δίκαιος in any Lukan sense. It is fanciful, as some journalists have done, to relate the name to Qumran and its community; that community is hardly likely to have chosen *Latin* names. One still hesitates to dismiss the possibility of the name's being relevant to this study because at Acts 18.7 Luke describes Titius Justus as σεβομένου τὸν Θεόν; cf. Col. 4.11 where Jesus Justus is ἐκ περιτομῆς (cf. also Hegesippus (Eus. *HE* ii.23) who claimed that, because of his commitment to *Torah*, James, the Lord's brother, was known as *the Just*). But Jackson and

The safest conclusion seems to be that Luke's use at 23.47 was *transitional*, reflecting both cases: it strongly related Jesus' humiliation and death to a *scriptural model* the writer shared with his readers; it confirmed that even at death this δίκαιος called God 'Father' just as the paradigm said he did (Wis. 2.16); if Luke knew the Markan tradition of the centurion's words (Mark 15.35), he did not displace it but subsumed it in a larger model in which the δίκαιος was resented because he said he was God's son (Wis. 2.18, cf. v. 13; but see Cadbury, 1933, p. 364); it affirmed the exemplary loyalty to and trust in God of a δίκαιος consistent to the end.

Consequently, to render δίκαιος at Luke 23.47 as 'innocent' is not only to ignore Luke's consistent practice but, worse, to obscure his *theologia crucis*.[38] After δοξάζειν τὸν Θεόν and δίκαιος, a third, confirmatory range of evidence must now be examined.[39]

Lake (*BC* IV, p. 14) indicate a Jewish practice of choosing a Latin *cognomen* similar to one's Hebrew *praenomen*. On balance, for present purposes, Ἰοῦστος may be set aside.

38 A sketched approach to Luke's *theologia crucis* is offered in chapter 8D.

39 This is confirmatory in the sense that it supports conclusions already reached – that Luke strongly related his thought about Jesus' death to Wisdom's δίκαιος-model. This present study *might* have begun by asking about the significance of Luke's choice of Ps. 30.6 as Jesus' final word, entering the hermeneutical circle at a different point.

6

'FATHER, INTO THY HANDS . . .'

A. Jesus' last word

Luke's account of Jesus' last word confirms that he was working with a δίκαιος-model. In Luke's version Jesus' final word was, Πάτερ, εἰς χεῖράς σου παρατίθεμαι τὸ πνεῦμά μου (Luke 23.46), which is entirely consistent with what Wisdom had affirmed would be the lot of God's δίκαιοι (Wis. 3.1). Whatever seems to be their loss or suffering, they are in God's hands. Whether Luke rewrote Mark's cry of dereliction because he had already begun to think of Jesus as *the* δίκαιος, or whether the tradition of Jesus' death that he received already treasured Psalm 30.6(31.5)[1] as Jesus' last word which then directed Luke's or his church's mind to Wisdom's model, is probably an insoluble problem. Significantly, in Luke, Jesus' last word schematically coheres with the centurion's recognition of Jesus as ὄντως ... δίκαιος; both changes probably originate in the same underlying model, each confirming the other.

This argument recognises that for Luke there was at this point only one word of Jesus from the cross. Attempts to show that Luke's saying was a supplementary form to that found in Mark or Matthew tend to founder on two hard facts. First, the structure of Luke's sentence seems to preclude the possibility of there being more than one 'final' word: ... καὶ φωνήσας φωνῇ μεγάλῃ ὁ' Ιησοῦς εἶπεν, Πάτερ ... τοῦτο δὲ εἰπὼν ἐξέπνευσεν (Luke 23.46–7). Second, those who seek to reconcile Luke's word with that of Mark and Matthew tend to become enmeshed in self-defeating arguments as do Bock (1987, p. 147f.) or Taylor (1937, p. 200). Grayston (1991, pp. 222f.) has also been confused by the synopticon. Most modern

[1] Throughout this chapter, Luke's citation of the psalm at Luke 23.46 will be referred to as Ps. 30.6, as in Rahlf's *Septuaginta*, Stuttgart, Deutsche Bibelgesellschaft, 1935 (1979). See also Léon-Dufour (1978a) and Powell, J. E. (1989) for comment on Jesus' last word.

synopticons probably contribute to this harmonising trend by placing Luke 23.46 parallel with Mark 15.37; the logic of the three accounts and their underlying structure points to Luke 23.46 belonging more naturally alongside Mark 15.34. This move clarifies the unity of thought within Luke's passion story, but it also involves provisionally working with the probability that Luke consciously corrected Mark at this point. Those who are sure that Markan priority is a lost cause should go straight to section B because the argument of this chapter stands without recourse to that hypothesis. On the other hand, waverers or Markan priorists may find it useful to reflect on some pointers to the possibility of Luke's having reworked one of his sources.

Excursus: Mark's passion narrative as Luke's principal source

An emendation needs to be made to the Lukan column in both Huck (250, p. 204) and Aland (Synopsis Quattuor Evangeliorum, 347, pp. 487ff.). Each synopticon prints Luke 23.46 parallel with Mark 15.37, effectively isolating Jesus' words drawn from Psalm 30.6 as 'additional' to those he has 'omitted' from Mark; this is possibly a visual illusion. It must be granted immediately that Mark's text gives the impression that there were *two* great cries from the cross – vv. 34 and 37 plainly refer to Jesus' 'great cries', so one can see why there is pressure to print them as they are. Alternatively, by printing Luke 23.46 in parallel with Mark 15.34, the new arrangement shows how Luke retained a strong underlying Markan structure while radically redrawing the scene of Jesus' death. Table 6.1, by setting out Luke 23.44–6 in parallel with Mark, illustrates how this evangelist handled his alleged sources.

From table 6.1 it becomes clear that although both Huck and Aland identified Luke 23.46 with Mark 15.37 they missed important structural links, particularly the way in which sections 1, 3, 5, 10–15 and 20 indicate Luke's dependence on Mark. Luke never uses βοάω (12) of Jesus, so it was natural for him to take up the cognate φωνέω implied in 14; that verb equally naturally became a participle because the evangelist was to emphasise (16) that Jesus' *saying* of the psalm was intelligible and not a confusing shout (*contra* Mark's reporting of the 'Elijah' material). The instrumental form at 14

Table 6.1. *Luke 23.44–6 and Mark 15.33–8*

	1	2	3	4	
Mk [33]	Καὶ	γενομένης	ὥρας ἕκτης		
Lk [44]	Καὶ	ἦν ἤδη ὡσεὶ	ὥρα ἕκτη	καὶ	
	5				
Mk	σκότος ἐγένετο ἐφ' ὅλην τὴν γῆν ἕως ὥρας ἐνάτης.				
Lk	σκότος ἐγένετο ἐφ' ὅλην τὴν γῆν ἕως ὥρας ἐνάτης				
	6	7			
Mk		(=23)			
Lk [45]	τοῦ ἡλίου ἐκλιπόντος,	ἐσχίσθη δὲ			
	8	9			
Mk	(=22)	(=24)			
Lk	τὸ καταπέτασμα τοῦ ναοῦ	μέσον.			
	10	11	12	13	14
Mk [34]	καὶ	τῇ ἐνάτῃ ὥρᾳ	ἐβόησεν	ὁ'Ιησοῦς	φωνῇ μεγάλῃ,
Lk [46]	καὶ		φωνήσας		φωνῇ μεγάλῃ
	15	16	17	18	
Mk	(=13)		Ελωι ελωι . . .	Mk 13.35, 36	
Lk	ὁ'Ιησοῦς	εἶπεν,	Πάτερ . . .	Lk 23.48	
	19	20	21		
Mk [37f.]	ὁ δὲ'Ιησοῦς ἀφεὶς φωνὴν μεγάλην	ἐξέπνευσεν.	[38]Καὶ		
Lk	τοῦτο δὲ εἰπὼν	ἐξέπνευσεν.			
	22	23	24		
Mk	τὸ καταπέτασμα τοῦ ναοῦ	ἐσχίσθη	εἰς δύο ἀπ ἄνωθεν ἕως κάτω.		
Lk	(=8)	(=7)	(=9?)		

must be given its proper force as a Markan element in the Lukan redaction.

Section 19 raises a problem which is probably insoluble but in relation to which one must take a stance. Luke *resumed* his narrative, τοῦτο δὲ εἰπών, *before* he reported that Jesus ἐξέπνευσεν (20 – identical with Mark but different from Matthew's ἀφῆκεν τὸ πνεῦμα). Is, then, Mark's ἀφεὶς φωνὴν μεγάλην also resumptive? It is just possible that Matthew sensed the difficulty here and settled it with his πάλιν (Matt. 27.50). Once one rearranges the synopticon the question 'How many cries?' becomes pressing.

Mark's meaning *may* be that although the mockers asked whether Elijah would come to save Jesus, Jesus, having uttered a great sound, the great sound referred to in Mark 15.34, *that sound which had brought about the mockers' misunderstanding,* expired. Matthew settled the matter for his readers: πάλιν[2] ensures that one understands that there were *two* cries from the cross. Luke settled the matter for his readers: τοῦτο δὲ εἴπων *implies that this evangelist knew of only one cry.*

Given Luke's transposition of Mark 15.38 to its new position before v. 34, the parallel Markan and Lukan sequences from section 10 to 20 are consistent, sharing a basic structure. Each begins with καὶ (10) followed by a verb (12), a reference to the subject (13 = 15) and an instrumental φώνῃ μεγάλῃ (14). A quotation from scripture follows (17), then a resumption of the subject's action (19) and, finally, ἐξέπνευσεν (20).

This underlying 'Markan' structure implies that Luke's redaction of section 17 and 18 was radical in the strictest sense of that word. *Assume* – before this probability is demonstrated in the remainder of this chapter – that Luke wished to remove Mark's Ελωι, ελωι . . . Such excision would entail the removal of Mark 15.35 and 36 simply because they depend *entirely* on the hearers' confusion of Ελωι and Ἠλιας (see Taylor, 1952, p. 593). This excision left Luke with Markan bystanders and their responses to the scene:[3] he tidied them into Luke 23.48–9. Once one recognises the inevitability of section 18's disappearance given a Lukan correction of 17, a rearrangement of the synopticon to give due weight to sections 12–15 seems more reasonable than the division in Aland and Huck.

The result of this rearrangement seems to be as follows:[4] Luke understood there to have been only one intelligible saying from the cross and he replaced Mark's desolate cry with an affirmation of trust derived from another psalm. Section 17 shows that one does not need to assume that Luke wanted to bypass Psalm 21(22); it is now clear that he *replaced* it. Whether Luke's was the theologically

2 Matt. 27.50

3 These bystanders play a more important part in Luke–Acts than is usually noted. Their 'seeing' function relates them naturally to the αὐτόπται of Luke's preface, giving a weight to this passion narrative which should not be undervalued. Mark's 'they all forsook him and fled' has no place in Luke where Jesus' friends *saw* what happened and could report the *manner* of his death. However one interprets the significance of this change, it gives strongly implied support to Luke's claim to have investigated these matters carefully, back to those who *saw* the events. Luke's differences from Mark's passion narrative demand careful reflection.

4 For the present, questions are left aside about Luke's placing the rending of the sanctuary veil to a point *before* Jesus' death. See Fitzmyer (1985, pp. 1518f.).

perceptive mind[5] which wrought this or whether he borrowed from a tradition which offered him this saying is less important than that his presentation of Jesus' death is made distinctive and coherent by the three elements examined in part II, including this last word.

If Luke's having considered accounts drawn up by 'many' (Luke 1.1–4) presented him with a variety of dominical 'last words', and he has studiously chosen to record both Jesus' word and that of the centurion in a form which echoes Wisdom's δίκαιος-model while differing from forms reported in the other canonical Gospels, then an interpreter is prompted to explore reasons for Luke's choosing as he did. First, what might dissuade Luke from staying with the 'cry of desolation'; second, what factors within the δίκαιος-model might lead Luke to choose something like Psalm 30.6; finally, is there a parallel tradition to Luke's concerning Jesus' death? Here, this excursus ends and the chapter's main argument resumes.

B. Why might Luke abandon Psalm 21(22).1?

Luke may simply have trusted and followed a tradition which included Psalm 30.6; but bracketing off that possibility, the question is put again. While there is no certain answer,[6] two lines of argument together constitute a strong case for Luke's intentional rejection of a tradition which used the word from Psalm 21(22). Each line of argument runs from what has already been established of Luke's composition: the centurion's glorifying God drew a reader's attention to Jesus' death as fulfilment of scripture (chapter 2); Jesus died as a δίκαιος, a term explored in Wisdom's model and in the Psalms (chapters 4 and 5 above); Luke knew of only one word of Jesus from the cross.

The essence of the following case is that once Luke had identified Jesus' passion, death and vindication as fulfilment of what scripture had said of a δίκαιος, the *character* of the δίκαιος portrayed in those scriptures

- **precluded** (if from the Psalms) any 'last word' which was not an affirmation of continuing trust in God;

[5] Scholars tend not to rate Luke very highly as a theologian (see, e.g., Barrett, 1979, p. 84), but he deserves more praise than he has been given for having told the story as a coherent whole.

[6] 'Luke's omission of Jesus' cry of dereliction on the cross (Mark 15.34–5) confirms for Dubois the association of Jesus with Elijah, for "si Jésus représente un Nouvel Elie, il ne peut pas s'appeler lui-même"' (Miller, 1988, p. 614).

– **required** (if from Wisdom) a final word exemplifying both Jesus' endurance in torment and his ἐπιείκεια.[7]

In practice, Luke seems to have drawn principally from Wisdom, turning to the Psalms for fuller information about the career of the δίκαιος.

Ἐγκαταλείπω in the Psalms

If one of Luke's pools of meaning for δίκαιος was in the Psalms, then one factor was probably sufficient to preclude Luke's use of the Markan cry of desolation: it employed a verb – ἐγκαταλείπω – which, to the psalmists, was the negation of vindication, itself an essential element in scripture's portrayal of God's δίκαιος. Some modern commentators, for example, Bock (1987, p. 147f.) and Taylor (1937, p. 200), have found difficulty in the cry of desolation's being Jesus' last word. The disturbed textual tradition exhibits a like difficulty for earlier Christians: for some copyists it was clearly the *verb* which was the problem. It was probably problematic for Luke whose systematic relating of Jesus' life to the fulfilment of scripture made considerable use of the Psalms. He was not averse from Psalm 21(22) *per se*; in fact he not only took over the bulk of traditional usage but also *developed* it. For example, he took over[8] the use of Psalm 21(22).19, but he knew that the psalm had also something to say of those who watched Jesus' sufferings:

> πάντες οἱ θεωροῦντές με ἐξεμυκτήρισάν με,
> ἐλάλησαν ἐν χείλεσιν, ἐκίνησαν κεφαλήν . . . (Ps. 21.8)

When Luke tidied his predecessors' narratives so that groups of people were sorted out and reported on separately, that verse from the psalmist, used *only* by Luke, was split between two groups:

> καὶ εἱστήκει ὁ λαὸς θεωρῶν (Luke 23.35a)
>
> ἐξεμυκτήριζον δὲ καὶ οἱ ἄρχοντες. (Luke 23.35b)

This Lukan echo from Psalm 21(22) exemplifies the evangelist's easy familiarity with scriptural passages which illuminated Jesus' suffer-

[7] In response to Stanton (1974, pp. 37f.) it may be urged that Jesus' patience and courage belong *together* with the fact of his death as fulfilment of scripture. Perhaps it is Stanton's 'merely' (1974, p. 38) which needs correction here. But Stanton had been convinced by Kilpatrick at Luke 23.47 (1974, p. 39 n. 1); the use of 'innocent' at this point destroys the scene's carefully crafted unity.

[8] But, if he borrowed from Mark, he altered Mark's *form* of the allusion, probably for stylistic reasons; see Marshall, 1978, p. 868.

ing and death and his willingness to summarise those events in scripture's words.[9]

A further example of Luke's willingness to summarise events surrounding Jesus' death in words from the Psalms is found at Luke 23.49, εἱστήκεισαν δὲ πάντες οἱ γνωστοὶ αὐτῷ ἀπὸ μακρόθεν.

Compare:

> οἱ φίλοι μου καὶ οἱ πλησίον μου ἐξ ἐναντίας μου
> ἤγγισαν καὶ ἔστησαν,
> καὶ οἱ ἔγγιστά μου ἀπὸ μακρόθεν ἔστησαν. (Ps. 37.12)

Luke's verse may conceivably echo Psalm 87.9

> ἐμάκρυνας τοὺς γνωστούς μου ἀπ' ἐμου ...

Luke's willingness to use psalms in this way is evident; that he was not averse from using Psalm 21(22) is equally clear. Why then did he not take over the cry of desolation? The answer is probably found in those psalms on which Luke drew as he spelled out how scripture had been fulfilled: those who were committed to God and lived trustingly *expected to be vindicated.* Bock, Taylor and some copyists looked for a different final word from the cry of desolation; so did the psalmists for whom the word ἐγκαταλείπω has profoundly negative connotations.

Louw and Nida (Vol. I.35.56, p. 465) have pointed out how 'to forsake' has senses which vary from language to language: desert, refuse to help, leave and refuse to care for. Usage within the psalms suggests the verb's covering this last sense – to desert and refuse to care for the suppliant. The following examples show how deeply negative this notion is to a Jew who trusts in God:

> ὅτι οὐκ εγ̓κατέλιπες τοὺς ἐκζητοῦντάς σε, Κύριε
> (Ps. 9.11)
> ὅτι οὐκ ἐγκαταλείψεις τηὺ ψυχήν μου εἰς ᾄδην
> οὐδὲ δώσεις τὸν ὅσιόν σου ἰδεῖν διαφθοράν.
> (Ps. 15.10 cf. Acts 2.25–28)

> ὅτι ὁ πατήρ μου καὶ ἡ μήτηρ μου ἐγκατέλιπόν με
> ὁ δὲ Κύριος προσελάβετό με ... (Ps. 26.10)

9 'Εξεμυκτήριζον appears in the NT only here and at Luke 16.14 where it is used of Pharisees who mocked Jesus' telling of the story of the Unjust Steward. Its use at 23.35–6 is most probably a direct echo of Ps. 21(22) because it stands immediately after an unquestionable allusion to that psalm reported in the Triple Tradition (Luke 23.34 = Ps. 21(22).19); see Chapter 7B, 'Criteria for allusion'.

νεώτερος ἐγενόμην καὶ γὰρ ἐγήρασα
καὶ οὐκ εἶδον δίκαιον ἐγκαταλελειμμένον . . . (Ps. 36.25)

ὅτι Κύριος ἀγαπᾷ κρίσιν
καὶ οὐκ ἐγκαταλείψει τοὺς ὁσίους αὐτοῦ (Ps. 36.28)

κατανοεῖ ὁ ἁμαρτωλὸς τὸν δίκαιον
καὶ ζητεῖ τοῦ θανατῶσαι αὐτόν,
ὁ δὲ Κύριος οὐ μὴ ἐγκαταλίπῃ αὐτὸν εἰς τὰς χεῖρας
αὐτοῦ . . . (Ps. 36.32–3)

μὴ ἐγκαταλίπῃς με, Κύριε·
ὁ Θεός μου, μὴ ἀποστῇς ἀπ' ἐμοῦ.
πρόσχες εἰς τὴν βοήθειάν μου, Κύριε τῆς σωτηρίας
μου. (Ps. 37.22)

Further, similar examples of the psalmists' horror of being forsaken by God are to be found at Psalms 70(71).9, 11; 93(94).14; 118(119).8; 139(140).9(NB).

Two of the extracts cited above need comment. **First,** in illustrating Luke's readiness to summarise in words of scripture events surrounding the cross, it was noted that he turned to Psalm 37.12 (Luke 23.49); might there also have been an echo of Psalm 37.22 in his mind (see the final citation above) – although Jesus' acquaintances stood aloof from him (v. 11) his prayer would have been that God would neither forsake him nor be aloof from him (37.22)? **Second,** at Acts 2.25–8, Luke turned to another psalm in this list, Psalm 15(16).10, to illustrate why death could not retain Jesus; scripture had affirmed that God would not abandon his holy one to death and corruption.[10] Luke, who made so much of scripture's

[10] REB's 'faithful servant' is positively misleading here. A *preacher* might also reflect on God's promise to another Ἰησοῦς, an earlier successor to Moses (Josh. 1.5–6):

καὶ ὥσπερ ἤμην μετὰ Μωϋσῆ, οὕτως ἔσομαι
καὶ μετὰ σοῦ καὶ οὐκ ἐγκαταλείψω σε
οὐδὲ ὑπερόψομαί σε. ἴσχυε καὶ ἀνδρίζου.

Given Luke's understanding of Jesus as the prophet like Moses (see the discussion above in chapter 2A 3. 'Luke 7.16'; see also chapter 2 note 14; cf. Luke 9.35; Acts 3.22; 7.37), it is difficult to believe that he did not know this promise. A *preacher* might also wonder whether Acts 10.38b (ὅτι ὁ Θεὸς ἦν μετ' αὐτοῦ) is not a sidelong glance at Josh. 1.5. But in his study a preacher might find it impossible to do more than note an interesting verbal echo which he can assign to a 'mood' of faith in God which permeates scripture: 'God does not abandon whom he calls.'

N-A 26, *Loci citati vel allegati*, has ten entries under Joshua for Luke–Acts, four of them in Stephen's speech. Because Luke clearly knew this book, may we infer

being fulfilled and who manifestly knew his psalms so well, could not have failed to see one fact – God would not *abandon* his saints and their confident prayer was that he would not do so.

Consequently, Luke's problem is clearer. First, Jesus was obviously a holy one, a δίκαιος in that his vindication was Luke's major theme: Jesus' resurrection, exaltation, his standing at God's right hand, his appearing to Stephen and to Paul, all witness to this central element in Luke's κήρυγμα. Second, however, equally obvious was scripture's testimony that God's saints had a horror of being abandoned by God and that their consistent prayer was that they might not be. Third, being vindicated was the contrary of being abandoned; Jesus had been vindicated, therefore he had *not* been abandoned. Fourth and consequently, Psalm 21(22).1 could not be Jesus' *final* word; it was so at odds with scripture, and, moreover, it was not drawn from that subset of psalms which overtly refer to the δίκαιος as their subject. Of course, Psalm 22 moves *through* despair to confidence; of course it echoes much of the crucifixion scene (or contributed to its detail); of course the citing of one verse might evoke awareness of the remainder with it. Those are all devices by which Christians have sought to explore the significance for themselves of Jesus' death.[11] Yet the textual tradition shows how difficult Christians have found the saying; Bock and Taylor illustrate how modern scholars seek an alternative climax (see Robinson, 1973, p. 84, n. 81). Arguably, Luke himself replaced this problematic citation with a more 'suitable' prayer, one which emphasised the loyalty and trust of 'a holy one' who hoped never to be abandoned, but, as will be argued below, Luke's version was probably controlled by the tradition that he knew (see D below).

The virtuous life of Wisdom's δίκαιος

If, however, Luke's principal scriptural pool of meaning was in Wisdom, Jesus' dying would be expected to reveal both his endurance under suffering and his ἐπιείκεια.

Luke's awareness of this firm inaugural promise of God to Ἰησοῦς? This would be confirmation of what God promised his δίκαιοι.

[11] Cotterell and Turner (1989, p. 72) distinguish carefully between two distinct elements within hermeneutics: the determination of *discourse meaning* or exegesis, that is, an interpreter's understanding of an author's intended meaning; the interpreting of the text, that is a search for understanding the significance *for one's own world* of a text's discourse meaning.

ἴδωμεν εἰ οἱ λόγοι αὐτοῦ ἀληθεῖς,
καὶ πειράσωμεν τὰ ἐν ἐκβάσει αὐτοῦ.
εἰ γάρ ἐστιν ὁ δίκαιος υἱὸς Θεοῦ, ἀντιλήμψεται αὐτοῦ
καὶ ῥύσεται αὐτὸν ἐκ χειρὸς ἀνθεστηκότων.
ὕβρει καὶ βασάνῳ ἐτάσωμεν αὐτόν,
ἵνα γνῶμεν τὴν ἐπιείκειαν αὐτοῦ
καὶ δοκιμάσωμεν τὴν ἀνεξικακίαν αὐτοῦ.
θανάτῳ ἀσχήμονι καταδικάσωμεν αὐτὸν,
ἔσται γὰρ αὐτοῦ ἐπισκοπὴ ἐκ λόγων αὐτοῦ.
(Wis. 2.17–20)

Within this section the major concern is with *pattern* rather than with verbal or structural dependence.[12] Drury, for example, comments on Luke's passion:

> Only in Luke does the end come so gently: in Mark and Matthew it is despair, in John, triumph ... Luke's account of Jesus' death is quieter and less distressing than Mark's, without the theological depth of John's. (1973, pp. 212f.)

Drury's response through *feeling* exemplifies an important element in any literary appreciation of the text; the reader *feels* that Luke's Jesus 'makes a good end'. Luke's account, however, also echoes the passage cited above from Wisdom. **First,** it is an account of a man *tested by his opponents* (πειράσωμεν).[13] Luke's narrative shows Jesus being tested by thorough and exhaustive examination (so Louw and Nida, 27.46) while being *systematically observed* by named groups (e.g. Luke 23.35–49; see chapter 7). At the close of the scene more observers are noted: the centurion, Jesus' friends and his women companions (Luke 23.47–9). This is a more ordered account than that found in Mark or Matthew. **Second,** Luke's is an account whose text might well have been ἔσται γὰρ αὐτοῦ ἐπισκοπὴ ἐκ λόγων αὐτοῦ: here is a distinct mood of quiet confidence in God. This narrative is, in a strict sense, preparatory to the vindication that stands at the heart of Luke's work, and it is not without its own

12 Wenham (1991, p. 54) comments that 'The only safe criterion of literary dependence is the plain man's test: Is there consistent evidence of either copying of order or copying of the actual wording?' In chapter 7B, 'Criteria for allusion', a very different group of criteria is suggested.

13 Verbal frequency tests support this judgment. Of the twenty-nine uses of πειράζω//πειρασμός in the Gospels and Acts, fourteen occur in Luke–Acts; that is, 48.2 per cent of the word group's occurrences are found in 45 per cent of the text. Πειρασμός is Luke's preferred use: 70 per cent of the noun's appearances in the Gospels and Acts are found in Luke–Acts. See further, chapter 7C below.

theological depth (*contra* Drury above). *This* death is a testing of the δίκαιος: εἰ γάρ ἐστιν ὁ δίκαιος υἱὸς Θεοῦ, ἀντιλήμψεται αὐτοῦ.[14] It is not Elijah who is to save Jesus, but God, and this death is to test the δίκαιος to the very end – 'he will be looked after, we have his word for it'. That this testing is also a testing by God is implied by Wisdom 3.5, and a nearby statement offered good reason why Jesus should commend his spirit to God – Wisdom 3.1 is another way of saying what the psalm said and has the virtue of demonstrating that Jesus was a δίκαιος. **Third,** Luke's account exhibits two features not obvious in the others: Luke has emphasised both Jesus' ἐπιείκεια and his ἀνεξικακία (cf. Wis. 2.17–20). The latter quality, according to Louw and Nida (25.170) is one of 'enduring difficulties without becoming angry or upset'; according to Liddell and Scott it is one of 'enduring torment'. By his rejection of the 'Markan' cry of desolation and his substitution of Psalm 30.6 Luke has unambiguously demonstrated Jesus' ἀνεξικακία – and one recalls that Luke's centurion, on seeing what had happened, is made to say

> Ὄντως ὁ ἄνθρωπος οὗτος δίκαιος ἦν. (Luke 23.47)

Luke's account also appears to emphasise Jesus' ἐπιείκεια. Louw and Nida (88.62) characterise the word as indicating gentleness, graciousness, forbearance. At least four elements in the Lukan narrative portray this quality in Jesus. First, at Luke 23.28–31 his word to the lamenting women points away from his own fate to that awaiting them and their friends; his concern is for the welfare of others. Second, at Luke 23.34 Luke records Jesus' word of forgiveness for his (unspecified) tormentors. There has been much discusssion of the 'rightness' of this saying in Luke's text: on balance, the saying is probably a Lukan element and may, consequently, be claimed as another example of Jesus' ἐπιείκεια (see section D below, 'Jesus and Stephen: Master and martyr'; see also Squires, 1993, p. 170). **Third,** Luke's cameo of Jesus' conversation with the penitent thief (Luke 23.40–3) is a further instance of this

[14] Wis. 2.18a. The second part of the verse also supports this argument–καὶ ῥύσεται αὐτὸν ἐκ χειρὸς ἀνθεστηκότων. The δίκαιος can trustingly commend himself to God's hands – a trust noted at Wis. 3.1. It is difficult to avoid an impression that the author of Wisdom deliberately contrasted *God's hands* with those of the ἀσεβεῖς. We shall later reflect on the place in Luke's narrative of the notion of Jesus' being betrayed, or handed over, into men's hands (e.g. Luke 9.44 and 24.19–20; 18.31–4; 20.20, although at 23.46 the evangelist makes a different point; see chapter 7).

quality in that the manner of his attention to the other is both gentle and gracious.[15] **Fourth,** as Neyrey (1980, revised 1985, pp. 49–68) and Squires (1992, p. 170) have strongly argued, Luke's version of Jesus' betrayal at night in an orchard has an emotionless quality which demands some sort of explanation. This scene includes not merely a noble attitude in the face of impending malign fate but a 'sweet reasonableness' toward both the disciples and those who arrest him; this is a living out of both ἀνεξικακία and ἐπιείκεια.

Given the initial clue that Luke held Jesus' death to be that of a δίκαιος (chapter 4) and his commitment to tell Jesus' story as fulfilment of scripture (Luke 1.1–4; 24.25–7, 44–7), one cannot but be impressed by the coherence of Luke's account with the paradigm drawn from Wisdom 2.10–3.5. Drury's judgment that Luke's account lacks the theological depth of John remains debatable, yet his narrative exemplifies Luke's theme of fulfilment. *This* death was a living out of the Wisdom δίκαιος-model: tested by scoffers, trusting himself into God's hands, as his witnesses testified, Jesus was really (ὄντως, Luke 24.34, see chapter 7A below) vindicated by God. But one more detail in Wisdom's model must be noted here. Luke, who drew on Wisdom's history in Stephen's speech, would probably have known what Wisdom had to say in detail of Joseph:

αὕτη πραθέντα δίκαιον οὐκ ἐγκατέλιπεν . . . (Wis. 10.13)

So Luke's Wisdom-model and the Psalms agreed that God (Σοφία) would not abandon, had not abandoned, his δίκαιος. *How far* Luke was influenced by Wisdom 10.13–14 is not a pressing concern, but its clear paradigmatic statement of God's vindication of a δίκαιος is impressive, leading to

. . . ἕως ἤνεγκεν αὐτῷ σκῆπτρα βασιλείας
. . . καὶ ἔδωκεν αὐτῷ δόξαν αἰώνιον.

It is enough to recognise that Joseph-δίκαιος was not abandoned.

Luke's earliest readers must have shared in his finding in Wisdom and the Psalms these two lines of argument leading from distinct, but conceptually convergent, scriptural sources to a model of the death of the δίκαιος. These two lines preclude a 'cry of desolation', demanding instead a final word expressive of unconditional com-

[15] Neyrey (1985, pp. 133–40) made much of this incident as an indicator of Lukan soteriology. Matthew Arnold understood ἐπιείκεια as 'sweet reasonableness'.

mitment to God by his δίκαιος. This Lukan 'final word' must now be examined.

C. Psalm 30.6 in Luke's composition[16]

According to Luke, Jesus' final word was:

Πάτερ, εἰς χεῖράς σου παρατίθεμαι τὸ πνεῦμά μου.
(Luke 23.46)

The psalmist's expression of confident trust had been only slightly different:

εἰς χεῖράς σου παραθήσομαι τὸ πνεῦμά μου ... (Ps. 30.6)

Luke, however, made two significant changes: first, Jesus' form of address to God, Πάτερ, is that of the prayer he taught his disciples (Luke 11.2), of the prayer of agony in Gethsemane (Luke 22.42) and of his prayer for God's forgiveness of his persecutors (Luke 23.34; see also D below). It is also the name by which Wisdom's δίκαιος addressed God.[17] Second, the psalmist's confident future tense has become an 'existential' present; in the moment of Jesus' death Luke saw scripture being fulfilled.

It is entirely possible that Luke chose this word rather than another because the tradition he trusted offered these as Jesus' final words. Another reason sometimes offered is that these words formed a regular Jewish evening prayer and that Jesus would habitually have used them in this way. Evidence for this suggestion is late (SB II.269) and not convincing for so early a period. A more compelling reason relates Jesus' words to Luke's matrix undergirding the death scene – the confident loyalty to God of the δίκαιος both in the face of his enemies and throughout his own undeserved suffering, together with his equally confident expectation of vindication *by* God: Psalm 30.6 coheres with Wisdom 3.1.

While Luke almost certainly would not have formally identified a subset of psalms which might be called δίκαιος-psalms, his own use

[16] Cf. Powell (1989).

[17] Given the fact that the use of this term by the δίκαιος was one important ground of the ungodly's hatred of him (e.g. Wis. 2.16b), the addition of Πάτερ to the psalmist's word at Luke 23.46 may be taken as confirmation of Luke's use of the Wisdom model. The ungodly purposed to *test* the δίκαιος with insult and torture, to explore his gentleness and forbearance, to see if his words (that God is his Father) were true (Wis. 2.12–20). See chapter 7 below for an exploration of 'sonship' (the correlative of Father) as fulfilment of God's promise.

of scripture points to an awareness that some words were particularly appropriate to events in Jesus' life. Psalm 30.6, however, clearly belongs to such a subset if one groups those psalms whose defining characteristic is a concern with the fortunes of, *and* the use of the word, δίκαιος:

> ἄλαλα γενηθήτω τὰ χείλη τὰ δόλια
> τὰ λαλοῦντα κατὰ τοῦ δικαίου ἀνομίαν
> ἐν ὑπερηφανίᾳ καὶ ἐξουδενώσει. (Ps. 30.19(31.18))

This suppliant was a δίκαιος. What is more he was certain that God had not abandoned him:

> καὶ οὐ συνέκλεισάς με εἰς χεῖρας ἐχθροῦ . . . (v. 9)

While there are certainly elements in it which 'reflect' the sufferings of the crucified Jesus, particularly vv. 9–13, it is an air of robust conviction that God *will* save his people which pervades this psalm, culminating in:

> ἀγαπήσατε τὸν Κύριον, πάντες οἱ ὅσιοι αὐτοῦ
> ὅτι ἀληθείας ἐκζητεῖ Κύριος
> καὶ ἀνταποδίδωσιν τοῖς περισσῶς ποιοῦσιν ὑπερηφανίαν.
> ἀνδρίζεσθε, καὶ κραταιούσθω ἡ καρδία ὑμῶν,
> πάντες οἱ ἐλπίζοντες ἐπὶ Κύριον (Ps. 30.24–5(31.23–4))

These verses cohere with the thrust of Luke's appeal to his readers for confident discipleship as he 'reported' Jesus' words:

> ἀρχομένων δὲ τούτων γίνεσθαι
> ἀνακύψατε καὶ ἐπάρατε τὰς κεφαλὰς ὑμῶν,
> διότι ἐγγίζει ἡ ἀπολύτρωσις ὑμῶν. (Luke 21.28)

> ἀγρυπνεῖτε δὲ ἐν παντὶ καιρῷ
> δεόμενοι ἵνα κατισχύσητε ἐκφυγεῖν ταῦτα πάντα τὰ μέλλοντα γίνεσθαι, καὶ
> σταθῆναι ἔμπροσθεν τοῦ υἱοῦ τοῦ ἀνθρώπου.
> (Luke 21.36)

Consequently, what may be said of Luke's choice of this saying as Jesus' final, conclusive, climactic word? **First**, it is drawn from a δίκαιος-psalm which belongs to a stratum of scripture known to have influenced his thinking about Jesus' death (cf. his composition at Luke 23.47; *contra* Conzelmann, 1960, pp. 88f.). **Second**, the overall thrust of this psalm is an appeal to God's people to be confident; the psalm moves from an individual saint's experience to a more general appeal. **Third**, this thrust is paralleled in Luke's reporting Jesus' appeal to his disciples to be confident. **Fourth**, this appeal came from one who, adopting the words of the psalmist, expressed his own trust in and commitment to God; Jesus, in Luke's presentation of him, *cannot have been less trusting and confident than he asked of his disciples.*

Although the question is probably unanswerable,[18] it is proper to ask why Luke chose this psalm rather than another. Section D below sheds some light on the question, but one further factor remains to be taken into account: if Luke was really working with Wisdom's model then he cannot have been unaware of the close parallel to Psalm 30.6 to be found at Wisdom 3.1 –

> Δικαίων δὲ ψυχαὶ ἐν χειρὶ Θεοῦ,
> καὶ οὐ μὴ ἅψηται αὐτῶν βάσανος ...

By his 'praying' Psalm 30.6 Jesus was clearly 'fulfilling' what Wisdom had shown to be the case with δίκαιοι; *this* δίκαιος, *in extremis*, was a model of God's trusting and faithful man.

Two recent writers offer support to this view. Both Beck and Neyrey have discerned the significance for Luke's theology of Jesus' appeal to Psalm 30.6. Neyrey's (1985) six chapters are loosely grouped in that they are based on Luke's passion narrative. Neyrey's treatment of Luke 23.46 emphasised Luke's redaction of Mark, tracing his prime reason for doing so to Psalm 16, one of the premier Lukan scriptural proofs that God had promised to raise the dead. By his redaction Luke had shown his church how to die; additionally, this redaction had clearly demonstrated Jesus' faith in God. Beck (1981), examining the centurion's confession in relation to this theme, actually isolated and briefly explored each of the elements identified in this study as significant for an assessment of what Luke apparently intended to convey at Luke 23.47. Beck rightly noted that δίκαιος can hardly be restricted to 'innocent'; that ἐδόξαζεν τὸν Θεόν most probably signifies the centurion's giving conscious praise to God; that δίκαιος 'hardly figures as a technical designation for the Servant' (p 43). He continues:

[18] An obvious and not to be too quickly dismissed possibility is that Luke 'chose' this psalm because the tradition he most respected, whether written or oral, assured him that this was what Jesus actually said; this possibility is discussed in section D below; see also note 3 above.

> Instead we must look elsewhere. It is surprising that, among the surviving early Jewish documents that deal with the sufferings of the righteous, more attention has not been given by commentators to Wisdom 1–5, particularly in view of the parallels contained in these chapters to the Passion narratives especially in the section 1:16–3:9. (1981, p. 43f.)

Building on this insight, Beck almost incidentally noted of Psalm 30.6:

> While commentators observe that this is the prayer of the pious Israelite before sleeping, it is also, in the context of the entire psalm, a prayer of the righteous (verse 19, τοῦ δικαίου) for deliverance, which is appropriate to the context of Wisdom 2. If Luke had the ideas of Wisdom in mind, this may have been part of the reason for the choice of these particular words to make up for the omission of the cry of dereliction (Mark 15:34). (1981, p. 45)

D. Discipleship, trust and Jesus' passion: 1 Peter and Acts

More important, however, than support from recent writers is confirmation of Luke's δίκαιος-matrix from within Luke–Acts and 1 Peter. Within Luke's own scheme and in a letter reflecting another NT writer's thought there is *a pattern of discipleship* in which Christians are called both to entrust themselves to God and to model their living and dying on Jesus who, in each case, is called δίκαιος; this modelling is overt in 1 Peter and strongly implied in the Acts. What is important for the present case is to note that this pattern of discipleship implies an underlying account of Jesus' death which must have included a word from the dying Jesus very like, if not identical with, that found at Luke 23.46.

Because this discipleship pattern is so deeply embedded in Luke–Acts and, more especially so, in 1 Peter it may be properly inferred that Luke's composition at Luke 23.46 was influenced by a body of Christian tradition in which Jesus' dying word was one of trust and confidence – e.g. Psalm 30.6. It may be that Luke systematically rewrote Mark's account, correcting his predecessor's portrayal of Jesus; if so, this correction is in a direction validated by someone claiming to be a witness of Jesus' sufferings (1 Peter 5.1) – and Luke also claims to stand within that tradition handed on from the αὐτόπται (Luke 1.2). How one assesses the value of these things belongs to another study than this; what is important is the existence of a parallel tradition testifying to an underlying passion narrative like Luke's. His passion narrative, consequently, is neither capricious nor bathetic, but moves systematically in a direction concerned not only with the fulfilment of scripture but also with what he learned from the αὐτόπται and ministers of the word of the manner of Jesus' dying.

A Δίκαιος-matrix in 1 Peter?

This epistle's 'preoccupation with suffering and with Christian behaviour under it, is unique to I Peter ... ' (Robinson, 1976, p. 152). Throughout the letter the theme of discipleship under stress is interwoven with recollections of and reflections on the story of Jesus' passion (Elliott, J. H., 1985, pp. 184–209). Within this complex pattern there are two probable linkings of the *thrust* of Psalm 30.6 with the disciples' calling, and in each case there is also a tight link with Jesus' dying. The clearer of the two allusions is found at 1 Peter 4.19:

> ὥστε καὶ οἱ πάσχοντες κατὰ τὸ θέλημα τοῦ θεοῦ πιστῷ κτίστῃ παρατιθέσθωσαν τὰς ψυχὰς αὐτῶν ἐν ἀγαθοποιΐᾳ.

N-A 26 notes this parallel at Luke 23.46, the target passage; there are distinct features of a δίκαιος-matrix in its context. **First**, it addresses suffering for the sake of goodness: 'for Christ', 'as Christians', 'for the Name' (4.14–16). **Second**, there is clear reminiscence of the age-long conflict between those who suffer for doing right and the 'ungodly' and 'sinners' (4.18b); those who suffer for right are characterised as δίκαιος (4.18a) as the author cites Proverbs 11.31[19]:

> εἰ ὁ μὲν δίκαιος μόλις σῴζεται,
> ὁ ἀσεβὴς καὶ ἁμαρτωλὸς ποῦ φανεῖται;

Third, as in Wisdom's matrix, so here also, suffering is God's *testing*: the disciples' *fiery ordeal* (4.12) is *God's judgment* (4.17) beginning with his own οἶκος. This understanding leads to a call to disciples –

[19] Although the Proverbs treatment of the concept δίκαιος differs from that in the Psalms and in Wisdom in that it has no humiliation/vindication dimension, it does have both a clear-cut contrast between *righteous* and *sinner* and an affirmation of God's care for the righteous. The difference is enough to require a *formal* exclusion of Proverbs from the scriptural pool on which Luke drew for his δίκαιος-model.

those who suffer according to God's will – to commit themselves by doing good to the God who can be trusted. There is much here that is redolent of Jesus' death scene, and it seems that according to this writer disciples who suffer for God's sake entrust themselves to God in words very like those of their dying Lord; it is notable that this author had earlier characterised Jesus' death as that of a δίκαιος (3.18).

A second and rather less clear allusion to Luke 23.46 stands at 1 Peter 2.23b:

> παρεδίδου δὲ [ἑαυτὸν] τῷ κρίνοντι δικαίως.

This falls within the *Haustafeln*, particularly within that group dealing with servants' behaviour under ill treatment. Discipleship here is overtly *imitatio Christi*:

> εἰς τοῦτο γὰρ ἐκλήθητε,
> ὅτι καὶ Χριστὸς ἔπαθεν ὑπὲρ ὑμῶν,
> ὑμῖν ὑπολιμπάνων ὑπογραμμὸν
> ἵνα ἐπακολουθήσητε τοῖς ἴχνεσιν αὐτοῦ. (2.21)

This pattern for servants to follow is probably intentionally expressed in language borrowed from Isaiah 53 (so Elliott, J. H., 1985, p. 193ff.), although its underlying soteriology is substantially different from Luke's. Its literary structure is formulaic (see Elliott, J. H., 1985, pp. 190f. and Selwyn, 1952, pp. 179f. and 268–81), hymnic or confessional, a fact clearly indicated in N-A 26:

> ὃς λοιδορούμενος οὐκ ἀντελοιδόρει,
> πάσχων οὐκ ἠπείλει,
> παρεδίδου δὲ τῷ κρίνοντι δικαίως. (2.23)

This possibly indicates a pattern of thought older than the epistle itself, a fact of special interest, since it discloses something fundamental in Jesus' dying which disciples must also embrace.[20]

Disciples are reminded that Jesus 'handed himself over' and was not simply 'delivered up'. He gave himself up to the One who judges justly – in contrast to those judges who encompassed or acquiesced

[20] Interestingly, 1 Pet. 5.5–6 alludes to another fundamental aspect of disciples' behaviour, ταπεινοφροσύνη, which its author shares with Luke: Ταπεινώθητε οὖν ὑπὸ τὴν κραταιὰν χεῖρα τοῦ θεοῦ, ἵνα ὑμᾶς ὑψώσῃ ἐν καιρῷ. This Lukan emphasis was explored in chapter 4C (and in note 31) above, concluding that for Luke one of the defining characteristics of a δίκαιος was that disposition marked out by ταπεινῶν ἑαυτὸν; this attitude seems to be deeply embedded in the tradition about Jesus.

in Jesus' ill-treatment and condemnation (see chapter 7E below). The letter's readers might be expected to know that the One who judges justly is that same One who also vindicates his faithful ones. It is difficult to avoid the impression that 2.23b is at least a paraphrase of what is more obviously at 4.19 an allusion to something like Luke 23.46. The underlying Petrine passion story knows that the dying Jesus entrusted himself to God. If the author was genuinely a witness of Jesus' sufferings – and there seems no good reason to doubt this (so Selwyn, 1952, pp. 30–33, 228f.) – then Luke's narrative at Luke 23.46 coheres with an apparently early testimony to 'what happened.' This first example comes from a source external to Luke–Acts; the second comes from within it.

Jesus and Stephen: Master and martyr

καὶ ἐλιθοβόλουν τὸν Στέφανον ἐπικαλούμενον καὶ λέγοντα, Κύριε Ἰησοῦ, δέξαι τὸ πνεῦμά μου. θεὶς δὲ τὰ γόνατα ἔκραξεν φωνῇ μεγάλῃ, Κύριε, μὴ στήσῃς αὐτοῖς ταύτην τὴν ἁμαρτίαν. καὶ τοῦτο εἰπὼν ἐκοιμήθη.

(Acts 7.59–60)

This scene, from within Luke's own work, also sheds light on his composition of Luke 23.46–7 because it offers a model of how Christians ought to die.[21] The model here is like that set out in 1 Peter: let those who suffer according to the will of God (e.g., Stephen) entrust themselves to a faithful Creator. There is also a widely acknowledged, close match between Stephen's death and that of Jesus (see table 6.2). It is *more likely* that a pattern of martyr-dying would grow up in the light of a passion narrative rather than precede it: the servant is not above his Lord nor the manner of his dying more δίκαιος-like. Consequently, in Luke's church, or among those with whom he had discussed the matter, or from whom he had learnt the tradition (αὐτόπται), Jesus' dying words can hardly have been less δίκαιος-like than those of this proto-martyr (Acts 7.60): the pattern of entrusting oneself to God's care while suffering 'in his Name' is built into the fabric of Luke's two-volume work.

It is quite clear, however, that Stephen's prayer, cited at the head of this section, is only a distant allusion to Psalm 30.6, recognisably transformed by Christian tradition. Its formal address is now Κύριε

[21] It also echoes the trust expressed in Wis. 3.1.

Ἰησοῦ *vice* Πάτερ; it seems that what is being stressed here is that God's δίκαιος, Jesus, who has suffered and been vindicated, is now, as Son of man, at God's right hand, the head and representative of all God's faithful saints who are one day to stand before him (Luke 21.36).[22] Those who live and die 'in his Name' expect to be gathered together with him before God in a like vindication and to inherit the Kingdom. Stephen's martyrdom actually links his vision of the Son of man at God's right hand (Acts 7.56) and his understanding of Jesus as δίκαιος (Acts 7.52). Haenchen's comment (1971, p. 296) is rather bland and obvious: 'Thus we encounter a specifically Christian devotion which is already so centred on Jesus that it is *his* name which is invoked in the hour of death.' Of course; but why? Devotion usually gathers around a 'vision' of what is greatly valued; what Stephen is said to have valued was his conviction that Jesus was God's man; his vision confirmed this – Jesus, the vindicated Son of man, was at God's right hand, *standing* before his accusers and waiting to be joined by God's saints, of whom Stephen prayed to be one.

The brief, but identical, phrase, τὸ πνεῦμά μου, links this passage, Luke 23.46 and Psalm 30.6. It is also possible that the verb – δέξαι – accents all that is said above of Jesus' place in God's economy of salvation. In this scheme, Jesus was the δίκαιος whose unconditional self-entrustment to God (Neyrey's 'faith') issued in his vindication; Stephen's prayer was that he might be joined with his Master (Κύριος, but see also Luke 21.36 for its link with 'the Son of man'.)

This proto-martyr's death was, as Conzelmann (1987, p. 61) noted, very reminiscent of the death of Christ (Fitzmyer, 1989, pp. 117–45 offers a penetrating essay on discipleship in Luke–Acts). Talbert (1974, pp. 96f.) claims that the scene is a key example of a principle of *imitatio Magistri* in Acts, one element in the succession motif. One does not have to accept Talbert's whole thesis about the genre of Luke to recognise that there is considerable structural parallelism between the Gospel and Acts. The parallels that he has highlighted (see table 6.2) between Stephen's death and that of Jesus are clear examples of Luke's interest in a close relationship between Christian discipleship and Jesus' death.

22 '[Luke] 23,34.46, when compared with Acts 7, 59.60, suggest that the disciple may and should imitate the suffering and dying Jesus' (Barrett, 1979, p. 77).

Table 6.2. *Parallels between the death of Jesus and that of Stephen*

	Jesus (Luke)	Stephen (Acts)
Trial before Sanhedrin	22.69–71	6.12–15
Martyr-death	.....	.....
'Commit/receive' word	23.46	7.59
'Forgive persecutors' word	23.34	7.60
Son of man *logion*	22.69	7.56
Converted others	23.39–43	8.1–4

To Talbert's list two other features should be added. First, just as each death is related to a saying about Jesus and the Son of man, so each is related to a reference to Jesus as δίκαιος (Luke 23.47 cf. Acts 7.52). Second, and not to be pressed too hard, each death has one saying which is uttered μεγάλῃ φωνῇ; this may or may not be significant, but given that Luke uses the term as a kind of stock rhetorical phrase, it should be noted. The parallelism of these two deaths appears intentional.

One may immediately object that an impressive case can be made for the Gospel's passion narrative having been accommodated to that in the Acts: the objection needs to be met. It rests on substantial textual evidence which points to Luke 23.34's being an interpolation, evidence which cannot be ignored. Some English translations omit Jesus' prayer that his tormentors might be forgiven because they did not know what they were doing; others send the saying to a footnote. The N-A 26 textual apparatus certainly gives one pause. To omit from the Gospel this saying about forgiveness would significantly diminish the 'Talbert' parallels, *but still leave enough to ensure that Luke's patterning remains part of the evidence.*

If this is the case, then the *logion*'s appearance at Acts 7.60 should be taken as one element in favour of the Lukan saying's rightful place in his Gospel. It is possible to see how, at a very early stage in the text's transmission, Christian scribes raised questions about their Lord's words: did Jesus' persecutors *really* not know what they were doing (*pace* the 'ignorance motif' in Acts; cf. chapter 7H below); since there was now a gulf between church and synagogue had Jesus *really* forgiven 'the Jews'? [*pace* his recorded teaching on reconciliation]; was it possible, some asked, that a church could continue to pray for the forgiveness of those who had rejected and brought about the death of the Lord?[23]

An argument that the internal structure of Luke–Acts adds considerable weight for the 'forgiveness' *logion*'s proper inclusion in the text of the gospel needs more detailed exploration than is possible here. Marshall (1978, pp. 867f.), Beck (1981, p. 45, n. 55) and Vermes (1993, p. 161, n. 11) incline to its inclusion although Fitzmyer's way of reporting matters (1985, pp. 1503f.) suggests his vote for exclusion. None of them, it seems, has drawn attention to the significance for this discussion of Luke's report of Jesus' ethical teaching, especially Luke 6.27–8.

> Ἀλλὰ ὑμῖν λέγω τοῖς ἀκούουσιν, ἀγαπᾶτε τοὺς ἐχθροὺς ὑμῶν, καλῶς ποιεῖτε τοῖς μισοῦσιν ὑμᾶς, εὐλογεῖτε τοὺς καταρωμένους ὑμᾶς, προσεύχεσθε περὶ τῶν ἐπηρεαζόντων ὑμᾶς.

Verses 29, 35 and 37 amplify the forgiving disposition commended in Luke's sermon – a disposition commended also, for example, in Romans 12.14 and in 1 Corinthians 4.12. In short, prayer for one's persecutors appears to have been a feature of discipleship among 'Pauline' churches, and, moreover, to have been derived from dominical authority. It is almost impossible to conceive of Luke's not having attributed to Jesus a virtue the evangelist manifestly held to be important in those who *followed* the Lord. This kind of consideration properly figures in the eclecticism now practised by textual critics: while the argument from *textual* evidence is very strong the *thematic* evidence tells against it.

Clearly, the character of Christian discipleship according to Luke (see Fitzmyer, 1989) and his reporting of Jesus' own life cohere. Equally clearly, there is a sense in which this passion scene coheres with what was found in 1 Peter – a Master-disciple modelling. In both the epistle and Acts disciple and Master share a trust in and

[23] Taylor (1954, pp. 216f.) cites Hort, Streeter, Rendel Harris and W.L. Knox in support of the 'authenticity' of this disputed *logion*. He notes that Streeter 'quotes with approval the suggestion of J. Rendel Harris, that the phrase was deleted because some Christian in the second century found it hard to believe that God could or ought to forgive the Jews. Recently, W.L. Knox has expressed the same view.' So also Vermes (1993, p. 161 n. 11). Sanders' charge of anti-Semitism is probably more soundly brought against those who *omitted* this *logion* about forgiveness than against Luke.

commitment to God conveyed in words cited from or very close in sentiment to Psalm 30.6.[24]

E. Summary

All of this implies that Luke's composition at Luke 23.46 both accorded with passion traditions valued by his own and at least one other Christian community, and was constrained by what scripture had said of the δίκαιος. Consequently, Luke's representing Jesus' death and vindication in conformity with a δίκαιος-matrix is not necessarily an editorial freedom of a sort to impugn his integrity as a historian. It is unlikely that Luke dealt in pure invention; a 'both/and' reflects what this chapter has shown of Luke's practice – he *both* celebrates scriptural fulfilment *and* affirms what tradition had to say of Jesus' dying word.

While this argument does not offer irrefragable proof that these things are so, it does offer a probable and coherent paradigm for Luke's version of the passion narrative so that his distinctive elements at Luke 23.46 and 47 support one another, each making more likely the others' place in a Wisdom model. If this be so, Kilpatrick's allegation against Luke – that his changes would make no sense to his readers or might prove mere bathos – is to be rejected. Part III will explore some consequences of rejecting Kilpatrick's case and affirming Luke's recourse at Luke 23.46–7 to a systematic δίκαιος-model, drawn principally from Wisdom but indebted also to the more diffuse picture of a δίκαιος drawn by the psalmists. Because, as chapter 7 will suggest, Luke's debt to Wisdom is more extensive than these two verses have revealed, in chapter 8 it becomes possible to infer that Luke's δίκαιος-model is also an implied *theologia crucis*.

24 Given this study's appeal to 1 Peter for support for Luke's version of Jesus' last word, should one appeal to Hebrews (e.g. Heb. 5.7) for support for Mark's? Moffatt (1924, pp. 64f.) relates this verse to an echo of Ps. 22, but does not specifically refer to the Markan cry of dereliction. N-A 26 notes a parallel to the Matthaean Gethsemane (Matt. 26.38–46).

PART III

Echoes of Wisdom in Luke's theology of the cross

7

WISDOM IN LUKE'S PASSION STORY

> Il y a beaucoup de raisons d'affirmer – constatait G. Kuhn il y a plusieurs années déjà – que le livre de la Sagesse jouissait d'une grande estime chez les auteurs du Nouveau Testament. On le lisait assidûment et ses traces se retrouvent aujourd'hui aussi bien chez saint Paul que dans l'Apocalypse, dans les Evangiles, et, peut-être, dans l'Epître aux Hébreux et dans l'Epître de Jacques.
>
> (Romaniuk, 1968, p. 498)

Starting with this quotation from Kuhn,[1] Romaniuk set out to identify traces of Wisdom in the New Testament. This chapter's purpose is more focused: it will examine whether in Luke's passion narrative there is evidence of the 'assiduous reading' of Wisdom alleged by Kuhn, whether 'traces' of the book can be found (hereafter called 'echoes'), and whether such echoes may count as evidence for Luke's knowing and using Wisdom. Romaniuk identified a trace of Wisdom in Matthew's passion narrative (1968, pp. 499f.) but turned to Luke's description of the end of the world, echoing God's judgment on the ungodly (Wis. 5.22–3), for evidence of Luke's use of the book. What follows is not so much a dialogue with Romaniuk's article, which offers no more than two sides of a page on three Synoptists, but rather a keeping in mind what he set out to do and occasional reflection on his findings.

Close study of Luke 23.46–7 clarified three issues which lead towards understanding Luke's *theologia crucis*. First, it was able to set aside a 'political' apologetic element and restore the 'religious' element to its proper place in Luke's thought, implying that Kilpa-

[1] Kuhn, G, 'Beitrage zur Erklärung des Buches der Weisheit,' *ZNW* XXVIII (1929) pp. 338ff. Maclachlan (1920) examined Luke's work in relation to Wisdom; see also Conzelmann (1976), Horbury (1994) and Sugirtharajah (1990) for perspectives on the issue. See also Winston (1979).

trick should not be followed in translating δίκαιος as 'innocent' unless compelling new reasons were adduced. Second, it concluded that the presence of ἐδόξαζεν τὸν Θεόν at this point highlights Luke's fundamental concern with the fulfilment of scripture, so his 'scriptural' emphasis turns out to feature also in his account of Jesus' cross. Third, it assumed that Luke addressed his story to a *corpus mixtum* in which Jew, God-fearer and Gentile sought confirmation in scripture that they were truly heirs of the promises of God so lately fulfilled among them. Further, these two verses (23.46–7) constitute a distinctive Lukan scene, significantly different from the accounts found in the other canonical Gospels; thus, Luke's choice of δίκαιος as a descriptor of Jesus, here and in his usage of the term in the Acts, demands consideration. It is Luke's emphasis on δίκαιος which becomes the present point of entry into an exploration of his larger debt to Wisdom.

A. Literary echoes and a Lukan dialogue with Wisdom

Pace Kuhn's opinion, this study does not seek to confirm that Wisdom was the popular, Sunday afternoon reading of first-century Christian congregations; it does, however, look for the 'traces' of which Kuhn wrote. What is already notable is that through the horizontal plane of these two Lukan verses pass a number of other literary planes, some of which carry Luke's *intra*-textual themes. Other literary planes, with more complex *inter*-textual surfaces, intersect Luke's work at varying angles which range through 'vertical' quotations from clearly identifiable scriptural sources to 'oblique' possible *allusions* to, or even echoes from, scripture.

Intra-textually, although writers like Tannehill (1961, 1986 and 1990) and Johnson (1991 and 1992) have exposed much of Luke's careful composition, much probably remains to be explored in these two volumes. Studies of the narrative unities of Luke–Acts have shown how complex a work Luke's is and how carefully he develops his themes. From within the two focal verses (Luke 23.46–7) one may look back on his 'Father' theme, beginning in the birth narratives and culminating in the last word from the cross; similarly, 'into thy hands' (23.46) stands in counterpoint to frequent Lukan references to Jesus' destiny as being 'delivered into the hands of men', while δίκαιος both sums up Luke's previous use of the word as it related to others and points forward to its three crucial occurrences in Acts in contexts which suggest that Luke is explaining for readers what he believed was 'really' happening at the cross.

Inter-textual relations are, however, a far more complex matter. Quotations are relatively simple to work with and both UBS3 and N-A 26 are helpful here, providing appendixes which identify widely agreed quotations; few are likely to question the rightness of identifying a citation from Psalm 30.6(31.5) at Luke 23.46 even though a verb has changed. No one can be altogether happy with the rogue 'only' in the Preface to the third edition of the UBS Greek New Testament (1975, p. ix, italics added):

> The Index of Quotations has been completely rewritten, now calling attention only to those passages which are clearly quotations from the Old Testament, and eliminating references to words and phrases which are *only* allusions or literary echoes.

Romaniuk carefully distinguished 'Les citations proprement dites' (1968, p. 504) from 'Citations libres et allusions' (1968, p. 505); the former occupied about one side of a page, concerning itself extensively with Romans 5.12, while the latter occupied pages 505–13. More significantly, R. B. Hays' work on echoes of scripture in Paul's letters (Hays, 1989) shows how powerfully allusions or echoes shape a text for both writer and reader. For example, the four tightly written lines of W. B. Yeats' *The Nineteenth Century and After* can stand on their own and speak to modern readers, but leap into new life when readers recognise in them Yeats in dialogue with Matthew Arnold's *Dover Beach*.[2] There is here no quotation, no shared word, but it is almost impossible to read Yeats without responding to the dialogue between these writers. The argument of this monograph is that Luke, similarly, held dialogue with the scriptures in his retelling of Jesus' story, and that he included among his scriptures Wisdom's biography of the δίκαιος. Although Luke does not quote Wisdom directly, once a reader mentally draws in the

[2] See Hays (1989, pp. 19–20). Hays' work has been a significant influence on my reading of Luke–Acts, but at this point I have deliberately avoided being caught up in the continuing, important debate about his methodology. For present purposes a precise distinction between 'echo' and 'allusion' is less important than our recognising both Luke's indebtedness to scripture and the effect that his indebtedness had on his shaping, and our reading, of his passion narrative. In his work on Mark, Joel Marcus (1993) has significantly developed Hays' approach; this approach puts a question against Wenham's principle (1991, p. 54); see chapter 2 note 20 above.

oblique allusions to or echoes of scripture passing through the horizontal of two Lukan verses (23.46–7), noting that only Wisdom 2–5 appears to 'transmit' the three 'Lukan' elements in Jesus' passion examined in part II, such density of allusion suggests both that something is happening in these verses which demands further exploration, and that this apparently important pattern or dialogue may also be discernible in other parts of Luke–Acts.

It may be accidental that in these *two* verses Luke reported the death of Jesus in terms which apparently echo Wisdom 2–5, but that is unlikely. First, his final assessment of Jesus, to the moment of his death, was that he was ὄντως . . . δίκαιος, the key category in the thinking of Wisdom's author, an important descriptor which Luke used later in the witness of three key figures in the Acts, and in contexts which share many characteristics of Luke's concern with the meaning of the cross and Jerusalem's responsibility for it. Second, the dying Jesus addressed God as 'Father' and, third, in words drawn from a δίκαιος-psalm, commended his spirit into God's hands where Wisdom was sure the souls of the departed righteous properly belonged (Wis. 3.1). These three elements belong together in Wisdom in an intimate and dynamic way, and this *patterning of ideas* is as evidential as shared language. It is probably more than coincidence that three key elements of *one* scriptural model should stand so closely interrelated in so small, yet so central and important, a Lukan space.[3]

One further clue needs to be taken up from the preceding paragraph: why does ὄντως make its appearance here, suggesting that strong affirmation of this man's being δίκαιος is important? Once Luke's characteristic use of ὄντως is understood, allusions to Wisdom in these verses appear even more probable.

Ὄντως

Ὄντως is a word which Luke uses only twice: at Luke 23.47 within the centurion's affirmation, and again at Luke 24.34 within the apostolic *praeconium paschale*. It may, of course, be coincidence that this is so; the word, once used, was hovering in the author's

[3] Cf. 'Bien évidemment, on ne peut pas affirmer que Paul n'était pas capable d'inventer lui-même une telle expression. Mais il reste à expliquer la nature et la cause de cette coïncidence étonnante entre lui et le livre de la Sagesse . . . Attribuer cette coïncidence à un simple hasard serait trop simpliste et peu convaincant' (Romaniuk, 1968, p. 505).

mind, emerging unconsciously when he next wanted to affirm something. Reflection on the word's function in each context suggests that one should explore the possibility that Luke *intended*[4] this usage by his centurion and that it plays a role in his narrative of the cross. How, then, does Luke usually affirm the 'thatness' of things?

Forms of asseveration in Luke–Acts

If one provisionally brackets off ὄντως, and ignores Acts 12.9, the semantic domain (real/unreal) with which this study is concerned is largely covered in Luke–Acts by three expressions, ἀμήν, ἀληθῶς and ἐπ' ἀληθείας. For Luke's Jesus, solemn affirmation of what is really the case is normally via ἀμήν (Luke 4.24; 12.37; 18.17, 29; 21.32; 23.43) with ἀληθῶς (Luke 9.27; 12.44; 21.3) as its less frequent alternative, although in the Nazareth sermon ἐπ' ἀληθείας is also found (4.25). In much the same way, characters other than Jesus normally affirm the 'thatness' of a case by ἐπ' ἀληθείας (Luke 20.21; 22.59; Acts 4.27; 10.34), although at Acts 12.11 Peter's surprised perception of the reality of his 'vindication' is expressed through ἀληθῶς (cf. Acts 12.9). So, Luke's Jesus does not use ὄντως and characters other than Jesus, including the narrator, do not use ἀμήν.

Ὄντως is thus marked out by its unusualness in Luke–Acts: it is also distinguished by its associations. At Luke 23.47 it expresses the Lukan centurion's evaluation of Jesus in his death as *really* δίκαιος, and at Luke 24.34 the word stresses the *reality* of the Lord's being raised as opposed to the disciples' earlier judgments that the women's talk of angels at an empty tomb was fantasy. In other words, Luke seems to have reserved *this* word of affirmation for the two key kerygmatic elements, death and vindication, in his telling the story of Jesus as God's agent. It is likely that the centurion and the apostles here speak with the authentic voice of the narrator because the remainder of Luke–Acts supports the centrality of these two ὄντως statements. The contrast within the repeated formula 'you put him to death but God raised him from the dead' forms the twin foci of a Lukan kerygmatic pattern which begins in the Emmaus story and runs through the Acts speeches (e.g. Luke 24.19–24; Acts 2.23–4; 5.30–1; 7.52–6; 10.39–40; 13.27–31; 26.23).

4 We cannot, of course, *know* what was in Luke's mind, but we can infer from what we understand of his work the probability of this word's belonging essentially to it. It is in that reduced sense that we use 'intended'.

At Luke 23.47 this asseveration is of Jesus' being δίκαιος; in other words, there is something in *this* descriptor to be attended to if one is properly to understand what Luke is saying about the cross. (Ὄντως thus supports the pressure already exerted on δίκαιος by ἐδόξαζεν τὸν Θεόν.) This conclusion is itself confirmed by Luke's own decision to have three major witnesses (Peter, Stephen and Paul) refer to Jesus as ὁ δίκαιος, continuing his narrative line through from the cross into the apostolic interpretation of what had happened there. Ὄντως dispels the doubts of those who could not believe that the women's tales of meeting the Lord were true (Luke 24.34; cf. 24.9–11, 22–3). Similarly, Luke may use ὄντως at the cross to dispel the doubts of those who, having learnt of the shameful end he met, could not see Jesus as God's agent. Is Luke's formulation an answer to a charge that one who hung on a tree could not conceivably be proclaimed as messiah (Deut. 21.22–3; cf. Wis. 2.20)? and is not a part of Christian answers to such complaints found in Wisdom's claim that while the opponents of the δίκαιος unjustly conspired to hound him to a shameful death, testing him in life and death, God vindicated him (Wis. 5.1–8)? Here is a paradox of salvation (Wis. 5.1): it was clear to the opponents of Wisdom's δίκαιος that he had been overwhelmed by his suffering and shameful death; it was clear to Wisdom's author that *in the end* God would vindicate the δίκαιος in the presence of those same oppressors. Within Wisdom this strongly implies that the δίκαιος would be *the first* to rise from the dead (cf. Acts 26.23).

If this is a plausible hypothesis, then one should examine whether Luke more extensively reshaped his story of Jesus' cross as a dialogue between traditions that the evangelist received, first from 'eyewitnesses and ministers of the word', and second, from the biography of Wisdom's δίκαιος. Is there evidence of wider Lukan use of this dialogue? What might count as evidence? Having established one probable allusion, one asks whether Kuhn's 'traces' of Wisdom play a larger part in Luke–Acts than Romaniuk uncovered.

B. Criteria for allusion

Romaniuk (1968) carefully distinguished between 'citations proprement dites' and 'citations libres et allusions'. This is not a straightforward distinction. Quotations within a text are relatively easy to handle,[5] but how may one be sure that an echo or allusion is just that? Is there really a dialogue between Luke and Wisdom in Luke 23.46–7, or is it imagined? There is need first to establish criteria by which to assess the likelihood of a specific Lukan passage's alluding to or echoing what Wisdom said of the δίκαιος. By such dialogue Luke would have been exploring the 'things fulfilled among us' (Luke 1.1); he would have been telling his story systematically (καθεξῆς, Luke 1.3); he would have been staying close to what had been handed on to him from the 'eyewitnesses and ministers of the word' (Luke 1.2); in other words, he would have been writing according to his declared purposes. This is not to suggest either that Luke's interest in scripture or his basis for the passion story was *confined* to Wisdom: Appendix III of N-A 26 shows that this evangelist quotes from a wide range of scriptural books. However, he tends not to announce his quotations, and uses them less heavy-handedly than, for example, John or Matthew. Why, then, might Luke lay such weight on *allusion* to an otherwise unquoted source at so crucial a point in his narrative?

Luke's thinking about Jesus' cross was probably 'attracted' by Wisdom's influence. An analogy drawn from astronomy may help us here: a number of previously unknown planets or stars have been 'discovered' by astronomers who, reflecting on an 'oddness' in the passage of a known body, inferred from its motion the presence of another, as yet unidentified body whose gravitational field attracted the known object from its predicted path. Similarly, it is entirely understandable that a writer may work with a basic pattern of thought discernible only obliquely through fundamental patterns and occasional words.

There is further evidence than that of Luke 23.46–7 that Luke's retelling of Jesus' passion was pulled into a variant orbit by Wisdom's model. For example, this enquiry *begins* with the proposition that Luke's composition shows that he used δίκαιος where others did not and that there is a coherence in his use which implies a common underlying pattern within each occurrence of the word. But how may one confirm that in his composition of Luke 23.46–7 Luke worked with such a conceptual model, that his orbit through his retelling of Jesus' story was 'attracted' by the strong, though formally unacknowledged, gravitational tug of Wisdom's biography

5 The force of *relatively* should not be overlooked. Reference to other works on the place of scriptural quotation in Luke–Acts may be found in: Cadbury (1958); Dodd (1952); Fitzmyer (1981); Hanson (1983); Hays (1989); Lindars (1961).

of the δίκαιος? In the rest of this chapter the following five criteria are brought into play in varying ways in an exploration of other apparent Lukan allusions to Wisdom's model.

1 **Does the allusion comprise at least two mutually supportive elements from the alleged source?** For example, allusion to Wisdom in Luke 23.46–7 has been claimed *solely* because out of all the inter-textual surfaces which may be thought to pass through Luke's writing at this point, only Wisdom's model contains all *three* Lukan compositional elements. Had δίκαιος alone featured in this verse, an allusion to Wisdom here might have been judged as improbable as Cadbury thought it.[6] But the reference to 'hands' adds weight to the possibility of allusion because of their relation in Wisdom's δίκαιος-model. As emerges below, 'Father' is another important element both in the death of Wisdom's δίκαιος and in the Lukan passion narrative. This conjunction of mutually supportive elements in so small a unit suggests that this is probably a clear allusion.

2 **How clearly does one hear echoes from the same model in contexts near to the 'primary' echo detected in Luke?** The word 'clearly' should be understood in the sense found in 1 above, and 'near' contexts are, for the present, those within the same narrative stage, Luke's account of Jesus' final visit to Jerusalem. Further echoes of Wisdom in this section of the Gospel tend both to confirm the allusion at Luke 23.46–7 and to be confirmed by it.

3 **How important to this author's telling of the passion are 'rare' words essential to the underlying model, but uncommon in his work and in the New Testament as a whole?** Gärtner (1912) drew up a list of thirty-eight terms found only in Wisdom and the New Testament, but while words do have evidential value, they need to be rooted in a firm conceptual context before they can count as an 'allusion'. Consequently, once one has begun to hear more surely echoes of an underlying model, words like ἐνεδρεύω, ἔξοδος, παράδοξος, ἑστῶτα take on stronger, additional roles as pointers to the model's use by Luke.

4 **How much of the primary model in Wisdom appears to be basic to the model this author offers of Jesus' death and life?**

[6] Cadbury (1933 p. 364, n. 3).

This is more difficult to determine, a question of delineation rather than of words, of shapes and patterns rather than quotations: it implies careful comparison between Wisdom's elements of the fate of the δίκαιος on one hand and the *Lukan* features of Jesus' passion and resurrection on the other. The extent to which these match will suggest how far Luke was indebted to his model.

5 **How far does the primary model go towards making sense of Lukan features noted by authors other than oneself?** This throws the accent on to what *others* have seen in Luke–Acts, introducing a more 'objective' selection of texts on which to focus.

With these criteria in mind, Luke's modelling of the final stage of Jesus' journey to death will be examined. The last criterion suggests the choice of topics: Luke's use of πειρασμοῖς at Luke 22.28; the noticeable absence of emotion in Luke's account of Jesus *face à la mort menaçante;* Luke's handling of the Sanhedrin's grounds for sending Jesus off to Pilate – these are all issues which have attracted detailed discussion by *Neutestamentler*, and which are probably clarified by perceiving their relation to Luke's δίκαιος-model. Luke's treatment of Jesus' entrapment will be explored, then the significance of ἔξοδος at Luke 9.31, and, finally, Luke's 'ignorance' theme. It will then be possible formally to compare the Lukan and Wisdom models, although this paragraph already points to the extent of Luke's modelling.

C. The testing of Jesus

> ὑμεῖς δέ ἐστε οἱ διαμεμενηκότες μετ' ἐμοῦ ἐν τοῖς πειρασμοῖς μου· κἀγὼ διατίθεμαι ὑμῖν καθὼς διέθετό μοι ὁ πατήρ μου βασιλείαν . . . (Luke 22.28–9)

This *logion* from Luke's account of Jesus' discourse at the Last Supper is taken up because, first, it stands as a Lukan construct in close relation to Jesus' approaching passion and thus to the focal allusion to Wisdom in Luke 23.46–7; second, there seems a strong probability that its place in Luke's thought is clarified when the passage is read in the light of Wisdom's δίκαιος-model and in relation to Luke's characterisation of Jesus' life; additionally, its issues have been explored by others.

Commentators tend to focus on the word πειρασμοῖς in response to Conzelmann's bold, though mistaken, assertion concerning Luke 4.13 that 'The expression συντελέσας πάντα πειρασμόν can scarcely be overemphasised. It really means that henceforth there will be no temptations in the life of Jesus' (1960, p. 28). Anticipating his treatment of the sayings at the Last Supper (1960, p. 80), Conzelmann continued, 'Thus his life as a whole is not regarded as a temptation either.' For present purposes, the central issues are threefold: first, what may be meant by πειρασμός; second, what is the force of διαμεμενηκότες? The third issue is closely related to each of the other two: in what sense, if any, is discussion of these two verses illuminated by reference to Wisdom's δίκαιος-model?

Conzelmann's understanding of Luke 4.13 is questionable because he assumed that πειρασμός had to do with the devil's seducing Jesus to infraction of *Torah*, on which he then built too emphatic a denial. Discussion of whether 'the Period of Jesus' is Satan-free tends to skew attempts to grasp what Luke is about at Luke 22.28.[7] It is also unhelpful to see πειρασμός as a Lukan way of speaking of apostasy and having to treat Luke 22.28 as an exception.[8] A natural way of reading πειρασμός is to think of it primarily as a testing rather than a seduction, and it will shortly be clear that this 'natural' way works in Lukan contexts.

Conzelmann's treatment of πειρασμοί is cavalier: 'We must beware, however, of deducing from v. 28 a picture of Jesus' whole life as a temptation, for this would be false. It is now that the πειρασμοί hold sway. Previously they were far away' (1960, p. 80). His footnote (n. 4, p. 80)[9] is not convincing; this study also is primarily interested in knowing what *Luke had to say about* πειρασμοί, and part of Conzelmann's problem is that he ignored the considerable force of Luke's use of διαμεμενηκότες. Commentators generally appreciate the problem posed to Conzelmann's findings by this Lukan verb whose sense of *continuity from the past*

[7] Possibly, in Luke talk of Satan's 'testing' has to do primarily with Jesus' *interior* life. Luke's symbolic treatment of Jesus' post-baptismal wilderness experience, borrowed from the Dual Tradition and echoing Israel's own desert-testing (e.g. Deut. 6.16; 8.2, 16 where the verb is ἐκπειράζειν) then gives way to testing by human opponents.

[8] So, e.g., Brown, S., *Apostasy and Perseverance in the Theology of Luke* Analecta Biblica 36, Rome: Pontifical Biblical Institute, 1969; see also Brown, S. (1972).

[9] 'In order to avoid misunderstanding, we repeat that in the following exposition we are concerned solely with the meaning these sayings have for Luke (on the objection raised by K.G. Kuhn, cf.. p. 16, n. 2). To what extent the whole ministry of Jesus was thought of as a "temptation" before, at the time of, and after Luke, is a question we can leave open at this point' (Conzelmann, 1960, p. 80, n. 4).

and into the present must be taken seriously.[10] Conzelmann asks that the force of συντελέσας be emphasised; interpreters should also take account of διαμεμενηκότες (see below).

Luke's account of the Last Supper, which has attracted long, varied and detailed discussion, seems to be essentially his own construct, making use of some traditional material. This study is focused firmly on the two verses cited at the head of this section. There seems little doubt these verses and that immediately following are related to a tradition which appears also at Matthew 19.28: ὁ δὲ Ἰησοῦς εἶπεν αὐτοῖς, Ἀμὴν λέγω ὑμῖν ὅτι ὑμεῖς οἱ ἀκολουθήσαντές μοι, ἐν τῇ παλιγγενεσίᾳ, ὅταν καθίσῃ ὁ υἱὸς τοῦ ἀνθρώπου ἐπὶ θρόνου δόξης αὐτοῦ, καθήσεσθε καὶ ὑμεῖς ἐπὶ δώδεκα θρόνους κρίνοντες τὰς δώδεκα φυλὰς τοῦ Ἰσραήλ. While the second part of this Matthaean *logion* is similar to what is found in Luke 22.30, its first part is more remote. Matthew's Ἀμὴν λέγω ὑμῖν ὅτι ὑμεῖς οἱ ἀκολουθήσαντές μοι is paralleled by Luke's ὑμεῖς δέ ἐστε οἱ διαμεμενηκότες μετ' ἐμοῦ ἐν τοῖς πειρασμοῖς μου· Matthew's 'following' is matched by Luke's 'persevering with me in my testing(s)'. Further, immediately before reference to thrones and judging the twelve tribes of Israel, a reference shared with Matthew, Luke has the statement: κἀγὼ διατίθεμαι ὑμῖν καθὼς διέθετό μοι ὁ πατήρ μου βασιλείαν. Luke's construct at this key moment in his passion narrative now strongly relates the disciples' persistent 'remaining with' Jesus to their sharing in a βασιλείαν. Throughout Luke–Acts concern with continuing contact between Jesus and his disciples stretches like a thread in the evangelist's 'witnessing' theme: according to Luke, from its beginning Jesus' followers witnessed his ministry; they did not forsake him and flee during the passion; after his ascension they affirmed that they were with him from John's baptism until his being taken up (Acts 1.21–2). Moreover, the πειρασμός theme relates also to the disciples: they are to pray that they do not enter into it (Luke 11.4;

[10] See, e.g., Marshall (1978, p. 816), 'The claim of Conzelmann . . . comes to grief on the meaning of the perfect tense . . .' Fitzmyer (1985, p. 1418), who, like Marshall, appeals to Brown (1972), concluding that Conzelmann's reading of the participle is grammatically indefensible. Schweizer, whose 'Zum Verständnis des Kreuzestodes Jesu' (1993, p. 225) is taken up in the final chapter, has nothing to add on this point, but Wiefel (1987, p. 372), who simply notes that διαμεμενηκότες replaces ἀκολουθήσαντες (Matt. 19.28), continues with a quotation from Conzelmann : 'Seit dem Anbruch der Passion ist das Christ-sein Kampf – *erst seit da* – und die Apostel sind die, welche jetzt bleiben. Das ist der Sinn des Perfekts in V.28. Dazu stimmt, dass sie nach Lukas nicht fliehen' (Mitte der Zeit, p. 73, italics added). See also Tannehill (1961, pp. 198–203).

22.40b, 46 cf. Acts 20.19). It is the presence of πειρασμός as a Lukan description of Jesus' ministry up to and into his present crisis, and its association with a βασιλεία for his faithful disciples, which suggests that underlying and shaping this Lukan construct is Wisdom's δίκαιος-model.

'Testing' in Wisdom

For Wisdom's author 'testing', a key dimension of his δίκαιος-model, has two sides. From the viewpoint of those who oppressed the δίκαιος, from their stance of wealth and power, 'testing' refers to their cynical pressing on the limits of the righteous one's faith and commitment; will his darker experience of a persecuted life still support the religious claims he seems to have made? The verb πειράζειν appears early in this model:

> ἴδωμεν εἰ οἱ λόγοι αὐτοῦ ἀληθεῖς,
> καὶ πειράσωμεν τὰ ἐν ἐκβάσει αὐτοῦ ... (Wis. 2.17)

Their methods for testing him are direct:

> ὕβρει καὶ βασάνῳ ἐτάσωμεν αὐτόν ...
> θανάτῳ ἀσχήμονι καταδικάσωμεν αὐτόν ...(Wis. 2.19–20)

The import of πειράζειν here is plain enough: it is the inflicting of ill-treatment on a person and bringing him to a shameful death, to assess the worth or soundness of his commitment. From the *writer's* perspective, however, the sufferings of the δίκαιος belong to God's plan, where πειράζειν now has God as its subject. Their experience of 'testing' is 'really' God's testing of his saints, as gold is tested in a furnace:

> ... ὅτι ὁ Θεὸς ἐπείρασεν αὐτοὺς
> καὶ εὗρεν αὐτοὺς ἀξίους ἑαυτοῦ ... (Wis. 3.5b)

Their *post mortem* vindication is that they are in God's hands (3.1); 'they seemed to have died' (3.2); they are 'at peace' (3.3); they will 'shine out' (3.7); they will (significantly; see below) 'govern nations and rule peoples' (3.8); they 'will remain with [God] in love' (3.9); 'they' (sing. δίκαιος) will stand confidently in the presence of their oppressors (5.1); they will be clearly seen by their astonished, former persecutors to be 'numbered among the saints' (5.5). This portrayal is an *apologia* for Israel's sufferings. While other aspects of this theme of 'testing' will emerge in later parts of this monograph, one element needs to be considered immediately.

In Luke's construct the disciples are assured by Jesus that they who have persevered with him in his πειρασμοῖς are to receive a kingdom:

> κἀγὼ διατίθεμαι ὑμῖν καθὼς διέθετό μοι ὁ πατήρ μου βασιλείαν ἵνα ἔσθητε καὶ πίνητε ἐπὶ τῆς τραπέζης μου ἐν τῇ βασιλείᾳ μου, καὶ καθήσεσθε ἐπὶ θρόνων τὰς δώδεκα φυλὰς κρίνοντες τοῦ Ἰσραήλ. (Luke 22.29–30)

As was noted above, this *logion* about the apostles' thrones and their function as judges probably derives from traditions about Jesus with which Luke had to work.[11] What makes this of more than passing interest, is that Luke has brought into close relation in one brief *logion* (*diff.* Matt.) reference both to the apostles' perseverance with Jesus in his 'testing' and to their receiving thrones. This relation of ideas is the kind of density of reference which probably constitutes allusion, so that a Lukan relating of these two would be reason enough to recall Wisdom's relating them (Wis. 3.8).

There is probably further cause for thought in, κἀγὼ διατίθεμαι ὑμῖν καθὼς διέθετό μοι ὁ πατήρ μου βασιλείαν. The appearance in this passage of ὁ πατήρ μου reminds a reader that reason for the humiliation of Wisdom's δίκαιος by his oppressors lay in his calling God 'Father' (Wis. 2.16). That is, talk of 'testing', of a 'kingdom' for the Lord and his faithful followers, and of 'Father' are clustered in this Lukan *logion;* they belong together also in the Wisdom model. It may be objected that in Daniel, similarly, a βασιλεία is reward for faithful suffering, although it is not called πειρασμός (Dan. 7.14, 18, 22, 27). This is so, but two considerations keep the Wisdom model in focus at this point. The first is that the constituent elements of Luke's tightly redrawn death scene (Luke 23.46–7) seem to point to Wisdom's δίκαιος, and the twin notions of πειρασμός and βασιλεία found in the Lukan narrative of the Last Supper belong organically to that same model. Second, because in Luke a closely associated term like ὁ πατήρ μου links both notions with the allusive core of the death scene and, *by implication*, with the trial of Jesus (see the discussion below), it is preferable temporarily to hold in view its connection with the dominant Lukan model, δίκαιος.

At present, one simply notes that at a significant moment in the

[11] The notion of the saints as 'judges' appears also at 1 Cor. 6.2a.

longer narrative of Jesus' sufferings and death – his Jerusalem days – Luke has chosen formally to associate a βασιλεία for the disciples with his characterisation of Jesus' previous career as a πειρασμός before his trial and death; this is probably an echo of Wisdom. And, according to Wisdom, the point of testing the δίκαιος is to see what kind of end he would make.

D. The Lukan Jesus' bearing in the face of death

Many writers have drawn attention to the particularity of Luke's portrayal of Jesus confronting his sufferings: it is a feature of Luke's narrative that has evoked recurrent interest.[12] Grayston can focus the issue here: noting the characteristics of Luke's *passio,* he affirms that this Jesus is not a hapless victim, but the *disturber of his enemies.*[13] He remarks that Luke's Gethsemane presents Jesus as a model of goodness and nobility, and that the Markan element of Jesus' distress has been excised from it. On trial, Jesus is noble-spirited in his innocence and then goes like a great prince to his execution. From this cross, no reproach is addressed to God; Jesus magnanimously forgives his executioners, promises paradise to a repentant criminal and finally commends himself into God's hands. His nobility sustains him to the end and is recognised by the Roman centurion (1990, p. 354f.). Grayston's thumb-nail sketch of a dignified, admirable person sets out what he believes to be distinctively Lukan in the telling.

Other scholars have also seen in Luke's threatened Jesus a marked absence of emotion. Johnson understood this to be a Lukan way of showing Jesus as a *sophos* unshaken amidst turmoil (1991, p. 354f.). Because Luke's portrayal of Jesus approaching his passion is significantly different from that in the other Gospels and in Hebrews, Johnson drew attention to the fact that Luke focuses sharply on Jesus rather than on the disciples and seems to remove Jesus' need for companionship; the terrible grief and fear in Mark are also absent from Luke. Neyrey (1980, revised in 1985, pp. 49–68)

[12] E.g. Grayston: 'Jesus is not Mark's distraught prophet, but Luke's impressive teacher and healer who attracts by his goodness and nobility ... In Luke's Gethsemane Jesus does not appeal to God or look for an omen or display extreme agitation: *he betrays knowledge of God and a controlling personal goodness*, both directed to the benefit of his followers' (1990, p. 215, italics added). See also Neyrey (1980, revised 1985, pp. 49–68).

[13] Cf. Wis. 2.12b, 14–16a. It is interesting that Grayston chose to include this phrase as a description of Luke's Jesus.

offers a much fuller examination of the significant difference between Luke and the other Gospels. Basically, Neyrey's redactional study of Luke's garden scene indicates that this evangelist has stripped from Jesus all hint of 'unworthy' emotion and transferred λύπη from Jesus to his disciples. He has removed those Markan details which suggest Jesus to be distraught or lacking in moral control. Neyrey found the reason for this editing in a practical concern that both the LXX and popular Hellenistic thought, as evidenced for example by Philo, held such emotions to diminish the character being described.

Some scholars have tried to identify literary models on which Luke's passion narrative was shaped. Collins (1993), primarily concerned with Mark's passion narrative, drew attention to the literary genre called τελευταί or *exitus illustrium virorum,* in which a writer explores the dying of a famous person. Because dying is an important part of life, interest in the ways in which people die is perennial, and one example of such a τελευτή is found in 4 Maccabees 5–7, where 'the emphasis on Eleazar's ability to endure pain and torture ... probably derives from the author's Stoic values'. Although the word is not used in the text, Eleazar's bearing well exemplifies ἀνεξικακία. While Collins may have identified a genre, the huge difference between that account of Eleazar's death and Luke's more restrained account of the sufferings of Jesus makes one hesitate. Neyrey also is certainly on to something important, but his reference to the LXX and the Hellenistic climate of thought leaves one wondering how from these beginnings Luke might have arrived at his distinctive portrayal of Jesus.

There is, possibly, a simpler, more satisfying, answer, one which draws attention to Jesus' positive virtues rather than to his want of emotion: opponents, oppressors of the δίκαιος in Wisdom's account put him to the test *to see what kind of end he would make*. It was a testing to discover whether he *really* (ὄντως, Luke 23.47) was δίκαιος. Moreover, as was shown in chapter 6, a good case can be made for identifying the elements of Jesus' dignified bearing in the face of suffering and death as ἀνεξικακία and ἐπιείκεια, virtues looked for by those testing Wisdom's δίκαιος. These virtues probably summarise in Wisdom what was also admired more widely in Greek and Latin thought. Neyrey *et al.* have probably identified elements which comprise all that was admired in the good man. Yet if Luke had decided to characterise his Jesus as δίκαιος; to have him commit his spirit into his Father's hands; to characterise his life as πειρασμοί, then it would not be surprising if this author's carefully crafted description of Jesus' progress through his sufferings matched the ἀνεξικακία and ἐπιείκεια of his primary model. One may take this distinctive element of Luke's portrait of Jesus as one more indicator of his basic scriptural model: it is an element *identified by others*; it appears within the *context* marked out on one side by the twofold πειρασμοί and βασιλεία of the Last Supper discourse and, on the other, by Luke's allusions to a δίκαιος-model in the death scene; the element is *explained more simply and naturally* by appeal to Luke's probable use of Wisdom than by reference to vaguer 'external' influences. This element also suggests *coherence* within Luke's presentation of Jesus and his cross, and relates that presentation firmly to an identifiable book within the LXX.[14] Such coherence embraces Luke's treatment of how his opponents brought *this* δίκαιος to his shameful death.

E. The Sanhedrin's decision: Luke 22.66–71

Luke's distinctive narrative of the processes which brought Jesus to his cross has often been explored, particularly those aspects of it which bear on the historicity of the reported events.[15] This section's concern, however, is exclusively with Stage III of the tradition, with the literary and theological implications of Luke's account, most especially with his apparently careful distinction between two descriptors of Jesus, ὁ Χριστός and ὁ υἱὸς τοῦ θεοῦ. A synopticon clearly shows Luke 22.70 standing out as an element which belongs to this evangelist and not to the others, but its context needs also to be seen as a whole.

> Καὶ ὡς ἐγένετο ἡμέρα, συνήχθη τὸ πρεσβυτέριον τοῦ λαοῦ, ἀρχιερεῖς τε καὶ γραμματεῖς, καὶ ἀπήγαγον αὐτὸν εἰς τὸ συνέδριον αὐτῶν, λέγοντες, Εἰ σὺ εἶ ὁ Χριστός, εἰπὸν ἡμῖν. εἶπεν δὲ αὐτοῖς, Ἐὰν ὑμῖν εἴπω οὐ μὴ πιστεύσητε: ἐὰν δὲ ἐρωτήσω οὐ μὴ ἀποκριθῆτε. ἀπὸ

[14] The question of Wisdom's place in the canon and among the earlier Christians remains open (see Winston, 1979; cf. Horbury, 1994).

[15] E.g., Catchpole, D.R., 'The Problem of the Historicity of the Sanhedrin Trial', in Bammel, E., *The Trial of Jesus* SBT 2/13, London: SCM Press, pp. 47–65; Goguel, M., 'À propos du procès de Jésus', *ZNW* 31 (1932), pp. 289–301; Tyson, J.B., 'The Lukan Version of the Trial of Jesus', *NovT* 3 (1959), pp. 249–58. The work of P. Winter is of great importance here.

> τοῦ νῦν δὲ ἔσται ὁ υἱὸς τοῦ ἀνθρώπου καθήμενος ἐκ δεξιῶν τῆς δυνάμεως τοῦ θεοῦ.
>
> Εἶπαν δὲ πάντες, Σὺ οὖν εἶ ὁ υἱὸς τοῦ θεοῦ; ὁ δὲ πρὸς αὐτοὺς ἔφη, Ὑμεῖς λέγετε ὅτι ἐγώ εἰμι. οἱ δὲ εἶπαν, Τί ἔτι ἔχομεν μαρτυρίας χρείαν; αὐτοὶ γὰρ ἠκούσαμεν ἀπὸ τοῦ στόματος αὐτοῦ. (Luke 22.66–71)

A number of intra-textual themes pass through this extract which deserve brief note before passing to this section's major concern with Luke's distinction between two christological terms. First, Luke has carefully avoided telling the Sanhedrin that *they will see* the Son of man seated at the right hand of God's power; in *Luke's* narrative it will be Stephen who later 'sees' Jesus' vindication as the same authorities continue their oppression of Jesus through his follower. Second, by his εἶπαν δὲ πάντες Luke has prepared the way for that succession of speeches in Acts which report in summary form the things concerning Jesus, in which he places responsibility for Jesus' death firmly on the Jerusalem authorities (Luke 22.66) and not on 'the Jews'. Third, Luke's account of what happened before the Sanhedrin lacks reference to the High Priest's tearing his clothes, to blasphemy, to other witnesses and to any form of judicial condemnation. This is a very different account from the other Gospels.

This distinctively Lukan retelling of events emphasises a distinction where there is a real difference – between Χριστός (Luke 22.67) and ὁ υἱὸς τοῦ θεοῦ (Luke 22.70). Whether first-century Judaism did or did not understand ὁ υἱὸς τοῦ θεοῦ as a messianic term is presently of peripheral concern to one's understanding of Luke's composition. Schweizer's discussion of the passage (1993, pp. 230–2), matched by Fitzmyer's (1985, pp. 1467f.) and elaborated by Johnson's (1991, pp. 359–63), focuses on the Lukan separation of these terms and shows that the effect of Luke's composition is to make the question of Jesus' being *Son of God* the precipitating factor in the Sanhedrin's unwittingly fulfilling the internal prophecies of Jesus' passion predictions: they handed him into the power and authority of the Gentile governor (Luke 20.20). This term, 'Son of God', belongs to the tradition Luke inherited, but in the birth narratives and in the kerygmatic speeches of Acts he has illustrated and explored its meaning for him, so those who claim that 'Son of God' is Luke's primary christological term have a strong case. It is, also, a correlative term to *Father*, which makes its appearance in the

Jerusalem context more frequently than elsewhere in Luke, and the two appear to interrelate dynamically in the passion narrative.

What may have prompted Luke to make this distinction between Χριστός and ὁ υἱὸς τοῦ θεου, to separate them in his narrative and consequently to place greater weight on Jesus' being 'Son of God'? Whatever may be meant by Jesus' Ὑμεῖς λέγετε ὅτι ἐγώ εἰμι there can be no doubt that it angered the Sanhedrin: οἱ δὲ εἶπαν, Τί ἔτι ἔχομεν μαρτυρίας χρείαν; αὐτοὶ γὰρ ἠκούσαμεν ἀπὸ τοῦ στόματος αὐτοῦ.

In the light of earlier discussions, the fact cannot be ignored that according to the author of Wisdom a prime reason offered by his opponents for pursuing the δίκαιος was that he called himself 'Son of God' and talked of God as his Father (Wis. 2.13, 16, 18). It would be surprising if this fundamental Lukan distinction between two terms, making *sonship* rather than the question of Jesus' *messiahship* the root cause of the Sanhedrin's decision, were not related to his indebtedness to Wisdom. This Lukan feature is noted and discussed by other scholars; it stands in the context of other, reasonably clear allusions to the underlying model; it relates Luke's compositional activity in this scene to an overall patterning and throws into sharper relief his interest in the term *Son of God.* If this may be sustained as an allusion to Wisdom's δίκαιος-model, then one is probably dealing with a two-way process within Luke's composing. First, elements in existing Christian traditions about Jesus reminded him of the suffering righteous one, and particularly of Wisdom's form of that figure, where key terms in Christian tradition like 'son', 'father', 'testing' and reference to shameful death already existed; second, Wisdom's δίκαιος then offered Luke a coherent scriptural matrix around which *to shape his own account* of the significance of Jesus' cross.

Romaniuk (1968, p. 499) found traces of Wisdom's *Son of God* in Matthew 27.43. 'On les retrouve dans le récit matthéen de la passion: "Il a compté sur Dieu; que Dieu le délivre maintenant, s'il s'intéresse à lui! Il a bien dit: Je suis fils de Dieu!"' Romaniuk rightly noted the connection between Matthew's *Fils de Dieu* and Wisdom 2.18 'où le Juste se déclare "Fils de Dieu".' Although v. 43a echoes Psalm 21(22).19, and thus relates to Jesus' word from the cross according to Matthew's passion narrative, it also echoes the remainder of Wisdom 2.18, εἰ γάρ ἐστιν ὁ δίκαιος υἱὸς Θεοῦ, ἀντιλημψεται αὐτοῦ καὶ ῥύσεται αὐτὸν ἐκ χειρὸς ἀνθεστηκότων. Because the two elements of Matthew's verse, sonship and rescue, appear together in Wisdom, not in the psalm, it is likely that the evangelist is recalling both Wisdom and the psalm, conflating ideas from both under the one model.

In Luke there is also the question of Jesus' entrapment which brought him to the point where Jerusalem's rulers decided to hand him over to Pilate.

F. Entrapment

According to Luke, those who delivered Jesus into the governor's hands had earlier vigorously sought to entrap him. Because Luke shares this element of his narrative with the other evangelists, it is not easy to notice the 'orbital shift' in his handling of the tradition, yet his careful crafting of this theme, making it leaner and more tightly integrated with his whole work, leaves some traces of Wisdom's influence. From his account of the cleansing of the Temple to that of the widow's offering, Luke develops the theme of entrapment that he had begun earlier in his Gospel. In the Lukan scheme it is the Jerusalem authorities who are primarily responsible for the death of Jesus, so in this sequence Pharisees drop from view and a combination of scribes, chief priests and aristocrats comes into focus as his opponents.

In Luke's Jerusalem sequence, it is both Jesus' cleansing of the Temple and his popular public teaching there (Luke 19.45–7) which provide his opponents with grounds to ask by what authority he does these things (Luke 20.1–8). Their refusal to answer Jesus' counter-question (Luke 20.3b–8) leads into his public telling of the parable of the Wicked Husbandmen (Luke 20.9–18), with its own Lukan agenda,[16] and to a consequent hardening of the authorities' attitude to him (Luke 20.19). This includes putting him under close observation, with the object of handing him over to the governor's jurisdiction, and sending spies (Luke 20.20) to pose a trick question about taxation, the answer to which silences them. An exegetical question about resurrection is then posed by Sadducees (20.27), the answer to which, a knock-down argument from *Torah*, is praised by scribes (20.39) who, although silenced like other opponents, are in turn offered a similar scriptural treatment of their position (20.41–4) before being savagely and publicly (ἀκούοντος δὲ παντὸς τοῦ

[16] Luke's telling is much more like his passion narrative; the son alone is killed. (See chapter 1, p. 8.)

λαοῦ) attacked (20.45–7). It seems likely that the poor widow's giving of two *lepta* illustrates the scribes' 'devouring of widow's houses' (21.1–4; cf. 20.47). This attack on them is strongly reminiscent of an earlier incident in Luke's journey narrative where scribes (11.45–52), there associated with, yet carefully distinguished from, Pharisees (11.37–44), are subjected to Jesus' fierce critique of their lives[17] and *plot how to trap him.*

This long sequence must be examined in rather more detail.

1. Luke 19.47–20.8

> Καὶ ἦν διδάσκων τὸ καθ' ἡμέραν ἐν τῷ ἱερῷ. οἱ δὲ ἀρχιερεῖς καὶ οἱ γραμματεῖς ἐζήτουν αὐτὸν ἀπολέσαι καὶ οἱ πρῶτοι τοῦ λαοῦ· καὶ οὐχ εὕρισκον τὸ τί ποιήσωσιν, ὁ λαὸς γὰρ ἅπας ἐξεκρέματο αὐτοῦ ἀκούων ... Καὶ ἐγένετο ἐν μιᾷ τῶν ἡμερῶν διδάσκοντος αὐτοῦ τὸν λαὸν ἐν τῷ ἱερῷ καὶ εὐαγγελιζομένου ἐπέστησαν οἱ ἀρχιερεῖς καὶ οἱ γραμματεῖς σὺν τοῖς πρεσβυτέροις ...

There are two references in as many verses to Jesus' public teaching in the Temple and it seems to be this as much as the 'cleansing' which constitutes the ταῦτα of Luke 20.2; Luke has drawn attention to this public nature of Jesus' teaching in his account of the arrest (22.53; cf. 21.37–8). He has also clarified the consortium which constituted Jesus' opponents: for some reason Luke has distanced Pharisees from responsibility for Jesus' death by excluding them altogether from the Jerusalem narrative.[18] He focused on Jerusalem and its authorities as those who did these things, and the authorities are named as scribes, priests and aristocracy.[19] This Lukan view of responsibility for Jesus' death is consistently maintained through the Emmaus story and into the speeches in Acts.

Jesus himself is represented as doing what God had anointed him to do (εὐαγγελιζομένου; cf. 4.18 and 7.22b). Readers know what Jesus' authority is even though his opponents do not understand it. Because Luke (*diff.* Mark, Matt.) has no intervening story about a fig tree, in this continuous narrative Jesus' telling of the parable of the vineyard follows closely on his opponents' refusal seriously to discuss their question about authority, and issues in their determination to do away with him. As already noted, this parable's detail

[17] See note 13 above. [18] See Ziesler (1978). [19] E.g. Luke 22.66.

reflects a Lukan passion story, but present concern is only with its effects on some of its hearers.

2. Luke 20.19–20

Καὶ ἐζήτησαν οἱ γραμματεῖς καὶ οἱ ἀρχιερεῖς ἐπιβαλεῖν ἐπ' αὐτὸν τὰς χεῖρας ἐν αὐτῇ τῇ ὥρᾳ, καὶ ἐφοβήθησαν τὸν λαόν· ἔγνωσαν γὰρ ὅτι πρὸς αὐτοὺς εἶπεν τὴν παραβολὴν ταύτην. Καὶ παρατηρήσαντες ἀπέστειλαν ἐγκαθέτους ὑποκρινομένους ἑαυτοὺς δικαίους εἶναι, ἵνα ἐπιλάβωνται αὐτοῦ λόγου, ὥστε παραδοῦναι αὐτὸν τῇ ἀρχῇ καὶ τῇ ἐξουσίᾳ τοῦ ἡγεμόνος.

Although the aristocracy have disappeared from his narrative, Luke has reaffirmed the nature of the opposition to Jesus – scribes and priests. There is a sense of urgency in the narrative; it was ἐν αὐτῇ τῇ ὥρᾳ that his opponents wanted to lay hands on Jesus. Luke's idiomatic ἐπιβαλεῖν ἐπ' αὐτὸν τὰς χεῖρας also has its echo in the story of the arrest (ἐξετείνατε τὰς χεῖρας, 22.53), possibly firming up Luke's theme about whose hands Jesus was really in.

By distinctive features in its opening and closing verses, Luke's account of the question concerning tribute to Caesar emphasises its place in the sequence of entrapment. Although both Mark and Matthew make use in this story of hunting verbs not found in Luke, in his version there is a strong, pervasive sense of close, narrow observation (παρατηρήσαντες; cf. 6.7; 14.1) and careful preparation of *agents provocateurs* (ἀπέστειλαν ἐγκαθέτους) whose task is to 'catch' Jesus (ἵνα ἐπιλάβωνται αὐτοῦ λόγου), with all the ambiguities of ἐπιλαμβάνομαι hanging in the air. Luke clearly wanted to sustain such ambiguity and used a variation on it to bring his telling of this story to a neat conclusion, with silenced opponents: καὶ οὐκ ἴσχυσαν ἐπιλαβέσθαι αὐτοῦ ῥήματος ἐναντίον τοῦ λαοῦ, καὶ θαυμάσαντες ἐπὶ τῇ ἀποκρίσει αὐτοῦ ἐσίγησαν (Luke 20.26; cf. 20.40).

3. Luke 20.39

ἀποκριθέντες δέ τινες τῶν γραμματέων εἶπαν, Διδάσκαλε, καλῶς εἶπας.

But silenced opponents are not vanquished opponents, and although they play no active part in the arrest of Jesus, Luke clearly identified the scribes as part of that group which questioned Jesus and handed him over to the governor (Luke 22.66). The *agents provocateurs* did not succeed in entrapping Jesus, and Sadducees who brought their own question appear to have been adequately answered because Luke's account (*diff.* Matt, Mark) has the scribes respond approvingly to Jesus' argument from *Torah*. Even though they no longer dared ask him anything, scribes found Jesus offering them exegetical insights into a psalm before, in the hearing of the people, he turned to his disciples to warn against the scribes' ostentatiousness and greed. But while he shared this short sequence with Mark, Luke also had a previous, longer incident (Luke 11.37–52) in which Jesus comprehensively attacked the scribes' behaviour.

4. Luke 11.53–4

> Κἀκεῖθεν ἐξελθόντος αὐτοῦ ἤρξαντο οἱ γραμματεῖς καὶ οἱ Φαρισαῖοι δεινῶς ἐνέχειν καὶ ἀποστοματίζειν αὐτὸν περὶ πλειόνων, ἐνεδρεύοντες αὐτὸν θηρεῦσαί τι ἐκ τοῦ στόματος αὐτοῦ.

These verses are the climax of an account (Luke 11.37–52) of controversy between Jesus and these two groups, Pharisees and scribes, in the context of a meal at which Jesus was a guest. In Luke the groups are formally separated and each criticised in specific terms; their manner of life is vigorously *attacked*. Not surprisingly, 'they began to have it in for him terribly', and to lead him on by questioning him. There is, moreover, the matter of the verbs in v. 54; they belong to the discourse of hunting and of trapping. Importantly, one of them, ἐνεδρεύω is used in the New Testament only by Luke (cf. Acts 23.21; cf. also Acts 25.3) and appears uniquely here in the Gospel as Jesus' abused and insulted opponents smart and plot, echoing their predecessors' thoughts:

> ἐνεδρεύσωμεν τὸν δίκαιον
> ὅτι δύσχρηστος ἡμῖν ἐστιν
> καὶ ἐναντιοῦται τοῖς ἔργοις ἡμῶν·
> καὶ ὀνειδίζει ἡμῖν ἁμαρτήματα νόμου
> καὶ ἐπιφημίζει ἡμῖν ἁμαρτήματα παιδείας ἡμῶν.
>
> (Wis. 2.12)

It may, of course, be coincidence that Luke used *this* verb at *this* point. However, given echoes already heard in Luke 23.46–7 and in associated passages, and given the continuity between this controversy and those in Jerusalem closer to Jesus' death, perhaps ἐνεδρεύω should be heard as another, more distant echo from the model that helped shape Luke's story.

There remains one more feature of this incident which calls for note, no more. At Luke 11.49 stands:

> διὰ τοῦτο καὶ ἡ σοφία τοῦ θεοῦ εἶπεν, Ἀποστελῶ εἰς αὐτοὺς προφήτας καὶ ἀποστόλους, καὶ ἐξ αὐτῶν ἀποκτενοῦσιν καὶ διώξουσιν . . .

Two matters deserve comment. First, God's sending of messengers who are to be killed and persecuted is the theme of that parable of the vineyard which triggered the formal Lukan portrayal of Jesus' entrapment by his enemies (see Luke 20.19–20 above). This theme, of course, belongs to the heart of Israel's prophetic tradition and is frequently treated in scripture; it is also the theme of the abstract, plural and 'historical' explorations of δίκαιος in Wisdom. Second, if this be the case, then one may be dealing with an *echo* of scripture rather than an elusive citation, and ἡ σοφία τοῦ θεοῦ *may possibly* be a way of speaking of what is presently called the Wisdom of Solomon.[20] That suggestion may be set aside for the present; all that need be carried forward from here is that in Luke 11.53–4 is a Lukan construct with a high density of the language of entrapment and, in ἐνεδρεύω, a possible echo from Wisdom 2.12. Here is one step on Jesus' journey to his ἔξοδος in Jerusalem (Luke 9.31).

These passages are supported by the language of *close observation*, παρατηρέω, in Luke 6.7 and 14.1, itself redolent of the oppressors of the δίκαιος in Wisdom's model; by the ἐκπειράζων of Luke 10.25 and the πειράζοντες of 11.16 (both *contra* 4.12?). They may also be supported by an echo detected much earlier in Luke's account of the first encounter of Jesus with scribes and Pharisees (Luke 5.17–26).

5. Luke 5.26

> καὶ ἔκστασις ἔλαβεν ἅπαντας καὶ ἐδόξαζον τὸν θεόν, καὶ ἐπλήσθησαν φόβου λέγοντες ὅτι Εἴδομεν παράδοξα σήμερον.

[20] See the discussion in Romaniuk (1968, pp. 498f.).

Because this passage was discussed at length in chapter 2, its context may safely be summarised; a highly formalised opening to Luke's story gives it an ominous air (Luke 5.17a); its ending implies that these 'opponents' shared with others in saying that they had seen παράδοξα (5.26). These are the same people who 'murmur' (5.30) about Jesus' teaching and activity and who shortly afterwards keep sharp watch on him: παρετηροῦντο δὲ αὐτὸν οἱ γραμματεῖς καὶ οἱ Φαρισαῖοι εἰ ἐν τῷ σαββάτῳ θεραπεύει, ἵνα εὕρωσιν κατηγορεῖν αὐτοῦ (Luke 6.7). Luke's theme of entrapment begins early in his Gospel and is tightly systematised in the Jerusalem narrative. Embedded in this theme are two words, ἐνεδρεύω and παράδοξα, peculiar to Luke yet basic to Wisdom's account of the entrapment and vindication of the δίκαιος – aerolites from a Wisdom heaven?

It was the disciples' following of Jesus in his journey, their sharing his experience of conflicts designed to entrap him and hearing the summons themselves to take up their cross daily, that constituted the διαμεμενηκότες μετ' ἐμοῦ ἐν τοῖς πειρασμοῖς μου of Luke 22.28, however badly they were about to behave – although Luke spares them the apostasy implied in Mark's account of their abandoning him. During, and at the end of, that journey, Luke drew clearer sketches of the entrapment of the δίκαιος, echoing its language as well as its pattern. Luke alone among the evangelists thought of that journey and its complex outcome of Jesus' death, resurrection and exaltation as his ἔξοδος, another Wisdom word, (Luke 9.31 cf. Wis. 3.2b) which he was to fulfil or accomplish in Jerusalem.

G. Jesus' ἔξοδος in Jerusalem: Luke 9.31

> οἳ ὀφθέντες ἐν δόξῃ ἔλεγον τὴν ἔξοδον αὐτοῦ ἣν ἤμελλεν πληροῦν ἐν Ἰερουσαλήμ.

Apart from 2 Peter 1.15, ἔξοδος makes only this appearance in the NT. What might have led Luke to use this word at this point in his narrative? The tradition's reference to Moses (cf. Matt. 17.1–8; Mark 9.2–8) might have prompted Luke to choose ἔξοδος as a euphemism for Jesus' death, but his version of the transfiguration reveals that his choice of the term emerged from the δίκαιος-model with which he was working.

'Transfiguration' in Luke (9.28–36)

While Luke shares the substance of his account of Jesus' 'transfiguration' with the other synoptists, his own narrative has distinctive features. His version sets the event firmly in a context of prayer (9.28–9); his alone speaks of the δόξα in which Moses and Elijah appeared (9.30) and of Jesus' δόξα (9.32), subtly reinforcing the 'exodus' elements in his account; and by specifying what the older prophets were discussing with Jesus – τὴν ἔξοδον αὐτοῦ – Luke's version characteristically links δόξα with suffering (9.31). Although Luke shares with Mark and Matthew the essence of the heavenly voice's message – καὶ φωνὴ ἐγένετο ἐκ τῆς νεφέλης λέγουσα, Οὗτός ἐστιν ὁ υἱός μου [ὁ ἐκλελεγμένος; *diff.* Mark, Matt.; see below], αὐτοῦ ἀκούετε (Luke 9.35) – his echo from Deuteronomy 18.15, αὐτοῦ ἀκούετε, is, perhaps, clearer than theirs because his word order reflects its 'source.'

Given earlier recognition of echoes from Wisdom's model, the word ἔξοδος alone might have made one suspect another:

> But the souls of the righteous are in the hand of God, and no torment will ever touch them. In the eyes of the foolish they seemed to have died, and their ἔξοδος was thought to be a disaster, and their πορεία from us to be their destruction; but they are at peace. (Wis. 3.1–3)

There are, however, further supporting elements in Luke's transfiguration narrative which also need to be considered. First, Jesus' ἔξοδος is sited *in Jerusalem*, the city that 'kills the prophets' (Luke 13.34), the destination of Jesus' journeying (Luke 9.51), the city whose authorities encompassed his death. It is Luke's reference to *what is about to be accomplished in Jerusalem* that so tightly links the word ἔξοδος at 9.31 to the Jerusalem context of earlier sections of this study's present chapter; by this one word Luke has also crystallised the significant events of the climax of his Gospel. Second, τὴν ἔξοδον αὐτοῦ is the object of an interesting verb, ἣν ἤμελλεν πληροῦν ἐν Ἰερουσαλήμ, which suggests accomplishment or, possibly, completion, so it is difficult not to associate this ἔξοδος with Luke's thoroughgoing treatment of God's plan of salvation and fulfilment of scripture. Third, shared tradition affirmed that at the transfiguration a heavenly voice confirmed Jesus' baptismal experience of *sonship,* a Lukan theme isolated at 22.68 as the immediate cause of Jesus' committal to the governor by the Sanhedrin. Luke's retelling of the transfiguration story is thus distinctive in its association of ἔξοδος, Jesus' sonship and a sense of completion in Jerusalem, placing all these things in a clear 'Exodus' context.

It is easy to see how Wisdom's model might have suggested to Luke a symbolic use of ἔξοδος, although Goulder (1989) holds that the Lukan 'web of associations' found in the narrative suggested 'Exodus' to him. While the word appears only once in the Gospel, the fact of Jesus' journeying to his specific goal, both literal and conceptual, is carefully prepared for and reemphasised while in progress (e.g. Luke 9.51–7; 10.1, 38; 13.22, 33; 17.11; 18.31, 35; 19.1, 11, 28–44). The harmonics of *Pesah* and the events of Holy Week are also to be heard in Luke's use of ἔξοδος. If ἔξοδος really derives from Wisdom's model, *then its use in that model suggests what it may point to in the Gospel.* This is an important step, allowing both contexts to determine the word's meaning at Luke 9.31.

Ἔξοδος in Wisdom 2–5

Schweizer is probably mistaken in limiting the word's reference to Jesus' death (1993, pp. 104f.), because Wisdom's usage seems to have taken up both overtones of the concept 'exodus' in Jewish use and a fuller pattern of the life, death and vindication to which God's δίκαιοι had been brought. This can be clearly seen in Wisdom's treatment of its own δίκαιος-model: a long passage describing his oppressors' plotting against the δίκαιος (Wis. 2.12–20) is followed by the author's reaffirmation that their reasoning was flawed (2.21–4; cf. 2.1); it was faulty because they were ignorant of God's secret purposes and were themselves unconcerned with holiness (3.1–9). In this section the writer contrasts 'their' defective reasoning with God's *shalom* for his δίκαιοι. For them, death is not death but an ἔξοδος (3.2; cf. 7.6) or a πορεία (3.3; cf. 5.11; 13.18) to God's hands, a going out from oppression into *shalom* where there is no more torment and where their 'testing' is perceived to be God's testing them, as he tested Israel during her ἔξοδος.[21] Given

[21] See Deut. 8.3; 6.13, 16. The Dual Tradition used this Deuteronomic 'testing' motif as the matrix for its recounting Jesus' 'temptation' experience. The ἔξοδος which Jesus was about to complete in Jerusalem had begun in Luke's appropriated account of the Lord's wilderness experience in which, as an Israelite, he shared Israel's temptations and proved loyal (δίκαιος). In fact, in an earlier work Schweizer had clearly seen this: 'and how can one understand correctly Luke's conception of Jesus' journey up to Jerusalem – a journey which the people thought

Wisdom's concern with the Exodus in chapters 8–19, its earlier imagery of journeying is not surprising, and a reader recognises that the concept 'Exodus' is a whole package, comprising testing, humiliation, journeying, suffering at the hands of the 'ungodly' and ultimate vindication by God (Wis. 19.22 is a significant motif). Unlike the 'ungodly', because they trust God the δίκαιοι understand truth, and because they are concerned with holiness they know his mercy and grace (Wis. 3.9; cf. 4.15). This leads to one more aspect to explore.

Ὁ ἐκλελεγμένος (Luke 9.35)

Although the three synoptists substantially agree in their report of the heavenly voice's affirmation of Jesus' sonship (Luke 9.35), Luke's extension of ὁ υἱός μου is probably ὁ ἐκλελεγμένος (*hap. leg.* in the NT; cf. Goulder, 1989, p. 442) rather than the ὁ ἀγαπητός of Mark 9.7 or Matthew's ἐν ᾧ εὐδόκησα (Matt. 17.5). These extensions tend to draw a reader's attention to specific scriptural contexts for ὁ υἱός μου; at this point Luke's account probably echoes Wisdom in that its vindicated δίκαιοι are also God's *elect*, those who understand, who know God's grace and mercy.

> οἱ πεποιθότες ἐπ' αὐτῷ συνήσουσιν ἀλήθειαν,
> καὶ οἱ πιστοὶ ἐν ἀγάπῃ προσμενοῦσιν αὐτῷ·
> ὅτι χάρις καὶ ἔλεος τοῖς ἐκλεκτοῖς αὐτοῦ. (Wis. 3.9)

This complex of understanding, grace, mercy and God's elect appears again:

> ἀρεστὴ γὰρ ἦν κυρίῳ ἡ ψυχὴ αὐτοῦ
> διὰ τοῦτο ἔσπευσεν ἐκ μέσου πονηρίας·
> οἱ δὲ λαοὶ ἰδόντες καὶ μὴ νοήσαντες
> μηδὲ θέντες ἐπὶ διανοίᾳ τὸ τοιοῦτο,
> ὅτι χάρις καὶ ἔλεος ἐν τοῖς ἐκλεκτοῖς αὐτοῦ
> καὶ ἐπισκοπὴ ἐν τοῖς ὁσίοις αὐτοῦ. (Wis. 4.14–15)

Summary

Luke's version of the transfiguration, anticipating the complex events of Jesus' final days during *Pesah* in Jerusalem, not only

would culminate in the immediate coming of the kingdom of God (19.11), while in fact the cross was waiting – without any knowledge of the wanderings of the patriarchs and of the Israelites, who were all on the way to the promised land?' (1971, p. 146). *Cf* Luke 11.20 for another hint of the Exodus motif in Luke.

named that complex ἔξοδος but further echoed Wisdom in speaking of this δίκαιος as God's chosen one. One can now be reasonably confident of this because many of the criteria for allusion are satisfied. This pair of rare words (criterion 3) in Luke–Acts standing close together (criterion 1) in a key, traditional passage already focusing on Jesus' sonship, itself firmly linked (criterion 2) to the closing chapters of the Gospel, sustain each other as echoes of Luke's underlying model of the humiliated, killed and vindicated δίκαιος. Discussion has also made coherent some elements in Luke's narrative which continue to command commentators' attention (criterion 5). To determine whether the fourth criterion can be satisfied, this study needs to compare Wisdom's model with Luke's presentation of Jesus' suffering and vindication. First, there is another echo to which to listen carefully.

H. Ignorance and guilt: a Lukan theme

Houlden (1984, pp. 64f.) highlighted this theme when, in a seminal note appended to his discussion of Luke's purposes, he wrote:

> The Wisdom of Solomon ... may have a bearing on the attitudes which are so problematic in Luke. In Wis. 2.22, we read of the ungodly who persecute the righteous: καὶ οὐκ ἔγνωσαν μυστήρια Θεοῦ. Read in conjunction with 3.10, this makes plain that the ungodly both act in ignorance and are punished for their deed. It is virtually the position of Luke, and it may incline us to ascribe his attribution of ignorance to the Jews less to his almost proverbial *mansuetudo* than to a kind of convention or at any rate to a less smiling attitude.

Houlden also wondered whether γνῶναι τὰ μυστήρια (Luke 8.10) might echo Wisdom 2.22, but his noting that Matthew has the same variant (13.11) on Mark (4.11) robs the point of much of its force; it is no longer a *Lukan* feature, although it may signal something happening in a wider circle of churches. For example, Paul probably knew this Wisdom passage, although in his survey of Pauline allusions Romaniuk (1968, pp. 503–13) seems to have ignored 1 Corinthians 2.6–9, where Paul's discussion of σοφία not only has verbal allusions to Wisdom, but highlights the 'rulers of this age' as those whose ignorance of God's plan was the cause of their crucifying the Lord of glory, precisely the attitude taken by Luke (see below). Paul probably expected Corinthian Christians to take his point.[22]

The issue is: does Luke's apparent emphasis on the ignorance of God's purposes of those who brought about Jesus' death echo Wisdom's model? There are other issues related to this theme, particularly, according to Luke, the question of who was responsible for Jesus' death. While this question has to be approached, its detailed discussion is not possible here. Perhaps all that can confidently be said is that there is a Lukan 'ignorance' theme; that this theme is closely associated in Luke–Acts with clear attribution to specific groups of responsibility for Jesus' death; that this pairing matches an element in Wisdom's biography of the δίκαιος; that there is other, substantial cumulative evidence that Luke shaped his narrative of Jesus' passion, highlighting features which seemed to him to fulfil what scripture had said of the δίκαιος; consequently, his 'ignorance' theme tends to support earlier evidence that Luke was working with an interpretative matrix drawn from Wisdom.

In this regard, the strongest clues to Luke's debt to Wisdom are: first, the tight connection between his references to ignorance and to an emphasised responsibility for Jesus' death; second, he roots this kerygmatic theme in a distinctively 'Lukan' word of the Lord at the heart of his passion story. If this 'ignorance' theme has to do with Jesus' oppressors, who were they? This question is put to the speeches in Acts before attention is focused on three specific passages.

Jesus' oppressors: speeches in Acts

It is evident from the speeches in Acts that at the heart of the matter lies *the city of Jerusalem*. Reflecting retrospectively on Jesus' passion, Paul, preaching in a Pisidian synagogue, placed direct responsibility for Jesus' death on the citizens of Jerusalem and on their rulers (Acts 13.27, see below; cf. 2.14; 4.16); that sermon is Luke's sole example of an address to a Jewish congregation outside Jerusalem and is, consequently, of great importance for reconstructing what Luke thought that Paul proclaimed. Identifying these 'rulers', Peter had placed them 'in Jerusalem' (Acts 4.16). By implication, both Stephen (Acts 6.8–15; 7.54–8:1) and Peter (Acts 3.1, 9;

[22] Particularly if Kuhn, *ZNW* 28 (1929), is right in holding that Wisdom was much respected and read assiduously by NT authors who, presumably, shared their passion for this book with Christian communities.

4.1–7) are presented as *directly* addressing people in Jerusalem. Luke's Gospel prepared readers for his focus on Jerusalem: it was where Jesus' ἔξοδος was to be fulfilled (Luke 9.31; cf. 18.31) and his lamenting over Jerusalem firmly relates to his own destiny (Luke 13.1–5, 31–5; 19.41–4; 23.27–31). Luke's Gospel has thirty references to Jerusalem by name, more than the sum of those in Matthew (twelve) and Mark (eleven) together. Of more importance than the total of references to this city – there are sixty more in the Acts – is their focus on Jerusalem's reputation and Jesus' destiny.

This city, however, is essentially its citizens and Luke has involved both its people (Acts 3.11; 4.27; 6.12; 13.27) and its ruling class (Acts 4.5; 5.21b, 27; 6.12; 13.27) in responsibility for Jesus' death, although it will later be seen that Luke moves to distance 'the people' from the 'rulers' (Acts 2.41, 47b; 4.4, 21; 5.13, 16, 26). However Luke may use ὁ λαός and ὁ ὄχλος, according to the speeches in Acts he clearly intended readers to understand Jerusalem's *inhabitants* to be directly responsible for Jesus' death.[23]

Further, Luke's preachers are shown *to emphasise* for their hearers in Jerusalem the grave responsibility for what they had done: the presence of ὑμεῖς throughout (Acts 3.13–15; 4.10; 5.28; 7.51–3) points this up. Things are other in Pisidian Antioch where 'they' replaces 'you', simply because Paul's hearers are not in Jerusalem and consequently not responsible for this deed (13.27). Indeed, this sermon is designed to summon this congregation to *hear* God's word and so escape the fate of those who do not hear (Acts 13.40–1). This emphatic attribution of responsibility is sharpened by the contrast between what Jerusalem's people did and what God was doing (e.g. 'you' – Acts 3.13–15; 4.10; 5.30; 7.51; contrast 'they' – 13.28–30; 'God'–3.15; 4.10b; 5.30a, 31).

There remains, however, a curious twist in Luke's narrative: the hearers undoubtedly did this dreadful thing, yet they did it *in ignorance* (Acts 3.17, which probably governs the following two chapters also). This reference to 'ignorance' apparently diminishes the hearers' guilt in so far as they recognise what they have done and repent (Acts 2.37–42; 5.12–16; cf. Wis. 11.23–6).

Echoes of Luke's passion narrative

These Acts speeches cohere with Luke's passion story; readers are given enough information to recall that longer narrative. Jesus was

[23] *Contra* Sanders (1987). This is an important consideration in deciding whether Luke–Acts is anti-Semitic.

denied and betrayed (Acts 3.13–15 cf. Luke 9.44; 23.25; cf. also Luke 20.20; 22.2); he was denied in favour of Barabbas (Acts 3.14, cf. Luke 23.25); he was killed or murdered (Acts 3.15; 7.52) by being crucified (Acts 4.10; cf. Luke 23.21, 23), that is, hung on a tree (Acts 5.30; 13.29), a term which draws attention to the shameful manner of this death (Deut. 21.22–3; cf. Wis. 2.20). Luke's 'distancing' of 'the people' from this process starts early in his passion narrative (Luke 23.27, 48, 50–3) and runs on into Acts (see above). Ascough (1993) has detected Lukan parallels among Peter's denial of Jesus, the people's uncharacteristic behaviour before Pilate and the repentance that both show later. Such Lukan treatment makes for further distance between the people of Jerusalem and their rulers. Ascough's article sets yet another question mark against readings of Luke–Acts which find an underlying anti-Semitism at work while ignoring distinctions drawn by Luke among diverse groups; this is also the thrust of O'Toole's 1993 article in *Biblica.*

Luke's theme of 'ignorance' in the Acts

Two principal passages in the Acts focus this theme, but do not exhaust it. The first, in Paul's synagogue address at Pisidian Antioch (13.16–41), is the only evidence in Acts of what Luke took to be Paul's message to Jews. This speech, an Acts parallel to that in the Nazareth synagogue (Luke 4.16–30), is probably paradigmatic and certainly addressed to Jews *outside* Jerusalem. The second, at the heart of Peter's speeches *in* Jerusalem, carefully distinguishes varying layers of responsibility for the death of Jesus. The core of Luke's 'ignorance' theme lies in its complex of responsibility for Jesus' death, the possibilities of penitence and, last, ignorance of God's plan of salvation revealed through scripture, particularly *Torah* and prophets. Within this complex stands also the irony that Jerusalem's ignorance of scripture and its rejection of Jesus made possible God's fulfilling of his plan; yet it is Jerusalem's ignorance which now makes possible, through the apostles' preaching, her belated recognition both of Jesus and of scripture's meaning and, consequently, the possibility of her penitence and salvation.

1. Acts 13.27

οἱ γὰρ κατοικοῦντες ἐν Ἰερουσαλὴμ καὶ οἱ ἄρχοντες αὐτῶν τοῦτον ἀγνοήσαντες καὶ τὰς φωνὰς τῶν προφητῶν τὰς κατὰ πᾶν σάββατον ἀναγινωσκομένας κρίναντες ἐπλήρωσαν ...

The syntax is not easily unscrambled, but this verse seems to mean: 'Jerusalem's residents and their rulers fulfilled [the prophetic scriptures] by judging him, because they did not comprehend [recognise?] him or the voices of the prophets which are read every Sabbath and although they found no reason for his death, they asked Pilate to have him done away with.' This is a hotly disputed area, but for the present this study works with the reasonable assumption that Luke held Jerusalem and her residents as primarily responsible for Jesus' death; this 'Pauline' kerygmatic statement speaks of Jerusalem, so does not directly address its Jewish hearers as those guilty of what happened. In this, it differs from Peter's address (see below) which emphasises his hearers' own part in Jesus' story. But the twofold ignorance of those responsible is made clear: **first**, they had failed to grasp the prophetic message. As is normally the case, this theme has been prepared for in the Gospel, for example, in its programmatic Nazareth incident.[24] Again, the ironic conclusion of Luke's tale of Dives and Lazarus not only generalises the moral importance of 'hearing' scripture, but one hears in it also a Lukan comment, anticipating the Acts, on those not moved by Jesus' being raised from the dead; εἰ Μωϋσέως καὶ τῶν προφητῶν οὐκ ἀκούουσιν, οὐδ' ἐάν τις ἐκ νεκρῶν ἀναστῇ πεισθήσονται (Luke 16.31). Of course, in Luke's Gospel disciples also are revealed as ignorant (Luke 18.31; 24.25–7, 32, 44–6) particularly in relation to Jesus' sayings about the Son of man (Luke 9.45 (cf. 8.10) cf. 18.34). **Second**, Jerusalem's residents had, consequently, not recognised Jesus; leaders and people together shared this failure in recognition. Luke's story of the walk to Emmaus takes up the same theme in relation to disciples and clearly demonstrates that only when the Lord had 'opened up the scriptures' could his disciples grasp what had been 'going on' during the puzzling events in Jerusalem. Presumably, the speeches of Acts are Lukan outworkings of his understanding of the disciples' new hermeneutic.

[24] Parallels between Pisidian Antioch and Nazareth (Luke 4.16–30) are important and numerous. One, that Paul's destiny is modelled on that of his Lord, is basic to Talbert's case. For our purposes, Luke's Nazareth narrative presents a synagogue that listens to the prophets read but does not hear them, that sees a prophet read but neither hears nor recognises him. Consequently, they anticipated this prophet's end (4.28–30), but it was impossible that a prophet should perish outside Jerusalem. (See also Anderson (1964); Grässer (1972); Hill (1971); Reicke (1973)).

The result of their ignorance of scripture and failure to 'recognise' Jesus is that Jerusalem's inhabitants 'brought to completion' what scripture had to say of him: ὡς δὲ ἐτέλεσαν πάντα τὰ περὶ αὐτοῦ γεγραμμένα, καθελόντες ἀπὸ τοῦ ξύλου ἔθηκαν εἰς μνημεῖον. (Acts 13.29). There is possibly an echo here of the shameful death (Deut. 21.22–3 cf. Wis. 2.20a) plotted by those who trapped the δίκαιος. But there is no hint in this speech that in Jerusalem's earlier ignorance lies also the possibility of her penitence; this congregation in Antioch needs only to be aware of the importance of *their* listening to the prophetic word (Acts 13.39–41) which warned them that even when God's work is spelt out clearly for them, as Paul had done in his sermon, demonstrating how God's promises had been worked out in Jesus' life and vindication, it remains possible not to believe it. Luke's ignorance theme is not always exculpatory; evidence of that emerged in an earlier focus.

2. Acts 3.17

> καὶ νῦν, ἀδελφοί, οἶδα ὅτι κατὰ ἄγνοιαν ἐπράξατε, ὥσπερ καὶ οἱ ἄρχοντες ὑμῶν.

This is the 'strong' form of Luke's theme. The immediate context of this extract shows that it is 'the people' who are here addressed and whose responsibility for Jesus' death is emphasised (Acts 3.13, 14, 15); but together with this charge Peter offers them 'mitigating circumstances' and calls on them to repent. Much of what needs to be said has been said above; what they did, the people did in ignorance, *as did their rulers*. A distinction between these two groups reflects Luke's recounting the passion where each has a different function, as Ascough (1993, pp. 362f.) has traced.

What commands one's closest interest here is the emergence of Luke's 'ignorance' theme in a context where Jesus is described as δίκαιος (Acts 3.14–17):

> ὑμεῖς δὲ τὸν ἅγιον καὶ δίκαιον ἠρνήσασθε ... τὸν δὲ ἀρχηγὸν τῆς ζωῆς ἀπεκτείνατε, ὃν ὁ θεὸς ἤγειρεν ἐκ νεκρῶν ... καὶ νῦν, ἀδελφοί, οἶδα ὅτι κατὰ ἄγνοιαν ἐπράξατε, ὥσπερ καὶ οἱ ἄρχοντες ὑμῶν.

Earlier, where two elements of this δίκαιος-model emerged in the same close context, the presence of two was judged to be more convincing than one. These elements are linked because in Wisdom it is *the narrator* who on both occasions (Wis. 2.21–2; 4.15–18) strongly comments on the 'not-knowing' of the ungodly that led them to oppression of and contempt for the δίκαιος; this attitude towards ignorance and moral responsibility for it belongs to Wisdom's author's perspective on God's dealing with Israel. Luke's perspective is less harsh: the apostolic mission in Jerusalem offers the preachers' hearers space for repentance and amendment of life.

There is oblique evidence that this Lukan perspective is deep-seated rather than cosmetic. Because δίκαιος features in the basic christology of three major witnesses, Peter, Stephen and Paul, it is a little surprising to note the 'ignorance' theme's apparent absence from Stephen's witnessing. Although it does not figure in the immediate context of Acts 7.52, the theme is present in the speech in two ways. First, the whole of Stephen's speech may be thought to epitomise God's successive δίκαιοι *contra* an unheeding or hostile Israel. But, second, and more importantly, an intrusive Lukan comment disrupts a sequence in such a way as to disclose his own underlying thought. The sequence is found in Acts 7.14–34 where early allusions to Genesis (vv. 14–16) give way to a run of indebtedness to Exodus, particularly Exodus 2.2–3.10. This second run begins at Exodus 2.2, after which only two verses appear not to be indebted to Exodus, Acts 7.22 and 25: v. 22 looks like the Lukan summarising formulae of Luke 1.80 and 2.52 with a longer side-glance at 24.19 (ὃς ἐγένετο ἀνὴρ προφήτης δυνατὸς ἐν ἔργῳ καὶ λόγῳ ἐναντίον τοῦ θεοῦ καὶ παντὸς τοῦ λαοῦ); this is probably further evidence of Luke's closely relating Jesus' story with that of Moses. Acts 7.25 is the narrator's plain, non-biblical intrusion between vv. 24 and 26 which would otherwise remain connected, sustaining their place in the author's sequence from Exodus. Acts 7.25 is thus a Lukan comment on Moses' story: 'He supposed that his kinsfolk would understand that God through him was rescuing them, *but they did not understand.*' (NewRSV, italics added). Not-understanding, being-ignorant is one element in Luke's theological perspective on Israel's treatment of the δίκαιος in every age and runs as a sub-text throughout Stephen's speech. Is it this sub-text which prompts this proto-martyr's prayer for his killers' forgiveness, Κύριε, μὴ στήσῃς αὐτοῖς ταύτην τὴν ἁμαρτίαν. καὶ τοῦτο εἰπὼν ἐκοιμήθη (Acts 7.60b)?

Lukan themes tend to link the two volumes: the presence of an 'ignorance' theme in Acts suggests that it also appears in the Gospel.

Luke's theme of 'ignorance' in the Gospel: Luke 23.34

ὁ δὲ Ἰησοῦς ἔλεγεν, Πάτερ, ἄφες αὐτοῖς, οὐ γὰρ οἴδασιν τί ποιοῦσιν: διαμεριζόμενοι δὲ τὰ ἱμάτια αὐτοῦ ἔβαλον κλήρους.

It was urged earlier (chapter 6D, 'Jesus and Stephen: Master and martyr') that despite its textual history there are good reasons, positive and negative, to sustain this verse as Luke's composition. The substance of that argument was that Stephen's generous forgiveness of his tormentors (Acts 7.60b) is more likely to reflect the model of Jesus' nobly bearing his suffering and death than the other way round. At this point, the argument for its authenticity takes up another thread: in Luke 23.34 Luke offers dominical authority for the apostolic 'ignorance' theme in Acts, a *logion* which follows immediately on Luke 23.32–3 – ἤγοντο δὲ καὶ ἕτεροι κακοῦργοι δύο σὺν αὐτῷ ἀναιρεθῆναι. καὶ ὅτε ἦλθον ἐπὶ τὸν τόπον τὸν καλούμενον Κρανίον, ἐκεῖ ἐσταύρωσαν αὐτὸν καὶ τοὺς κακούργους, ὃν μὲν ἐκ δεξιῶν ὃν δὲ ἐξ ἀριστερῶν, echoing Wisdom 2.20–2:

'Let us condemn him to a shameful death,
for, according to what he says, he will be protected.'[25]
Thus they reasoned, but they were led astray,
for their wickedness blinded them,
and they did not know the secret purposes of God,
nor hoped for the wages of holiness,
nor discerned the prize for blameless souls.

Thus Luke's description of Jesus' execution is linked with a strong statement of the ignorance of those who plotted and did these things; in three verses Luke echoes three verses of Wisdom's model. Peter's speech expressly embraces both people and rulers as having acted in ignorance when they delivered up Jesus to death; Paul's sermon reiterates that fact. Luke's measured telling of Jesus' bearing at his death (see above) now also links Jesus' prayer to the Father for forgiveness for his persecutors with *a strong assertion of their ignorance of what they were doing*; such prayer probably exemplifies Jesus' ἐπιείκεια (Wis. 2.19). As already noted, the increased use of

[25] Does one assume the δίκαιος to have in mind Ps. 22.9? At Matt. 27.43 the margin of N-A 26 picks up to an allusion to Wisdom's model as well as to Isa. 36.7, 20.

'Father' in Luke's passion narrative is probably associated with Wisdom's model.

Summary

At the outset it was acknowledged that one could do little more than note Luke's use of this 'ignorance' theme and place it within the context of what an interpreter can be more sure of, namely Luke's retelling Jesus' story as the fulfilling of Wisdom's δίκαιος-model. If, however, Luke 23.34 may reasonably be claimed for Luke's composition, then the enigmatic 'ignorance' theme of the speeches in Acts finds its roots at the heart of Luke's creative, distinctive moulding of his passion narrative around Wisdom's δίκαιος-matrix. Houlden's tentative suggestion is made much more likely when set within this larger context, and Kuhn's confidence[26] vindicated just a little in respect of one evangelist.

By the criteria formulated earlier it seems safe to hear another echo of that model. First, because this 'ignorance' element can be placed within Luke's overall δίκαιος-model, Houlden's suggestion that Wisdom may explain some problematic features of Luke–Acts should be both welcomed and taken as satisfying the fifth criterion. This argument is cumulative rather than circular, building on Houlden's original suggestion. Combining Luke's 'ignorance' theme with his using Wisdom's δίκαιος-model certainly helps to make sense of Luke's telling of his story: it associates this theme with Luke's interest in the fulfilling of God's plan revealed by scripture. Second, because it seems likely that the disputed *logion* at Luke 23.34 belongs organically to Luke's composition, Luke's 'ignorance' theme in Acts is linked overtly and directly to his passion narrative where were detected his first, dense allusions to Wisdom's δίκαιος-model. If that be the case, the second criterion is satisfied. Third, in one 'ignorance' context (Acts 3.17) the near presence of δίκαιος as a descriptor of Jesus (Acts 3.14) was noted, which satisfies the first criterion. It is also possible that Paul's sermon in the Antioch synagogue (Acts 13.16b–41) is woven around its unexpressed text, Habakkuk 2.4b – ὁ δὲ δίκαιος ἐκ πίστεώς μου ζήσεται – which would, though more distantly, relate δίκαιος and ignorance in this Pauline context also.[27] But this possibility cannot be argued in detail

[26] See the quotation with which this chapter opens.
[27] This argument is worked out in detail in Doble (1992, chapter 6C2).

here, nor is there need of more support than that already offered in the Petrine speech. Fourth, because among the evangelists this theme is distinctively Lukan, evidenced by its unique appearance in the gospel tradition at Luke 23.34; because it is closely related to Luke's overarching theme of scripture's fulfilment and God's plan; because Wisdom's abstract model makes much of the ungodly oppressors' ignorance of God's purposes (Wis. 2.22; 4.15; cf. 3.10), one may be confident that this theme at least *supports* earlier evidence that Luke was working with Wisdom's δίκαιος-matrix. Luke's attribution of ignorance to 'the Jews' is not a conventional thing,[28] but a studied contribution to his own *theologia crucis*.

I. Criterion four

One can now assess how much of Wisdom's primary model appears to be basic to the model underlying Luke's retelling of Jesus' death and life. There were both an 'orbital shift' in Luke's passion narrative and some significant 'verbal remnants' that probably confirm the presence of a model that determined the 'shift'.

'Orbital shift'

The distinctiveness of Luke's retelling the story of Jesus' death (Luke 23.46–7) is widely recognised. It portrays one who, rather than rail against 'that great absence', entrusted his spirit to the hands of God whom he addressed as 'Father' (a word appearing often in Luke's story of the passion), one whom Luke's centurion consequently described as ὄντως ... δίκαιος. It portrays one whose magisterial dignity is better described positively as ἐπιείκεια and ἀνεξικακία than as the absence of emotion. In his testament at the Passover meal, Jesus described experience shared with his disciples as 'testings'. Following sustained attempts to entrap him, at his appearance before the Sanhedrin the Lukan Jesus was directly asked, 'Are you Son of God'? His answer ensured that this phrase was the reason for his committal to Pilate and to death. This Jesus sought his oppressors' forgiveness on the grounds that they did not know what they were doing and, from Emmaus into the Acts, the authorities' responsibility for his shameful death was attributed to their ignorance of God's plan.

[28] *Contra* Houlden (1984, p. 64).

Perhaps telling evidence for this shift also lies in the three-fold use of δίκαιος as a christological descriptor in Acts: each instance is in a speech by a significant witness; in each case the word focuses an encounter with those who persecuted Jesus; in two instances the word directly relates to their responsibility for Jesus' death.[29] Luke thus uses δίκαιος of Jesus four times, and on each occasion it has to do with his persecution and death.

Verbal remnants

The model that redirected his passion narrative was in Luke's mind at the beginning as at the end of its trajectory: one can see why at the transfiguration he spoke of events to be realised in Jerusalem as an ἔξοδος and at Stephen's martyrdom his Jesus was standing (ἑστῶτα) rather than sitting. It is just possible that when formally assembled authorities first carefully watched Jesus' deeds and heard his words Luke used παράδοξα proleptically and, when shortly into his narrating the Jerusalem journey he focused further conflict, he echoed ἐνεδρεύω from the same model.

Luke used this term probably because its associated scriptural model helped him grasp and communicate what was really happening in Jesus' shameful death. He knew well that the Lord himself spoke of *Son of man*, but that term could not counter complaints that Jesus' death was under God's curse; Wisdom's model of the δίκαιος effectively placed such a shameful death within God's purposes. The paradox of salvation is that Jesus, the humiliated δίκαιος, died *according to the scriptures*[30] and was vindicated by God's ensuring that his death was entrance to God's presence. Paradoxically, from one point of view his was a shameful death, from another it was noble; from one point of view he suffered an ἔξοδος, from another his was an ἔξοδος to standing at God's right

[29] In note 24 to chapter 5, 'Paul's apologia in Jerusalem', certain parallels are indicated between the description of Paul as a persecutor and Wisdom's conflict passages; these may be another, supporting strand of evidence for Luke's echoing Wisdom.

[30] Perhaps our identification of Luke's reliance on Wisdom's δίκαιος-model may go some way to writing a footnote to Vermes' comments on early Christian attempts to account for Jesus' death (1993, p. 210). Vermes, like Bruce, rightly notes that one looks in vain for scriptural warrant for a suffering messiah; Luke probably knew that, which may account for his turning to Wisdom. But he also knew that Christians had filled the word 'messiah' with the 'things concerning Jesus', because that was a term which most focused their sense of fulfilment.

hand in the presence of those who persecuted him. Luke's *theologia crucis* is built on this paradox of salvation.[31]

[31] An early draft of this chapter was presented as a paper to the annual seminar on the Use of the Old Testament in the New. I am grateful to Mrs Wendy Sproston and to Dr Lionel North, both of the University of Hull, for inviting me to this seminar at Hawarden, and my thanks are due to its many members who offered comments, but most particularly to Dr Alan Lowe of the University of Leeds for his perceptive and helpful criticism, both in word and in letters. This chapter owes much to him; its deficiencies remain mine. I am also grateful to the Revd Dr W.H. Burns who has not only discussed the final version of this chapter with me, but read the manuscript and commented on it in detail.

8

TOWARDS A LUKAN *THEOLOGIA CRUCIS*

Previous chapters examined detailed evidence for Luke's use of Wisdom in shaping his passion narrative.[1] This chapter briefly reflects on ways in which Luke's choice of δίκαιος as a key christological term points to his distinctive *theologia crucis*. Although he used δίκαιος of Jesus anarthrously at Luke 23.47, Luke firmly placed this word on the lips of his three major witnesses, Peter, Stephen and Paul, specifically in 'Jerusalem' contexts as they confronted Jesus' opponents who were now opponents of his *sheluchim* also.[2] Affirming that Jesus was the Δίκαιος was probably Luke's way of dealing with problems and possibilities posed by Jesus' shameful death; it may not be all that Luke had to say on this matter,[3] but appreciating the contribution of Wisdom's δίκαιος-model to his two volumes constitutes a defence of Luke against accusations that he has no *theologia crucis*.[4] Δίκαιος, one christological descriptor among many, sharply focuses Luke's position that Jesus was *truly just* and *truly raised*. Because Luke affirmed these facts to be uniquely true of Jesus, δίκαιος contributes one element to Kümmel's defence that for Luke the cross was final event: for Luke, cross and resurrection were a paradox of salvation that laid claim on Jesus' followers.

1 In one sense all narration is interpretation and Luke's perspective means that he tells the story of Jesus' passion, not neutrally, but as an element in God's fulfilling his plan of salvation. Beck (1981) rightly identified many Wisdom elements in this Lukan perspective but stopped well short of attempting to describe Luke's *theologia crucis*. That, of course, was not his purpose in writing, but he sharply focused for one reader the place of *imitatio Christi* in Luke's work.

2 Peter and Stephen make their statements in Jerusalem *directly* to Jerusalem's citizens and their leaders. Paul's defence in Jerusalem is of his own, earlier encounter with the exalted Jesus, an oppressor meeting the vindicated one.

3 We leave open, e.g. the question of Paul's farewell to the Ephesian elders (Acts 20.18–38) with its 'unLukan' v. 28, which possibly represents what Luke believed to be Paul's position (so Tannehill, 1961, p. 198, n. 11), just as the ταπεινοφροσύνη of v. 19 echoes Paul (see chapter 4 above, n. 31). So it is with Acts 8.26–40.

4 See chapter 1A above, esp. notes 1 and 11.

A. Δίκαιος among christological descriptors

Δίκαιος occupies a distinctive place among Luke's christological descriptors. The term carries a corporate dimension (Wisdom's δίκαιοι) yet focuses on Jesus' unique place in Luke's thought about salvation. Luke knew and used a variety of christological descriptors, but Wisdom's δίκαιος-model enabled him to tell the story of Jesus' humiliation and shameful death as an essential part of God's plan of salvation; and since christology seems to be ultimately dependent on soteriology[5] δίκαιος is a key christological term. Some of his other descriptors were introduced in Luke's prologue and developed in the rest of his work: Son of God, Lord, Saviour, Christ. While these are all 'scriptural' words drawn from Israel's experience and from her hope that God would once more act to save, for Luke these are words now filled by Christians with experiences and convictions associated with their own κήρυγμα that God acted through Jesus. 'Prophet' is another key term in Luke's portrayal of Jesus and is tightly linked with his suffering and death in Jerusalem.[6] Yet neither 'Christ' nor 'prophet' was a term which readily related such suffering and death to God's plan revealed in scripture. Further, except for bringing the sequence to its end in the Stephen-unit, Luke observed what appears to be Christian tradition's handling of the term 'Son of man', restricting the phrase to Jesus' lips, so it cannot function as a *Lukan* christological term,[7] although he is prepared to edit such sayings to conform to his own passion tradition (e.g. Mark 10.45 seems very like Luke 19.10[8] and there are Lukan fingerprints all over Luke 18.31–4). Δίκαιος

[5] This case was urged by Young (1977, pp. 13–47, esp. pp. 13, 30 and 38); cf. her note in Goulder, M., *Incarnation and Myth: The Debate Continued*, London: SCM Press (1979), pp. 101–3. While δίκαιος as a christological term appears only four times in Luke–Acts, its importance in the Lukan scheme is much greater than its numerical value because of its contexts. In key incidents δίκαιος is an explanatory descriptor indicating what Luke believed God to be doing to save people in and through the life, ministry and especially the death of Jesus. Luke's concept of salvation includes elements drawn from Moses and Joshua, from the prophet of Deutero-Isaiah and from Wisdom, in both of which an Exodus of the People of God from bondage to liberty is a central notion. To identify Luke's *theologia crucis* one needs to spell out what Luke thought God to be doing through Jesus' story.

[6] Luke 13.33 is a key *logion* here, sharply focusing Luke's great construct of the journey *to Jerusalem* and what awaited Jesus there (cf. Luke 4.24; 6.23; 11.47, 49, 50; 13.34; Acts 7.52).

[7] It is, obviously, a christological term which Luke uses and possibly adapts (e.g. Luke 18.31).

[8] See, e.g., Doble (1992, pp. 349–56).

remains the one *Lukan* christological descriptor closely associated with Jesus' death.

Luke's decision to produce two volumes probably emerged from a problem created for him by a rift with the local synagogue:[9] how might he deal with the story of Jesus' shameful death in his presentation of the apostles' preaching? He was committed to retelling Jesus' story as the fulfilment of God's plan, and that in a world where crucifixion was commonly held to be evidence of criminality or of God's curse. Although, in post-resurrection contexts, Luke could have Jesus or Paul speak of *the Christ's* destiny to suffer (e.g. Luke 24.46, cf. Acts 26.22–3), apart from equating Χριστός with terms such as *'ebed Yahweh* or Son of man, there is little evidence of scriptural roots of this notion.[10] Δίκαιος, however, as understood in the Wisdom of Solomon, comprised such elements as God's plan, 'son' and 'father', plotting by ungodly opponents, a virtuous life crowned by endurance of a shameful death, and a glorious *post mortem* vindication. The Christian traditions known to Luke were already made up of such material and the author of 1 Peter also knew how a δίκαιος-matrix made sense of it. Both Ruppert (1972, pp. 15–26, 72–5) and Schweizer (1993, pp. 225–6, 241, 253) have affirmed the place of the suffering prophet and *righteous one* in Lukan thought; neither, however, teased out Luke's use of Wisdom's model. It is in this model underlying both Luke's passion narrative[11] and the speeches in Acts that the internal logic of Luke's *theologia crucis* is to be found. How might this be?

For Luke, the term δίκαιος, both at Luke 23.47 and in the three

[9] Many reasons have been suggested for Luke's producing two volumes; our work suggests another – that he modelled his scheme on the twofold story of Wisdom's δίκαιος (see D below). Luke's emphasis in the Gospel on Jesus' death and his systematic use of δίκαιος in Acts suggests that he countered adverse comment on Jesus' death by showing how the earliest witnesses rooted it firmly in God's plan, expounding scripture to make sense of it. *Theological* pressure emerging from a rift with the local synagogue should be added to the social and political pressures identified by Esler (1987) – who, incidentally, cast his vote for Kilpatrick in the matter of Luke 23.47 (1987, p. 203).

[10] See Bruce (1952, p. 111), Vermes (1993, p. 210); cf. chapter 5 above. This was also a problem for Creed (1930, p. lxxii): 'There is indeed no *theologia crucis* beyond the affirmation that the Christ must suffer, since so the prophetic scriptures had foretold.' They had not. Luke, however, seems to have realised that Wisdom's scriptural model potentially constituted a *theologia crucis* which made sense of the scandal of the cross.

[11] Because, as was argued in chapters 2–7, Luke's passion narrative echoes Wisdom's model, its 'telling' is not neutral (*contra* Cadbury, 1958, p. 280). In shaping his narrative Luke *explains* what is happening just as he does by his choice of δίκαιος as his descriptor.

target speeches in Acts,[12] made possible his bringing together of four strands of thought:

First, δίκαιος *directly confronted the scandal* of Jesus' suffering and shameful death which was probably a problem for Luke's community as it was for the Corinthian church – 'a stumbling block to Jews and nonsense to Gentiles' (1 Cor. 1.23). If, with Esler,[13] we postulate a *corpus mixtum* recently estranged from its neighbouring synagogue, then Luke's *accenting the shame of the cross* by speaking of Jesus' 'hanging on a tree' (Deut. 21.22–3; cf. Acts 13.29 *et al.*) may be seen as part of his strategy to make sense of Jesus' *death* and to counter protests that so shameful a death could only be of one cursed by God. Luke found in Wisdom's δίκαιος a scriptural model of Jesus' death detailed enough to eradicate all suspicion that Jesus' death was ultimately shameful.

Second, δίκαιος *roots Jesus' shameful death firmly in scripture and in the plan of God.* Both Acts 2.23 and 4.27–30, for example, unambiguously place Jesus' death within God's plan, while Acts 13.29 relates it to unspecified scripture. While scripture says nothing of *the messiah's* death, Luke's defence of Jesus' humiliation and execution is rooted in another basic term and model. The complex of oppression, death and resurrection which characterises Wisdom's δίκαιος-model emphasised the shameful nature of the death to be endured (Wis. 2.19–20). It was, however, ignorance of God's μυστήρια which led 'the ungodly' to ill-treat the δίκαιος as they did (Wis. 2.22; cf. 1 Cor. 2.6–8); his was an unjust, profoundly wicked death (cf. Acts 7.52–60). Probably, when Luke reflected on Israel's scripture in the light of what had befallen Jesus, he recognised a remarkable affinity with Wisdom's δίκαιος and reshaped his own retelling of Jesus' passion around that model.[14] In doing this, Luke was not creating something new: other Christian writers had thought of Jesus as δίκαιος,[15] although their uses of δίκαιος both vary among themselves and differ from Luke's use.[16] With so clear a scriptural statement of God's plan to hand, Luke could confidently face detractors who found Jesus' death offensive or repulsive, and

[12] Acts 6.8–8:2 (esp. 7.52); 22.1–21 (esp. 22.14); 3.12b–26 (esp. 3.14).

[13] See chapter 1E above.

[14] See chapter 7, sections C to H, above, *contra* Conzelmann (1960, p. 201): 'The fact that the death itself is not interpreted as a saving event of course determines the account given of it.'

[15] E.g. 1 Pet. 3.18; 1 John 2.1, 3.2; James 5.6.

[16] See chapter 6D above for comment on 1 Pet. 3.18.

demonstrate that this apparently shameful death actually fulfilled God's saving purposes.

Third, Wisdom's model *set Jesus' suffering and death in the context of the persecution of the δίκαιος by his ungodly oppressors* and of their astonishment at the 'paradox of his salvation'. What was clear in other Gospels was sharpened by Luke's formalising Jerusalem's guilt – 'you did it' – and by his portrayal of Israel's leaders plotting to do away with Jesus. At this point one needs to comment finally on the persistent, quite mistaken claim that Luke intensified the anti-Judaism of his sources and that he is, consequently, one of the roots of a traditional, disastrous Christian anti-Semitism.[17] However much one may loathe anti-Semitism, with its long, tragic tale that led to the Holocaust, and wish to foster reading of the Christian scriptures which positively undoes prejudiced attitudes, it remains the case that Luke is reporting the tensions of his own time which seem mostly to belong to disputes *within* a Judaism of which 'the Way' was still a part.[18] *Contra* Beck (1994), it is the sensitive interpreting of Christian scripture, particularly its passion narratives, which is called for, not their radical redrafting. It is not Luke who is the problem but his interpreters. According to Luke, this death was not the execution of a villain, but the betrayal and murder of God's prophet, himself a Jew, by some of his fellow Jews, particularly leaders, who plotted his humiliation because he alleged their manner of life was not 'worthy of their calling' (cf. Acts 7.52 -60). This tragedy belongs essentially within a plural Judaism's varied and changing life.

Fourth, Wisdom's model *related Jesus' ἔξοδος in Jerusalem to his summoning others to take up their cross daily* and to follow him. Essentially, Luke presents Jesus as head of a community responding to his renewed vision of God, a pattern for others to follow.[19] Taking up one's cross *daily* (Luke 9.23) is not a reduced requirement of discipleship from that found, for example in Mark,[20] but rather a

[17] See, e.g., Beck, N.A. (1994); Sanders, J.T. (1987); cf. Ascough (1993), O'Toole (1993).

[18] See, e.g., Dunn (1991), Bauckham (1993).

[19] This in no sense implies a moral influence theory of the cross. Luke's position seems to be that Jesus, as head of the new community gathering around his proclamation of God's Kingdom, was God's agent whose own faithfulness to death was matched by God's faithfulness in vindicating him. Barrett (1979, pp.75f.) has urged that due weight be given to the distinctiveness of Luke 9.23, adding: 'Luke deliberately extends the decision of faith through a lifetime of daily following described in terms of cross-bearing.'

[20] So, e.g. Barrett (1979, p. 76)

recognition that within the longer time-span envisaged by Luke's *schema*, discipleship after Jesus' ascension was no longer their sharing in a single journey to Jerusalem and its crisis, but a protracted, persevering stance for God's Kingdom, a stance modelled on their Lord and teacher. There would be other conflicts, other journeys and other crosses (e.g. Luke 21.16). 'Following' now has an extended sense and commitment to Jesus may be naturally spoken of as 'the Way'. Jesus' ἔξοδος, completed in Jerusalem, was the passage of a prophet like Moses, at the head of a renewed People, now including 'the nations', following the command of God to live as sons and daughters of the Father, anticipating his Kingdom, and ultimately experiencing his salvation. Luke's portrayal of Jesus as the Leader,[21] the first among many, in death as in resurrection, is an essential element in his *theologia crucis*. Just as Wisdom's author oscillated between δίκαιος and δίκαιοι, their fates and fortunes intertwined, so Luke's *schema* first set out Jesus' story before, second, presenting his tradition lived out in his earliest followers;[22] these had already been identified as those who had continued with Jesus in his testings, and who were to be covenanted a kingdom by Jesus as he had been by God; these are the community of 'those being saved' (Acts 2.47).

This *identity* of the exalted Jesus with his followers is sharply focused for readers in Luke's thrice-told story of the encounter of Saul, the erstwhile persecutor, with the vindicated Lord:

> Ὁ δὲ Σαῦλος, ἔτι ἐμπνέων ἀπειλῆς καὶ φόνου εἰς τοὺς μαθητὰς τοῦ κυρίου, προσελθὼν τῷ ἀρχιερεῖ ᾐτήσατο παρ' αὐτοῦ ἐπιστολὰς εἰς Δαμασκὸν πρὸς τὰς συναγωγάς, ὅπως ἐάν τινας εὕρῃ τῆς ὁδοῦ ὄντας, ἄνδρας τε καὶ γυναῖκας, δεδεμένους ἀγάγῃ εἰς Ἰερουσαλήμ. ἐν δὲ τῷ πορεύεσθαι ἐγένετο αὐτὸν ἐγγίζειν τῇ Δαμασκῷ, ἐξαίφνης τε αὐτὸν περιήστραψεν φῶς ἐκ τοῦ οὐρανοῦ,

21 Ἀρχηγός (Acts 3.15, followed by ὃν ὁ θεὸς ἤγειρεν ἐκ νεκρῶν; 5.31– τοῦτον ὁ θεὸς *ἀρχηγὸν καὶ σωτῆρα ὕψωσεν τῇ δεξιᾷ αὐτου* τοῦ δοῦναι μετάνοιαν τῷ Ἰσραὴλ καὶ ἄφεσιν ἁμαρτιῶν). *With* Haenchen (1971, p. 206, n. 4) *contra* Bruce (1952, p. 109), cf. Johnson (1992, p. 68). Barrett ended his essay '*Imitatio Christi* – in Acts' (Green and Turner, 1994, pp. 251–62): 'In general, however, the apostles and their colleagues are witnesses rather than examples and the Jesus to whom they bear witness is a savior rather than an example, though the precise sense in which he is a savior is never clarified as it is for example by Paul; it is clear that those who are saved must follow their Ἀρχηγός, even if to follow means to suffer.'

22 See, e.g., Talbert (1988, pp. 2–6)

> καὶ πεσὼν ἐπὶ τὴν γῆν ἤκουσεν φωνὴν λέγουσαν αὐτῷ, Σαοὺλ Σαούλ, τί με διώκεις; εἶπεν δέ, Τίς εἶ, κύριε; ὁ δέ, Ἐγώ εἰμι Ἰησοῦς ὃν σὺ διώκεις.
>
> (Acts 9.1–5; cf. 22.4–8 and 26.9–15)

Towards the end of that *apologia*, Luke presented Paul's clear statement that (Jesus) was to be 'the first to rise from the dead' (Acts 26.23), the hope of all Israel (Acts 26.6–8); this clear 'first among many' principle depends on Luke's affirmation of Jesus' being *truly* δίκαιος and *truly raised.*

B. 'Truly just and truly raised'

Although Luke appears to think of him as essentially one of God's People, in Luke's thought Jesus' being God's agent marks him out for a unique place in God's unfolding plan of salvation. This 'placing' begins systematically in the first two chapters of the Gospel. In his second volume, Luke focuses on Jesus' cross and exaltation as the essence of the apostolic κήρυγμα. These two happenings are aspects of one event, so it is a mistake to view the Lukan cross as 'merely' a prelude to the resurrection.[23] In Lukan terms resurrection and cross belong together, linked by Luke's distinctive use of ὄντως; Jesus was 'truly δίκαιος and truly raised',[24] the only one of whom both these things might be said, thus embodying the δίκαιος-model of Wisdom 2–5. Because Luke holds both these things to be true of Jesus, *this* scripture has been fulfilled and God has kept his promises to the forefathers (Acts 26.6–8). Consequently, those who follow the vindicated Jesus in his Way, taking up their cross daily, may trust God to raise them also. The essence of Luke's *theologia crucis* is that Jesus' life of commitment to God was crystallised in the manner of his suffering and dying;[25] there was an ἐπιείκεια and an ἀνεξικακία that Luke celebrated in this death. While, for Luke, the cross is a pattern for Christians in their commitment, he sees it as more than that. While his portrayal of the cross evokes pity, admiration and respect for so noble an *exitus*, Luke offers more than that. In Lukan terms, Jesus' cross is his living out, *and thereby fulfilling*, the life of the δίκαιος of the

[23] *Contra* Barrett (1994, p. 256), Cadbury (1958, p. 280), Franklin (1975, p. 67 cf. p. 99, n. 36), Kiddle (1935, p. 273). In this matter at least, Luke is quite 'Johannine'.

[24] Luke 23.47; 24.34; see chapter 7 above, 'Ὄντως'.

[25] See chapter 7C and D above.

earlier chapters of Wisdom, and, for Luke, what is the case for the δίκαιος will be so for the δίκαιοι who persevere to the end.

For Luke, as was argued in chapter 7C above, Jesus' cross is essentially the testing of one whose life and suffering showed him to be ὄντως ... δίκαιος. There was a δεῖ about this death; it had to happen because it was an element in God's plan (Luke 9.22; 13.33; 17.25; 22.37; 24.7, 26, 44; Acts 2.23; 4:27–8; 13.29). Luke's account of Jesus' death shows that it validated his commitment to God as 'Father', consummating his commitment to live, witness and die as one authentically Θεοῦ υἱὸς (Luke 23.46–7; cf. Wis. 2.13, 16, 18). Unlike the other synoptists, Luke's Jesus affirmed God as 'Father' even in the bitterest moment before death (Luke 23.46); unlike their cry of abandonment, his last word is one of trusting confidence, probably modelled on Wisdom 3.1.[26] Further, Wisdom's author emphasised that the δίκαιος knew himself to be Θεοῦ υἱός,[27] and that not in some metaphysical sense,[28] but in the same way that Israel was. For Luke, Jesus' followers also might be God's children (Luke 6.35–6) and Christian tradition was that Jesus taught his disciples also to call God 'Father' (e.g. 11.2–4).

The manner of Jesus' death and his consequent resurrection also authenticated his teaching about the Kingdom of God and the Kingdom's values. Wisdom's telling of the conflict between the δίκαιος and his ungodly opponents centres on conflict between two ways of life, two sets of values: the δίκαιος is hated and persecuted because his lived account of godly values judges his opponents' way of life. Similarly, Luke's conflict stories, particularly of conflict with scribes (e.g. Luke 11.45–52; 20.39–47; cf. Wis. 2.12, 14–16), although marginally less bitter than Matthew's attacks on scribes and Pharisees (Matt. 23), portray the tense resentment of those whose manner of life Jesus attacked. So for Luke this δίκαιος, anointed with God's spirit (Luke 3.21–2; 4.1–13, 16–30; cf. Acts 10.37–8), dying on his cross with integrity and trust, is the one God

[26] See chapter 6C above.

[27] Wis. 2.18; cf. 2.13 and 5.5 where παῖς seems to convey the same sense.

[28] This denial is sustainable because in the oscillation between the sing. and pl. forms of δίκαιος in Wisdom the pl. tends to relate to faithful Israel, and in the central chapters each δίκαιος is one of Israel's human forefathers; so also Israel might be παῖδες Θεοῦ. It is important to recognise that Wisdom's own usage is that the δίκαιος 'παῖδα Κυρίου ἑαυτὸν *ὀνομάζει*'. Luke's use of Θεοῦ υἱὸς is discussed by Fitzmyer (1981, pp. 205–8) who, while affirming a uniqueness of filiation in Luke's thought, remains clear that 'it does not yet carry the later connotations of physical or metaphysical sonship or identity of substance associated with the later Nicene or Constantinopolitan creeds' (1981, p. 207).

summoned to this prophetic task. Luke's centurion affirmed that Jesus died δίκαιος (Luke 23.47; cf. Acts 10.38, 'God was with him') as did Peter, Stephen and Paul.[29] That Jesus was truly raised is spelt out by Luke 24.33–5 and in the speeches of Acts (e.g. Acts 2.22–4, 29–33; 3.14–15, 26; 4.8–10; 5.29–32; 13.27–31 *et al.*). These two focal events are central: ὄντως … δίκαιος, ὄντως ἠγέρθη. For Luke, the cross *shows* Jesus to be genuinely δίκαιος in Wisdom's way and his resurrection *confirms* it. The raised one could be none other than the one who was authentically δίκαιος in life and death since these elements belong together in Wisdom's model (e.g. Wis. 4.20–5.5) as they belong together conceptually in Luke's work. This cross is not merely a prelude to Jesus' resurrection,[30] but has its own significance originating in Luke's twofold model drawn from Wisdom. For Luke, those who commit themselves to follow in his Way, taking up their cross daily, may be confident that Jesus' teaching about God and his Kingdom, his *mitzvot* and parables, his pattern of living are all to be trusted and lived.

Δίκαιος belongs to the same general semantic domain as *'ebed Yahweh* and 'Son of man', so Luke's theology of the cross has more in common with the prophet of Deutero-Isaiah and the book of Daniel than it has with Paul. Each descriptor is one attempt to come to terms with the persistent problem of the terrible suffering of those faithful to God, and these two post-Maccabaean writers were probably deeply indebted to the theology which underpins Deutero-Isaiah. Their exploring that book's humiliation-vindication patterning also grapples with the apparently irrational, immoral suffering of those faithful to God, and is focused in their terms 'Son of man' and δίκαιος. Consequently, it is important to recognise the significance of Luke's choice of the δίκαιος-model: through it he constructs his own theology as he shapes his own narrative of Jesus' death. Luke distanced himself from sacrificial or vicarial strands of thought,[31] concentrating on Jesus' δίκαιος-like suffering and death as God's bringing about his plan of salvation through the fulfilling of scripture. Luke's *theologia crucis* is that the δίκαιος has died and

[29] Acts 3.12b–26; 6.8–8:2; 22.1–21.　　[30] See note 20 above.

[31] See chapter 1A above. For discussion of Jesus' death in Luke–Acts see also Barrett (1979); Benoit (1969); Betz (1968); Cassidy (1983); Ford (1983); Garrett (1992); George (1973); Grayston (1990); Karris (1986); Larkin (1977); Matera (1985); Robbins (1988); Ruppert (1972); Tyson (1986); Zehnle (1969). Franklin (1975, p. 66) puts the matter plainly: 'Why has Luke avoided all references to the redemptive significance of the death of Jesus and the vicarious expressions that should have been suggested by his use of the Servant idea?'

been raised, so Jesus' followers can be sure that God's plan of salvation is nearing fulfilment.

C. The cross as 'final event'

Kümmel's response (1975, p. 141) to the accusation that Luke has no *theologia crucis* was: *does Luke understand the history of Jesus as final event?* Because Luke does, there is a distinct, different, supporting range of evidence to rebut the charge against Luke. Luke's emphasis[32] on Jesus' cross as an element in the fulfilment of the δίκαιος-model, although different from Paul's understanding, confirms that he does have a consistent *theologia crucis*. Luke may not conceive of Jesus' death as an atonement,[33] but he does understand this death and resurrection as a 'turning of the ages'. The remainder of this section examines ways in which the pattern and language of Wisdom's δίκαιος-model supports Kümmel's claim that Luke understood the cross as final event.

It is its place in the complex of cross and resurrection which makes the Lukan cross if not 'final event' in God's plan of salvation, then at least 'penultimate event', an *essential* element in the process of 'final event' beginning in the death and resurrection of this δίκαιος yet destined to end in a larger drama (Luke 21.7–36 cf. Acts 4.1–30). **First**, Luke's story is of one prophet who not only spoke out for God but who lived out what it means to call God 'Father' and to conceive of oneself as 'son'. In one sense this is simply to repeat that Jesus' life was of a piece with his dying and was sufficient ground for his being the first to be raised. Yet this, however, is also Luke's affirming that what Israel had hoped for had truly happened (e.g. Acts 26.6, 23), that is, Jesus' death and resurrection is an inaugural stage in God's completing his plan of salvation. **Second**, Stephen testified to his *seeing* Jesus, who as the ὄντως ... δίκαιος of Luke 23.47 was now spoken of as ὁ δίκαιος (Acts 7.52), standing at God's right hand. Within Wisdom's δίκαιος-model such *post mortem* vindication of the δίκαιος is an unambiguously eschatological event, God's reckoning of sins (Wis. 5.1–8). **Third**, and directly associated with his δίκαιος theme, Luke's Son of man

32 See chapter 1A above, 'A Lukan emphasis'. Tannehill (1961, p. 198) goes so far as to speak of 'the unusual emphasis on the divine necessity of the suffering and death of Jesus'.

33 See Barrett (1979, p. 73). It is possible to have a 'salvific' *theologia crucis* without its being thought of as atonement.

sequence has also been formally (and uniquely) brought to its conclusion, an eschatological event according to both Daniel 7.13–27 and Luke 21.27. **Fourth**, by citing Joel (2.28–32), Luke's report of Peter's Pentecost speech (Acts 2.14–21) also sets all these events – e.g. the outpouring of the Spirit[34] – in 'the last days'.

There is yet another dimension to a Lukan sense of 'last days'. Within Luke's *schema* stands an emphasis on the 'incoming' of the Gentiles, so this Isaianic element within Simeon's canticle[35] has its fulfilment in Acts. The Cornelius episode (especially Acts 11.18) and Paul's Pisidian Antioch experience (especially Acts 13.46–9) witness to this Lukan thrust: in each case 'incoming' is closely tied to Jesus' story in detail, and the cross is where Luke focuses it. Just as his prologue set out its 'Isaianic' hope of light for Gentiles and glory for Israel (Luke 2.29–32), so in his account of Paul at Antioch in Pisidia Luke reminded his readers of this great hope of salvation (Acts 13.46–7). Again, before 'his' Paul's voyage to Rome (Acts 26.22–3), before Acts' enigmatic ending, he epitomised the Pauline message as he understood it. As Luke presented Jesus' resurrection as a proleptic eschatological event, so his theme of the ingathering of Gentiles is further evidence that God was fulfilling his plan.

In this matter of 'final' or penultimate event, Luke drew important inferences from apostolic *witness* to Jesus' resurrection and exaltation. He reports that Jesus *appeared to* Simon (Peter) (Luke 24.34); that Stephen *saw* Jesus at God's right hand (Acts 7.55); that on his way to Damascus, Saul (Paul) *encountered* the exalted Jesus (Acts 9.1–6; 22.3–10; 26.9–20). Peter confidently asserted that 'God has made both Lord and Christ this Jesus *whom you crucified*' (Acts 2.36), both terms which point in some sense to the ultimacy of what had happened. Echoing both Wisdom 3.8 and Daniel 7.14 (cf. vv. 18, 27), both Peter (Acts 10.42) and Paul (Acts 17.31) affirmed that God had appointed Jesus to be judge of all. Both of these assessments of Jesus' significance point *towards* the end of the Lukan time scheme, although 'the end is not yet' (see Talbert, 1970).

[34] For fuller discussion of Luke's position on the Spirit's activity as evidence that God's salvation has been substantially fulfilled see Maddox (1982, pp. 132–45).

[35] Riesner (1994) throws light on a possible link between James' speech (Acts 15.13–21) and Simeon's canticle (Luke 2.29–32) in relation to 'the incoming of the Gentiles'. He returned to the question of 'Συμεων' at Acts 15.14, querying its identity with 'Peter' and asking whether in his speech James might be not in dialogue with Peter but rather offering independent support from old (Amos) and new (Simeon) prophets for his judgment (Acts 15.19–21). In view of the use we

There is yet another, more obvious sense in which the Lukan narrative of Jesus' death and resurrection points to final event: the word 'resurrection' belongs to the language of eschatology and, since the core of Luke's case is that *this unique* resurrection is of *this one who died thus,* the twofold event may be understood to stand at the turn of the ages. But this 'final event' is also 'first event' in that δίκαιος both precedes and comprehends δίκαιοι; Jesus' disciples are called to follow him, to embody his vision and his teaching and to persevere in the face of oppression. If, like him, they humble themselves, they, like him, will also be exalted (Luke 21.12–19, 34–6; cf. Acts 5.30–1). While the Lukan cross is no ransom and effects no forgiveness – which Luke understands as God's direct gift to the penitent[36] – this cross is the proving of *the* δίκαιος and a model of how those who follow him might expect to die. Additionally, in the speeches in Acts, Jesus' cross is not separated from affirmation of his resurrection; their resurrection is the hope of his followers, indeed, the hope of all Israel (e.g. Acts 26.4–8; 28.20). For Luke, Jesus is the first of a company gathered to walk in his Way: if the 'final event' is the resurrection of the saints or the δίκαιοι, then Jesus' resurrection and exaltation is their guarantee of what is to come. God raised Jesus because his dying proved him δίκαιος. The disciples' salvation is their assured resurrection; this is the language of eschatological salvation.[37]

D. Paradox and salvation[38]

At the very heart of Wisdom's conceptual model of the δίκαιος is the language of salvation (Wis.. 5.1–5). Here, the word σωτηρία

have made in part II of Simeon's canticle, Riesner's essay, which provokes many lines of thought, deserves careful reading, although at present I am not persuaded.

[36] In Luke's Gospel forgiveness is not contingent upon Jesus' death, but in the Acts being in 'the Way' *puts one in the realm of forgiveness* (Acts 2.38; 5.31; 10.43; 13.38); see esp. 26.18 where, in an expansion of Paul's encounter with the vindicated Jesus one finds 'forgiveness of sins' associated with κλῆρον ἐν τοῖς ἡγιασμένοις πίστει τῇ εἰς ἐμέ. There is a clear picture in Acts 2.43–7 both of the kind of community Luke conceived the People of the Way to be and of its daily increase: ὁ δὲ κύριος προσετίθει *τοὺς σῳζομένους* καθ' ἡμέραν ἐπὶ τὸ αὐτό.

[37] The clear statement about resurrection found in Dan. 12.1–3 is anticipated in the visions of Dan. 7.9–27. Although the *concept* of resurrection is present in, e.g. Wis. 4.16–20, the *language* is not; but ἀθανασία (Wis. 3.4) should be understood in the context of 4.16–5.20 with its *post mortem* judgment.

[38] Luke's two volumes are essentially a theology of salvation (Marshall, 1970, esp. chapter IV; Fitzmyer, 1981, esp. pp. 179–92).

carries a sense of surprising, unexpected, astonishing reversal of the ill fortune of the δίκαιος. His opponents,

> ἐλεύσονται ἐν συλλογισμῷ ἁμαρτημάτων δειλοί,
> καὶ ἐλέγξει αὐτοὺς ἐξ ἐναντίας τὰ ἀνομήματα αὐτῶν.
> Τότε στήσεται ἐν παρρησίᾳ πολλῇ ὁ δίκαιος
> κατὰ πρόσωπον τῶν θλιψάντων αὐτὸν
> καὶ τῶν ἀθετούντων τοὺς πόνους αὐτοῦ.
> ἰδόντες ταραχθήσονται φόβῳ δεινῷ
> καὶ ἐκστήσονται ἐπὶ τῷ παραδόξῳ τῆς σωτηρίας . . .
> (Wis. 4.20–5.5)

This, however, is not the only appearance of σωτηρία in Wisdom; at 16.6 and 7 both 'salvation' and 'Saviour' are rooted in the story of the Exodus:

> . . . they were troubled for a little while as a warning, and received a symbol of salvation to remind them of your law's command. For the one who turned toward it was saved, not by the thing that was beheld, but by you, the Saviour of all.

The accent here is on God as the author of salvation; in 18.7 salvation is said to be of the righteous, clearly Israel:

> The salvation of the righteous (σωτηρία μὲν δικαίων) and the destruction of their enemies were expected by your people.

Wisdom's conceptual model (chapters 2–5) is probably a distillation of faithful Israel's experience throughout the ages, in the Exodus as in the Maccabaean struggles, and the text for the whole book might well be its concluding verse (19.22):

> Κατὰ πάντα γάρ, Κύριε, ἐμεγάλυνας τὸν λαόν σου καὶ ἐδόξασας καὶ οὐχ ὑπερεῖδες ἐν παντὶ καιρῷ καὶ τόπῳ παριστάμενος.

That sentence displays a vast confidence drawn from reflection on a highly legendary form of the Exodus story: God always saves. But such was all too evidently not the case for the Maccabaean martyrs for whom only a *post mortem* vindication was possible, in God's eschatological court when their persecutors were arraigned. According to Wisdom's author, as in some ways for Daniel's, salvation for such as Eleazar and the seven brothers[39] would consist

[39] Eleazar (2 Macc. 6.18–31; cf. 4 Macc. 5:4–6:30); the brothers (2 Macc. 7.1–42).

in their *ultimate* vindication, that is, in their being with God, in their obviously being God's saints, in their ruling nations, in their being at peace. In Wisdom's conceptual model this realistic perspective shows a new, refined understanding of what 'salvation' might mean; Wisdom moved Israel's Exodus faith into the longer perspective of a resurrection hope.[40]

'Salvation' is also Luke's perspective on the Jesus-event:[41] from Simeon's canticle and its association with Isaiah's vision of 'salvation' for all nations, through the 'save' taunts offered the suffering Jesus, to the appeals of the apostles,[42] Luke is concerned with salvation. His concept of salvation may be inferred, but is nowhere defined; it is broad, ranging from personal healings through to the nature of that widening company who aligned themselves with Jesus' 'Way'. Luke's *theologia crucis* turns out to be a subset of his *theologia salutis*; Jesus' cross is one element in God's plan to 'save' all people (Isa. 42.6; 49.6; cf. 60.1–3).

The very structure of Luke's two-volume work may reflect this underlying Wisdom model of an extraordinary, unexpected salvation. It is worth asking yet again why Luke chose to offer two volumes. Perhaps, to answer this, it is worth suggesting that if one of the reasons that prompted him to write was a need to reply to complaints that a Jesus who died as he did was no leader to follow, then Luke was aware of two basic experiences of his Christian community on which to build. First, there was the life, ministry and death of Jesus that pressingly needed to be related to God's plan in scripture. Second, there was the presence of Gentiles within the *corpus mixtum* which was Luke's community, leading to the social and political pressures identified by Esler. There were, naturally, other features Luke needed to address[43] – for example, their experience of the now-democratised Spirit – but his explaining Jesus' death and accounting for the presence of Gentiles is our concern here. These two basic experiences are focused in the word 'salvation', a concept central both to Deutero-Isaiah and to

40 While Wisdom does not use the word 'resurrection' a form of the concept is found in Wis. 4.20–5.13. There is a central notion of God's judgment (cf. 2 Macc. 6.34–36; Dan. 7.1–28; 12.1–3), unmistakably *post mortem*, in which those faithful to God are vindicated and their oppressors judged.

41 So, e.g. Fitzmyer (1981, pp. 179–192, 219–27); Marshall (1970); Bovon (1987). Each of these offers extensive bibliographies.

42 So, e.g. Acts 13.38–42, 44–9. Although words drawn from σῴζ- do not appear in the appeal at the end of each apostolic speech, many of its conceptual elements do.

43 See chapter 1E above.

Wisdom, and each experience fits naturally into Luke's twofold scheme.

First, Luke's scheme offers a straightforward 'before' and 'after', echoing Wisdom's δίκαιος-model with its 'amazing reversal' theme: Luke's Gospel offers an account of the prophet whose life and death revealed him to be ὄντως . . . δίκαιος; Acts spells out what God did in vindicating Jesus, and in doing so offers its own vindication scenes to Jerusalem and her leaders (e.g. the Stephen-unit). There is another, corporate dimension to Luke's scheme for, according to his Gospel, the δίκαιος Jesus had through word and deed gathered around him a community focused on God's Kingdom, and taught its members that commitment to God required their daily cross-bearing, patterned on his life and teaching. According to the Acts, by deed and word his followers continued the gathering of God's community around Jesus' renewed vision of God; they conceived themselves to be witnesses[44] to the reality of the exalted Jesus. Barrett has persuasively urged that a *theologia crucis* in Acts may be found in the lived-out commitment of Jesus' followers and there is certainly truth in that; he has later suggested that Acts shows how Luke 9.23 worked out in the earlier community.[45] But there is more than that:[46] these are followers in his Way; they act in his name; they

[44] Acts 1.8, 22; 2.32; 3.15; 5.32; 6.13; 7.58; 10.39, 41; 13.31; 22.15; 26.16.

[45] Barrett (1979).

[46] Barrett (1994); because Barrett's essay appeared after the body of this monograph had been completed, it has not been possible to deal in the text with Barrett's penetrating critique of an *imitatio Christi.* The force of his argument must be conceded immediately. Perhaps our understanding of Luke's *theologia crucis* may contribute to a response to Barrett. If Luke worked with an unacknowledged model drawn from Wisdom, he did so because he shared that model with those likely to read his work, and there is some evidence that Wisdom was excluded from the canon of rabbinic Judaism because of the use Christians made of it. Given Luke's placing of δίκαιος at key points in his work, he seems to have been overtly confronting the problem of Jesus' death. Given the mirror patterning of Luke's Gospel and the Acts; given the underlying 'attraction' by Wisdom with its oscillation between singular and plural δίκαιος concepts; given the basic 'paradox' reflected in the two-volume structure of Luke's work, it is not unlikely that Luke's readers would have in mind the larger context implied by his use of Wisdom's δίκαιος. If Acts is read by those who already share a Wisdom perspective on these things, then the connections between the two volumes are implied and Luke is absolved from internal sign-posting (although the word δίκαιος may itself be sufficient). Perhaps it is also of some significance that he speaks of members of the community as 'saints' (Acts 3.21; 9.13, 22, 41; 26.10), a word which also appears in the 'paradox' context of Wis. 5.5 (cf. 18.9) to speak in an alternative way about the δίκαιοι. It is important to note, however, that in this monograph we have been exploring only one aspect of Luke's thinking and that many other terms and concepts contribute to an account of Luke's theology.

explore the scriptures to show how these happenings belong to God's plan and they summon people to repentance by proclaiming what God has done in Jesus to fulfil his plan of salvation. In other words, at the heart of Luke's scheme is his affirmation of the solidarity of the one and the many: the salvation of Jesus heralds and guarantees the salvation of his community.

Second, there is another dimension to this twofoldness. From an early moment in his Gospel, Luke spelled out his broad view of the concept of salvation: Simeon's canticle set the scene for an 'Isaianic' understanding of salvation that was to include 'the nations'. The Acts shows how this came to be, from the Ethiopian eunuch (Acts 8.26–38)[47] through Cornelius (Acts 10.1–46) to the few at Athens (Acts 17.34) and beyond. As Isaiah said, God's *saving acts* were for all nations – φῶς είς ἀποκάλυψιν ἐθνῶν καὶ δόξαν λαοῦ σου Ἰσραήλ (Luke 2.32) – so the growth of the Church could be described as ὁ δὲ κύριος προσετίθει τοὺς σῳζομένους καθ' ἡμέραν ἐπὶ τὸ αὐτό (Acts 2.47).

But how, precisely, might Theophilus understand that people were being saved? And since Luke avoided vicarial and atonement language, what, if anything, had Jesus' death to do with their being saved? Although he thought of Jesus in terms of a suffering prophet or righteous man, Schweizer's summary[48] of what was happening at Jesus' cross lacks an organising principle such as Wisdom's δίκαιος-model provides.

'Being saved' and the death of Jesus

The Acts shows that people were being saved by responding to the message of salvation first by 'turning their backs'[49] on that way of

[47] This man, rather than Cornelius, is the prototype of the Gentile entering into the number of those being saved. Just as Luke's Jesus stretched the boundaries of *mitzvot* to include those otherwise excluded from 'Israel' by some Jewish groups (Luke 14.21–4), so among his *sheluchim* is now a *castrato* whose presence in Israel is excluded by Deut. 23.1.

[48] 'Lukas sieht also 1. Jesu Wirken in Vollendung alttestamentlichen Prophetenschicksals als bewussten Gang ins Leiden. Er betont die Grösse der Versuchung, die "Macht der Finsternis" und Jesu Unterordnung unter Gottes Willen. Das wird 2. heilswirksam in Jesu Zuwendung zum Menschen und ermöglicht so 3. den nach-österlichen Weg der Gemeinde ins Dienen und Leiden ... Nur er kann vollmächtig das Reich (22,29f.) und das Paradies (23,43, s.d. Schl.), also das Heil zusprechen.' (1993, p. 226).

[49] ὑμῖν πρῶτον ἀναστήσας ὁ θεὸς τὸν παῖδα αὐτοῦ ἀπέστειλεν αὐτὸν εὐλογοῦντα ὑμᾶς ἐν τῷ ἀποστρέφειν ἕκαστον ἀπὸ τῶν πονηριῶν ὑμῶν (Acts 3.26). This ἀποστρέφειν is a Hebraic image of μετάνοια (cf. Wis. 5.3).

life which led to destruction (e.g. Acts 3.26, cf. Wis. 5.6–8). They were then invited to participate in the paradox of salvation. Luke does not use this language, but the pattern he presents of life in the community of 'those being saved' largely reflects their Lord's life. Like Jesus, they were to be baptised and, like him, to receive the Holy Spirit.

Like Jesus with his disciples, they were to walk in his Way. Christians held to the apostles' διδαχή because they understood apostles to be authentic carriers of Jesus' tradition:[50] his disciples had been with him; they had received from Jesus himself his hermeneutic[51] and were consequently able to open up the scriptures to show how the Jesus they proclaimed conceived his place in God's purposes; they had continued with him throughout his testing[52] and, from a distance, witnessed his end;[53] they had met with – and were therefore witnesses to – the raised Lord before his ascension and had been taught by him (e.g. Acts 10.39–43; cf. 1.3, 21–2); to hold fast to the apostles' teaching was, like them, to enter into Jesus' way of being.[54] They held to the κοινωνία (Acts 2.42, cf. 2.44; 4.32) which reflects both the disciples' experience of their journey with Jesus to Jerusalem[55] and Luke's account of Jesus' teaching about wealth

50 So, e.g., Talbert (1988, pp. 2–6).

51 Luke 24.25–7, 32, 44–8. The last extract raises again the question of the sources underlying this thinking. The reference to 'all nations' is most probably to the Isaianic strand beginning with Simeon's canticle. We have already seen the problem about the sufferings and resurrection of 'the Christ': since 'Christ' appears to be a post-resurrection Christian term in Luke–Acts, then it had possibly already become a larger semantic basket into which elements of other models, like δίκαιος, have been placed.

52 Luke 22.28. See chapter 7B above.

53 Luke carefully reworked his passion narrative so that it has no parallel to Mark's καὶ ἀφέντες αὐτὸν ἔφυγον πάντες (Mark 14.50); his narrative implies that 'his friends' saw all that happened, εἱστήκεισαν δὲ πάντες οἱ γνωστοὶ αὐτῷ ἀπὸ μακρόθεν, καὶ γυναῖκες αἱ συνακολουθοῦσαι αὐτῷ ἀπὸ τῆς Γαλιλαίας, ὁρῶσαι ταῦτα. (Luke 23.49). This is important for Luke's basic 'witnessing' theme as a constituent element in the apostles' bearing of Jesus' authentic tradition, and leaves no part of his career unwitnessed: δεῖ οὖν τῶν συνελθόντων ἡμῖν ἀνδρῶν ἐν παντὶ χρόνῳ ᾧ εἰσῆλθεν καὶ ἐξῆλθεν ἐφ' ἡμᾶς ὁ κύριος Ἰησοῦς, ἀρξάμενος ἀπὸ τοῦ βαπτίσματος Ἰωάννου ἕως τῆς ἡμέρας ἧς ἀνελήμφθη ἀφ' ἡμῶν, μάρτυρα τῆς ἀναστάσεως αὐτοῦ σὺν ἡμῖν γενέσθαι ἕνα τούτων (Acts 1.21–2). This contributes to the ἵνα ἐπιγνῷς περὶ ὧν κατηχήθης λόγων τὴν ἀσφάλειαν of Luke 1.1–4.

54 See Morris, L., 'Disciples of Jesus', in Green, J.B. and Turner, M., (1994, pp. 112–27). Morris suggests that 'while [μαθητής] could signify simply a learner, [it] came to have the fuller meaning of one who accepted the teacher' (1994, p. 113). This sense is strongly implied throughout Luke–Acts.

55 E.g. Luke 9.58, cf. 8.1–3; 10.1–7; 18.28–30; 23.49–55.

(e.g. Luke 12.33–4). They held to the prayers, thus reflecting Luke's account of Jesus' own practice, of which the Lord's Prayer is a pattern. They were reminded that they were to enter God's Kingdom through many θλίψεις (Acts 14.22) and Stephen's story modelled for them what that might mean (Acts 6.8–8.2), a living out of Luke 9.23 and a clear reflection of their Lord's death as it was portrayed in Luke's first volume. In short, they were very like the δίκαιοι described by Luke in his first volume,[56] although they now lived on the other side of God's saving acts. It was not for them to know times and seasons and when the end was to come (Acts 1.6); they were simply to get on with walking in Jesus' Way which led to the kind of salvation which his life story confirmed.

According to Luke's narrative, the witnesses who continued to gather a community in Jesus' name did so by life and word. Their κήρυγμα could be called ὁ λόγος τῆς σωτηρίας ταύτης (Acts 13.26), pointing to a ὁδὸν σωτηρίας (Acts 16.17). Within that κήρυγμα they explored scripture and ways in which it pointed to and explained the things concerning Jesus, but at its heart is the consistently presented, twofold central event which echoes Wisdom's παράδοξος τῆς σωτηρίας and in which Jesus' death is rooted in scripture (e.g. Acts 13.29 cf. Luke 18.31). The protagonist in this drama is God: God raised Jesus. As in Wisdom so in Luke–Acts, salvation's author is God; the tested δίκαιος is the model of those being saved; the δίκαιος *represents* those like him and he may be thought of as like Moses, at the *head* of those walking in his Way, saved but awaiting salvation; their liberation lies at the end of their exodus with him.

Because Luke's 'echoes', heard in language and in pattern, strongly suggest that he shaped his story of Jesus' death around the armature of Wisdom's δίκαιος-model, his readers may infer that Luke probably intended to affirm that Jesus' death stood in God's plan of salvation as *that willing act of faithful response to God's call which turned the ages*; and that sounds very like a coherent *theologia crucis*. Luke is not Paul, nor is he a John, but his substantial, two-volume work offers a narrative theology of the cross, firmly rooted in Israel's scripture, which stands as one more witness beside those of the other great writers of the New Testament, offering his own interpretation of Jesus' story, particularly of his death, so that

[56] See chapter 1A above. I am grateful to Mary Hayward and William Burns for perceptive criticism of successive drafts of this chapter – which has now become more of an agenda than a report.

readers may know the ἀσφάλειαν of the things about which they have been taught, which have been fulfilled among them.

> Ἰδὼν δὲ ὁ ἑκατοντάρχης τὸ γενόμενον ἐδόξαζεν τὸν θεὸν λέγων, Ὄντως ὁ ἄνθρωπος οὗτος δίκαιος ἦν.

BIBLIOGRAPHY

Achtemeier, P. (1978) 'The Miracles of Jesus' in Talbert (1978)

Aland, K. (1976) *Synopsis Quattuor Evangeliorum*, Stuttgart: Deutsche Bibelstiftung

Alexander, L. (1986) 'Luke's Preface in the Context of Greek Preface-Writing' *NovT* 28, pp. 48–74

(1993) *The Preface to Luke's Gospel: Literary Convention and Social Context in Luke 1.1–4 and Acts 1.1*, SNTSMS 78, Cambridge: CUP

Anderson, H. (1964) 'Broadening Horizons: The Rejection at Nazareth Pericope of Luke 4:16–30 in Light of Recent Critical Trends', *Interpretation* 18, pp. 259–75

Andresen, C. and Klein, G. (1979) *Theologia Crucis – Signum Crucis*, Tübingen: JCB Mohr [Paul Siebeck]

Arndt, W.F. and Gingrich, F.W. (1957) *A Greek-English Lexicon of the New Testament and Other Early Christian Literature*, Cambridge

Ascough, R.S. (1993) 'Rejection and Repentance: Peter and the People in Luke's Passion Narrative', *Biblica* 74, pp. 349–65

Athyal, A.P. (1988) 'Towards a Soteriology for the Indian Society: Guidelines from Luke–Acts', *Biblebhashayam* 14, pp. 132–48

Aune, D.E. (1981) 'The Problem of the Genre of the Gospels: A Critique of C.H. Talbert's *What is a Gospel?*' in France and Wenham (1981)

Bailey, K.E. (1976/80) *Poet and Peasant* and *Through Peasant Eyes*, Grand Rapids, Michigan: Eerdmans Combined Edn

Balz, H. and Schulz, S. (1973) *Das Wort und die Wörter*, Stuttgart

Bammel, E. and Moule, C.F.D. (eds.) (1984) *Jesus and the Politics of His Day*, Cambridge: CUP

Barr, J. (1961) *The Semantics of Biblical Language*, London: OUP

Barrett, C.K. (1961) *Luke the Historian in Recent Study*, London: Epworth Press

(1979) 'Theologia Crucis – in Acts?' in Andresen and Klein (1979), pp. 73–84

Bauckham, R. (1993) 'The Parting of the Ways: What Happened and Why', *Studia Theologica* 47 (2.1993), pp. 131–5

Baumbach, G. (1972) 'Gott und Welt in der Theologie des Lukas', *Bibel und Liturgie* 45, pp. 241–55

Beck, B.E. (1977) 'The Common Authorship of Luke & Acts', *NTS* 23, pp. 346–52

(1981) '*Imitatio Christi* and the Lucan Passion Narrative' in Horbury and McNeil (1981)
(1989) *Christian Character in the Gospel of Luke*, London: Epworth
Beck, N.A. (1994) *Mature Christianity in the 21st Century: The Recognition and Repudiation of the Anti-Jewish Polemic in the New Testament*, New York: Crossroad
Benoit, P. (1969) *The Passion and Resurrection of Jesus Christ*, London: DLT
Berry, D.L. (1988) 'Revisioning Christology: The Logic of Messianic Ascription', *ATR* 70, pp. 129–40
Beskow, P. (1962) *Rex Gloriae: The Kingship of Christ in the Early Church*, Uppsala: Almquist and Wicksells
Betz, H.D. (1969) 'The Origin and Nature of Christian Faith According to the Emmaus Legend (Luke 24: 13–22)', *Interpretation* 23, pp. 32–46
Betz, O. (1968) 'The Kerygma of Luke', *Interpretation* 22, pp. 131–46
Bock, D.L. (1987) *Proclamation from Prophecy and Pattern: Lucan Old Testament Christology*, Sheffield: JSOT Press
Borsch, F.H. (1967) *The Son of Man in Myth and History*, London: SCM
Bovon, F. (1978) *Luc le Théologien: Vingt-cinq ans de recherches (1950–1975)*, Neuchâtel: Delachaux & Niestle
(1987) *Luke the Theologian: Thirty-three years of Research (1950–1983)*, Allison Park, PA: Pickwick Publications
Bowker, J.W. (1967) 'Speeches in Acts: A Study in Proem and Yelammedenu form', *NTS* 14, pp. 96–110
Brawley, R.L. (1987) *Luke–Acts and the Jews: Conflict, Apology and Conciliation*, SBLMS 33, Atlanta
(1990) *Centering on God: Method and Message in Luke–Acts*, Louisville, Kentucky: Westminster/John Knox Press
Brodie, T.L. (1986) 'Towards Unravelling Luke's Use of the Old Testament: Luke 7.11–17 as an *Imitatio* of 1 Kings 17.17–24', *NTS* 32, pp. 247–67
Brown, R.E. (1979) *The Birth of the Messiah*, Image Books, New York: Doubleday
(1986) 'The Passion According to Luke', *Worship* 66, pp. 2–9
Brown, S. (1972) 'Apostasy and Perseverance in the Theology of Luke', *The Bible Today* 63, pp. 985–93
(1978) 'The Role of the Prologues in Determining the Purpose of Luke–Acts' in Talbert (1978)
Bruce, F.F. (1952) *The Acts of the Apostles*, London: Tyndale Press
(1984) 'Render to Caesar' in Bammel and Moule (1984)
(1987) 'Paul's Apologetic and the Purpose of Acts', *BJRL* 69, pp. 379–93
Buttrick, D.G. (1970) *Jesus and Man's Hope*, Pittsburgh: Pittsburgh Theological Seminary
Cadbury, H.J. (1921) 'The Purpose expressed in Luke's Preface', *The Expositor* 21, pp. 431–441
(1922) 'Commentary on the Preface of Luke' in Jackson and Lake (1922)
(1933) 'The Titles of Jesus in Acts' in Jackson and Lake (1933b)
(1958) *The Making of Luke–Acts* (second edition), London: SPCK
Caird, G.B. (1963) *Saint Luke*, Harmondsworth: Penguin Books

(1980) *The Language and Imagery of the Bible*, London: Duckworth
Carpenter, S.C. (1919) *Christianity According to S. Luke*, London: SPCK
Carroll, J.T. (1988) 'Luke's Portrayal of the Pharisees', *CBQ* 50, pp. 604–21
Cassidy, R.J. (1983) 'Luke's Audience, the Chief Priests, and the Motive for Jesus' Death' in Cassidy and Scharper (1983)
Cassidy, R.J. and Scharper, P.J. (1983) *Political Issues in Luke–Acts*, Maryknoll, New York: Orbis Books
Cassirer, H.W. (1989) *God's New Covenant: A New Testament Translation*, Grand Rapids, Michigan: Eerdmans
Charlesworth, J.H. (1989) *Jesus within Judaism*, London: SPCK
Chilton, B. (1981) 'Announcement in Nazara: An Analysis of Luke 4:16–21' in France and Wenham (1981)
(1984) *A Galilaean Rabbi and His Bible*, London: SPCK
Clarke, W.K.L. (1922) 'The Use of the Septuagint in Acts' in Jackson and Lake (1922)
(1929) *New Testament Problems*, London: SPCK
Coleridge, M. (1993) *The Birth of the Lukan Narrative*, JSNTSS 88, Sheffield: JSOT Press
Collins, A.Y. (1993) 'The Genre of the Passion Narrative', *Studia Theologica* 47 (1.1993), pp. 3–28
Combrink, H.J.B. (1973) 'The Structure and Significance of Luke 4:16–30', *Neotestamentica* 7, pp. 27–47
Conzelmann, H. (1960) *The Theology of Saint Luke*, London: Faber and Faber
(1976) 'Wisdom in the NT', *IDB* Supp. Vol., pp. 956–60
(1987) *Acts of the Apostles*, Philadelphia: Fortress Press
Cotterell, P. and Turner, M. (eds.) (1989) *Linguistics and Biblical Interpretation*, London: SPCK
Creed, J.M. (1930) *The Gospel According to St Luke*, London: Macmillan & Co. Ltd
Cribbs, F.L. (1971) 'St. Luke and the Johannine Tradition', *JBL* 90, pp. 422–50
Cullmann, O. (1963) *The Christology of the New Testament*, London: SCM Press
Danker, F.W. (1988) *Jesus and the New Age: A Commentary on St Luke's Gospel*, Philadelphia: Fortress Press
Davies, W.D. (1987) 'Canon and Christology' in Hurst and Wright (1987)
Dawsey, J.M. (1986) *The Lukan Voice*, Macon, GA: Mercer University Press
(1989) 'The Literary Unity of Luke–Acts: Questions of Style – a Task for Literary Critics', *NTS* 35
Delebecque, E. (1976) *Etudes Grecques sur l'Evangile de Luc, Société d'Edition «Les Belles Lettres»*, Paris
(1976a) *Evangile de Luc, Société d'Edition «Les Belles Lettres»*, Paris
Derrett, J.D.M. (1988) 'The Son of Man Standing (Acts 7,55–56)', *Biblica & Orientalia* 30, pp. 71–84
Descamps, A. (1950) *Les justes et la justice dans les évangiles et le christianisme primitif hormis la doctrine proprement paulinienne*, Universitas

Catholica Lovaniensis 2:43, Gembloux: Publications Universitaires de Louvain

Dillon, R.J. (1978) *From Eye-witnesses to Ministers of the Word*, Analecta Biblica 82, Rome: Biblical Institute Press

(1981) 'Previewing Luke's Project from his Prologue', *CBQ* 43, pp. 205–27

Doble, P. (1960) 'The Temptations', *ExpT* 72, pp. 91–3

(1985) 'The Son of Man Saying in Stephen's Witnessing: Acts 6.8–8.2', *NTS* 31, pp. 68–84

(1992) 'Δίκαιος at Luke 23:47 as a Lukan Christological Term', unpublished doctoral thesis, University of Leeds

Dodd, C.H. (1935) *The Bible and the Greeks*, London: Hodder and Stoughton

(1952) *According to the Scriptures*, London: Nisbet

Donahue, J. (1976) 'Introduction: From Passion Traditions to Passion Narrative' in Kelber (1976)

Downing, F.G. (1988) '*A Bas Les Aristos*: The Relevance of Higher Literature for the Understanding of the Earliest Christian Writings', *NovT* 30, pp. 212–30

Drury, J. (1973) *Luke*, Glasgow: Fontana Press

(1976) *Tradition and Design in Luke's Gospel*, London: DLT

(1985) *The Parables in the Gospels*, London: SPCK

Dubois, J.-D. (1973) 'La Figure d'Elie Dans La Perspective Lucanienne', *RHPR* 53, pp. 155–76

Dunn, J.D.G (1975) *Jesus and the Spirit*, London: SCM Press

(1977) *Unity and Diversity in the New Testament*, London: SCM Press

(1987) '"A Light to the Gentiles": the Significance of the Damascus Road Christophany for Paul' in Hurst and Wright (1987)

(1987a) *The Living Word*, London: SCM

(1989) *Christology in the Making* (second edition), London: SCM

(1991) *The Partings of the Ways*, London and Philadelphia: SCM/TPI

Dupont, J. (1953) 'L'Utilisation Apologétique de l'Ancien Testament dans les discours des Actes', *Ephem Theol Lovan*, pp. 289–327

(1985) 'La structure oratoire du discours d'Etienne (Actes 7)', *Biblica* 66, pp. 153–67

Easton, B.S. (1926) *The Gospel According to St Luke*, New York: Scribner

Edwards, R.E. (1969) 'The Redaction of Luke', *JnlRel* 49, pp. 392–405

Ehrhardt, A.A.T. (1963) 'The Disciples of Emmaus', *NTS* 10, pp. 182–201

Ellingworth, P. (1990) 'Translations (Modern)' in Houlden and Coggins (1990)

Elliott, J.H. (1985) 'Backward and Forward "In His Steps": Following Jesus from Rome to Raymond and Beyond. The Tradition, Redaction and Reception of 1 Peter 2:18–25' in Segovia (1985)

Elliott, J.K. (1969) 'The use of ἕτερος in the New Testament', *ZNW* 60, pp. 140ff.

(1972) 'When Jesus was Apart from God: an Examination of Hebrews 2.9', *ExpT* 83 (1971–2), pp. 339–41

(1972a) 'Does Luke 2.41–52 anticipate the Resurrection?', *ExpT* 83 (1971–2), pp. 87–89

(1972b) 'Κηφας· Σιμων Πετρος· ὁ Πετρος: An Examination of the New Testament Usage', *NovT* 14, pp. 241–56
(1980) 'Textual Criticism, Assimilation and the Synoptic Gospels', *NTS* 26, pp. 231–42
(1986) 'An Examination of the Text and Apparatus of Three Recent Greek Synopses', *NTS* 32,, pp. 557–82
(1991) 'Which is the Best Synopsis?', *ExpT* 102, pp. 200–4
Ellis, E.E. (1974) *The Gospel of Luke*, London: Oliphants
Esler, P.F. (1987) *Community and Gospel in Luke–Acts*, SNTSMS 57, Cambridge: CUP
Evans, C.F. (1955) 'The Central Section of St Luke's Gospel' in Nineham (1955)
(1990) *Saint Luke*, London: SCM
Evans, D. (1987) 'Academic Scepticism, Spiritual Reality, and Transfiguration.' in Hurst and Wright (1987)
Farris, S. (1985) *The Hymns of Luke's Infancy Narratives: their origin, meaning and significance*, Sheffield: JSOT Press
Feuillet, A. (1958) 'Les Perspectives propres à chaque Evangéliste dans les Récits de la Transfiguration', *Biblica* 39, pp. 281–301
Fiorenza, E.S. (1983) *In Memory of Her: A Feminist Theological Reconstruction of Christian Origins*, New York: Crossroad
Fitzmyer, J.A. (1960) 'The Use of Explicit Old Testament Quotations in Qumran Literature and in the New Testament', *NTS* 7 (1960–1), pp. 297–333
(1970) 'The Priority of Mark and the "Q" Source in Luke' in Buttrick (1970)
(1981) *The Gospel According to Luke (I–IX)*, Anchor Bible 28, New York: Doubleday and Co.
(1985) *The Gospel According to Luke (X–XXIV)*, Anchor Bible 28A, New York: Doubleday and Co.
(1989) *Luke the Theologian*, London: Geoffrey Chapman
Ford, J.M. (1983) 'Reconciliation and Forgiveness in Luke's Gospel' in Cassidy and Scharper (1983)
France, R.T. (1968) 'The Servant of the Lord in the Teaching of Jesus', *TB* 19, pp. 26–52
France, R.T. and Wenham, D. (1981) *Gospel Perspectives II: Studies of History and Tradition in the Four Gospels*, Sheffield: JSOT Press
Franklin, E. (1975) *Christ the Lord*, London: SPCK
Frein, B.C. (1994) 'Narrative Predictions, Old Testament Prophecies and Luke's Sense of Fulfilment', *NTS* 40 (1.1994), pp. 22–37
Garrett, S.R. (1990) 'Exodus from Bondage: Luke 9:31 and Acts 12:1–24', *CBQ* 52 (4.90), pp. 656–80
(1992) 'The Meaning of Jesus' Death in Luke', *WordWorld* 12, pp. 11–16
Gärtner, E. (1912) *Komposition und Wortwahl des Buches der Weisheit*, Berlin
George, A. (1973) 'Le Sens de la Mort de Jésus pour Luc', *Revue Biblique* 80, pp. 186–217
(1978) *Etudes sur l'Oeuvre de Luc*, Paris: Gabalda

Gerhardsson, B. (1991) 'If We Do Not Cut the Parables out of Their Frames', *NTS* 37, pp. 321–35
Goulder, M.D. (1978) *The Evangelists' Calendar*, London: SPCK
(1989) *Luke – A New Paradigm* (2 vols.), Sheffield: JSOT Press
Grässer, E. (1969) 'Jesus in Nazareth (Mc 6:1–6a)', *NTS* 16 (1969–70), pp. 1–23
Grässer, E. *et al.* (1972) *Jesus in Nazareth*, BZNW 40, Berlin & New York: W. de Gruyter
Grayston, K. (1990) *Dying, We Live*, London: DLT
Green, J.B. and Turner, M. (eds.) (1994) *Jesus of Nazareth: Lord and Christ*, Grand Rapids, Michigan: Eerdmans
Grundmann, W. (1961) *Das Evangelium nach Lukas*, THzNT 3, Berlin: Evangelische Verlagsanstalt
Haenchen, E. (1971) *The Acts of the Apostles*, Oxford: Basil Blackwell
Hamm, D. (1984) 'Acts 3:12–26: Peter's Speech and the Healing of the Man born lame', *PerspRelStud* 11, pp. 199–217
Hanson, A.T. (1983) *The Living Utterances of God*, London: DLT
Hanson, R.P.C. (1942) 'Does δίκαιος in Lk xxiii.47 Explode the Proto-Luke Hypothesis?', *Hermathena* 60, pp. 74–8
Hart, H. St John (1984) 'The Coin of "Render unto Caesar ..."', in Bammel and Moule (1984)
Hatch, E. and Redpath, H.A. (1897) *A Concordance to the Septuagint and the other Greek Versions of the Old Testament* (2 vols.), Graz: Academische Druck und Verlagsanstalt
Hauerwas, S. (1977) 'The Politics of Charity', *Interpretation* 31, pp. 251–62
Hays, R.B. (1989) *Echoes of Scripture in the Letters of Paul*, New Haven & London: Yale University Press
Hemer, C.J. (1977) 'Luke the Historian', *BJRL* 60, pp. 28–51
(1989) *The Book of Acts in the Setting of Hellenistic History*, Tübingen: Mohr
Hick, J. (ed.) (1977) *The Myth of God Incarnate*, London: SCM
Hill, D. (1967) *Greek Words and Hebrew Meanings*, Cambridge: CUP
(1971) 'The Rejection of Jesus at Nazareth (Luke iv:16–30)', *NovT* 13, pp. 161–80
Hooker, M.D. (1959) *Jesus and the Servant*, London: SPCK
Horbury, W. (1994) 'The Wisdom of Solomon in the Muratorian Fragment', *JTS* 45.1, pp. 149–59
Horbury, W. and McNeil, B. (eds.) (1981) *Suffering and Martyrdom in the New Testament*, Cambridge: CUP
Horsley, G.H.R. (1989) *New Documents Illustrating Early Christianity*, vol. 5, Sydney: Macquarie University
Horton, F.C. (1977) 'Reflections on the Semitisms of Luke–Acts' in Talbert (1977)
Houlden, J.L. (1979) 'The Development of Meaning', *Theology* 82, pp. 251–9
(1984) 'The Purpose of Luke', *JSNT* 21, pp. 53–65
Houlden, J.L. and Coggins, R.J. (eds.) (1990) *A Dictionary of Biblical Interpretation*, London: SCM
Houston, W. (1987) '"Today In Your Very Hearing": Some Comments on

the Christological Use of the Old Testament' in Hurst and Wright (1987)
Huck, A. (1951) *Synopsis of the First Three Gospels*, Oxford: Basil Blackwell
Hull, J.M. (1974) *Hellenistic Magic and the Synoptic Tradition*, London: SCM
Hultgren, A.J. (1976) 'Interpreting the Gospel of Luke', *Interpretation* 30, pp. 353–65
Hurst, L.D. and Wright, N.T. (eds.) (1987) *The Glory of Christ in the New Testament*, Oxford: Clarendon Press
Jackson, K.F.J. and Lake, K. (eds.) (1922) *The Beginnings of Christianity Part I: The Acts of the Apostles* vol. II, London: Macmillan and Co. Ltd
(1933) *The Beginnings of Christianity Part I: The Acts of the Apostles* vol. IV, London: Macmillan and Co. Ltd
(1933b) *The Beginnings of Christianity Part I: The Acts of the Apostles* vol. V, London: Macmillan and Co. Ltd
Jeremias, J. (1958) *Jesus' Promise to the Nations*, SBT 24, Naperville: Allenson
(1969) *Jerusalem in the Time of Jesus*, London: SCM
(1972) *The Parables of Jesus* (revised edition), London: SCM
(1980) *Sprache des Lukas Evangelium*, Göttingen: Vandenhoeck & Ruprecht
Jervell, J. (1972) *Luke and the People of God*, Minneapolis: Augsburg
Johnson, L.T. (1989) 'The New Testament's Anti-Jewish Slander and the Conventions of Ancient Polemics', *JBL* 108, pp. 419–41
(1991) *The Gospel of Luke*, Sacra Pagina 3, Collegeville, Minnesota: The Liturgical Press
(1992) *The Acts of the Apostles*, Sacra Pagina 5, Collegeville, Minnesota: The Liturgical Press
Jones, D.L. (1984) 'The Title "Servant" in Luke–Acts' in Talbert (1984), pp. 148–65
Just, A.A. (1993) *The Ongoing Feast: Table Fellowship and Eschatology at Emmaus*, Collegeville, Minnesota: The Liturgical Press
Karris, R.J. (1978) 'Poor and Rich: the Lukan *Sitz im Leben*' in Talbert (1978)
(1985) *Luke, Artist and Theologian*, New York: Paulist Press
(1986) 'Luke 23:47 and the Lukan View of Jesus' Death', *JBL* 105, pp. 65–74
Keck, L.E. (1967) 'Jesus' Entrance Upon His Mission: Lk 3:1–4:30', *RevExp* 64, pp. 465–83
Keck, L.E. and Martyn, J.L. (eds.) (1968) *Studies in Luke–Acts*, London: SPCK
Kee, H.C. (1990) *Good News to the Ends of the Earth*, London & Philadelphia: SCM/TPI
Kelber, W.H. (1976) *The Passion in Mark: Studies on Mark 14–16*, Philadelphia: Fortress Press
Kiddle, M. (1935) 'The Passion Narrative in St Luke's Gospel', *JTS* 36, pp. 267–80

Kilgallen, J. (1976) *The Stephen Speech*, Analecta Biblica 67, Rome: Biblical Institute Press
Kilgallen. J.J. (1988) 'Acts 13, 38–39: Culmination of Paul's Speech in Pisidia', *Biblica* 69, pp. 480–506
Kilpatrick, G.D. (1942) 'A Theme of the Lucan Passion Story and Luke xxiii.47', *JTS* 43, pp. 34–6
(1945) 'Acts vii.52 ΕΛΕΥΣΙΣ', *JTS* 46 (1945), pp. 136–45
(1965) 'Acts vii.56: Son of Man?', *TZ* 21, p. 14
(1978) 'Again Acts vii.56: Son of Man?', *TZ* 34, p. 232
Kloppenborg, J.S. (1992) '*Exitus clari viri*: The Death of Jesus in Luke', *Toronto Journ Theol* 8, pp. 106–20
Klostermann, E. (1929) *Das Lukasevangelium*, Tübingen
Knox, R.A. (1946) *The New Testament*, London: Burns & Oates
Kremer, J. (1979) *Les Actes des Apôtres: Tradition, rédaction, théologie*, BETL 48, Éditions Duculot, Gembloux: Louvain Univ. Press
Kümmel, W.G. (1972) *The New Testament: The History of the Investigation of its Problems*, London: SCM
(1975) 'Current Theological Accusations against Luke', *ANQ* 16, pp. 131–45
Kurz, W.S. (1993) *Reading Luke–Acts: Dynamics of Biblical Narrative*, Louisville, Kentucky: Westminster/John Knox Press
Lagrange, M.-J. (1921) *Evangile selon Saint Luc*, Paris: Libraire Lecoffre
Lake, K. and Cadbury, H.J. (1933) 'English Translation and Commentary' in Jackson and Lake (1933)
Lampe, G.W.H. (1955) 'The Lucan Portrait of Christ', *NTS* 2 (1955–6), pp. 160–75
Larkin, W.J. (1977) 'Luke's Use of the Old Testament as a Key to his Soteriology', *JETS* 20, pp. 325–35
Lash, N. (1986) *Theology on the Way to Emmaus*, London: SCM
Laurentin, R. (1966) *Jésus au Temple*, Libraire Lecoffre
Léon-Dufour, X. (1978) 'Jésus face à la mort menaçante', *Nouvelle Revue Théologique* 100, pp. 802–21
(1978a) 'Le dernier cri de Jesus', *Etudes* 348 (5.1978), pp. 666–82
Lin, J. van (1985) 'Christology and Christologies in India', *Exchange* 14 (1985), pp. 1–33
Lindars, B. (1961) *New Testament Apologetic*, London: SCM
(1965) 'Elijah, Elisha and the Gospel Miracles' in Moule (1965)
Linnemann, E. (1966) *Parables of Jesus: Introduction and Exposition*, London: SPCK
Lohfink, G. (1975) *Die Sammlung Israels: Eine Untersuchung zur lukanischen Ekklesiologie*, StANT 39, Munich
Longenecker, R.N. (1968) 'Some Distinctive Early Christological Motifs', *NTS* 14, pp. 526ff.
(1970) *The Christology of Early Jewish Christianity*, SBT (second series) 17, London: SCM
Louw, J.P. and Nida, E.A. (eds.) (1988) *Greek-English Lexicon of the New Testament based on Semantic Domains* (2 vols.), New York: United Bible Societies
Lüdemann, G. (1987) *Early Christianity according to the Traditions in Acts*, London: SCM

Maclachlan, H. (1920) *St Luke the Man and his Work*, Manchester: Manchester University Press
Maddox, R. (1982) *The Purpose of Luke–Acts*, Edinburgh: T. & T. Clark
Mánek, J. (1958) 'The New Exodus in the Books of Luke', *NovT* 2, pp. 8–23
Manson, T.W. (1949) *The Sayings of Jesus*, London: SCM
(1951) *The Teaching of Jesus*, Cambridge: CUP
(1962) *Studies in the Gospels and Epistles*, Manchester: Manchester University Press
Manson, W. (1930) *The Gospel of Luke*, The Moffatt New Testament Commentary, London: Hodder & Stoughton, Ltd
(1943) *Jesus the Messiah*, London: Hodder & Stoughton
Marcus, J. (1993) *The Way of the Lord*, Edinburgh: T. & T. Clark
Marshall, I.H. (1965) 'The Synoptic Son of Man Sayings in Recent Discussion', *NTS* 12 (1965–6), pp. 327–51
(1969) 'Tradition and Theology in Luke (Luke 8:5–15)', *TB* 20, pp. 56–75
(1969a) 'Recent Study of the Gospel According to St Luke', *ExpT* 80, pp. 4–8
(1969b) 'Recent Study of the Acts of the Apostles', *ExpT* 80, pp. 292–96
(1970) *Luke – Historian and Theologian* (third edn), Exeter: Paternoster Press
(1970a) 'The Son of Man in Contemporary Debate', *EQ* 42, pp. 67–87
(1973) 'The Resurrection of Jesus in Luke', *TB* 24, pp. 55–98
(1976) *The Origins of New Testament Christology*, Illinois: IVP
(1978) *The Gospel of Luke*, Exeter: The Paternoster Press
(1980) *The Acts of the Apostles*, Leicester: IVP
(1983) 'Luke and his Gospel' in Stuhlmacher (1983), pp. 289–308
(1989) 'The Present State of Lucan Studies', *Themelios* 14, pp. 52–7
Martin, R.P. (1976) 'Salvation and Discipleship in Luke's Gospel', *Interpretation* 30, pp. 366–80
Matera, F.J. (1985) 'The Death of Jesus according to Luke: A Question of Sources', *CBQ* 47, pp. 469–85
(1986) *Passion Narratives and Gospel Theologies: Interpreting the Synoptics Through Their Passion Stories*, New York
Mattill, A.J. (Jnr) (1975) 'The Jesus-Paul Parallels and the Purpose of Luke–Acts: H.H. Evans Reconsidered', *NovT* 17 (1975), pp. 15–46
McDonald, J.I.H. (1990) 'Hermeneutical Circle' in Houlden and Coggins (1990)
Mealand, D.L. (1990) 'The Close of Acts and its Hellenistic Vocabulary', *NTS* 36
Meeks, W.A. (1983) *The First Urban Christians: The Social World of the Apostle Paul*, New Haven & London: Yale University Press
Miller, R.J. (1988) 'Elijah, John, and Jesus in the Gospel of Luke', *NTS* 34, pp. 611–22
Minear, P.S. (1968) 'Luke's Use of the Birth Stories' in Keck and Martyn (1968)
(1973) 'Dear Theo: The Kerygmatic Intention and Claim of the Book of Acts', *Interpretation* 27, pp. 131–50
(1974) 'Jesus' Audiences according to Luke', *NovT* 16, pp. 81–109
Moessner, D.P. (1988) 'The "Leaven of the Pharisees" and "This Gener-

ation": Israel's Rejection of Jesus According to Luke', *JSNT* 34, pp. 21–46

(1989) *Lord of the Banquet: The Literary and Theological Significance of the Lukan Travel Narrative*, Philadelphia: Fortress Press

Moffat, J. (1924) *A Critical and Exegetical Commentary on the Epistle to the Hebrews*, Edinburgh: T & T. Clark

Morgan, R. (1990) 'The Historical Jesus and the Theology of the New Testament' in Hurst and Wright (1987)

Moule, C.F.D. (1965) *Miracles: Cambridge Studies in their Philosophy and History*, London: Mowbray

(1967) *The Phenomenon of the New Testament*, SBT(2) 1, London: SCM

(1968) 'The Christology of Acts' in Keck and Martyn (1968), pp. 159–85

Moulton, H.K. (1957) *The Acts of the Apostles*, CLS

Mowinckel, S. (1959) *He That Cometh*, Oxford: Basil Blackwell

Neirynck, F. *et al.* (1973) *L'Evangile de Luc*, BETL XXXII, Gembloux: Duculot

Neusner, J. *et al.* (1988) *The Social World of Formative Christianity and Judaism*, Philadelphia

Neyrey, J. (1985) *The Passion According to Luke*, New York: Paulist Press

Neyrey, J.H. (ed.) (1991) *The Social World of Luke–Acts*, Peabody, MA: Hendrickson

(1991a) 'The Symbolic Universe of Luke–Acts: "They Turn The World Upside Down"' in Neyrey, J.H. (ed.) (1991)

Nickelsburg, G.W.E. (1972) *Resurrection, Immortality and Eternal Life in Intertestamental Judaism*, Harvard Theological Studies XXVI, Cambridge, MA: Harvard University Press

(1980) 'The Genre and Function of the Markan Passion Narrative', *HTR* 73, pp. 153–84

Nicol, W. (1973) 'Tradition and Redaction in Luke 21', *Neotestamentica* 7, pp. 61–71

Nineham, D.E. (1955) *Studies in the Gospels: Essays in Memory of R.H. Lightfoot*, Oxford: OUP

(1963) *Saint Mark*, Harmondsworth: Penguin Books

O'Fearghail, F. (1991) *The Introduction to Luke–Acts*, Analecta Biblica 126, Rome: Editrice Pontificio Istituto Biblico

Oliver, H.H. (1964) 'The Lucan Birth Stories', *NTS* 10 (1963–4), pp. 202–26

O'Neill, J.C. (1970) *The Theology of Acts in its Historical Setting*, London: SPCK

O'Toole, R.F. (1977) 'Why did Luke write Acts (Lk–Acts)?', *Biblical Theology Bulletin* 7, pp. 66–76

(1993) 'Reflections on Luke's Treatment of Jews in Luke–Acts', *Biblica* 74, pp. 529–55

Parker, P. (1962) 'Luke and the Fourth Evangelist', *NTS* 9 (1962–3), pp. 317–36

(1965) 'The "Former Treatise" and the Date of Acts', *JBL* 84, pp. 52–8

Parsons, M.C. (1987) *The Departure of Jesus in Luke–Acts*, JSNTSS 21, Sheffield: JSOT Press

Pelikan, J. (1988) *The Melody of Theology: A Philosophical Dictionary*, Cambridge MA and London: Harvard

Phillips, J.B. (1952) *The Gospels in Modern English*, Glasgow: Fontana Books
Piper, R.A. (1989) *Wisdom in the Q-Tradition*, Cambridge : CUP
Plooy, G.P.V. du (1988) 'The Design of God in Luke–Acts', *Scriptura* 25, pp. 1–6
Plummer, A. (1922) *A Critical and Exegetical Commentary on The Gospel According to St Luke*, The International Critical Commentary, Edinburgh: T. & T. Clark
Powell, J.E. (1989) 'Father, Into Thy Hands . . .', *JTS* 40, pp. 95–6
Powell, M.A. (1989) 'Are the Sands Still Shifting? An Update on Lukan Scholarship', *Trin Sem Rev* 11, pp. 15–22
(1990) 'The Religious Leaders in Luke: a Literary-Critical Study', *JBL* 109, pp. 91–110
Ravens, D.A.S. (1988) 'The Setting of Luke's Account of the Anointing: Luke 7.2–8.3', *NTS* 34, pp. 282–92
(1990) 'Luke 9.7–62 and the Prophetic Role of Jesus', *NTS* 36, pp. 119–29
Reicke, B. (1973) 'Jesus in Nazareth – Lk 4,14–30' in Balz and Schulz (1973), pp. 47–55
Reiling, J. and Sweelengrebel, J.L. (eds.) (1971) *A Translator's Handbook on the Gospel of Luke: Helps for Translators prepared under the auspices of the United Bible Societies*, vol. X, Leiden: E. J. Brill
Rese, M. (1969) *Alttestamentliche Motive in der Christologie des Lukas*, Gütersloh: Gerd Mohn
Resseguie, J.L. (1974) 'The Lukan Portrait of Christ', *Studia Biblica et Theologica* 4, pp. 5–20
Riesner, R. (1994) 'James's Speech (Acts 15:13–21), Simeon's Hymn (Luke 2:29–32), and Luke's Sources' in Green and Turner (1994), pp. 263–78
Ringe, S.H. (1983) 'Luke 9:28–36: The Beginning of an Exodus', *Semeia* 28, pp. 83–99
Robbins, V.K. (1978) 'By Land and by Sea: The We-Passages and Ancient Sea Voyages' in Talbert (1978)
(1979) 'Prefaces in Greco-Roman Biography and Luke–Acts', *PerspRelStud* 6, pp. 94–108
(1988) 'The Crucifixion and the Speech of Jesus', *Forum* 4, pp. 33–46
Robinson, B.P. (1984) 'The place of the Emmaus story in Luke–Acts', *NTS* 30, pp. 481–97
(1956) 'The Most Primitive Christology of All?', *JTS* 7, pp. 177–89
(1973) *The Human Face of God*, London: SCM
(1976) *Redating the New Testament*, London: SCM
Robinson, J.M. (1970) 'On the *Gattung* of Mark (and John)' in Buttrick (1970)
Rodd, C.S. (1961) 'Spirit or Finger?', *ExpT* 72 (1960–1), pp. 157f.
Romaniuk, C. (1968) 'Le livre de la Sagesse dans le Nouveau Testament', *NTS* 14, pp. 498–514
Ruppert, L. (1972) *Jesus als der leidende Gerechte?*, Stuttgart: KBW Verlag
Sabbe, M. (1979) 'The Son of Man Saying in Acts 7.56' in Kremer (1979)
Salo, K. (1991) *Luke's Treatment of the Law*, Helsinki: Suomalainen Tiedeakatemia

Sanders, E.P. and Davies, M. (1989) *Studying the Synoptic Gospels*, London: SCM

Sanders, J.A. (1975) 'Torah and Christ', *Interpretation* 29, pp. 372–90

Sanders, J.T. (1987) *The Jews in Luke–Acts*, London: SCM

(1991) 'Who Is a Jew and Who Is a Gentile in the Book of Acts?', *NTS* 37 pp. 434–55

Sandmel, S. (1974) *A Jewish Understanding of the New Testament*, London: SCM

(1978) *Judaism and Christian Beginnings*, London: OUP

Schmidt, D. (1983) 'Luke's "Innocent" Jesus: A Scriptural Apologetic' in Cassidy and Scharper (1983)

Schweizer, E. (1960) *Lordship and Discipleship*, SBT 1/28, SCM (1960), London

(1968) 'The Concept of the Davidic "Son of God" in Acts and its Old Testament Background' in Keck and Martyn (1968), pp. 186–93

(1968a) 'Concerning the Speeches in Acts' in Keck and Martyn (1968), pp. 208–16

(1971) *Jesus*, London: SCM

(1993) *Das Evangelium nach Lukas*, Das Neue Testament Deutsch 3, Göttingen and Zurich: Vandenhoeck and Ruprecht

Segbroeck, F. van (1989) *The Gospel of Luke: A Cumulative Bibliography*, Leuven: Leuven Univ. Press

Segovia, F.F. (1985) *Discipleship in the New Testament*, Philadelphia: Fortress Press

Selwyn, E.G. (1952) *The First Epistle of St Peter*, London: Macmillan

Sheeley, S.M. (1992) *Narrative Asides in Luke–Acts*, JSNTSS 72, Sheffield: JSOT Press

Soards, M.L. (1987) *The Passion According to Luke: The Special Material of Luke 22*, JSNTSS 14, Sheffield: JSOT Press

Sparks, H.F.D. (1943) 'The Semitisms of St Luke's Gospel', *JTS* 44, pp. 129–38

Squires, J.T. (1993) *The Plan of God in Luke–Acts*, SNTSMS 76, Cambridge: CUP

Stanton, G.N. (1974) *Jesus of Nazareth in New Testament Preaching*, SNTSMS 27, Cambridge: CUP

Stempvoort, P.A. van (1958) 'The Interpretation of the Ascension in Luke and Acts', *NTS* 5 (1958–9), pp. 30–42

Stendahl, K. (1963) 'The Apostle Paul and the Introspective Conscience of the West', *HTR* 56, pp. 199–215

Steyn, G.J. (1990) 'Intertestamental Similarities between Septuagintal pre[-] texts and Luke's Gospel', *Neotestamentica* 24, pp. 229–46

Strack, H. and Billerbeck P. (1922–61) *Kommentar zum Neuen Testament* (6 vols.), Munich: Beck

Streeter, B.H. (1924) *The Four Gospels: A Study of Origins*, London: Macmillan & Co.

Stuhlmacher, P. (1983) *Das Evangelium und die Evangelien*, Tübingen: Mohr

Sugirtharajah, R.S. (1990) 'Wisdom, Q, and a Proposal for a Christology', *ExpT* 102 (Nov. 1990), pp. 42–5

Talbert, C.H. (1970) 'The Redaction Critical Quest for Luke the Theologian' in Buttrick (1970)
(1974) *Literary Patterns, Theological Themes, and the Genre of Luke–Acts*, Missoula, MT: Society of Biblical Literature and Scholars
(1976) 'Shifting Sands: the Recent Study of the Gospel of Luke', *Interpretation* 30, pp. 381–95
(1978) *Perspectives on Luke–Acts*, Edinburgh: T. & T. Clark
(1983) 'Martyrdom in Luke–Acts and the Lukan Social Ethic' in Cassidy and Scharper (1983)
(1984) *Luke–Acts: New Perspectives from the Society of Biblical Literature Seminar*, New York: Crossroad
(1985) 'Discipleship in Luke–Acts' in Segovia (1985)
(1988) *Reading Luke: A Literary and Theological Commentary on the Third Gospel*, New York: Crossroad
Tannehill, R. (1961) 'A Study in the Theology of Luke–Acts', *ATR* 43, pp. 195–203
Tannehill, R.C. (1972) 'The Mission of Jesus according to Luke IV 16–30', BZNW 40, Berlin & New York: W. de Gruyter
(1985) 'Israel in Luke–Acts: A Tragic Story', *JBL* 104, pp. 69–85
(1986) *The Narrative Unity of Luke–Acts: A Literary Interpretation*, vol. I – *The Gospel according to Luke*, Philadelphia: Fortress Press
(1990) *The Narrative Unity of Luke–Acts: A Literary Interpretation*, vol. II – *The Acts of the Apostles*, Philadelphia: Fortress Press
(1991) 'The Functions of Peter's Mission Speeches in the Narrative of Acts', *NTS* 37, pp. 400–14
Tatum, W.B. (1967) 'The Epoch of Israel: Luke I–II and the Theological Plan of Luke–Acts', *NTS* 13 (1966–7), pp. 184–95
Taylor, V. (1926) *Behind the Third Gospel*, London: OUP
(1937) *Jesus and His Sacrifice*, London: Macmillan
(1945) *The Atonement in New Testament Teaching*, London: Epworth Press
(1952) *The Gospel According to St Mark*, London: Macmillan
(1953) *The Names of Jesus*, London: Macmillan
(1954) *The Life and Ministry of Jesus*, London: Macmillan
(1958) *The Person of Christ*, London: Macmillan
Thrall, M.E. (1970) 'Elijah and Moses in Mark's Account of the Transfiguration', *NTS* 16, pp. 305–17
Tiede, D.L. (1988) '"Glory to Thy People Israel": Luke–Acts and the Jews' in Neusner *et al.* (1988)
Trites, A.A. (1987) 'The Transfiguration in the Theology of Luke: Some Redactional Links' in Hurst and Wright (1987)
Trocmé, A. (1973) *Jesus and the Nonviolent Revolution*, Scottdale PA: Herald Press
Tuckett, C.M. (1987) *Reading the New Testament: Methods of Interpretation*, London: SPCK
Tyson, J. (1984) 'The Jewish Public in Luke–Acts', *NTS* 30, pp. 574–83
Tyson, J.B. (1986) *The Death of Jesus in Luke–Acts*, New York: Columbia SC

Unnik, W.C. van (1968) 'Luke–Acts, A Storm Center in Contemporary Scholarship' in Keck and Martyn (1968), pp. 15–32
Vermes, G. (1993) *The Religion of Jesus the Jew*, London: SCM Press
Walaskay, P.W. (1983) *And So We Came to Rome: The Political Perspective of St Luke*, SNTSMS 49, Cambridge: CUP
Warner, M. (ed.) (1990) *The Bible as Rhetoric*, London: Routledge
Weber, H.-R. (1979) *The Cross: Tradition and Interpretation*, London: SPCK
(1986) *Living in the Image of Christ*, Geneva: WCC
Wenham, J. (1991) *Redating Matthew, Mark and Luke*, London: Hodder & Stoughton
Weymouth, R.F. (1903) *The New Testament in Modern Speech*, London: James Clarke & Co.
Wiefel, W. (1987) *Das Evangelium nach Lukas*, Theologischer Handkommentar zum Neuen Testament III, Berlin: Evangelische Verlagsanstalt
Wilcox, M. (1981) 'The Godfearers in Acts – a Reconstruction', *JSNT* 13, pp. 102–22
Wilkens, W. (1966) 'Zur Frage der literarische Beziehung zwischen Matthaus und Lukas', *NovT* 8, pp. 48–57
Williams, C.B. (1937) *The New Testament in the Language of the People*, Nashville: Holman Bible Publishers
Williams, C.K. (1952) *The New Testament: A New Translation in Plain English*, London: SPCK & Longmans
Williams, C.S.C. (1964) *The Acts of the Apostles*, London: A. & C. Black
Williamson, R. (1989) *Jews in the Hellenistic World: Philo*, Cambridge: CUP
Wilson, S.G. (1979) *Luke and the Pastoral Epistles*, London: SPCK
Winston, D. (1979) *The Wisdom of Solomon*, Anchor Bible 43, New York: Doubleday and Co., Inc.
Yoder, J.H. (1972) *The Politics of Jesus*, Grand Rapids, Michigan: Eerdmans
York, J.O. (1991) *The Last Shall Be First: the Rhetoric of Reversal in Luke*, JSNTSS 46, Sheffield: JSOT Press
Young, F. (1977) 'A Cloud of Witnesses' in Hick (1977)
(1990) *The Art of Performance*, London: DLT
Young, F.W. (1949) 'Jesus as Prophet: a Re-examination', *JBL* 68, pp. 285–99
Young, R. (1900) *Literal Translation of the Bible: The Holy Bible; consisting of the Old and New Covenants, translated according to the Letter and Idioms of the Original Languages* (first edn 1862), Edinburgh: G.A. Young and Co
Zehnle, R. (1969) 'The Salvific Character of Jesus' Death in Lucan Soteriology', *TS* 30, pp. 420–44
Ziesler, J. (1978) 'Luke and the Pharisees', *NTS* 25 (1978–9), pp. 146–57

INDEX OF BIBLICAL REFERENCES

Sirach

2 Maccabees

3 Maccabees

4 Maccabees

Psalms of Solomon

Romans

1 Corinthians

2 Corinthians

Ephesians

Philippians

Colossians

INDEX OF AUTHORS